Apocalyptic
Thought in
Early Christianity

HOLY CROSS STUDIES
IN PATRISTIC THEOLOGY AND HISTORY

Editorial Board
Robert J. Daly, SJ, Chair
Bruce N. Beck
François Bovon
Susan R. Holman
Demetrios S. Katos
Aristotle Papanikolaou
James Skedros

published under the auspices of
The Stephen and Catherine
PAPPAS PATRISTIC INSTITUTE
of
HOLY CROSS GREEK ORTHODOX SCHOOL OF THEOLOGY
BROOKLINE, MASSACHUSETTS

APOCALYPTIC
THOUGHT IN
EARLY CHRISTIANITY

EDITED BY

ROBERT J. DALY, SJ

Baker Academic
a division of Baker Publishing Group
Grand Rapids, Michigan

ORTHODOX
PRESS

© 2009 by Holy Cross Greek Orthodox School of Theology

Published by Baker Academic
a division of Baker Publishing Group
P.O. Box 6287, Grand Rapids, MI 49516-6287
www.bakeracademic.com

Printed in the United States of America

Library of Congress Cataloging-in-Publication Data
Apocalyptic thought in early Christianity / edited by Robert J. Daly.
    p.   cm. — (Holy Cross studies in patristic theology and history)
    Includes bibliographical references and indexes.
    ISBN 978-0-8010-3627-9 (pbk.)
    1. End of the world—History of doctrines—Early church, ca. 30–600. 2. Bible. N.T. Revelation—Criticism, interpretation, etc.—History—Early church, ca. 30–600. 3. Apocalyptic literature—History and criticism. I. Daly, Robert J., 1933–
    BT877.A66 2009
    220′.046—dc22   2008053463

CONTENTS

FOREWORD

FATHER NICK TRIANTAFILOU

*President of Holy Cross Greek Orthodox School
of Theology and Hellenic College*

Holy Cross Studies in Patristic Theology and History is the first publication project of the Pappas Patristic Institute of Holy Cross Greek Orthodox School of Theology in Brookline, Massachusetts. This institute, founded in 2003 from a generous gift from Stephen and Catherine Pappas, has as its goal the advancement of patristic studies in the service of the academy and of the church. It does this by supporting ecumenically sensitive and academically open research and study in the Greek patristic tradition in conversation with other ancient Christian traditions. The Institute carries forward its mission through the leadership of its board of directors comprised of scholars from the Orthodox, Roman Catholic, and Protestant traditions and headed by Rev. Dr. Robert Daly, SJ, and its director, Dr. Bruce Beck.

One of the primary ways in which this Institute works toward this goal is through a series of annual fall conferences focusing on patristic themes that have the power to shed light on contemporary concerns. Each year, in collaboration with Baker Academic, established scholars are invited to contribute papers on the theme of the conference. Themes chosen for the early years include wealth and poverty, apocalyptic thought, the Trinity in the life of the church, evil and suffering, sickness and healing, family and children, and creation and ecology. In order to disseminate to a broad readership the insights achieved by scholars participating in these conferences, the Institute invited Baker Academic, in cooperation with Holy Cross Orthodox Press, to publish the fruits of these annual conferences in a series of attractive volumes.

A prominent characteristic of the orthodox tradition is its understanding that patristic theology is integral to all of Christian thought and life. It is our hope that the volumes published in this series will effectively mediate the rich legacy of the early church to our contemporary world—including Christians of all traditions—that is thirsting and hungering for such food.

PREFACE

Almost every epoch in the history of Christianity has been affected by apocalyptic tensions. With writings like the "Left Behind" series rivaling the Bible itself as best sellers, the present age is clearly no exception. Millions read with fear the book of Revelation as a violent blueprint for the terrible things to come or, perhaps worse, read it with glee as a scriptural warrant for violence in God's name. Such literal readings of the Apocalypse have been and still are among the most tragic aspects of the later history of the Apocalypse and its reception. This is doubtless why so many contemporary Christians want to forget about the last book of the Bible, or just give up and leave it to the fundamentalists. However, the authors who came together to produce this book know that there is a better option, namely to look more carefully at the whole Bible, and then take a good look at the way the great teachers of the early church taught us to look ahead, not with fear and foreboding at terrible things to come, but with loving trust in the coming into our lives of the One at whose arrival "the wolf shall live with the lamb" (Isa. 11:6).

I will now introduce the scholars whose presentations and discussions have become the various chapters of this book, outline the principal themes of their respective contributions, and then highlight the way in which they happily come together to produce, contrary perhaps to much popular expectation, a remarkably positive and upbeat impression of early Christian attitudes toward the end of time.

Beginning at the "beginning," Theodore Stylianopoulos, professor of New Testament at Holy Cross Greek Orthodox School of Theology, in his "'I Know Your Works': Grace and Judgment in the Apocalypse," points out how the book of Revelation pushes further the Pauline trajectory of beginning to transcend the distinction between moral and ritual commandments. For Paul, contrary to common assumptions, sees "works" not negatively but positively, as involving not casuistical "counting" but as whole-hearted devotion and obedience to God, that is, to Christ and his works rather than to Rome and its works. Revelation actually teaches a unity between grace and judgment, seeing it as two sides of the same reality (analogous, in this respect, to Paul's *dikaiosynē*). Stylianopoulos emphasizes that the well-known objections to the Apocalypse are not so much to its *message* as to the overwhelming character of its *medium*, its overwhelming apocalyptic character. For its message is actually quite positive: "The core hope of Revelation," Stylianopoulos points out, is not in "the literal unfolding of historical events, whether past or future, but in the eschatological reality of God's triumph over evil in which God's very presence and glory will shine through all things."

This notably positive attitude toward what we in our day are now calling "apocalyptic themes" is strikingly supported by the findings of what is—at least geographically—our most comprehensive chapter, "Apocalyptic Themes in the Monumental and Minor Art of Early Christianity," by John Herrmann of the Boston Museum of Fine Arts and Annewies van den Hoek of Harvard Divinity School. This chapter begins with pre-Constantinian biblical and pagan sources and continues to the early Middle Ages, collecting evidence from all corners—except for the very far East—of the ancient Christian world, and organizing a daunting mass of evidence under helpful religio-graphic themes (e.g., the Lamb on Mount Zion, saints offer their crowns to Christ, the twenty-four elders of the Apocalypse, coming through the clouds and gathering the elect, the Virgin Mary as an "apocalyptic" ascension, etc.). It illustrates all this with more than four dozen sets of figures, most of them original photographs published here for the first time. The authors begin by pointing out an apparent principle of selection in the production of the earliest materials: what was selected by the producers of these mosaics, paintings, and graphic artifacts, were for the most part elements that enhance the majesty and dignity of Christ. Thus in what is perhaps the most striking finding of this incredibly detailed study, a finding that counters the popular assumption that apocalyptic themes are dominated by signs of fearsome judgment, punishment, and foreboding, the authors find just the opposite. They conclude: "In the terrifying world of the late Roman Empire and the early Middle Ages, carefully crafted apocalyptic works of art were intended to provide the viewer with gratification and freedom from anxiety."

The next two chapters are by scholars already well known for their work on this theme, Bernard McGinn of the University of Chicago and Brian E. Daley, SJ, of the University of Notre Dame. McGinn's chapter—actually the source of some of the remarks with which we opened this preface—is titled "Turning Points in Early Christian Apocalypse Exegesis." He identifies the main starting point of this exegesis at around 150 CE, and the tensions produced by the crisis over the nonappearance of the parousia. At this time, and in what became the basic Christian picture of the last events, we find side by side both a chiliastic and a nonchiliastic eschatology. However, not all early Christians comfortably accepted the canonicity of the Apocalypse. For example, Eusebius and Jerome were skeptical; the Eastern Church in general, associating the Apocalypse with the dangers of Montanism, remained suspicious; and the Marcionites, seeing it as a "Jewish book," were totally negative. But in the early third century we encounter in Hippolytus a critical turning point in the history of apocalyptic exegesis: he reads Revelation 12 in a basically ecclesiological and christological way, that is, as referring to the present and not to some awesome future. This line of interpretation, which basically spiritualizes the millennium and makes the present life of the church the main point of reference, continues with Origen, Dionysius, and Methodius, and eventually constitutes the baseline for what one might call mainstream or "orthodox" readings of the Apocalypse.

Brian Daley, in "'Faithful and True': Early Christian Apocalyptic and the Person of Christ," notes that New Testament apocalyptic was transformed by the early Christians, losing its urgency in an apocalypticism that had become a vehicle for acknowledging Jesus as Lord of history. This doctrinal, openly christocentric transformation of apocalyptic themes that remained influential in the development of Christian thought took the form of an apocalyptic cosmology (in Irenaeus), an apocalyptic Christology (in Irenaeus, Hippolytus, and Origen), and an apocalyptic ecclesiology (in Origen, Oecumenius, and eventually Maximus). In other words, the Apocalypse came to be read as "less a revelation of unknown things to come than as an affirmation of the victory of Christ and a representation of the life of the church, his body, in its present time of struggle."

Next come three studies from before the patristic golden age. Dragoş-Andrei Giulea of Marquette University, in "Pseudo-Hippolytus's *In Sanctum Pascha*: A Mystery Apocalypse," sees this work of Pseudo-Hippolytus as part of a general Christian response to mystery religions that combines three elements common to very early Christian writings: paschal celebration, apocalyptic language, and (what is here clearly developed) mystery language. This seems to indicate that Asia Minor of the second to the fourth century was the place of a decisive synthesis of two traditions: apocalypse and mystery.

In the second of these chapters, Bogdan G. Bucur, also of Duquesne University, in "The Divine Face and the Angels of the Face: Jewish Apocalyptic Themes in Early Christology and Pneumatology," outlines the occurrence of "face" Christology in Clement of Alexandria, Aphrahat the (early fourth-century) Persian sage, and in the seven spirits of the book of Revelation. In contrast to "name" Christology, "wisdom" Christology, and "glory" Christology, he notes that "face" Christology, one of the early building blocks for emerging Christian doctrine, never became a major player, but was replaced by more precise vocabulary shaped by the christological controversies of the third and fourth centuries.

In the third chapter of this group, J. A. Cerrato in "Hippolytus and Cyril of Jerusalem on the Antichrist: When Did an Antichrist Theology First Emerge in Early Christian Baptismal Catechesis?" notes that, to the three more widely known Antichrist literature genres of Apocalypse—namely, tractate, biblical commentary, and homily—we need to add another, less-noticed genre: that of baptismal instruction or catechetical homily. He argues that Cyril got this from Hippolytus's *On the Antichrist*, who contextualizes it as a part of the *disciplina arcani*. In doing this Cyril is reflecting the anxiety characteristic of early Christian baptismal instruction.

Still in the early period, we have from Ute Possekel, the 2007–2008 visiting fellow at the Pappas Patristic Institute, "Expectations of the End in Early Syriac Christianity." In her study of Bardaisan of Edessa and of the *Odes of Solomon* and of the *Acts of Thomas*, all coming from before the middle of the third century, she finds, despite clear evidence that apocalyptic imagery was known to these authors, a surprising absence of such imagery. The reason for this, Possekel suggests, might be both theological and sociological. We cannot be sure about the origin, the *Sitz im Leben*, of the *Odes* and the *Acts*. But Edessa, at least in those early Christian centuries, prosperously balancing between the empires of Rome and Parthia, neither of which could easily be thought of as all good or all evil, was not a marginalized community, and Bardaisan's Christian community was definitely not at the margins of society. Yes, there is a natural affinity between marginalized existence and apocalyptic musings; but studies such as this prompt us to ask whether the connection is a necessary one.

Next we have two "hinge" chapters. First, Alexander Golitzin of Marquette University, in "Heavenly Mysteries: Themes from Apocalyptic Literature in the Macarian Homilies and Selected Other Fourth-Century Ascetical Writers," shows how the mid-fourth-century Syriac writer Aphrahat portrays "the Christian sage" as becoming the *locus Dei*, that is, as experiencing, because of the changed situation brought about by Christ, not just a heavenly ascent but a journey *ad intra* into a state or place that later writers would call *theosis*. Golitzin finds a continuation of this kind of thinking a generation later in the Syrian writer known as the Macarian Homilist. He propounded what Golitzin calls an "interiorized apocalyptic" that, although interior, is both real and transforming. The raw material for all this was the super-saturate apocalyptic solution that was late Second Temple Judaism and the catalyst was the Christ-event. But the transmitters to later Christian ages were the monks who continued copying this literature despite the often thundering denunciations of such guardians of orthodoxy as Athanasius of Alexandria.

John A. McGuckin of Union Theological School/Columbia University then provides the second hinge chapter in this book, between what comes before and what comes after, with his "Eschatological Horizons in the Cappadocian Fathers." After some initial terminological clarifications, McGuckin points to Luke as an example of "de-eschatologizing," that is, the faltering of the translation of Semitic idiom—through which the early church was aware of the non-linearity of the eschatological drama—into a (Greek) linear taxonomy, out of which actually developed the liturgical year. As for the Cappadocians, he notes that Origen's eschatological agenda, whether they are correcting or following him, determines all their thinking. Gregory of Nazianzus (more Origenian than Gregory of Nyssa), far from being inconsistent—as has commonly been thought—with his two doctrines of the afterlife, one gloomy, one bright, is actually theologically quite substantive and sophisticated. He appropriates Origen's technique of the juxtaposed parallelism of doctrines that invite the proficient to a deeper understanding, which in this case inclines toward seeing punishment not as eternal but, teleologically, in terms of eventual purification. Gregory of Nyssa, whom McGuckin calls an "eschatological visionary," with his doctrine of *epektasis* (that has dominated recent scholarly discussion), moves toward the overcoming of the *diastasis* between creature and creator, toward "the impossible paradox of creaturely participation in the divine." This enables him to see *metousia theou* and *theosis* as "the same thing seen from different viewpoints: moral and ontological." Summing up, and quite in contrast to the Lukan "de-eschatologizing" mentioned above, both Gregorys were "strenuously attempting to resist the reification of eschatology in their time as fixed dogma, and to preserve its vitality as a luminous 'dissolver' of categories and, as such, an authentic vehicle for the language of *theologia* which can only (impossibly) be spoken of apophatically."

Georgia Frank of Colgate University, in her "Christ's Descent to the Underworld in Ancient Ritual and Legend," begins by reviewing accounts of underworld journeys in Greco-Roman religions, and then accounts of Jesus' descent in the New Testament and other early Christian writings. She then focuses on the *kontakia*/hymns of Romanos the Melodist in sixth-century Constantinople. These imaginative hymns, sung during all-night vigils, were filled with graphic descriptions of bodily punishments and wails of lamentation. But it is not the dead, neither the righteous nor the wicked, who are being punished. The victims are Hades and Death personified who, with the arrival of Christ, are forced to give back (graphically to vomit back from their tortured bellies) the dead whom they have consumed. What had begun as a story told about Jesus developed into a tale narrated by a host of voices of those who simulated Jesus' journey, and formed "a running underground commentary that will shape the faithful's perceptions of Jesus' final days."

Next, Lorenzo DiTommaso of Montréal's Concordia University, in "The Early Christian Daniel Apocalyptica," surveys a vast body of Eastern Mediterranean literature (at least twenty-four examples in eight languages) that recount first-person visions like those found in Daniel 7–12. None of these simply retell visions of the book of Daniel; they are all new compositions reflecting different historical circumstances. Although it is difficult to identify their precise *Sitz im Leben*, the earliest of them seem to coincide with the barbarian migrations in late antiquity, and many seem to reflect the concerns of the population of Constantinople under seige. Finally, DiTommaso notes that there is now serious doubt about the standard view that most or all of the Daniel Apocalyptica are descendents from a single Greek Apocalypse of Daniel.

As we move toward the close of the patristic period, we encounter the chapter of Elijah Nicolas Mueller of Marquette University: "Temple and Angel: Apocalyptic Themes in the Theology of St. John Damascene." Living in what had become a "disestablished" Christian community some one hundred years after the advent of Islam, St. John, not primarily an apocalyptic writer, imported in an apologetic tone some apocalyptic themes from primitive Christianity. He saw ultimate human destiny as being in angelic communion with God through sight. This begins in the here-and-now, in a liturgical experience of "the mystical vision of Christ, using the mediation of angels, angelic states of humanity, and the angelomorphic appearance of the Word and Image of God."

Closing this volume with a richly illustrated chapter is Nancy Patterson Ševčenko's "Images of the Second Coming and the Fate of the Soul in Middle Byzantine Art." First, carefully analyzing a twelfth-century Last Judgment icon on Mount Sinai, and puzzling over its obviously deliberate ignoring of the usual conventions for depicting time and space, she concludes that its purpose was to strike terror, yes, not into normal folk but into the hearts of those who administer the highly structured Byzantine world. She finds this confirmed in both graphic and literary evidence from this period, evidence that indicates that imagery of the Last Judgment was deeply embedded in the consciousness of Byzantine rulers. Then, as Last Judgment scenes became more numerous as time went on (but mostly in large-scale depictions, and only rarely in manuscripts and icons) she notes that depictions of individual punishments for individual crimes slowly enter into the iconographic repertory. While the grand Last Judgment scenes address a dire warning to the public at large, especially to those in positions of authority, one finds that some twelfth-century private manuscripts, along with these warnings, also depict, for example, by way of the image of the "heavenly ladder," the idea of a possible immediate entrance into paradise, especially for the monk.

Stepping back a bit from the individual chapters, we find that one of the striking contributions of this book as a whole is the strength of what has turned out to be its central thesis, namely, that in early Christianity apocalyptic ideas are not heavily dominated by negative and terrifying ideas of a terrible, fearsome end-event. Quite the contrary! By the end of the second century the early Christian writers were interpreting the Apocalypse as pointing not toward some awe-inspiring and future event, but to the challenges of contemporary life in the church. In addition, the material evidence from countless graphic artifacts regarding death and the future life (see chap. 2) is also predominantly positive, reflecting an apparently widely shared selectivity that emphasized the positive and the comforting rather than the negative and the threatening.

This was not a thesis that this book set out to support, but rather what was discovered as the cumulative result of the papers delivered at the first of the annual conferences of the Stephen and Catherine Pappas Patristic Institute at Holy Cross Greek Orthodox School of Theology in Brookline, Massachusetts in the fall of 2004—the papers that have been gathered and edited to become the chapters of this book. But, as is typically the case with such discoveries, they not only highlight important but often neglected verities but also suggest other potentially fruitful avenues of investigation.

We are reminded of the serendipitous creativity that is at work when scholars start sharing with others what they have been learning as they laboriously build up the silos that constitute their research. The bridges between these silos are so often the places where the most exciting discoveries are made. We are reminded how deeply anchored in the Bible are the themes that occupied the attention of the Fathers of the church. We are reminded how self-deceptively we tend to project back into earlier times and data our own assumptions and experiences. We are reminded how much more we can learn when we attend to the graphic data and material evidence of earlier times. And finally, we are reminded how important is every effort we can make to enter into the socio-politico-religio *Sitz im Leben* of the people whose works and lives we are attempting to understand, and from which we are now attempting to learn.

This book also helps us to identify and start naming the many silos of research still to be constructed and bridged in this area of apocalyptic themes in the early church. We could only begin to look into the Syriac tradition. Other traditions, like the Coptic and the Armenian, cry out for attention. None of these particular chapters were produced by liturgical scholars; yet the entire volume, indeed many volumes, could fruitfully be devoted to studying apocalyptic themes in early Christian liturgy. And the same could be said of what the sociologist could bring to the study of this theme. We have, excitingly, only begun to scratch the surface.

Robert J. Daly, SJ
March 2008

ACKNOWLEDGMENTS

The publisher wishes to acknowledge the following institutions or individuals for providing permission to use illustrations. Unless otherwise indicated, the figures appearing in chapter 2 are reproduced through the courtesy of Annewies van den Hoek.

Fig. 2.1   Metropolitan Museum of Art, New York, Rogers Fund, 24.240

Fig. 2.2   Classical Numismatic Group, *Triton V* (Lancaster, PA, 5 January 2002) lot 2180

Fig. 2.3   Ensoli, Serena, and Eugenio La Rocca, eds. *Aurea Roma: Dalla città pagana alla città cristiana*. Roma: L'erma di Bretschneider, 2000, 414, fig. 1

Fig. 2.5   Dr. Busso Peus Nachfolger, *Auction 378* (Frankfurt, 28 April 2004) lot 643

Fig. 2.6   Numismatik Lanz, *Auction 128* (Munich, 22 May 2006) lot 208

Fig. 2.7   Classical Numismatic Group, *Mail Bid Sale 72* (Lancaster, PA, and London, 14 June 2006) lot 1891

Fig. 2.8   Vatican Museums

Fig. 2.9   Louvre, Paris, Ma2980

Fig. 2.12a   Collection of Sir Charles Nuffler, Bart

Fig. 2.12b   Harlan J. Berk, Ltd., Chicago

Fig. 2.13   Collection of Sir Charles Nuffler, Bart

Fig. 2.14   Djemila, Algeria, Museum

Fig. 2.15   Collection of Sir Charles Nuffler, Bart

Fig. 2.16   Private collection, Medfield, MA

Fig. 2.17   Private collection, Dedham, MA

Fig. 2.22   Louvre, Paris, Ma1662

Fig. 2.23a   Numismatica Ars Classica, *Auction 25* (Zürich, 25 June 2003) lot 424

Fig. 2.23b   Astarte S. A., *Auction 19* (Lugano, 6 May 2006) lot 975

Fig. 2.23c   Gorny and Mosch Giessener Munzhandlung, Auction 169
               (Munich, 12 October 2008) lot 336. Luebke and Wiedemann,
               Studios für Fotografie, Stuttgart

Fig. 2.25   *Ambrogio e Agostino: Le sorgenti dell'Europa*. Milan: Olivares,
               2004, cat. no. 14

Fig. 2.28   Ciampini, Giovanni Giustino. *Vetera monumenta*. Rome, 1693,
               pl. 68

Fig. 2.34   Garden of the Archaeological Museum, Istanbul, inv. no. 5478

Fig. 2.35   Coptic Museum, Cairo, inv. no. 7102

Fig. 2.36   Coptic Museum, Cairo, inv. no. 12089

Fig. 2.38   Coptic Museum, Cairo, inv. no. 7110

Fig. 2.39   Private collection, Dedham, MA

Fig. 2.41   Scala/Art Resource, NY

Fig. 2.42   Kourkoutidou-Nikolaïdou, E., and A. Tourta, *Wandering in Byz-
               antine Thessaloniki*. Athens: Kapon, 1997, 92–93

Fig. 2.43   Coptic Museum, Cairo, inv. no. 753

Fig. 2.44   Deutsches Archäologisches Institut, Rome, 61.2579

Fig. 2.45a   Coptic Museum, Cairo, inv. no. 7118

Fig. 2.45b   Coptic Museum, Cairo, inv. no. 7118

Fig. 2.45c   Coptic Museum, Cairo, inv. no. 7118

Fig. 14.1   The Michigan-Princeton-Alexandria Expedition to Mount Sinai

Fig. 14.2   © Dumbarton Oaks, Image Collections and Fieldwork Archives,
               Washington, DC

Fig. 14.3   Bibliothèque nationale de France

Fig. 14.4   Bibliothèque nationale de France

Fig. 14.5   Bibliothèque nationale de France

Fig. 14.6   © All Rights Reserved. The British Library Board. License Num-
               ber: BAKACA01

Fig. 14.7   © Dumbarton Oaks, Image Collections and Fieldwork Archives,
               Washington, DC

Fig. 14.8   Nancy Patterson Ševčenko

Fig. 14.9   Nancy Patterson Ševčenko

Fig. 14.10   Robert Garrett Collection of Medieval and Renaissance Manu-
               scripts. Department of Rare Books and Special Collections.
               Princeton University Library

Fig. 14.11   © Dumbarton Oaks, Image Collections and Fieldwork Archives,
               Washington, DC

Fig. 14.12   Makis Skiadaresis

Fig. 14.13   Makis Skiadaresis

Fig. 14.14   Makis Skiadaresis

Fig. 14.15   Erich Lessing/Art Resource, NY

Fig. 14.16   © Biblioteca Apostolica Vaticana (Vatican)

1

"I Know Your Works"

Grace and Judgment in the Apocalypse

Theodore Stylianopoulos

In the inaugural vision of the prophet John, the exalted Christ thunders a series of seven oracles or prophetic messages to the seven Asian churches (Rev. 1:12–3:22). Five of those messages contain the refrain "I know your works."[1] The third message explicitly warns, "I will give to each of you according to your works" (Rev. 2:23c). Throughout the Apocalypse numerous scenes depict horrific punishments for sinners and celestial blessings for the righteous distributed respectively on the basis of deeds. In the account of the Last Judgment, God's books are opened and all humans are judged "according to their works" (Rev. 20:12–13). The final oracles of Christ include the utterance: "Behold, I am coming soon, and my reward is with me, to repay each according to his own work" (Rev. 22:12). It seems that in the scope of the Apocalypse the standard by which God dispenses eschatological rewards or punishments is the principle of judgment according to works.

My task in this essay is twofold. At one level I want to examine the meaning of "works" (*erga*) in the Apocalypse. Does Revelation teach salvation by

---

1. οἶδα τὰ ἔργα σου or οἶδά σου τὰ ἔργα (Rev. 2:2, 19; 3:1, 8, 15). Unless otherwise indicated, all biblical translations are my own.

works? It certainly seems so, but in what sense? At a deeper level I want also to engage the question of grace and judgment, an issue dramatically prominent in the Apocalypse and problematic particularly for those who seek to read Revelation as God's word.[2] Because the Apocalypse presents itself as a book of "prophecy" (1:3; 22:7, 10, 18–19), and for many the climax of biblical prophecy,[3] to raise the question of the theological significance of its message in the light of the gospel is of no small consequence. And I propose to accomplish this double task with an eye on the greatest preacher and theologian of the gospel—the apostle Paul.

Judgment according to Works

Several years ago Kent L. Yinger published an insightful monograph[4] in which he analyzed what he calls the motif of judgment according to deeds in the Jewish Scriptures, the Pseudepigrapha, the Qumran literature, as well as the letters of Paul. Building on the "new perspective" on Judaism and Paul advocated by E. P. Sanders, James D. G. Dunn, and now others,[5] Yinger argued that all this Jewish literature, with minor variations and developments, evidences the same covenantal perspective of grace and judgment familiar in the biblical tradition. The focus of Yinger's interest was Paul. His main purpose was to demonstrate the thesis, outrageous for the Reformation tradition, that the principle of justification by grace through faith and the principle of

2. The horrific visions of divine judgment in the book of Revelation were, as is well known, already theologically problematic among ancient interpreters and a significant factor behind the book's difficult entry into the canon of the New Testament in Eastern Orthodox Christianity. Although early writers such as Justin and Irenaeus, both millenarians, held the Apocalypse in high regard, later authors such as Origen, Gregory of Nyssa, Basil, Gregory the Theologian, and John Chrysostom exercised great reserve toward the Apocalypse. The lectionary of the Orthodox Church still excludes readings from Revelation.

3. For example, Richard Bauckham, *The Climax of Prophecy: Studies in the Book of Revelation* (Edinburgh: T&T Clark, 1992), xvi, who cogently argues that the climax of prophecy, centered on Jesus Christ, the final coming of the kingdom is integrally connected to the conversion of the nations predicted by the Old Testament prophets and proclaimed by Revelation, an eschatological event taking place amid pagan oppression and faithful Christian witness as interactive elements in God's paradoxical purposes.

4. Kent L. Yinger, *Paul, Judaism, and Judgment according to Deeds* (Cambridge: Cambridge University Press, 1999).

5. I am thinking largely of N. T. Wright and his writings: *The Climax of the Covenant: Christ and the Law in Pauline Theology* (Philadelphia: Fortress, 1991); *What Saint Paul Really Said: Was Paul of Tarsus the Real Founder of Christianity?* (Grand Rapids: Eerdmans, 1997); and *The Letter to the Romans: Introduction, Commentary, and Reflections*, NIB 10 (Nashville: Abingdon, 2002). For E. P. Sanders, see *Paul and Palestinian Judaism* (Philadelphia: Fortress, 1977); and *Paul, the Law, and the Jewish People* (Fortress: Philadelphia, 1983). For James D. G. Dunn, see *The Theology of Paul the Apostle* (Grand Rapids: Eerdmans, 1998). These authors have significantly influenced my own thinking about early Judaism, early Christianity, and Paul.

judgment according to deeds stand next to each other in Paul's major letters with astonishing comfort.[6] According to Yinger, Paul's thought in this respect is in complete continuity with what Yinger calls the "fundamental and living axiom"[7] of judgment according to deeds widely attested in Jewish literature. Further, according to Yinger, Paul reinforces the concept of judgment according to deeds by reviving the parallel concept of *reward* according to deeds, something that "had nearly died out in Judaism of the last two centuries of the pre-Christian era."[8]

Works in Paul's Letters

I acknowledge my indebtedness to Yinger's background work pertinent to this essay on grace and judgment in the Apocalypse. I begin by raising the question about "works" or "deeds" (*erga*). What is the nature and content of those works or deeds that serve as basis of God's judgment in the Jewish tradition, Paul, and the Apocalypse? In the case of Second Temple Judaism, the works in question are the works of the Law, the Torah, viewed in its unity and totality. In the case of Paul things, of course, are quite different. In Paul the centrality of the Torah has been replaced by the centrality of Christ, a fundamental position of which Yinger is fully aware. Nevertheless, Yinger, influenced in part by the "new perspective" on Judaism and Paul, does not fully grasp the role and implications of the "works of the Law" (*erga nomou*) in Paul. While Yinger, following the "new perspective," rightly rejects the erroneous view of Judaism as a religion of meritorious works, he does not clearly see that Paul implicitly marks the first sign of the breakup of the unity of the Torah or Law (*nomos*),[9] an assumption that the author of the Apocalypse also significantly shares with Paul.

6. The specific texts analyzed by Yinger are Rom. 2:6–11; 4:4–5; 6:23; 8:1–4; 14:1–12; 1 Cor. 3:5–9a, 9b–15, 27–28; 4:1–5; 2 Cor. 5:10; 11:15b; Col. 1:22–23a; 3:6, 22–25.

7. Yinger, *Paul, Judaism, and Judgment*, 286.

8. Ibid., 287. In the Pseudepigrapha, Qumran documents, and other Jewish writings of that era, the eclipse of the older Old Testament concept of reward according to deeds was due, Yinger argues, to a deepened sense of human sinfulness beyond any thought of deserving rewards; and the revival in Paul was due to the new sense of transformation and life in the Spirit.

9. I am not claiming that Paul's breakup of the unity of the Torah is distinctly conscious and explicit on his part. Paul mainly deals with the Torah as an entire dispensation in its totality and in the perspective of the history of salvation (Rom. 3:21–31; 5:20; 6:15; 7:6; 10:4; Gal. 3:10–4:5). However, Paul's argumentation at key points discloses specific differentiations between the ethical and cultic aspects of the Torah (esp. Rom. 2:6–26; 13:8–10; 1 Cor. 7:19) that amount to a breakup of its unity. The first signs of the relativization of the Torah occur in Stephen the Hellenist, whose proclamation was judged to amount to rejection of the Temple and apostasy from the Jewish traditions by his detractors (Acts 6:14). In Paul the controversy intensified because of the proclamation of the gospel to Gentiles apart from the Law. The account of the Apostolic Council, not without critical problems, suggests that the Jerusalem "pillar" apostles endorsed at least formally Paul's position and thereby the implicit relativization of the Law. The explicit breakup of the unity of the Law first occurs during

This point needs further clarification. The apostle Paul, as is well known, holds to the authority of the Torah as Scripture but sets aside the old order of the Torah as the standard of salvation. Yet at the same time he attests to what Yinger calls the Jewish "axiom" of judgment according to works as an operative soteriological principle. But the decisive difference has to do with Paul's understanding of the content of those works. The works that Paul asserts to be a standard of judgment are no longer the "works of the Law" (*erga nomou*), namely, circumcision, festivals, kosher foods, and other such Jewish practices.[10] Nor can it be demonstrated that, as the "new perspective" would have it, such Jewish practices were for Paul an expression of "ethnic" claims that could be set aside by virtue of the universality of the gospel. Paul in no way thinks in those terms. For him the whole Law is God's holy Law given for life.[11] Yet, for Paul those God-given religious practices that fundamentally defined the identity of God's elect people are now, at God's own initiative in Christ and by reason of their inefficacy due to the power of sin, put aside as the criteria of salvation.[12] For Paul the soteriological function of works as a formal principle is still operative and in continuity with Second Temple Judaism, but the *nature* and *content* of works is decisively different. The meaning of works pertains no longer to the observance of the corpus of the Law as a unity but to a new spiritual and ethical understanding of God's law determined by God's revelation in Christ. The new basis of judgment according to works in Paul has to do with the keeping of what he instructively calls "commandments of God" (*entolai Theou*, 1 Cor. 7:19). These are drawn from the Torah, particularly the Decalogue (Rom. 13:8–10), but yet differentiated from circumcision and other Jewish religious practices.[13] The commandments of God which are still obligatory under the new order of Christ, and which elsewhere Paul calls "good work" or "well-doing" (*ergon agathon*, Rom. 2:7,

---

the second century among the Gnostics (e.g., Basilides and Ptolemy). Justin Martyr (*Dial.* 44.2) lays out a tripartite division of the Law in terms of prophecy, moral law, and historical dispensation for the Jews. See Theodore Stylianopoulos, *Justin Martyr and the Mosaic Law*, SBLDS 20 (Missoula, MT: Scholars Press, 1975), 51–68.

10. These practices of the Torah in particular are the focus of contention in Paul's major arguments in Romans and Galatians (Rom. 2:25; 4:11; 14:2–6; Gal. 2:3; 4:10; 5:2–4; 6:12–14).

11. Paul's basic point in Rom. 7:7–23 is that God's Law is holy, just, good, and spiritual. However, according to Paul, because of the overpowering nature of sin and human weakness, the Law tragically did not fulfill its intended purpose.

12. Rom. 3:21; 4:13–15; 6:15; 7:7–13; 8:1–4; 10:1–11; Gal. 3:23–25; 5:1–4.

13. Paul declares in 1 Cor. 7:19: "Circumcision is nothing, and uncircumcision is nothing; but observance of the commandments of God [is everything]." But is not circumcision a commandment? Surely, but Paul now is assuming a radical differentiation between the ritual injunctions and the moral commandments of the Decalogue (Rom. 13:9). Compare Gal. 6:15: "For neither circumcision nor uncircumcision is anything; but a new creation [is everything]!" See also the crucial passage of Rom. 2:17–29 for the implicit differentiation between moral and ritual commandments.

10),[14] are of a spiritual and ethical nature having to do with the transformed life of the "new creation."[15] Those commandments for Paul sum up the "just requirement of the Law" and must be fulfilled by those who now are in Christ and walk according to the Spirit (Rom. 8:4; 13:8–9; Gal. 5:13–26).

I do not claim that we find in Paul an explicit distinction between moral and ritual commandments, or that the apostle advocates a universal moral law as clearly as later patristic authors do. But I am contending that Paul has made a critical, though implicit, move in that direction. Paul's sweeping condemnation of humanity in Romans 1–2 pivots around idolatry and immorality. His whole argument about the impartiality of God's judgment on both Gentiles and Jews, whether reward or wrath, rests precisely on doing those things required by the Torah that are also written on Gentile hearts (Rom. 2:5–15). The lists of vices in several Pauline letters,[16] which suggest contrasting virtues, implicitly make the same point. For Paul, the required works under Christ as standards of God's judgment are of a new nature and content—for lack of a better expression "spiritual and ethical"—drawn from the Torah but now transformed in the context of the new creation in Christ and the Spirit.[17] Thus while the principle of judgment according to works as a formal theological principle is attested in Paul in continuity with Judaism, the nature and content of those works are in significant discontinuity with the traditional understanding of the Torah and its injunctions as a unity.[18] That, of course, explains the magnitude of the controversy in early Jewish and Christian circles over Paul's ministry, and charges of apostasy against him (Acts 21:20–21, 28), because of his proclamation of the gospel to the

14. References to "well-doing" or "good work," sometimes contrasted to "evil-doing" or "evil" (τὸ κακόν), are frequent in Paul: Rom. 2:7–10; 3:8; 9:11; 12:21; 13:3–4; 15:2; 2 Cor. 5:10; Gal. 6:10.

15. See, e.g., Rom. 6:12–14; 7:6; 8:1–4, 12–14; 12:1–2.

16. Rom. 1:28–31; 1 Cor. 6:9–11; Gal. 5:19–21.

17. The implicit distinction between ritual and ethical aspects of the Torah is evident time and again in Paul and, as well, his insistence on ethical works (ἔργα ἀγαθά, τὸ ἀγαθόν, Rom. 2:7, 10; 13:3; 2 Cor. 5:10) as a criterion of judgment, distinguished from the former (Rom. 2:21–29; 13:8–10). Above all, in the whole argument of Galatians, Paul's vehemence is directed against observance of "works of the Law," that is, circumcision, Jewish festivals, and the like (Gal. 3:9–10), not against ethical works. Paul in Galatians mightily argues against observance of Torah ritual practices by Gentile Christians, not against moral effort and moral works that he clearly requires for salvation in tandem with the Spirit's transformational power (Gal. 5:16–24). Apart from this implicit but crucial distinction, Paul's teaching on justification by faith and not works is usually misinterpreted by losing sight of Paul's insistence on the necessity of ethical works for salvation. Still, for Paul, salvation is a gift and also a reward for faith and ethical working together. See his marvelous declaration, "For in Christ Jesus neither circumcision counts for anything nor uncircumcision, but [what really counts] is faith *working* through love" (Gal. 5:6; italics mine).

18. By referring to discontinuity I mean in terms of Paul's radical rejection of Torah practices for Christian Gentiles as part of God's people, resulting in his being persecuted as an apostate by fellow Jews and Jewish Christians. I do not by any means suggest that Paul's understanding of Christ and the new creation is in theological discontinuity with the Old Testament heritage according to Paul.

Gentiles based on faith in Christ and life in the Spirit and free from the yoke of the Mosaic Law.

Works in the Apocalypse

The author of Revelation stands on similar ground as does Paul, but he relativizes the authority of the Jewish Scriptures even more radically. On the one hand, the prophet John is enormously indebted to the Jewish Scriptures through his use of scriptural vocabulary, images, concepts, as well as fundamental theological categories. On the other hand, unlike Paul, he neither appeals to the authority of, nor explicitly cites, the Scriptures. Being the direct recipient of the living word of God from Christ and angelic figures, the seer seems to claim an authority higher than that of the scriptural word. At the same time, however, just as in the case of Paul, the seer requires faithful obedience to the "commandments of God" (*entolai Theou*, Rev. 12:17; 14:12). These commandments are nowhere explicitly defined in the Apocalypse. Certainly they have nothing to do with keeping or not keeping Jewish religious practices. Revelation evidences no conflict whatever over the "works of the Law" that mightily troubled Paul's ministry. For John and his communities, that issue is long dead. The controversy with Jews alluded to in the oracles to Smyrna and Philadelphia (Rev. 2:9; 3:9) involves other matters.[19]

An overview of the Apocalypse shows that the author's major concerns are virtually identical with Paul's—idolatry and immorality. Thus for the prophet John, too, for whom the breakup of the Torah is by now an established presupposition, the content of those required commandments of God are of an ethical nature. John unarguably shares with both Second Temple Judaism and Paul the formal soteriological principle of judgment "according to deeds," a standard repeated time and again in the Apocalypse.[20] But those deeds, though drawn from the Torah, are now redefined by the new situation in Christ and particularly the requirement of keeping the "witness" (*martyria*, Rev. 12:17) and the faithfulness (*pistis*, Rev. 14:12) of Jesus. In the case of the seer, just as in the case of Paul, we find continuity with Judaism on the formal principle of judgment according to works, but striking discontinuity as regards the understanding of the nature and content of those works.

19. Those reasons have to do with competitive claims over who constitutes the true people of God and can claim legal status under Roman law. Jews in Asia Minor were a thriving community and full participants in the economic and cultural life of Greco-Roman society, while enjoying legal exemption from emperor worship. The Christians were an upstart group with competitive claims and apparently exposed as deserving neither legal protection under the cover of Judaism nor exemption from emperor worship. See Leonard L. Thompson, *The Book of Revelation: Apocalypse and Empire* (New York: Oxford University Press, 1990), 137–45; and idem, *Revelation*, ANTC (Nashville: Abingdon, 1998), 24–30.

20. Κατὰ τὰ ἔργα (Rev. 2:23; 18:6; 20:12, 13); ὡς τὸ ἔργον (Rev. 22:12).

The meaning of "works" in Revelation is not denoted as much as it is connoted. The understanding of works, whether deserving reward or punishment, is connected to the familiar biblical division of humanity into two groups, saints and sinners, insiders and outsiders, a view also occurring in Paul.[21] In the Apocalypse this division is depicted in a far more pronounced apocalyptic perspective. Nevertheless, as also in Paul it is not strictly sectarian because God's judgment—and so too the standard of judgment according to works—applies equally to both insiders and outsiders on the basis of the impartiality of God. The saints are praised for their commendable works but they are also severely rebuked for condemnable works. The sinners, who are repeatedly designated with the telling characterization "inhabitants of the earth" or "earth-dwellers" (lit. "those who dwell on the earth")[22] do works for which they are severely punished but are assumed also to be capable of repentance,[23] and therefore of deeds for which they would be rewarded. The works themselves, whether positive or negative, are defined in polar relationship to each other.

With respect to the saints, the meaning of "works" in Revelation is bound up with the meaning of a whole series of words occurring in the same contexts such as "labor" or "toil" (*kopos*), "patience" or "endurance" (*hypomonē*), "affliction" or "tribulation" (*thlipsis*), "poverty" (*ptōcheia*), "love" (*agapē*), "faith" or "faithfulness" (*pistis*), and "service" (*diakonia*). On the one hand, the Christian communities are variously praised and encouraged on account of their works that evince such attributes. On the other hand, the communities are admonished and threatened with extreme judgment on account of the lack of such attributes. John's primary purpose is hortatory in line with the epistolary character of the Apocalypse. The ultimate intent is not to condemn and punish but to praise and chastise in order to bring about a way of life that God will crown with eschatological blessings. The standard of judgment according to works functions, on the one hand, as praise and promise of reward and, on the other hand, as critique and admonition leading

21. 1 Cor. 5:12; Col. 4:5; 1 Thess. 4:12.

22. Οἱ κατοικοῦντες ἐπὶ τῆς γῆς (Rev. 3:10; 6:10; 8:13; 11:10; 13:8, 14; 17:8; cf. 13:12; 17:2). See A. B. Luter and E. K. Hunter, "The 'Earth Dwellers' and the 'Heaven Dwellers': An Overlooked Interpretive Key to the Apocalypse," *Faith and Mission* 20, no.1 (2002): 3–18, who take Rev. 7:9–15 as the probable location of the rapture of the saints. However, Rev. 18:4 ("Come out of her, my people") addresses the saints who are still on earth, calling them to an alternative life distinct from that of pagan society symbolized by Rome. Revelation is not at all concerned with the concept of rapture. On the contrary, one of its main themes is that the saints on earth are God's witness on earth through suffering up to the final eschatological events.

23. Along with demonstrating God's vindication of the saints, part of the divine purpose behind the cosmic judgments against the "earth-dwellers" is to drive them to repent of their evil deeds (Rev. 9:20–21; 16:9). The angel's dramatic announcement of the "eternal gospel" of salvation from mid-heaven is addressed strikingly to the "earth-dwellers"—who oppress and persecute the saints (Rev. 14:6–7).

to correction. In line with the author's rhetorical purposes, the conclusion of each of the seven oracles, and the conclusion of the whole book, highlight the eschatological blessings promised to those who achieve victory through commendable works.

Here we may connect with Yinger's study on several points. The understanding of works in Revelation signifies a whole way of life, just as Yinger finds true of the entire Jewish tradition and Paul. The issue is not one of counting and weighing individual works and their merits in a casuistic way, but one of whole-hearted devotion and obedience to God. Revelation also takes for granted the biblical principle that God's judgment begins with the household of God. This principle, however, though it distinguishes true and false members in the same faith community, does not achieve in Revelation or Paul's letters the same kind of sectarian significance that Yinger finds prominent in the Pseudepigrapha and Qumran where salvation is for the faithful alone. For Paul and the prophet John the main dichotomy is not between true and false Christians as much as between Christians and outsiders for whom the hope of salvation still remains. Nevertheless, that God's judgment according to deeds begins with God's own household entails the considerable implication that the security of the saints in Paul as well as in the Apocalypse provides no immunity from God's judgment, just as in the Jewish tradition according to Yinger. Finally, Revelation abundantly attests to the principle of not only judgment but also reward according to works that Yinger sees revived in Paul because of the new confidence of believers who already enjoy in part the new creation in Christ and the Spirit.[24]

The more specific aspects of the understanding of works in the Apocalypse are related to the author's major concerns about false teaching within the communities and persecution against Christians from without. Throughout the Apocalypse both concerns are linked in a particular way to the recurring terminology of toil, affliction, endurance, faithfulness, and witness. Neither reason nor space here calls for attention to these issues that have been taken up by numerous commentaries and studies.[25] As regards false teaching, suffice it to say that the false teachers, signified by the code words Balaam, Nicolaitans, and Jezebel (Rev. 2:14–15, 20), are influential rivals to John who

24. According to Yinger (*Paul, Judaism, and Judgment*, 88), judgment by deeds in the Pseudepigrapha and the Qumran literature normally signifies punishment for the sinners and mercy (rather than reward) for the righteous. In this literature, Yinger found not a single instance of reward for the righteous on the basis of good deeds because of a profound sense of sinfulness that could not countenance such claims.

25. For example, Bauckham, *Climax of Prophecy*; idem, *The Theology of the Book of Revelation* (New York: Cambridge University Press, 1993); Adela Yarbro Collins, *Crisis and Catharsis: The Power of the Apocalypse* (Philadelphia: Westminster, 1984); Elisabeth Schüssler Fiorenza, *The Book of Revelation: Justice and Judgment* (Minneapolis: Fortress, 1998); and major commentaries by David E. Aune, *Revelation*, WBC 52a–c (Dallas: Word Books, 1997–98); and G. K. Beale, *The Book of Revelation: A Commentary on the Greek Text* (Grand Rapids: Eerdmans, 1999).

advocate more or less free interaction with pagan culture and its attendant idolatrous practices.[26] In biblical perspective, the seer's references to fornication (*porneia, porneuein*, Rev. 2:14, 20–21), and also the parallel references to either soiled or white garments (Rev. 3:4, 5, 18), have most likely in view not sexual matters alone as much as a compromised way of life pertaining to the dominant Greco-Roman culture. It is Rome, the "great harlot," that has intoxicated and corrupted the nations and "the earth-dwellers" with the "wine of its fornication."[27]

As regards persecution, the disputed issue of the nature and intensity of persecution in Asia Minor in the late first century is not central to this essay.[28] I take it for granted that, just as in the case of 1 Thessalonians, 1 Peter, and later Pliny's letter to Trajan (112 CE), there is early evidence of significant forms of social oppression and specific instances of violent persecution against Christians. The prophet John seems to presuppose such experiences for himself and for some of his communities (Rev. 1:9; 2:10, 13) and anticipates greater suffering in the imminent future. What I underscore here is that John's particular view of the principle of judgment according to works is directly linked to the interlocked questions of fornication as cultural accommodation and of affliction or persecution resulting from active resistance to such accommodation. In other words, John's distinctive view of works, both positive and negative, have to do with his view of a person's and community's basic stance to the dominant culture driven by Rome and its vacuous claims of peace, justice, and prosperity benefiting universal humanity.

From this perspective, according to the prophet John, the greatest positive work is to worship God and follow God's moral commandments. John's essential message is that the creator and almighty God (*pantokratōr*),[29] not caesar, is the true ruler of the universe. The "eternal gospel"[30] announced to the world by the angelic messenger in Rev. 14:6–7 proclaims: "Fear God and give him glory; . . . worship him who made heaven and earth." The prominent

---

26. Whether these false teachers are soft accommodators with respect to the eating of idol meats and giving honor to the emperor in harmony with the teaching of Paul (Rom. 13:1–7; 1 Cor. 10:25–26) or outright Gnostics wholly accommodated to Greco-Roman idolatrous practices under the premise that such practices require no explicit verbal confessions of faith is an important question but not directly relevant here.

27. Ἐκ τοῦ οἴνου τῆς πορνείας αὐτῆς, Rev. 17:2. See also Rev. 17:4; 18:3, 9; 19:1–2.

28. Most scholars agree that various forms and degrees of persecution occurred in Asia Minor and are historically presupposed by the author of Revelation. Of a sharply different view is Thompson, *Book of Revelation*, 128–32, 171–81, who finds most Christians in Asia Minor comfortably accommodated to the prevailing culture and deems that the theme of persecution in Revelation is but an apocalyptic literary motif without historical substance.

29. Lit. "one who holds all things [in his hands]" or "who has dominion over all things." See esp. Rev. 11:17; 15:3; 16:7, 14; 19:6, 15.

30. Εὐαγγέλιον αἰώνιον.

role of the throne room (chaps. 4–5), as well as the frequent scenes of the worship of God and of the Lamb throughout the Apocalypse,[31] drive home the same message about the worship of God. On two occasions the prophet himself is pointedly instructed to worship none but God (Rev. 19:10; 22:9). In contrast to the worship of God, the greatest condemnable work is to worship the beast and follow its idolatrous and immoral ways. The "earth-dwellers" are defined precisely as those who are enthralled by the wondrous works of the beast and worship its image (Rev. 13:4–8). At the forefront of their evil works is the worship of demons and idols (Rev. 9:20). The series of divine calamities against the "earth-dwellers" functions both as punishment on account of their idolatry as well as extreme correctives to lead to the worship of God, which for the most part they refuse to do and suffer continuous disasters (Rev. 11:13; 16:8, 21).

For the seer, there is no room for compromise. The choice is either between Rome and its works (Rev. 18:6) or Christ and his works (Rev. 2:26).[32] The two ways are irreconcilable. Rome's ways are marked by self-glorification ("goddess Roma"), wealth, luxury, and prosperity by which it deceives and corrupts the nations while concealing its abominations of violence, injustice, wantonness, lies, and slavery (Rev. 18:1–19). Not least, Rome is accountable to God for the blood of the saints who are killed for resisting its idolatrous practices.[33] To follow Rome, as the "earth-dwellers" do, is to participate in its abominations of murder, sorcery, immorality,[34] thefts, all motivated by the worship of demons (Rev. 9:20–21). Thus the saints are commanded: "Come out of her, my people, lest you take part in her sins, lest you share in her plagues" (Rev. 18:4). This call, of course, is not for physical withdrawal but for a distinctly countercultural way of life in the midst of Greco-Roman society. In contrast, Christ's way is the way of the slain Lamb bearing testimony to God's truth and achieving victory through suffering and death. To follow the slain Lamb, as the saints do, is to participate in Jesus' witness to God's word and in Jesus' suffering because of their own witness and suffering in active resistance to the prevailing culture. The assumption is that to live as a Christian is to live *in* the world and not *apart* from it. However, the choice provokes conflict and entails suffering, even the prospect of death (Rev. 13:9–10). The supreme ideal is symbolized by the 144,000 martyrs who stand victorious and sing praises before God's throne. The recurrent calls for faithfulness to God and the Lamb, and the exhortations to patient endurance to the point of death, signify that for the author of the Apocalypse the greatest commendable work is martyrdom itself.

31. Rev. 7:9–17; 11:15–18; 15:3–4; 19:1–8.
32. Τὰ ἔργα αὐτῆς ("her works," Rev. 18:6) and, with Christ speaking, τὰ ἔργα μου ("my works," Rev. 2:26).
33. Rev. 16:3; 17:6; 18:24.
34. In Rev. 9:21, "fornication" may signify specifically sexual immorality.

Grace and Judgment

The expectation of judgment is the most prominent theme in the Apocalypse centered on God's imminently awaited eschatological day. This great day is variously announced as "the hour of trial or testing,"[35] "the great day of the wrath" of God and of the Lamb,[36] "the mystery of God,"[37] and God's "hour of judgment."[38] The global calamities against humanity reach a crescendo in the imagery of the winepress and of Christ himself, bearing a two-edged sword, coming to tread on the winepress of "the fury of the wrath of God" (Rev. 14:10, 19; 19:15).[39] God's day of wrath is intensified by the opposing "fury" of the Dragon, Babylon, and their partner nations that also "raged" (Rev. 11:18) against God, all involved as aggressive participants in the apocalyptic drama. At the heart of all this is God's eschatological day of judgment involving the defeat of the evil forces, the final judgment of humanity, and God's crowning triumph through the epiphany of the new world (Rev. 19:19–21; 20:7–15; chap. 21).

The Unity of Grace and Judgment

However, if judgment is the most prominent theme, grace is theologically the most significant one. In the Apocalypse grace and judgment are two sides of the same reality, something comparable to Paul's understanding of God's righteousness. For Paul, God's righteousness or justice (*dikaiosynē*) involves not only a forensic aspect but also a powerful present reality—God's ongoing saving activity bringing about the new creation in Christ. Paul tells us that God's righteousness is "being revealed" as saving power to those who by faith accept the gospel (Rom. 1:16–17), and at the same time "being revealed" as the "wrath of God" to those who suppress God's truth by clinging to idolatry, falsehood, and all manner of moral evil (Rom. 1:18–32). If allowances are made for the extreme apocalyptic imagery of Revelation, the prophet John advocates the same truth. In John's symbolic world, where all aspects of time and space fuse into one reality, God's grace and judgment are viewed as simultaneous activities. For example, the repeated scenes of heavenly worship interjected in the series of catastrophic visions function not only as comfort and encouragement to the saints (and stylistic relief in the narrative) but also as signs of God's ever-present transcendent world, the greater reality of grace always at hand. The most notable illustration of the

---

35. Τῆς ὥρας τοῦ πειρασμοῦ (Rev. 3:10).

36. Ἡ ἡμέρα ἡ μεγάλη τῆς ὀργῆς αὐτῶν (Rev. 6:17). The plural pronoun in this context refers to God and the Lamb, not to the human recipients of God's judgments.

37. Τὸ μυστήριον τοῦ Θεοῦ (Rev. 10:5–7).

38. Ἡ ὥρα τῆς κρίσεως αὐτοῦ (Rev. 14:7).

39. Τοῦ θυμοῦ τῆς ὀργῆς τοῦ Θεοῦ (Rev. 19:15), where "fury" (θυμός) and "wrath" (ὀργή) are coupled.

integral relationship of grace and judgment is Christ himself depicted in the striking alternate metaphors of slain lamb, warrior judge, and bridegroom. In the seer's apocalyptic world, the relationship of grace and judgment is like looking at a gigantic thunderstorm in which ample spaces of glorious light and ominous dark clouds paradoxically mix in the same awesome spectacle, but grace and light have the last word.

The unity between grace and judgment is grounded in the very nature of God as creator, ruler, and judge.[40] In the seer's biblical perspective, God is praised not only for the attributes of holiness, glory, honor, and power, but also for God's actions that exhibit faithfulness, truth, deliverance, justice, and salvation.[41] In particular God's attribute of justice is emphatically celebrated as the series of global judgments reach their zenith (Rev. 15:3; 16:5, 7; 19:2). The warrior Christ, who comes to judge and make war, comes to do so precisely on behalf of justice (Rev. 19:11).[42] The seer's fervent hope is for God to manifest the divine attributes not by arbitrary self-assertion but by means of justice in order to put the world right. Revelation is above all a call for justice, a cry for the kingdom, a prayer for the disclosure of God's rule on earth as it is in heaven.[43] This call for justice is meant first of all for the persecuted saints. But it is also meant for all those who are killed, oppressed, and corrupted by superpower Rome (Rev. 17:1–2; 18:24). At the heart of the matter is "a global struggle for truth,"[44] that is, whether the ultimate meaning of existence lies with the creator God and the way of the Lamb or with Caesar and Rome's policies in ruling the world. However, the actualization of God's justice in the face of opposing forces necessarily entails both grace and judgment. Grace and judgment are authentic aspects of the same manifestation of God's reign. This is, of course, the core theological theme of the Apocalypse and the ground of its enduring message.[45]

Eschatological Favoritism

The prophet John, just as other New Testament authors, admittedly features a distinct "eschatological favoritism" toward the saints. Christ has already

40. The Apocalypse is a literary and theological paean to the true, living, creator God of the Scriptures disclosed in triadic mystery. God is the Alpha and the Omega, the possessor of the sacred name Yahweh/Kyrios, the one "who is and who was and is to come," the sole ruler who sits on a single heavenly throne and controls all things as almighty (παντοκράτωρ). See, e.g., Rev. 1:4–5; 4:8–11; 5:6.

41. Rev. 11:17–18; 15:3–4; 16:5–7.

42. Ἐν δικαιοσύνῃ κρίνει καὶ πολεμεῖ (Rev. 19:11).

43. The focal theme in Schüssler Fiorenza's superb work, *Book of Revelation*.

44. Richard Bauckham, *Bible and Mission: Christian Witness in a Postmodern World* (Grand Rapids: Baker Academic, 2003), 100.

45. On the theme of judgment in the Scriptures, see Stephen H. Travis, *Christ and the Judgment of God: Divine Retribution in the New Testament* (Basingstoke, Hants: Marshall Pickering, 1986); and Christopher D. Marshall, *Beyond Retribution: A New Testament Vision for Justice, Crime, and Punishment* (Grand Rapids: Eerdmans, 2001).

shown his love for the saints and has already redeemed them by his blood, making them a holy kingdom to God (Rev. 1:4–5; cf. 5:9; 14:3–4). The saints already possess the crown and can only lose it (Rev. 3:11). The sealing of the saints, in contrast to the marking of the followers of the beast, is the most graphic symbol of belonging to God and of enjoying the privileged status as God's elect people.[46] Most telling of all is that the saints already share in Christ's royal rule and, by means of their prayers, participate in God's judgments against the "earth-dwellers" (Rev. 1:6, 9; 3:21; 5:10; 6:10; 8:3–4). However, this feature of "favoritism" in the Apocalypse is qualified by an "eschatological reservation" also found in Paul and other New Testament authors. For the seer, as mentioned above, God's judgment begins with God's people for whom the possibility of loss of status is real. The horrific chastisements against sinful humanity are in the first place meant as admonitions to the Christian communities themselves, the direct addressees and recipients of the book. Moreover, the saints are promised no exemption from persecution and suffering at the hands of Rome and the nations. On the contrary, the Christians are no less vulnerable to suffering and death than the slain Lamb himself. To put it in Pauline terms, the way of the saints on earth is the way of the crucified and exalted Christ. Just as the saints share in the royal and judging attributes of Christ over against the "earth-dwellers," so also they participate in the suffering and the blood sacrifice of Christ for the redemption of the world.[47]

Thus we see that, on the one hand, the prophet John celebrates salvation as a glorious gift. "Salvation belongs to God and the Lamb" (Rev. 7:10). On the other hand, the seer also emphatically insists that the saints must "conquer," just as Jesus "conquered,"[48] through concrete deeds of faithful witness unto death in their daily engagement with the prevailing culture. The theological structure of Revelation is the same as that of Paul, Hebrews, and 1 Peter. It rests squarely on the biblical themes of election and covenant, promise and fulfillment, and the dialectic of "already" and "not yet," deeply rooted in the biblical tradition. On this basis, God's grace and judgment, and the requirement of obedience and victory through works, the standard of God's

---

46. The sealing of the saints is apparently also a sign of special protection from God's catastrophic judgments that harm only the "earth-dwellers" according to the paradoxical logic of the apocalyptic seer (Rev. 3:10; 7:3; 9:4; 16:2). The author never raises the question of how it is possible for believers to be protected from the impact of such cosmic disasters when living on the same planet as do sinners who are being punished. The suggestion by Beale (*Book of Revelation*, xii, 404) that the sealing of the saints is protection against loss of faith is unlikely because πίστις in Revelation signifies faithfulness in terms of conduct. The sealed saints, too, despite their sealing, enjoy no presumed security but are subject to the same divine judgment as Rome and its followers unless they depart from evil ways (Rev. 18:4).

47. See Bauckham, *Theology of the Book of Revelation*, 98–114. A striking parallel is a similar motif of sharing in the sufferings of Christ in Paul (2 Cor. 4:10–12; Gal. 6:17; Phil. 3:10–11; Col. 1:24).

48. The same verb "to conquer" (νικᾶν) is used. See Rev. 2:26; 3:21; 5:5; 12:11.

impartial judgment, are symbiotic rather than opposing elements in the covenant relationship between God and God's people. The heart of God's covenant with his people is love and mercy, not cold justice and punishment. God's judgment always bears a remedial intent toward repentance, restoration, and salvation.

The grace perspective of the Apocalypse embraces all creation. The goal of the disclosure of God's rule through Christ's death, enthronement, and coming is the liberation of the whole cosmos from the powers of evil. The "earth-dwellers" are part of God's creation and thus the objects of God's grace, too. In several places Revelation indicates that the judgments against sinful humanity, just as the threats of judgment against the saints, bear a disciplinary and remedial purpose, that is, to bring about repentance and presumed reward (Rev. 3:19; 11:13; 15:4). To be sure, for the most part the "earth-dwellers" do not show repentance but keep to their wickedness and stubborn cursing of God (Rev. 9:20–21; 16:9, 11, 21). This motif of human rebelliousness against God is of course well attested in the Scriptures. At the same time, however, the prophet's perspective is prominently inspired by the scriptural promise that the nations, too, will have a share in God's day of salvation. The victory song in Revelation 15:3–4, which exalts God's "just and true ways,"[49] ends with the proclamation that "all nations shall come and worship you, for your just judgments" or "righteous deeds" (*dikaiōmata*) "have been revealed." The unity of grace and judgment could not be more powerfully expressed. The eschatological disclosure itself of God's "just judgments" serves as means by which salvation comes to the nations. For the author, this offer of salvation to the nations through God's "just deeds" stands in contrast to what the author unmasks in his book: Rome's "unjust deeds" (*adikēmata*, Rev. 18:5), which deceive and bring corruption and death to humankind.

Objections to Apocalyptic

Objections to the prophet's apocalyptic style and thought are well known. The radical opposition to mainstream culture, the division of humanity into two groups, the portrayal of horrific violence, the calls to rejoice and celebrate over God's judgments against Rome and the "earth-dwellers,"[50] all these elements have variously given cause for offense in both ancient and modern times. The assessment of such questions is largely dependent on one's own presuppositions. Decades ago D. H. Lawrence contemptuously dismissed the Apocalypse as a book of Christian envy and of the rejection of civilization

---

49. Δίκαιαι καὶ ἀληθιναὶ αἱ ὁδοί σου (Rev. 15:3).

50. With regard to this last element some commentators have observed that, in view of the Apocalypse's emphasis on and witness to justice, it seems a loss of proportion to critique the Apocalypse for its occasional element of apparent vengeful joy over the judgment of evildoers.

itself. More recently Leonard L. Thompson, while a noted biblical scholar, characterized John's thought as essentially "deviant" not only from pagan culture but also from mainstream Christianity in Asia Minor.[51] For Thompson, John's profound sense of suffering and crisis was entirely of his own imagination, a mere literary topos of apocalyptic literature, with little or no basis in the historical circumstances of the Asian churches that had already happily joined the cultural mainstream. John therefore "deviates" from the "majority knowledge" of both the dominant society and the Christian community, and thus draws sectarian "hard boundaries," which "close the gate" to outsiders.

The issue of how far the Asian churches may have accommodated to the prevailing culture is historically debatable. The sensibilities of the apocalyptic seer toward pagan society were no doubt exceedingly sharper than those of the rank-and-file Christian. However, the author of the Apocalypse does not close the gates of God's mercy and salvation to outsiders. On the contrary he pointedly exults in the expectation that the New Jerusalem will bring "healing for the nations" and that the nations will "walk in its light" and "its gates will never be shut" (Rev. 21:24–26; 22:2). If any gate is closed, as in the case of the Laodicean Christians, it is closed from within and still Christ stands at the door knocking, ready to enter (Rev. 3:20). From God's side, the gates of God's grace are always open to saints and sinners alike. If John's theological position is deemed "deviant," then it is no more "deviant" in substance than Paul's proclamation of grace and judgment in the crucified and exalted Christ. If the gospel itself is viewed as "deviant," then there would be no gospel at all to proclaim. In that case, the gospel evaporates into a mist of innocuous moral appeals to justice, peace, and freedom while evil wreaks havoc on earth. Then the dire warnings of the Apocalypse concerning the dark and ugly side of reality prove equally true. Evil, through human self-assertion, exploitation, conflict, and war, continues to torture humanity in desperate need of divine deliverance because of humanity's own refusal to heed God's word of grace and judgment and thus to be accountable for its choices and actions before God.

What is to be critiqued is not the message but the medium of the Apocalypse, not its theology but its overwhelming apocalyptic character. The integration of the two elements in a book of symbols and images requires both clear distinctions and balanced interpretation. A literal reading of Revelation as a code book for deciphering maps in history is a distortion and betrayal of its message. The greater Eastern thinkers had an eloquent reserve toward this book, some of whom conducted the first demythologization of biblical apocalyptic imagery.[52] To this day the Orthodox Church excludes the

51. Thompson, *Book of Revelation*, 181–85, 191–97.

52. A tradition begun by Origen and developed by Gregory of Nyssa and others such as, most notably, Isaac the Syrian. For Origen and Gregory, see Brian E. Daley, *The Hope of the Early Church: A Handbook of Patristic Eschatology* (Cambridge: Cambridge University Press, 1991), 47–60, 85–89.

Apocalypse from liturgical recitation. N. T. Wright has proposed that the apocalyptic imagery may not have been taken literally by the biblical authors themselves.[53] According to Wright, such imagery was intended as a way of investing historical events with theological significance and not as a scenario of the end of the space-and-time universe. Whatever the case—and here is the call to the saints for epistemological humility—the apocalyptic images and metaphors concern realities whose nature and timing are beyond human speculation. The core hope of Revelation is not in the literal unfolding of historical events, whether past or future, but in the eschatological reality of God's triumph over evil in which God's very presence and glory will shine through all things.

For Isaac, see Hilarion Alfeyev, *The Spiritual World of Isaac the Syrian* (Kalamazoo: Cistercian Publications, 2000), 283–97. For many of these writers, particularly Isaac the Syrian, hell is not a physical place but a spiritual condition. Moved by the depth of love and the eternal goodness of God, Isaac most boldly contemplates that hell itself (as spiritual separation from God) and all its residents, including the demons, will, in the end of their own, turn to God and be redeemed, for otherwise God's will and plan for creation would be thwarted.

53. N. T. Wright, *Jesus and the Victory of God* (Minneapolis: Fortress, 1996), 96.

2

Apocalyptic Themes in the Monumental and Minor Art of Early Christianity

John Herrmann and Annewies van den Hoek

Introduction

It is widely agreed that apocalyptic writings, such as the book of Revelation, Ezekiel, and the "synoptic apocalypse" (Matt. 24:4–36; Mark 13:5–37; Luke 21:8–36), exerted a significant influence in early Christian art. The influence of Revelation, the most conspicuous of these texts, was great in the Latin West but less evident in parts of the East, where the book was regarded with suspicion from the third century onward.[1] The influence of the gospel apocalypse may have been somewhat undervalued in previous presentations, and apocalyptic passages in the Epistles may have to be added to those deserving

---

1. Suspicion was caused by Christian sects employing the text for their own purposes—especially for predictions of the imminent end of the world: see Helmut Koester, *Introduction to the New Testament*, 2 vols. (Philadelphia: Fortress; Berlin: de Gruyter, 1982), 2:256–57; Bernard McGinn, "Introduction: John's Apocalypse and the Apocalyptic Mentality," in *The Apocalypse in the Middle Ages*, ed. Richard K. Emmerson and Bernard McGinn (Ithaca, NY: Cornell University Press, 1992), 18.

attention. Many other apocalypses were available in the period,[2] but their influence (if any) on the arts has not yet come to general attention.

By and large, apocalyptic texts seem to have been taken up only in fragmentary form by artists, craftsmen, and their theological advisors. As Dale Kinney has pointed out, details tend to be lifted out of their context and adapted or mixed into traditional iconographies.[3] These selections, however, were used in impressive compositions in the most sacred and visually dramatic parts of churches: the apse, the wall above the apse, vaults, and the façade. The apocalyptic components supplement or enhance the visions of paradise or divinity that are shown in these areas.[4] Apocalyptic subject matter also made its appearance on many kinds of sculpture and minor arts, and these, too, should be given their due.

Artistic citations from apocalyptic texts draw on a narrow spectrum of the contents of the passages or books involved. Only those elements are chosen that tend to enhance the majesty and dignity of Christ. In contrast to medieval treatments of apocalyptic themes, tribulations, devastation, plagues, and personifications of evil are omitted from early Christian works. Monsters are admitted only to a limited degree.

It will be argued that the influence of the biblical apocalypses can be subtle and indirect as well as overt. Even when texts are not followed literally, the structure of the action in artistic compositions can be apocalyptic. Persons or objects may be changed to suit contemporary local interests and traditions, but their actions and relationships echo situations in the biblical visions of the second coming.

In this flexible environment, images are also drawn from non-Christian sources. Some of these motifs have emblematic meanings that enrich the transcendent scenes created in the service of the new religion. Others reflect contemporary practices of the late Roman and early Byzantine court.

The precise meanings of works of art with allusions to apocalyptic texts are often ambiguous, and authors have discussed at length whether they represent the second coming, the last judgment, the ascension, or a stable paradise.[5] In general, the thornier interpretive problems will be avoided here. Instead, the emphasis will be on mapping the presence of apocalyptic material and searching beyond the most salient elements of borrowings to spotlight peripheral material and underlying structures that stem from the same apocalyptic texts.

2. For a survey, see Philipp Vielhauer and Georg Strecker, "Apocalypses and Related Subjects," in *New Testament Apocrypha*, ed. Wilhelm Schneemelcher, trans. and rev. R. McLaren Wilson, 2 vols. (Cambridge: Clarke, 1992), 2:542–752.

3. Dale Kinney, "The Apocalypse in Early Christian Monumental Decoration," in Emmerson and McGinn, *Apocalypse in the Middle Ages*, 200–201. For a convenient though not exhaustive list of monumental examples, see ibid., 211–16.

4. On apse compositions, see Christa Ihm, *Programme der christlichen Apsismalerei vom vierten Jahrhundert bis zur Mitte des achten Jahrhunderts* (Wiesbaden: Steiner, 1960; 2nd ed. 1992); Margaret Frazer, in Kurt Weitzmann, ed., *Age of Spirituality: Late Antique and Early Christian Art, Third to Seventh Century*, exhibition catalog (New York: Metropolitan Museum of Art, 1979), 556–57.

5. The case of the S. Pudenziana apse is exemplary; see Kinney, "Apocalypse," 209–10.

Biblical and Pagan Sources in the Latin West

Pre-Constantinian Times: The Sheep and the Goats

Figure 2.1. Marble sarcophagus lid with the separation of the sheep from the goats, late third or early fourth century, from Rome.

Christ's revelations about the end of the world, his second coming, and the heavenly kingdom are "apocalyptic" in the same sense as the more bizarre visions of Revelation.[6] Apocalyptic texts from the Gospels begin to have an impact on art in pre-Constantinian times with the representation of the separation of the sheep from the goats, an allegory of the Last Judgment (Matt. 25:31–46), on a sarcophagus of about 300 in the Metropolitan Museum of Art (fig. 2.1).[7] The composition continues the allegorical language of biblical references to the shepherd and the sheep: texts that were popular sources for the art of the catacombs. References to the Last Judgment remain rare in early Christian art, and it hardly exists apart from the allegory of the sheep and goats, which returns in the early sixth-century mosaics of St. Apollinare Nuovo, Ravenna.[8]

After 350: the A and Ω

One of the first unmistakable borrowings from Revelation is the use of the letters alpha and omega as a symbol of God's eternity (Rev. 1:8; 21:6; 22:13). Possibly the first firmly datable examples appear on bronze coins of the emperor Magnentius, minted in 353 CE in various cities of Gaul and the Rhineland (fig. 2.2).[9] The coin's reverse shows the chi and rho

Figure 2.2. Bronze coin of Magnentius, 353 CE: obverse, bust of the emperor; reverse, chrismon with alpha and omega.

6. An apocalyptic vision permeates Christ's sayings in the Gospels; see D. Allison Jr., "The Eschatology of Jesus," in *The Encyclopedia of Apocalypticism*, vol. 1, *The Origins of Apocalypticism in Judaism and Christianity*, ed. John Collins (New York: Continuum, 1998), 267–302.

7. Frazer, in Weitzmann, *Age of Spirituality*, 556, 558, cat. no. 501; J(osef) Engemann, "Images parousiaques dans l'art paleochrétienne," *L'Apocalypse de Jean: Traditions exégétiques et iconographiques: IIIe–XIIIe siècles* (Geneva: Droz, 1979), 77–78, fig. 4.

8. F. W. Deichmann, *Frühchristliche Bauten und Mosaiken von Ravenna* (Baden: Grimm, 1958), pls. 173–74; Wolfgang Fritz Volbach, *Early Christian Art* (New York: Abrams, 1962), pl. 151; Engemann, "Images," 78, fig. 5. Some Coptic apocalyptic imagery, however, may imply judgment: see below, p. 77, note 150, fig. 2.45.

9. C. H. V. Sutherland and R. A. G. Carson, eds., *The Roman Imperial Coinage*, rev. ed. (London: Spink, 1984–), vol. 8, cat. nos. 34, 160, 198, 319, 320; David Vagi, *Coinage and History of the Roman*

of Christ's name flanked by the apocalyptic letters. In the West, the use of this embellished monogram became endemic in the art of 350–450. Sometimes it may have been a symbol of Christ in an anti-Arian sense,[10] but in other cases, it may have been little more than a proclamation of Christian allegiance. In the East it seems to have had less currency than in the West. It appears in a fourth-century tomb painting in Sofia, Bulgaria,[11] in funerary inscriptions in Macedonia,[12] on the Column of Arcadius in Constantinople,[13] and on sixth-century liturgical silver.[14]

The Lamb on Mount Zion

In the second half of the fourth century, complex compositions set in paradise began to draw—and draw heavily—on concepts and details inspired by Revelation. The literal borrowings may be limited, but the atmosphere is permeated with an apocalyptic spirit. A fresco in the Catacomb of Saints Marcellinus and Peter presents some unmistakable borrowings (fig. 2.3).[15] Christ's halo is flanked by the A and Ω, and below his throne is the Lamb of God, whose halo is also marked with the apocalyptic letters and with a small monogrammatic cross. The Lamb stands on a hill, which must be Mount Zion (as in Rev. 14:1). At the foot of Zion is the River Jordan, identified by the inscription IOR/DAS, which flanks the Lamb's halo. Zion is simultaneously the mountain of paradise, since four rivers of Eden (Gen. 2:10–14) flow from it. In the context of this fresco, the springs may be an allusion to the "water of life . . . flowing from the throne of God and of the Lamb" in the New Jerusalem (Rev. 22:1). Even in these citations, however, there are differences of detail from the text. The rivers are the four of Genesis rather than the one of Revelation, and the Lamb lacks the seven horns and seven eyes that it has elsewhere in Revelation (e.g., Rev. 5:6). In

---

Empire, 2 vols. (Sidney, OH: Amos, 1999), cat. no. 3293. See also Jochen Garbsch and Bernhard Overbeck, *Spätantike zwischen Heidentum und Christentum*, Ausstellungskataloge der Prähistorischen Staatssammlung 17 (Munich: Prähistorische Staatssammlung, 1989), cat. nos. M149, M150; www.coinarchives.com/a/results.php?results=100&search=ric+magnentius+34.

10. Kinney, "Apocalypse," 202.

11. Velizar Velkov, in Beat Brenk, ed., *Spätantike und frühes Christentum* (Berlin: Propyläen Kunstgeschichte, Supplementbände, 1977), cat. no. 396b.

12. E.g., Denis Feissel, *Recueil des inscriptions chrétiennes de Macédoine du IIIe au Vie siècle* (Athens: École Française d'Athènes; Paris: de Boccard, 1983), cat. nos. 12, 25, 180.

13. André Grabar, *Christian Iconography: A Study of Its Origins* (Princeton, NJ: Princeton University Press, 1980), fig. 128.

14. Helmut Buschhausen, in Weitzmann, *Age of Spirituality*, cat. no. 543, and Jack Schrader, in Weitzmann, *Age of Spirituality*, cat. no. 546. The Dumbarton Oaks pyxis, apparently of earlier date, is of unknown provenance; see Susan Boyd, in Weitzmann, *Age of Spirituality*, cat. no. 550.

15. Kinney, "Apocalypse," 202–3, 211; Maria Andalor, "I prototipi pagani e l'archetipo del volto di Cristo," in *Aurea Roma: Dalla città pagana alla città cristiana*, ed. Serena Ensoli and Eugenio La Rocca (Roma: L'erma di Bretschneider, 2000), 414, fig. 1.

Figure 2.3. Christ, Lamb of
God, Peter, Paul, and saints
of the catacomb, fresco,
late fourth century, Catacomb of SS. Marcellino e
Pietro, Rome.

all probability, the Lamb's attributes were not multiplied because doing so
would violate, on the one hand, traditions of Greco-Roman naturalism and,
on the other hand, traditions of shepherd allegory established in previous
Christian art.[16]

Many such theologically sophisticated compositions developed after about
350 are infused with the compositional principles of non-Christian Roman
art. Flanking Christ in this fresco are Saints Peter and Paul, and on the level
below are four lesser saints, whose relics lay in the catacomb: Gorgonius, Peter,
Marcellinus, and Tiburtius.[17] All six saints gesture with veneration toward
Christ or the Lamb. As has been frequently noted, such compositions recall
Late Roman court ceremonial.[18] As in the emperor's distribution of largess
on the Arch of Constantine,[19] figures in two ranks and in virtually identical
poses gesture toward an authoritative central figure.

16. Kinney, "Apocalypse," 202.

17. For a gold-glass medallion at Oxford with Christ seated between Peter and Paul and six saints
who are not limited to the twelve apostles (the preserved names are Timothy, Sixtus or Justus, Simon,
and Florus), see Charles Rufus Morey, *The Gold-Glass Collection of the Vatican Library with Additional Catalogues of Other Gold-Glass Collections*, ed. Guy Ferrari (Vatican: Biblioteca Apostolica
Vaticana, 1959), cat. no. 364; Grabar, *Christian Iconography*, fig. 171; Frazer, in Weitzmann, *Age of
Spirituality*, cat. no. 472.

18. Johannes Deckers, "Constantin und Christus," in *Spätantike und frühes Christentum*, exhibition catalog, ed. Herbert Beck and Peter C. Bol (Frankfurt am Main: Liebieghaus, 1983), 274, fig. 113,
hereafter Liebieghaus 1983. Kinney, "Apocalypse," 203.

19. Grabar, *Christian Iconography*, 44, fig. 116; Diana Kleiner, *Roman Sculpture* (New Haven and
London: Yale University Press, 1992), 452, fig. 413.

While the composition makes use of the formal language of non-Christian art of the time, biblical sources dictate many of the basic relationships and actions. Christ may be enthroned and wear clothing of purple, but unlike Christian emperors of the fourth to sixth centuries he has a long beard, long hair, and wears no crown. In the presence of the apocalyptic Lamb, he evokes the enthroned God of Revelation 4:2. He may have a book in his left hand, not a scroll in his right, as in Revelation, but the composition remains apocalyptic in structure if not in detail. In a similarly loose sense, the six saints of the fresco evoke the twenty-four elders of Revelation who adore the enthroned one.[20] The garlands (*serta*), fillets (*vittae* or *taeniae*), and flowers in the field around them recall the crowns (*coronae*) that the elders cast down before him (Rev. 4:10–11). On another level, these festive ornaments may also symbolize homage to the burials and relics in the catacomb, but the two references do not exclude each other.[21] Thus the composition of the fresco as a whole can be considered a structural parallel to the book of Revelation. The composition is broadly inspired by the text but modifies it according to local traditions and interests.

Christ Coming through the Clouds and the traditio legis

Figure 2.4. *Traditio legis*, mosaic, ca. 400 CE, baptistery, Naples.

Some compositions created around or not long after 350 show a high degree of theological manipulation of biblical sources, and apocalyptic material is worked into them to present an action in paradise. In one of these conceptual (rather than biblical) compositions— usually called the *traditio legis*—Christ is shown standing between Peter and Paul, handing the scroll of the law to Peter. The scroll is frequently inscribed "Dominus legem dat," as in the mosaics of the baptistery of Naples (fig. 2.4).[22] The composition, which was popular primarily in the second half of the fourth

20. Dale Kinney also sees the acclamatory context influenced by Rev. 5:8 ("Apocalypse," 203). For an extension of the elders' gesture of homage to other figures in early Christian art, see Beat Brenk, *Die frühchristlichen Mosaiken in S. Maria Maggiore zu Rom* (Wiesbaden: Franz Steiner, 1975), 16.

21. On the polyvalence of early Christian art, see Eduard Stommel, *Beiträge zur Ikonographie der konstantinischen Sarkophagplastik* (Bonn: Peter Hanstein, 1954), 66; Brenk, *Mosaiken*, last paragraph of the foreword (unpaged); Engemann, "Images," 79.

22. Jean-Louis Maier, *Le baptistère de Naples et ses mosaiques* (Fribourg: Éditions universitaires, 1964), 42–43, 108–20, pl. 8; Grabar, *Christian Iconography*, 42, fig. 102; Hugo Brandenburg, in Brenk, *Spätantike*, cat. no. 22a. For the theme in apses, see Ihm, *Programme*, 33–39.

century, is generally regarded as nonbiblical or biblical in only an indirect sense.[23] On the one hand, it is thought to conflate Christ giving the keys to Peter and God giving the law to Moses,[24] and on the other, it represents Christ giving the new law through the Gospels.[25] The first *traditio legis* may have been created for a redecoration of the apse of St. Peter's around the middle of the fourth century. Others have seen the *traditio* as the creation of workshops producing marble sarcophagi at that time.[26] In any case, the setting for the scene is otherwordly and in some sense apocalyptic in spite of the absence of a clear biblical source.

Figure 2.5. Bronze as of Faustina the Elder, after 141 CE.

In the *traditio legis* in the Naples baptistery, datable around 400, traditional imperial imagery is also used to evoke an ideal world above time and space, since Christ stands on the globe of the heavens (fig. 2.4).[27] In pagan art, the celestial sphere can have a variety of iconographic settings but usually includes the meanings of eternity and universality. In coinage, the globe is usually small and held in the hand of Aeternitas, various other personifications, or the Roman emperor. On coins issued

Figure 2.6. Denarius of Augustus, ca. 32–29 BCE.

to commemorate the death and deification of the Empress Faustina I, Aeternitas sits on the globe, which clearly represents the heavens since stars and the zodiac are indicated (fig. 2.5).[28] The emperor Alexander Severus (222–235 CE) is seated on the celestial globe on a bronze medallion, inscribed "temporum felicitas."[29] Virtually the only pagan divinity or personification who actually stands on the globe is Victoria.[30] Most commonly she awards emblems of triumph, a wreath

23. Walter Nikolaus Schumacher, "Dominus legem dat," *Römische Quartalschrift* 54 (1959): 1–39; Frazer, in Weitzmann, *Age of Spirituality*, 556, 559–60, cat. no. 503; Lucrezia Spera, "Traditio legis et clavium," in *Temi di iconografia paleocristiana*, ed. Fabrizio Bisconti (Rome: Vatican, 2000), 288–93, with bibliography; Fabrizio Bisconti, "Le basiliche cristiane e i nuovi programmi figurative," in Ensoli and La Rocca, *Aurea Roma*, 188–89.

24. The *traditio legis* has also been seen as a contamination of the assembly of the apostles with the giving of the law to Moses: Umberto Utro, "Le immagini e il culto dei santi sui vetri dorati romani durante il pontificato di Damaso e Siricio (366–399)," in *Ambrogio e Agostino*, 137.

25. Maier, *Baptistère de Naples*, 109–11.

26. M. Sotomayor, SJ, "Über die Herkunft der 'Traditio legis,'" *Römische Quartalschrift* 56 (1961): 215–30.

27. Grabar, *Christian Iconography*, 42, figs. 103–4.

28. Sutherland and Carson, *Roman Imperial Coinage*, 3:1159. For this and other types of coins included in this study, see www.coinarchives.com/a/.

29. Grabar, *Christian Iconography*, 42, fig. 104.

30. *LIMC* 8 (Zurich and Düsseldorf, 1997), s.v. "Victoria" (Rainier Vollkommer), cat. nos. 56–82. On rare occasions, the gods of the week can be shown on globes, as in bronze appliqués with Helios/

and a palm branch, as on a denarius of Augustus (fig. 2.6).[31] In late Roman times, the emperor, Jupiter, or Roma holds a small globe with Victoria. The image was perpetuated well into the fifth century, as on an issue of Theodosius II of 408 (fig. 2.7).[32] There was undoubtedly a carry-over of the composition's traditional meaning in the Naples baptistery. The globe on which Christ stands evokes his eternal victory over death, and he awards the law to Peter as a prize for martyrdom and primacy. The palm trees at the side of the Naples mosaic (see fig. 2.4) continue the Greco-Roman triumphal symbolism of the palm tree and

palm branch.[33] The palms also place the scene in paradise, a symbolic meaning that has different roots, as will be seen below.

Figure 2.7. Solidus of Theodosius II, 408 CE.

A biblical and apocalyptic element has been added to enrich the setting. Clouds tinted red above and blue below appear around Christ. They are inspired by Christ's prediction of his second coming: "They will see 'the Son of Man coming on the clouds of heaven' with power and great glory" (Matt. 24:30). The statement has a very similar form in Mark 13:26 and Luke 21:27. The words are then echoed at Christ's return in Revelation 1:7: "Look! He is coming with the clouds."[34] Colorful clouds become a staple of apocalyptic representations in the West. In this case, the precise meaning of the apocalyptic motif seems ambiguous; it may set the scene either at Christ's second coming or in the stable glory of heaven.

The Heavenly Jerusalem, the Heavenly Bethlehem, and the traditio legis

A gold-glass bowl fragment in the Vatican, datable in the span 366–399 CE, adds another element of apocalyptic origin to the *Dominus legem dat*

Sol and Venus from Sion, Switzerland; see *LIMC* 4 (Zurich and Munich, 1988), s.v. "Helios/Sol" (Cesare Letta), cat. no. 290; *LIMC* 8, s.v. "Venus" (Evamaria Schmidt), cat. no. 142.

31. H. Mattingly and E. A. Sydenham, *The Roman Imperial Coinage*, vol. 1, *Augustus to Vitellius* (London: Spink, 1926), Augustus, no. 255. For this and other types of coins included in this study, see www.coinarchives.com/a/lotviewer.php?LotID=224781&AucID=325&Lot=1227.

32. R. A. G. Carson, John Kent, and Andrew Burnett, *Roman Imperial Coinage*, vol. 10, *The Divided Empire and the Fall of the Western Parts, AD 395–491* (London: Spink, 1994), cat. no. 1320. The precise year of the issue can be determined since three *augusti* are indicated by the legend on the reverse. Roma holding the victoriola appears on a siliqua coined by a Vandal king of Africa in the name of Honorius between 450 and 484; see Cécile Morrisson, in *Ambrogio e Agostino*, cat. no. 287.

33. Fernand Cabrol and Henri Leclercq, *Dictionnaire d'archéologie chrétienne et de liturgie* (Paris: Letouzey, 1907–53), vol. 13, pt. 1, col. 949, s.v. "Palm, palmier"; Schumacher, "Dominus legem dat," 7.

34. Frederik van der Meer, *Maiestas Domini: Théophanies de l'Apocalypse dans l'art chrétien*, Studi di antichità cristiana, pubblicati per cura del Pontificio istituto di archeologia cristiana 13 (Città del Vaticano, Roma: Pontificio istituto di archeologia cristiana, 1938), 179–85, fig. 40.

Figure 2.8. Gold glass with *traditio legis*, 366–399 CE.

theme (fig. 2.8).[35] Christ stands on Mount Zion, hands a scroll to Peter, and gestures toward Paul. From the mountain flows water, which is designated as the River Jordan by the inscription IOR/DANES below the ground line. In the palm tree behind Paul is a phoenix, the bird of eternity; another palm would have appeared behind Peter in the missing part of the glass. The bird's presence reinforces the paradisiacal meaning of the palms, without excluding the triumphal meaning. In the exergue, the Lamb of God stands on the mountain of paradise (or Mount Zion once again), from which emerge the four rivers of Eden, or the water of life. On each side, three more lambs, representing apostles, proceed from two small and highly abbreviated city walls with crenellated towers, which are labeled ERVSALE and BECLE. This conception must surely have been inspired by the descent of the heavenly Jerusalem in Revelation 21:9–14. The names of the "apostles of the Lamb" are inscribed on its foundations (Rev. 21:14), a concept that may well have stimulated the procession of lambs in this gold glass and in other similar monuments.[36] Nowhere in Revelation, however, is the descent of a heavenly Bethlehem mentioned, and the addition of the second city, which is seen in other examples of the *traditio legis* as well,[37] must have been made in response to contemporary theological needs: that is, to articulate the distinction and the harmony between the churches *ex circumcisione* and *ex gentibus*.

35. Morey, *Gold-Glass*, cat. no. 78; Ihm, *Programme*, 36, fig. 6; Utro, "Immagini," 137, fig. 2.
36. For example, the mosaic of S. Costanza: Grabar, *Christian Iconography*, fig. 101; Bisconti, "Programmi," in Ensoli and La Rocca, *Aurea Roma*, 189, fig. 10.
37. See previous note.

Figure 2.9. Sarcophagus with the *traditio legis*, late fourth century.

Palm Trees and Ezekiel

The heavenly Jerusalem is visualized more forcefully on a late-fourth-century sarcophagus in the Louvre from the Mausoleum of the Anicii (an appendage of Old St. Peter's), and the *traditio legis* takes place with a grander cast of characters (fig. 2.9).[38] The central triad is essentially the same: Christ stands on the mountain of paradise/Mount Zion with its four rivers and hands the scroll of the law to Peter, who carries the cross of his martyrdom and receives the sacred scroll with covered hands, as in other examples of the scene (figs. 2.4, 8).[39] Paul and a palm tree appear at Christ's right. Two tiny figures at Christ's feet are probably the original owners of the sarcophagus. The other ten apostles now flank the central unit, and behind them are stretches of simulated masonry with towers, archways, and the crenellations of a fortress or a city's wall. This architectural backdrop must again have been inspired by the heavenly Jerusalem of biblical revelation. In the text, twelve angels, symbolizing the twelve tribes of Israel, stand at the twelve gates of the city (Rev. 21:12). Here, however, apostles replace the angels. There is a gap in the city wall at the center of the composition, where Christ is framed by a pair of columns carrying an entablature. This unit links the two sections of city wall, and the division suggests that not one but two cities may have been intended: Jerusalem and Bethlehem, as on the gold glass in the Vatican (see fig. 2.8).

38. François Baratte and Catherine Metzger, *Musée du Louvre: catalogue des sarcophages en pierre d'époque romaine et paléochrétienne* (Paris: Réunion des Musées Nationales, 1985), 316n212, 312–16 with bibliography; Catherine Metzger, in Ensoli and La Rocca, *Aurea Roma*, cat. no. 308. For the typology, see J. Dreskan-Weiland, *Repertorium der christlich-antiken Sarcophage, 2. Italien mit einen Nachtrag Rom und Ostia, Dalmatien, Museen der Welt* (Mainz: von Zabern, 1998), 52–64.

39. Usually considered a custom transferred from Roman court ceremonial: see, for example, Josef Engemann, "Die imperialen Grundlagen der frühchristlichen Kunst," in Liebieghaus 1983, 265, fig. 95.

Details of this and other "city gate sarcophagi,"[40] suggest that Revelation was not the only biblical and apocalyptic source behind the *traditio legis*. The palm tree between Christ and the column on the Louvre sarcophagus seems out of place in the urban setting evoked by the architectural background (fig. 2.9). The tree could perhaps be regarded simply as a motif transferred from *traditio legis* compositions without architectural backgrounds, such as the Naples mosaic and the Vatican gold glass (figs. 2.4, 8). The palm tree, however, takes on a specific meaning in the context of one of Ezekiel's visions. In his last vision, God reveals the future walled temple of Jerusalem to him (Ezek. 40–42). This extensive structure, which is like a city, has many gates, and on the jambs of these gateways are palm trees (Ezek. 40:16, 22, 26, 31, 34, 37). This embellishment goes back to the palm trees at the doors of Solomon's temple (1 Kings 6:29, 32, 35; 7:36). The palm trees, however, are left out of John's vision. In early Christian art, including other examples of the *traditio legis* (figs. 2.4, 8), palm trees define location (the heavenly Jerusalem and paradise) at least as much as they proclaim victory. This in itself evokes Ezekiel, where the palms are characteristic of the Lord's temple in an ideal future, rather than the Lord's victory. Edward Bleiberg derives the palms of paradise from the tree of knowledge and the tree of life in Genesis 2:16 and 3:22.[41] The species of these unique trees, however, is not defined; they are called *lignum*, not *palma*, and there were many other fruitful trees in the original paradise. The palm was associated with Judea in Roman and Jewish art,[42] but a geographic symbol could not by itself have reached such potent levels of eschatological symbolism in Christian art. The association with the historical and future temples must have been necessary to transform it into a symbol of paradise.

The parallel between Ezekiel's vision and the composition on the sarcophagus of the Anicii (fig. 2.9) can go further. After describing the temple, God details the practices that the Israelites must follow in the temple, and he delineates the land of Israel and his own land and city (Ezek. 43–48). Moreover, he charges Ezekiel to transmit these ordinances and laws (*leges*) to the Israelites (Ezek. 43:10–12). Transmission of the law, of course, takes place on the Louvre sarcophagus, although Peter, not Ezekiel, is the recipient. It

40. For the *traditio legis* on sarcophagi at Rome with bibliography, see Friedrich Wilhelm Deichmann, Giuseppe Bovini, and Hugo Brandenburg, *Repertorium der christlich-antiken Sarcophage, 1. Rom und Ostia* (Wiesbaden: Franz Steiner, 1967) cat. nos. 28, 200, 675–77, 679, 724, 1008.

41. Edward Bleiberg, *Tree of Paradise: Jewish Mosaics from the Roman Empire* (Brooklyn: Brooklyn Museum, 2005), 37.

42. Beat Brenk, "Die Christianisierung des jüdischen Stadtzentrums von Kapernaum," in *Byzantine East, Latin West: Art-Historical Studies in Honor of K. Weitzmann*, ed. Doula Mouriki et al. (Princeton, NJ: Department of Art and Archaeology, 1995), 24–26; S. Fine, "On the Development of a Symbol: The Date Palm in Roman Palestine and the Jews," *Jewish Studies Program* 4 (1989): 105–18; idem, *Journal for the Study of the Pseudepigrapha* 4 (1989): 105–18; Moshé Fischer, "Kapharnaum: Eine Retrospektive," *Jahrbuch für Antike und Christentum* 44 (2001): 152.

seems likely that the idea of connecting the heavenly Jerusalem with the transmission of the law to Peter could have been inspired by Ezekiel. In this context, the transmission of the law in the heavenly Jerusalem finds its best biblical foundation, and it becomes less of an arbitrary theological invention that tends to usurp Moses's historical function in favor of Peter's. Moses's reception of the law on Mount Sinai may lie somewhere in the background, but the composition is much more a conflation of the apocalyptic visions of Revelation and Ezekiel—modified, of course, by replacing the recipients and witnesses in those visions with figures from the New Testament.

City gate sarcophagi, such as that of the Anicii, date from late in the fourth century, several decades after the *traditio legis* had made its first appearance. Nonetheless, the theological thought and the apocalyptic sources behind the composition seem to be formulated more clearly in them than in other redactions, and these thoughts and sources may have been involved from the creation of the theme.

The Sign of the Son of Man in Heaven and the Four Living Creatures

Around the year 400, two new apocalyptic elements appear in the mosaics of the baptistery at Naples. In the center of the dome are a starry sky and a monogrammatic cross, that is, a "Latin" cross with the rho of Christos (fig. 2.10). The rho is surrounded with a halo as if it were the head of Christ. The cross is flanked by the apocalyptic letters and the hand of God places a wreath on it as an emblem of victory. As Friedrich Wilhelm Deichmann and others have noted, the basic elements of such a composition evoke Matthew 24:29: "Immediately after the suffering of those days the sun will be darkened and the moon will not give its light; the stars will fall from heaven, and the powers of the heavens will be shaken. Then the sign of the Son of Man will appear in heaven."[43] The text prescribes the elimination of the stars. Without the stars, however, it would have been impossible to establish a location for the cross, and it seems fair to consider their inclusion poetic license. Once again, the composition seems to be apocalyptic both in structure and inspiration even though it does not follow the text literally in every detail.

In the squinches or quarter-domes supporting the baptistery's vault are the living creatures of Revelation 4:6–8. Only two are well preserved, the winged man and the winged lion. They each have six, featherlike wings, but they are not quite as much like a peacock's tail as the text of Revelation would have them; the wings are not covered with eyes.

---

43. Apropos of the mausoleum of Galla Placidia: F. W. Deichmann, *Ravenna, Hauptstadt des spätantiken Abendlandes: Kommentar, 1. Teil* (Wiesbaden: Franz Steiner, 1974), 84–86; Engemann, "Images," 92–93, fig. 15.

Figure 2.11. Dome mosaic, 400–450 CE, Mausoleum of Galla Placidia, Ravenna.

Figure 2.10. Monogrammatic cross in sky, ca. 400 CE, baptistery, Naples.

A similar apocalyptic conception appears in the Mausoleum of Empress Galla Placidia (400–450). In the dome, a plain Latin cross floats in a starry sky, and the four living creatures circle around it (fig. 2.11).[44] The creatures have two wings rather than the six of the apocalyptic text, a modification that became standard in the Latin West during early Christian times.

Some versions of the sign appearing in heaven exclude the four creatures. A gold cross in a wreath emerges in a field of stars in the dome mosaic of a small memorial chapel at Casanarello near Lecce in south Italy.[45] A triple chrismon (three monograms, one superimposed on the other) floats in a starry sky in mosaic in a niche of the baptistery at Albenga on the Ligurian coast. At Albenga each monogram has an alpha and omega, and around the triple chrismon are twelve doves and a small Latin cross.[46] The sarcophagus of Aemiliana from Capri of the fifth or sixth century has three crosses carved on a starry field.[47] In this funerary context an announcement of the second coming has a particularly clear message of hope and anticipation.

44. For a full discussion of the various interpretations of the mosaic, see Deichmann, *Kommentar, 1. Teil*, 84–86. For the date, see ibid., 66. For illustrations, see Deichmann, *Bauten*, pls. 19–25.

45. Renato Bartoccini, "Casanarello e i suoi mosaici," *Felix Ravenna*, new series 4 (45)(1934): 157ff.; F. van den Meer and Christine Mohrmann, *Atlas of the Early Christian World*, trans. Mary Hedlund and H. H. Rowley (London, Edinburgh, New York, Toronto, Johannesburg, Melbourne, Paris: Nelson, 1959), 144–45, fig. 469; Deichmann, *Kommentar, 1. Teil*, 85–86; Brandenburg, in Brenk, *Spätantike*, cat. no. 19a.

46. Van den Meer and Mohrmann, *Atlas*, fig. 415; Brandenburg, in Brenk, *Spätantike*, cat. no. 20.

47. Deichmann, Bovini, and Brandenburg, *Repertorium der christlich-antiken Sarkophage, 1*, cat. no. 813 (Rome, Musei Capitolini).

African Red Slip Ware, Popular Art, and Imperishable Crowns

Some apocalyptic themes turn up in African red slip ware, a very widely distributed kind of ceramics produced in the area of modern Tunisia. Ceramics are earthy and popular by nature, and their imagery generally is concrete rather than literary or visionary. By and large, the influence of Revelation is mild. The apocalyptic letters attached to a monogrammatic cross, a popular motif throughout early Christian art in the West, also appears in African red slip ware in the fifth century (figs. 2.12a, b).[48] Strangely, the alpha

and omega are almost never associated with the chrismon or the Latin cross in African ceramics.[49] The Lamb of God (who is identified by a chrismon or a cross) appears on plates and lamps of 350–530 (fig. 2.13), but he does not stand on Mount Zion.[50] The

Figure 2.12a. Fragment of an African red slip ware trial piece with monogrammatic cross, 400–440 CE.

living creatures and Christ's ring of radiance of apocalyptic texts are cited on a type of African lamp with the ascension (fig. 2.39), but this unusual composition is better treated with other objects showing the same subject.

Visionary texts from the Epistles seem to have influenced the designers of African red slip ware. A fragmentary bowl in Djemila, Algeria, presents the best example (fig. 2.14). A long-haired youth lounges casually on a chair and holds out a wreath in his right hand. To his left, a balding, bearded man wrapped in a *pallium* makes a gesture of acclaim. A second such figure probably

Figure 2.12b. Fragment of an African red slip ware plate with monogrammatic cross, 440–510 CE.

48. John Hayes, *Late Roman Pottery* (London: British School at Rome, 1972), 272–74, types 289–90, figs. 54a–d; Abdelmajid Ennabli, *Lampes chrétiennes de Tunisie (Musés du Bardo et de Carthage)* (Paris: CNRS, 1976), cat. nos. 996–1004; Garbsch and Overbeck, *Heidentum und Christentum*, cat. nos. 113, 124; J. Herrmann and A. van den Hoek, *Light from the Age of Augustine: Late Antique Ceramics from North Africa (Tunisia)* (1st ed., Cambridge: Harvard Divinity School 2002; 2nd ed., Austin: Institute for the Study of Antiquity and Christian Origins at the University of Texas at Austin, 2003), cat. nos. 14, 53.

49. For a rare exception, see a lamp reflector with a chrismon and the apocalyptic letters in Garbsch and Overbeck, *Heidentum und Christentum*, cat. no. 152.

50. Ibid., cat. nos. 89–91; Herrmann and van den Hoek, *Light*, cat. no. 39.

completed the scene at the youth's right. Jan Willem Salomonson has recognized the agonistic character of the scene, seeing a victorious poet in the seated youth and an actor in the old man.[51] In Greek representations of award ceremonies for victorious athletes and poets, however, judges are often seated, while the winning competitor stands both to compete and to receive his award.[52] Thus the seated youth on the vase fragment seems to be the judge awarding the prize, not the contestant. This is nevertheless an abnormal situation, since judges are usually old and competitors young.

Figure 2.13. African lamp with the Lamb of God, 420–530 CE.

The role reversal seems to project the situation into the Christian realm. Since the old man resembles St. Paul and the youth wears his hair long like Christ, the composition could well represent Christ rewarding his faithful apostle. Paul speaks metaphorically of athletic training to receive an imperishable crown (1 Cor. 9:25). In more con-

Figure 2.14. Christ with wreath and an apostle, African red slip ware bowl fragment, 350–430 CE.

crete terms the Pastoral Letters have Paul declare "I have fought the good fight, I have finished the race, I have kept the faith. From now on there is reserved for me the crown of righteousness, which the Lord, the righteous judge, will give me on that day, and not only to me but also to all who have longed for his appearing" (2 Tim. 4:7–8). As Thomas Mathews points out, Ambrose used the metaphor of Christ awarding a crown to his athletes in connection

51. Jan Willem Salomonson, "Spätrömische rote Tonware mit Reliefverzierung aus nordafrikanischen Werkstätten," *Bulletin van de Vereeniging tot bevordering der kennis van de antieke beschaving* (1969): 59–60, 65, fig. 86. The suggestion that the old man is an actor seems unlikely since he does not seem to be wearing a mask.

52. E. Kakarouga-Stassinopoulou, in D. Vanhove, ed., *Le Sport dans la Grèce Antique: Du Jeu à la Compétition* (Brussels: Palais des Beaux-Arts, 1992), cat. no. 125; E. Kephalidou, "Victory Ceremonies and Post-Victory Celebrations," in *Agon*, ed. Nicholas Kaltsas (Athens: National Archaeological Museum, 2004), 77; L. Utkina, in Kaltsas, *Agon*, cat. no. 159; John J. Herrmann Jr., Christine Kondoleon, and Lisa Buboltz, *Games for the Gods: The Greek Athlete and the Olympic Spirit* (Boston: Museum of Fine Arts, 2004), 144, 148, 189–90, cat. nos. 140, 150.

with baptism.[53] On gold-glass cups of the fourth century, Christ was frequently shown placing wreaths on the heads of Peter, Paul, other saints, and married couples.[54] Rewards for the saints surely locate the scene in the afterlife and make the composition eschatological if not apocalyptic—in a small-scale, personal sense, not necessarily tied to the fate of the entire world at the second coming.

Figure 2.15. Apostle and Christ or a martyr with a wreath, African red slip ware bowl fragment, 350–430 CE.

It is very likely that the same action of heavenly reward is represented on an African red slip ware platter rim where Christ stands as he extends a wreath to an aged apostle or martyr (fig. 2.15). Numerous fragments exist of bowls and platters with this scene.[55] The figure of Christ standing and holding out a wreath appears on a well-preserved lamp in a private collection (fig. 2.16).[56] To some degree the action parallels imperial ceremonies, as on Roman coins where the Emperor Caracalla, wearing military costume and standing on a high platform, awards wreaths in various *fora* of Asia Minor,[57] but award ceremonies at athletic and theatrical festivals must have been much more common occurrences. In mosaics martyrs receive wreaths of victory from the hand of God, as in the dome of St. Victor, Milan (late fifth century),[58] and S. Vitale, Ravenna (547 CE; fig. 2.32).

Figure 2.16. African lamp with Christ holding a wreath, 420–530 CE.

53. Thomas Mathews, *The Clash of Gods: A Reinterpretation of Early Christian Art* (Princeton, NJ: Princeton University Press, 1993), 163–64. On wreaths, see Karl Baus, *Der Kranz in Antike und Christentum* (Bonn: Peter Hanstein, 1940), cited in Ihm, *Programme*, 20n28.

54. Morey, *Gold-Glass*, cat. nos. 29, 37, 50 (Christ identified by label), 66, 74, 102, 109, 241, 272, 278 (Christ identified by label), 286, 314, 397, 450; Nancy Patterson Ševčenko, in Weitzmann, *Age of Spirituality*, cat. no. 507; Utro, "Immagini," 136–37.

55. A rectangular platter (lanx) with the old apostles and the young martyr or Christ has been reconstructed on paper from fragments; see Garbsch and Overbeck, *Heidentum und Christentum*, cat. nos. 93–94; Herrmann and van den Hoek, *Light*, cat. nos. 45–46.

56. Herrmann and van den Hoek, *Light*, cat. no. 47.

57. Grabar, *Christian Iconography*, 42, fig. 103. See also the coin of Laodicaea in the Museum of Fine Arts, Boston 1971.45, viewable at www.mfa.org.collections.

58. Brandenburg, in Brenk, *Spätantike*, cat. no. 27.

On another bowl fragment St. Paul venerates the wreath of Jesus' victory or reaches out for his own leafy crown (fig. 2.17).[59] A crown or the chrismon is frequently shown above or between saints or married couples on gold glass of the fourth century. The wreath can be a substitute for the figure of Christ, and the composition suggests both a transcendent reward and unity in Christ.[60] The African red slip ware tradition seems to present much the same transcendent thoughts as the gold glass but formulates them in its own distinctive manner.

Figure 2.17. St. Paul venerates a wreath, African red slip ware bowl fragment, 350–430 CE.

After ca. 390: Saints Offer Their Crowns to Christ

In early Christian art, saintly victors not only receive wreaths but also return them to Christ as an act of homage. This action might have some prototypes in pagan tradition, but its roots in apocalyptic thinking and biblical texts are even stronger. Early examples of the motif can be seen in the Naples baptistery. Between the squinches with the living creatures are windows flanked by apostles or martyrs holding out their crowns of golden leaves fastened with gems (fig. 2.18).[61] Saints offering crowns to Christ have been interpreted as mimicking the imperial tradition of *aurum coronarium*: conquered peoples or the Senate offering tribute to the emperor in the form of gold wreaths.[62] It is difficult to see this theme as the sole source for the action of these saints. Bringing tribute is tinged with an evocation of barbarian submission, and senatorial tribute is scarcely documented in Roman imperial art before the column of Arcadius around 400 CE. Thomas Mathews has suggested that ancient religious traditions of bearing wreaths, garlands, or ritual vessels to cult images could have played a part.[63] Could not the elders of the Apocalypse, who throw down their crowns before the throne of Christ (Rev. 4:10), have

59. Herrmann and van den Hoek, *Light*, cat. no. 44. For more examples of the same basic idea, often called the "Kreuzwache," see Garbsch and Overbeck, *Heidentum und Christentum*, cat. nos. 92, 98–100.

60. Ševčenko, in Weitzmann, *Age of Spirituality*, cat. nos. 506, 508; Utro, "Immagini," fig. 1.

61. Maier, *Baptistère de Naples*, 45–52 (apostles); Brandenburg, in Brenk, *Spätantike*, cat. no. 22b.

62. Theodor Klauser, "Aurum Coronarium," *Römische Mitteilungen* 59 (1944): 129–43; Engemann, "Grundlagen," in Liebieghaus 1983, 264, 266, fig. 91.

63. Citing Michael McCormick, *Eternal Victory* (New York: Cambridge University Press, 1986), 19, 210; Mathews, *Clash*, 200–201n20.

Figure 2.18. Martyrs
with crowns, mosaic,
ca. 400 CE, baptistery,
Naples.

also influenced the sudden popularity of this action in Christian iconography? The biblical text would have given both prominence and highly positive connotations to the gesture of offering crowns. Beat Brenk has argued that the four living creatures offering crowns in the mosaics of S. Maria Maggiore also draw their inspiration from the elders.[64] Thus while saints offering crowns are not a literal citation from the book of Revelation, they again present what can be called an apocalyptic structure and betray the influence of Revelation. The motif became very widespread in early Christian art of the Latin West, as in the Baptistery of the Arians at Ravenna, where the apostles present their crowns to the throne of Christ (fig. 2.27).

The Row of Living Creatures and the Throne with Symbol

A tradition of stately apocalyptic imagery develops in Italy in the late fourth century and evolves toward more literal biblical citation throughout the fifth and sixth centuries. The key element is a row of apocalyptic monsters from Revelation centered on either a symbol or a bust of Christ. The main vehicle of this Italian tradition is mosaic decoration in the churches of Rome and Ravenna. In the apse mosaic of S. Pudenziana in Rome (390–398), the four living creatures (Rev. 4:6–7; 5:6) hover in the sky on either side of a jeweled cross rising from Golgotha (fig. 2.19).[65] Below the creatures are the buildings of the heavenly Jerusalem (Rev. 21:9–14), and probably the heavenly Bethlehem.[66] Within the holy cities, a majestic Christ is enthroned among his apostles, who gesture toward him in acclamation. Peter and Paul are crowned

64. The four living creatures of the apocalypse: Brenk, *Mosaiken*, 16.

65. Volbach, *Early Christian Art*, pl. 130; Ihm, *Programme*, 130–32, pl. 3; Richard Krautheimer, *Corpus basilicarum christianarum Romae* (Rome: Pontificio istituto di archeologia cristiana, 1967), 3:279, fig. 248; Mathews, *Clash*, 97–114, figs. 71, 72, 74.

66. Richard Krautheimer has legitimately identified the basilica with a pyramidally roofed annex in the mosaic as the Church of the Nativity at Bethlehem (*Early Christian and Byzantine Architecture* [Harmondsworth, Baltimore, Ringwood: Penguin, 1965], 38, pl. 8b). Thomas Mathews mentions

Figure 2.19. Christ and the apostles in the heavenly Jerusalem, mosaic, about 400 CE,
S. Pudenziana, Rome.

by the *ecclesia ex gentibus* and the *ecclesia ex circumcisione*. Formerly visible
in the lower part of the mosaic were the Lamb of God on Mount Zion and
the dove of the Holy Spirit.[67]

The row of apocalyptic monsters is normally centered on a roundel with
a symbol or a bust of Christ. This composition is usually located at the end
of the nave above the apse (a surface for convenience called the "triumphal arch"). Under Pope Sixtus III (432–440) the triumphal arch of S. Maria
Maggiore was decorated with events from the childhood of Christ, but an
apocalyptic composition largely based on Revelation interrupts it at the
center and at the lower corners.[68] Over the apex of the arch, the row of living creatures flanks a roundel enclosing a throne (fig. 2.20). The roundel is
bordered with blue, green, and white rings, which evoke "the rainbow that
looked like an emerald" that surrounds the throne of Revelation 4:3.[69] In the
mosaic the throne is empty except for the cross and a wreath. Crosses or
chrisma are often used as replacements for a depiction of Christ in human

only Jerusalem (*Clash*, 98, fig. 71). Ecclesia and Synagoga, however, should be balanced by the two
cities.

67. Recorded in drawings of 1595 and ca. 1630; see preceding note.

68. Ihm, *Programme*, 12–15, 132–35; Brenk, *Mosaiken*, 14–19; Bisconti, "Programmi," in Ensoli
and La Rocca, *Aurea Roma*, 189–90, fig. 11.

69. On biblical and nonbiblical sources for the mosaic, see Brenk, *Mosaiken*, 15–19.

Figure 2.20. Apocalyptic emblems, mosaic, 432–440 CE, triumphal arch of S. Maria Maggiore, Rome.

Figure 2.21b. New Jerusalem, 432–440 CE, triumphal arch of S. Maria Maggiore, Rome.

Figure 2.21a. New Jerusalem, 432–440 CE, triumphal arch of S. Maria Maggiore, Rome.

form.[70] On the footstool below the throne lies a scroll with seven seals (Rev. 5:1). Jerusalem and Bethlehem appear at the lower corners of the triumphal arch, and their walls are bejeweled, as in Revelation 21:18–21 (figs. 2.21a, b). As pointed out by Beat Brenk, the mosaics display many variations from the text of Revelation. The living creatures hold out crowns, which, as noted

70. Cf. Deichmann, *Kommentar, 1. Teil*, 41.

Figure 2.22. Marble relief with the throne of Saturn, 117–138 CE.

above, must have been inspired by the action of the twenty-four elders (Rev. 4:9–10).[71] As is customary in Rome, the princes of the apostles are present. Twelve sheep crowd around the gates of Jerusalem and Bethlehem, evoking the names of the "apostles of the Lamb" inscribed on the foundations of the gates (Rev. 21:14).

The throne surmounted by symbols at S. Maria Maggiore (fig. 2.20) is an image patently borrowed from pagan or secular Roman art of earlier times. The empty throne could be used as an emblem of an invisible God, as in the Hadrianic marble reliefs with the thrones of Neptune and Saturn (fig. 2.22).[72] In the latter, cupids carry the pruning hook and another symbol of the divinity toward the throne, which is draped with the god's mantle, and the celestial globe is placed below it. An empty throne could also be an emblem of worldly power and office, as on a denarius of Titus minted between 79 and 81 (fig. 2.23a).[73] A throne with symbol could symbolize the heavenly reign of dead and divinized emperors and empresses. The Empress Faustina the Elder was commemorated numismatically as *diva* in 146, five years after her death (fig. 2.23b). Her throne has the attributes of Juno: the peacock and the scepter.

Figure 2.23a. Empty throne, silver denarius of Titus, 79–81 CE, Rome.

71. Brenk, *Mosaiken*, 16.

72. Jocelyn M. C. Toynbee, *The Hadrianic School: A Chapter in the History of Greek Art* (Cambridge: Cambridge University Press, 1934); Guido Mansuelli, *Galleria degli Uffizi, Le sculture* (Roma: Libreria dello Stato, 1958), 1:172–73; idem, "Rilievi romani di Ravenna," *XV corso di cultura sull'arte ravennate e bizantina* (Ravenna: Edizioni Dante, 1968), 205–15, figs. 2–5.

73. H. Mattingly and E. A. Sydenham, *The Roman Imperial Coinage*, vol. 2, *Vespasian to Hadrian* (London: Spink, 1926), Titus, no. 24a, p. 119, pl. III, 48; I. A. Carradice and T. V. Buttrey, *The Roman Imperial Coinage*, vol. 2, pt. 1, *Vespasian to Domitian*, 2nd rev. ed. (London: Spink, 2007), Titus, no. 124, p. 206, pl. 87; www.coinarchives.com/a/results.php?results=100&search=ric+24a.

Figure 2.23b. Throne with symbols, silver
denarius of Faustina the Elder, after 141 CE.

Figure 2.23c. Silver denarius of Septimius
Severus, 211 CE.

The legend is *aeternitas*, evoking her eternal blessedness and authority.[74] In
a denarius of Septimius Severus, which was issued not long after his death
in 211, the throne is shown with the oak wreath of Jupiter and a footstool
(fig. 2.23c).[75] While the symbolic thrones on coin and mosaic are highly similar formally, their allegorical message differs in several important respects.
While both the pagan and the Christian throne and wreath imply an eternal
and celestial reign, the Christian image also signifies Christ himself and his
eventual return to the earth. This kind of symbolism must have been widely
recognized, since at several church councils a throne with the Gospels was
placed in the hall for deliberations.[76] In Syria in the fifth century, stone stands
for biblical books took the form of thrones and were an integral part of the
bema or exedra for the clergy and elite members of the congregation.[77]

Fifth and Sixth Centuries: Apocalyptic Images in Italy with Symbolic Thrones

Impressive compositions including thrones without occupants in human
form appear throughout Italy. A program with many of the core elements
of Revelation 4–5 appears in the vaulting zone of the fifth-century chapel
of S. Matrona attached to S. Prisco at S. Maria in Capua Vetere (north of
Naples).[78] In the mosaics of one lunette, two of the living creatures—here with

74. Carl-Otto Nordström, *Ravennastudien: Ideengeschichtliche und ikonographische Untersuchungen über die Mosaiken von Ravenna* (Stockholm: Almqvist and Wiksell, 1953), 51, pl. 12f–j,
13j; H. Mattingly and E. A. Sydenham, *The Roman Imperial Coinage*, vol. 3, *Antoninus Pius to
Commodus* (London: Spink, 1930), Faustina the Elder, no. 353; www.coinarchives.com/a/results
.php?results=100&search=ric+353.

75. H. Mattingly and E. A. Sydenham, *The Roman Imperial Coinage*, vol. 4, pt. 1, *Pertinax to
Geta* (London: Spink, 1936), Septimius Severus, no. 191E; www.coinarchives.com/a/results.php?
results=100&search=ric+191e.

76. Nordström, *Ravennastudien*, 51; Spiro Kostof, *The Orthodox Baptistery of Ravenna* (London
and New Haven: Yale University Press, 1965), 80.

77. As at Qirqbizzé, Kfeir, and the West Church at Behyo: Jean Lassus and Georges Tchalenko,
"Ambones syriennes," *CaA* 5 (1950): 103ff.; J. Lassus, "Syrie," in Cabrol and Leclercq, *Dictionnaire*,
vol. 15.2 (1953), 1865, 1881, figs. 11001, 11011, 11012; G. Tchalenko, *Villages antiques de la Syrie
du nord* (Paris: Geuthner, 1953), I, 328; III, pl. 10; 103, 105–6, 111, 113.

78. Brandenburg, in Brenk, *Spätantike*, cat. no. 23.

Figure 2.24a. Mosaic, fifth century, Chapel of S. Matrona, Church of S. Prisco at S. Maria in Capua Vetere, Campania.

six wings—flank a throne, which in this case is not enclosed in a roundel (fig. 2.24a). In the background are gloriously colorful clouds inspired by the synoptic apocalypse and Revelation 1:7. On the throne are the scroll with seven seals (Rev. 5:1) and the dove of the Holy Spirit, who is not mentioned in Revelation. Facing this mosaic is a lunette with a bust of Christ

Figure 2.24b. Mosaic, fifth century, Chapel of S. Matrona, Church of S. Prisco at S. Maria in Capua Vetere, Campania.

in a blue, green, and white roundel, which recalls the "rainbow that looks like an emerald" of Revelation 4:3, flanked by A and Ω (fig. 2.24b). Two more living creatures were in the side lunettes of the chapel. Elements extracted from Revelation and from pagan tradition have been skillfully distributed throughout the small chapel to create an elegant vision of the second coming.

An ivory reliquary of about 440 from Pola in Istria, now in the Venice Archaeological Museum, has an empty throne with the Lamb of God below it (fig. 2.25).[79] A cross may have surmounted the throne, as in S. Maria Maggiore (fig. 2.20). In the Roman church Peter and Paul flank the throne, while on the casket,

79. Anna Angiolini, *La capsella eburnea di Pola* (Bologna: Patron, 1970), 52–66, 101–4, fig. 9; Maria Cristina Dossi, in *Ambrogio e Agostino*, cat. no. 14.

four other saints join them. The gesturing martyrs, who do not carry wreaths, are in the tradition of the fourth century. The Lamb of God on Mount Zion is below the throne, and palms of paradise form the backdrop for the figures.

In the two baptisteries of Ravenna, thrones with symbols are stripped of explicit references to biblical apocalypses, but they project an apocalyptic vision nonetheless. In the dome of the Orthodox Baptistery of 458, four thrones—empty except for crosses—are placed in the four cardinal directions of the building, and according to Friedrich Wilhelm Deichmann, they allude to Christ's dominion throughout the universe (fig. 2.26).[80] They are lodged in fanciful garden pavilions that represent the architecture of paradise. In the Baptistery of Arians, of the early sixth century,[81] a single symbolic throne has become the goal of the procession of apostles (fig. 2.27), as it had been on the Pola Casket (fig. 2.25), and again the proces-

Figure 2.25. Ivory reliquary from Pola, about 440 CE, Archaeological Museum, Venice.

Figure 2.26. Throne with cross, mosaic of dome, ca. 458 CE, Orthodox Baptistery, Ravenna.

sion takes place among the palms of paradise. In the mosaic, however, the Lamb is missing, and the apostles do not gesture but present crowns and other emblems (keys of St. Peter and scrolls of St. Paul). The throne is surmounted by a cross, which is draped with the purple mantle of Christ.[82] The

---

80. Deichmann, *Kommentar, 1. Teil*, 42. For illustrations, see Volbach, *Early Christian Art*, pls. 140–41; Deichmann, *Bauten*, pls. 62–71.

81. Deichmann, *Bauten*, pls. 251, 256–73.

82. Deichmann, *Kommentar, 1. Teil*, 254–55.

Figure 2.27. Apostles present crowns to throne with symbols, mosaic of dome, early sixth century, Arian Baptistery, Ravenna.

action offers a distant echo of the elders of the Apocalypse and increases the suggestion that the mosaic presents a vision of the second coming.

Finally, an actual throne of marble too small for a human occupant was covered with apocalyptic images. The throne from Grado, which is now in Venice and dates from the late sixth century, would, as in Syria, have been a stand for a biblical manuscript. It has the six-winged living creatures distributed in starry fields on the back and sides, and two angels with trumpets make the allusion to the second coming unmistakable (Rev. 8:6–9:14).[83]

The Twenty-Four Elders of the Apocalypse, Angels, and Trumpets

The burial church of St. Paul at Rome was burned in 1823, but it is clear from a print of 1693 that it had an apocalyptic image on the archway between the nave and transept (fig. 2.28).[84] After the fire the church was rebuilt in a "classical Christian style," which transformed the imagery stylistically but not iconographically. The mosaic, which was created between 440 and 450 under Pope Leo I, again has the row of living creatures, and a bust of Christ fills the central roundel. The local favorites Peter and Paul have been moved well

83. Engemann, "Images," 96–97, figs. 19–22.
84. Giovanni Giustino Ciampini, *Vetera monumenta*, vol. 1 (Rome: Komarek, 1693), pl. 68; Krautheimer, *Corpus basilicarum christianarum Romae*, 5:98–99, 138, 162–63, fig. 132.

Figure 2.28. Drawing of lost mosaic of triumphal arch, 440–450 CE, St. Paul's Outside the Walls, Rome.

below to make space for the twenty-four elders of Revelation. Inclusion of the elders represents a new detail from the text, but even so there are deviations; the elders don't fall on their faces or actually throw down their crowns: they offer them. Two angels now flank Christ; they evoke the angels who give commands in Revelation 14 or the angels who gather the elect in Matthew 24:31. They genuflect in adoration as they approach, perhaps inspired by the angelic voices praising God in Revelation 5:11–12.

The façade of Old St. Peter's was also decorated by Pope Leo I (440–461) with an apocalyptic mosaic based on selected details from Revelation. A drawing of the eleventh century in Eton College gives an approximate idea.[85] The composition included the Lamb, the row of four living creatures, and the twenty-four elders.

Angels with a clearer relationship to the text of Revelation appear in the mosaic of S. Michele in Africisco, Ravenna (now in Berlin) datable 545.[86] On the triumphal arch Christ sat enthroned between two angels carrying lances and the seven angels with trumpets of Revelation 8:2. Two angels with trumpets appear along with the living creatures on the marble throne from Grado in Venice.[87]

The Seven Candelabra

The mosaic decoration of the triumphal arch of Sts. Cosmas and Damian at Rome, which dates from either 527 or 530, builds on the composition at

---

85. Kinney, "Apocalypse," 204, fig. 18.
86. Ihm, *Programme*, 161–63, pl. 8.2.
87. See above, note 82.

Figure 2.29a. Mosaics of apse and triumphal arch, 527–530 CE, Sts. Cosmas and Damian, Rome.

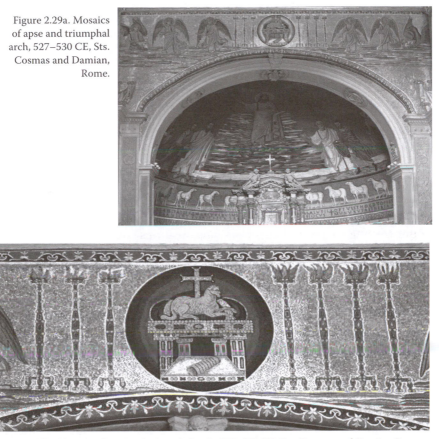

Figure 2.29b. Mosaics of apse and triumphal arch, 527–530 CE, Sts. Cosmas and Damian, Rome.

S. Paolo (fig. 2.28) and incorporates new motifs from Revelation (figs. 2.29a, b). The mosaic is topped by a row of apocalyptic motifs floating on colorful clouds. At the center of the row is a roundel enclosing a throne with the cross and the Lamb of God. The colors of the roundel again evoke "the rainbow that looked like an emerald" around the throne of Revelation 4:3. On the footstool is the scroll with seven seals. For the first time seven candelabra accompany the throne, as in Revelation 4:7. Pairs of angels flank the candelabra. Beyond them were the four living creatures. In this case, they carry books, which characterize them as the four evangelists.[88] Two of the symbolic monsters were concealed when the church was remodeled in 1632. At that time the original nave was narrowed when chapels were added on either side. Below

88. On Irenaeus's role in establishing the link between the creatures and the evangelists, see Robin Jensen, "Of Cherubim and Gospel Symbols," *BAR* 21 (July/August 1995): 42, 65.

the band of clouds are the remains of the twenty-four elders, who were almost entirely concealed in the remodeling.

Seven lampstands had already appeared along with the living creatures in the (lost) mosaic of the triumphal arch of S. Giovanni Evangelista in Ravenna (ca. 430).[89] Seven lampstands are also shown in mosaic between the windows of the façade of the Basilica Euphrasiana at Poreç (Parenzo), Croatia (543–553).[90]

Reduced Rows of Living Creatures in Sixth-Century Italy

In the sixth and seventh centuries, the row of monsters centered on a theophoric roundel did not always aim at such an ambitious and detailed citation of Revelation. The mosaic on the triumphal arch above the apse of S. Apollinare in Classe of 533–549 (fig. 2.30) displays the apocalyptic elements seen at S. Maria Maggiore (fig. 2.20), with one significant alteration.[91] The roundel at the center of the row of living creatures contains a bust of Christ rather than symbolic allusion to him. The New Jerusalem and the New Bethlehem are again present, but the twenty-four elders are missing. This time the lambs (apostles) march in procession toward the bust of Christ at the center. The palms of paradise complete the apocalyptic composition. The apse of S. Apollinare has a version of the transfiguration (Matt. 17:1–6), in which the cross and a tiny bust in a roundel replace the full figure of Christ and lambs

Figure 2.30. Triumphal arch mosaic, 533–549 CE, S. Apollinare in Classe, Ravenna.

89. Ihm, *Programme*, 15–17, 169–71, fig. 2.

90. Pairs of apostles flank the windows, but the main, pedimental zone of the mosaic is largely missing. In all probability, however, it displayed an apocalyptic composition; see van den Meer and Mohrmann, *Atlas*, fig. 272; Nenad Cambi, in Brenk, *Spätantike*, cat. no. 373. See also www.mein-kroatien.info/Euphrasius-Basilika.

91. Deichmann, *Bauten*, pls. 383, 410–13.

replace the disciples witnessing the scene. Below the cross, St. Apollinaris prays in paradise.[92]

Coming through the Clouds and Gathering the Elect: The "Gospel" Apocalyptic Tradition

There is an alternative, more naturalistic apocalyptic Roman tradition in which Christ in human form comes through the clouds without the extravagant trappings of Revelation. These images seem to evoke the parousia or second coming of the synoptic apocalypse (Matt. 24:29–31; Mark 13:24–27; Luke 21:21–28). Christ is not enthroned, nor is he surrounded by a ring of radiance other than a halo. In these compositions the influence of the Gospel parousia may well have gone beyond the central motif. Saints and donors flank Christ in a way that suggests the gathering of the elect, as in Matthew 24:31. The act of gathering may have been transformed in terms of contemporary court ceremonial, but the way that saints are actively guided toward Christ is a structural parallel with the text.

These simpler, synoptic conceptions usually appear in the apses of churches. Some details of their compositions may also be taken from the book of Revelation, and compositions inspired by this book can appear on adjoining wall surfaces.

This synoptic conception of the second coming can already be traced in *traditio legis* scenes, as in the Naples baptistery (fig. 2.4), where Christ's majesty is enhanced by colorful clouds. Colorful clouds are frequently present in triumphal arches with the four living creatures (figs. 2.19, 20, 24a, 30). In the apse of Sts. Cosmas and Damian, Rome, decorated in 527–530, Christ floats down in even more impressive and more illusionistic fashion through intensely colored clouds (fig. 2.29).[93] The clouds form a pathway for him so that they are not simply background; they are, as the Gospel texts imply, the means by which he arrives. On either side of him, Sts. Peter and Paul introduce SS. Cosmas, Damian, and Theodore, who bear wreaths of martyrdom, and Pope Felix IV, who offers a model of the church. The princes of the church in a sense take over the roles of the angels who gather the elect. The assemblage of "local" saints and dignitaries harks back to earlier local pictorial traditions, such as the fresco in SS. Marcellino e Pietro (fig. 2.3), but the action of gathering and Christ's descent through the clouds casts the scene more in terms of Matthew than Revelation. The action of gathering the elect has, of course, been translated into contemporary terms. Christa Ihm

92. Ibid., pls. 12–14, 385–93; Brandenburg, in Brenk, *Spätantike*, cat. no. 36; Mathews, *Clash*, 150, figs. 119–20.

93. Grabar, *Christian Iconography*, 32–33, fig. 66; Brandenburg, in Brenk, *Spätantike*, cat. nos. 37–38; Mathews, *Clash*, 169, fig. 133; Bisconti, "Programmi," in Ensoli and La Rocca, *Aurea Roma*, 190, fig. 12.

Figure 2.31a. Mosaics of triumphal arch and apse, 640–649 CE, chapel of S. Venanzio, Lateran Baptistery, Rome.

has pointed out how such scenes correspond to late Roman court ceremonial: the official *praesentatio*.[94] Martyrs venerated in the church (or adjoining catacomb, when one is present) are the usual subjects of these presentations. Active introductions, however, had not been seen previously. Processions of saints, as in the Arian Baptistery at Ravenna (fig. 2.27), represent a different situation, which finds its biblical justification in the offerings of the twenty-four elders and its existential inspiration in (different) court and religious ceremonies.[95] In both cases, however, a biblical text has been translated into a contemporary social form.

While the Gospel parousia is the dominant source for the apse of Sts. Cosmas and Damian, the imagery of the book of Revelation is also present within the apse, as on the triumphal arch. In the zone below Christ (and segregated from him by the River Jordan), the Lamb of God stands on the mountain of paradise, from which gush the Geon, Fison, Tigris, and Euphrates (concealed by the Baroque altar in fig. 2.29a).

Figure 2.31b. Mosaics of apse, 640–649 CE, chapel of S. Venanzio, Lateran Baptistery, Rome.

94. Ihm, *Programme*, 25, 27.
95. Mathews, *Clash*, 150–57.

A variation on the synoptic parousia appears in the chapel of S. Venanzio attached to the Lateran Baptistery. In the apse of this structure, datable 640–649, a bust, rather than a full figure of Christ, appears in a field of gaudy polychrome clouds (figs. 2.31a, b).[96] Flanking him are the busts of two angels, who raise both hands in a gesture of prayer or appeal. The angels can be interceding for the seventeen saints that they have gathered in the row below. At the center of the row, which extends from the apse onto the triumphal arch, is Mary, whose presence was probably inspired by Eastern representations of the ascension and the second coming (figs. 2.41, 43, 45a). On the triumphal arch, the evangelist symbols and Jerusalem and Bethlehem set the scene at the second coming.

Christ Seated on the Celestial Globe

The apse of S. Vitale, of 547, has a composition derived from the Gospel parousia, but it is given a more supernatural tone through the addition of abstract, symbolic elements (fig. 2.32).[97] Echoing the Gospels, gloriously colorful clouds hover above Christ's head, and angels gather the

Figure 2.32. Mosaics of apse and triumphal arch, 547 CE, S. Vitale, Ravenna.

96. Sergio Ortolani, *S. Giovanni in Laterano* (Rome: Le Chiese di Roma illustrate, N. 13, no date), 109, fig. 48; Grabar, *Christian Iconography*, 43, 133, fig. 107, 322.

97. Deichmann, *Bauten*, pl. 8, 351–57; Volbach, *Early Christian Art*, pl. 158; F. W. Deichmann, *Ravenna, Hauptstadt des spätantiken Abendlandes: Kommentar, 2. Teil* (Wiesbaden: Franz Steiner, 1976), 178–80; Grabar, *Christian Iconography*, 43, fig. 106; Mathews, *Clash*, 150, figs. 112, 116.

elect, which in this case consists of only two persons of local interest: the martyr St. Vitalis, who receives his crown of victory from Christ, and Bishop Ecclesius, who presents a model of the church. Christ has the scroll with the seven seals in his hand (Rev. 5:1), placing the scene at the second coming. The lovely landscape with its four rivers (as well as the gold background) identifies the location as paradise.[98] Antinaturalistic elements are the gold background and the blue celestial globe on which Christ sits.[99] The latter scheme had already appeared at S. Costanza in Rome in the fourth century[100] and S. Agata dei Goti, Rome, between 460 and 470.[101] Figures seated on the celestial globe represent a survival of a pagan iconographic tradition (fig. 2.5). In a Christian context, the composition evokes Isaiah's vision of the Lord, who declares, "Heaven is my throne and the earth is my footstool" (*Caelum sedes mea, terra autem scabellum pedum meorum*; Isa. 66:1).[102]

Christ is seated on a globe in a composition similar to that of S. Vitale in the apse mosaic of S. Teodoro in Rome (sixth century); clouds are above him, and a martyr is introduced on each side of him.[103] As in the Roman church of Sts. Cosmas and Damian (fig. 2.29a–b), Peter and Paul rather than angels do the introducing. Christ seated on a globe soon appears on triumphal arches. The clouds disappear, diluting the connection with Gospel texts and increasing the sense of abstraction. In S. Lorenzo-fuori-le-mura, Rome, built by Pope Pelagius (579–590; figs. 2.33a, b), Peter and Paul introduce four of the elect with Roman connections.[104] The heavenly Jerusalem

Figure 2.33a. Mosaic of triumphal arch, 579–590 CE, S. Lorenzo-fuori-le-mura, Rome.

98. The paradise of the martyrs (based on passages of Cyprian): Ihm, *Programme*, 27, 37–38.

99. At times misleadingly called the globe of the world: Ihm, *Programme*, 164 ("Weltkugel"); Grabar, *Christian Iconography*, 43 ("sphere of the world"; more properly "universe" on the same page).

100. Ihm, *Programme*, 18, 129–30, pl. 5.2; Volbach, *Early Christian Art*, pl. 33a.

101. Ihm, *Programme*, 15, 153–54, pl. 4.1.

102. Quoted or echoed in Matt. 5:34–35; 23:22; Acts 7:49. These biblical connections for the globe have generally been ignored or underplayed in the traditional drive to interpret the image of Christ as cosmocrator, on the model of a Roman or Byzantine emperor.

103. Ihm, *Programme*, 24, 140–41, pl. 6.2.

104. Volbach, *Early Christian Art*, pl. 185.

Figure 2.33b. Mosaic of triumphal arch, 579–590 CE, S. Lorenzo-fuori-le-mura, Rome.

and Bethlehem at the sides are the only notes from traditional Johannine triumphal arch iconography. In the triumphal arch of the Euphrasiana at Poreç (543–553), Christ is seated on the celestial globe at the center of a row of twelve apostles.[105]

Christ within a Ring Carried by Flying Angels: East and West

Symbols and Busts

One of the oldest and simplest ways to represent a Christian theophany is to enclose the image of the holy being in an honorific ring lifted by angels. A wreathed symbol of Christ is carried by angels on several sarcophagi in Istanbul,[106] including a fragmentary but richly detailed example in the garden of the Archaeological Museum (fig. 2.34).[107] The Victories carry the wreath with an honorary veil or napkin hanging below it, perhaps an extension of the custom of receiving a sacred object with veiled hands (figs. 2.4, 8, 9). This kind of image is ambivalent; at first glance it appears more triumphant

105. Van den Meer and Mohrmann, *Atlas*, fig. 271; Ihm, *Programme*, 5, 168, pl. 15.2. See also www.mein-kroatien.info/Euphrasius-Basilika.

106. David Talbot Rice, *The Art of Byzantium* (New York: Abrams, 1959), pl. 9; Hans-Georg Severin, in Brenk, *Spätantike*, cat. nos. 112a, b (date is mistakenly made a century too late, as is evident from the author's comparisons).

107. Nezih Firatli, *La sculpture byzantine figurée au Musée Archéologique d'Istanbul*, edited and presented by C. Metzger, A. Pralong, and J.-P. Sodini (Paris: Librairie d'Amérique et d'Orient Adrien Maisonneuve, 1990), cat. no. 82. The cloth below the wreath is interpreted as the covering of a throne, but well-preserved Coptic images, such as fig. 2.36, make it clear that it is a loose veil or napkin.

Figure 2.34. Chrismon elevated by Victories, marble sarcophagus front, early fifth century.

than apocalyptic: a proclamation of Christian victory. In the sarcophagi, the chrismon is enclosed in a victor's wreath and the angels are indistinguishable from Roman Imperial Victories. The scheme of chrismon born by Victories or angels was used around 400 CE on the column of Arcadius in Constantinople, a purely secular victory monument.[108] In a funerary context, however, the composition must have both expressed hope for the resurrection and alluded to the sign in heaven before the second coming (Matt. 24:30). As pointed out by Josef Engemann, St. Augustine compares the cross as the sign of the *secundus adventus* to the triumphal *vexillum* carried by a victorious army entering a city.[109] An apocalyptic meaning was almost certainly intended in the mosaics of S. Vitale in Ravenna, where flying angels carry a radiant monogram of Christ above the triumphal arch (fig. 2.32). The allusion to the second coming is explicit since the heavenly Jerusalem and Bethlehem appear on either side.[110] The imagery is also seen in Coptic Egypt, where in limestone reliefs angels fly holding wreathes with equal-armed crosses.[111]

Christ is often shown in human form in a roundel carried by angels or cherubim. This nonbiblical scheme for a theophany was popular in Coptic Egypt from the fifth to the seventh century. Busts of Christ in wreaths or rings carried by angels appear

Figure 2.35. Bust of Christ or an evangelist carried by angels, limestone relief from Bawit, first half of fifth century.

108. Known only from Renaissance drawings; see Grabar, *Christian Iconography*, 46–47, figs. 128, 129, 131; Engemann, "Grundlagen," in Liebieghaus 1983, 263, figs. 92–93.

109. Augustine, *Sermon* 155 (PL 39, col. 2051f.); Engemann, "Images," 83–84, fig. 6.

110. Deichmann, *Kommentar*, II *Teil*, 180.

111. For example, Severin, in Brenk, *Spätantike*, cat. no. 279b. Severin's mid-fourth-century date is surely too early.

Figure 2.36. Bust of Christ elevated by angels, fresco from Bawit.

in wooden door panels,[112] limestone reliefs,[113] and frescos. In a relatively early relief, a pair of angels carries a medallion enclosing a bust of either Christ or an evangelist, who holds a book with a cross at his left shoulder (fig. 2.35). Another book with a cross is attached to the veil hanging below the wreath. The veil is like that seen in the marble relief in Istanbul (fig. 2.34). A relatively late example of the medallion with bust carried by angels is provided by a sixth- or seventh-century lunette from Bawit (fig. 2.36).[114]

True seraphim with six wings carry a bust of Christ in an oval wreath on the portal of the Evangelists' Basilica at Ala-han, Cilicia (on the south coast of Turkey) of the fifth or sixth century (fig. 2.37a).[115] The apparition may represent either the ascension or the second coming. The seraphim are biblical, but no biblical text describes them carrying Christ, nor is

Figure 2.37a. Bust of Christ elevated by seraphim, lintel front, 450–530 CE, Evangelists' Basilica, Ala-han Monastery, Cilicia.

112. From St. Barbara, ca. 500, in Coptic Museum, Cairo: *L'Art Copte* (Paris: Petit Palais, 1964), cat. no. 92; Severin, in Brenk, *Spätantike*, cat. no. 286b; Gawdat Gabra and Anthony Alcock, *Cairo: The Coptic Museum, Old Churches* (Cairo: Egyptian International Publishing Company, Longman, 1993), cat. no. 45.

113. Severin, in Brenk, *Spätantike*, cat. no. 279b.

114. Gabra and Alcock, *Coptic Museum*, cat. no. 39.

115. Gerard Bakker, "The Buildings at Alahan," in *Alahan: An Early Christian Monastery in Southern Turkey*, ed. Mary Gough (Toronto: Pontifical Institute of Mediaeval Studies, 1985), 87–88, pl. 19; John J. Herrmann Jr. and Annewies van den Hoek, "Two Men in White: Observations on an Early Christian Lamp from North Africa with the Ascension of Christ," in *Early Christian Voices In Texts, Traditions, and Symbols*, ed. David H. Warren et al. (Boston and Leiden: Brill, 2003), 304, fig. 6.

Figure 2.37b. Tetramorph and prophet, soffit of lintel, 450–530 CE, Evangelists' Basilica, Alahan Monastery, Cilicia.

God surrounded by a wreath. In biblical visions God is surrounded by "splendor" (Ezek. 1:27–28) or a "rainbow that looks like an emerald" (Rev. 4:3). The artistic scheme employed at Alahan goes back to pagan sarcophagi in which a pair of cupids transports to celestial immortality a roundel with the bust of the deceased.[116] Even without biblical authority, the composition effectively conveys an apocalyptic message.

Full Figures in a Mandorla

Frequently Christ is shown in full figure within a roundel or mandorla carried by angels. He is usually seated on a throne, as in a fifth- or sixth-century limestone relief in Cairo (fig. 2.38). In the Coptic relief, curtains are pulled back at the sides to reveal the revelation. The curtains could be intended to dramatize the exceptionality of

Figure 2.38. Enthroned Christ elevated by angels, limestone relief from Bawit.

116. See, e.g., a sarcophagus of ca. 230 CE in the Gardner Museum, Boston; see Cornelius Vermeule, in Cornelius C. Vermeule, Walter Cahn, and Rollin Hadley, *Sculpture in the Isabella Stewart Gardner Museum* (Boston: Isabella Stewart Gardner Museum, 1977), cat. no. 62; Herrmann and van den Hoek, "Two Men," 304, fig. 8; Vassiliki Gaggadis-Robin, *Les sarcophages païens du Musée de l'Arles antique* (Arles: Éditions du musée de l'Arles et de la Provence antique, 2005), cat. no. 71, with bibliography.

the sacred event and were probably modeled on court ceremonial.[117] In another reflection of court custom, each angel holds the mandorla with one covered hand. On two fifth-century sarcophagi in Marseille, the enthroned Christ is enclosed in a ring carried by angels.[118] On one of the sarcophagi, Peter and Paul look on with excitement at either side. In lamps produced in Tunisia about 440–470, Christ stands in a mandorla, which is supported from below by two flying angels (fig. 2.39).[119] He is ascending to heaven, since the hand of God at his right assists him upward. The "two men in white" of Acts 1 are shown below. Although the ascension is depicted on the lamp, the four living creatures of Revelation are present, arranged, as in Italian tradition, in a curving row at the top of the composition. The apocalyptic trappings are justified, since the two men in

Figure 2.39. African lamp with the ascension.

white declare that "Jesus . . . will come in the same way as you saw him go into heaven" (Acts 1:11). Jesus' return in the book of Revelation provided the model and the source for living creatures and the mandorla.

In sixth-century theophanies from the Eastern Mediterranean, four angels usually support the mandorla enclosing the enthroned Christ, as in an icon in the Vatican,[120] lead ampullae in Monza,[121] and a gold medallion in a private collection.[122] Four angels support the image of divinity in a roundel when it is located at the center of a dome or vault. In S. Vitale in Ravenna, the Lamb of God appears in a wreath of fruit supported by four angels on celestial globes (fig. 2.40).[123] The angels are inspired by Roman Victories,

117. Theodor Klauser, "Der Vorhang vor dem Thron Gottes," *Jahrbuch für Antike und Christentum* 3 (1960): 141–42; Julie Märki-Boehringer, F. W. Deichmann, and Theodor Klauser, *Frühchristliche Sarkophage in Bild und Wort*, Antike Kunst, Beiheft 3 (Olten: Urs Graf, 1966), 88, pl. 39, 2.

118. Geneviève Drocourt-Dubreuil, *Saint Victor de Marseille: Art funéraire et prière des morts aux temps paléochrétiennes (IVe-Ve siècles)* (Marseilles: de Boccard, 1989), 70–79; Herrmann and van den Hoek, "Two Men," 304, fig. 7.

119. Garbsch and Overbeck, *Heidentum und Christentum*, 76, 138; Fathi Bejaoui, *Céramique et religion chrétienne. Les thèmes bibliques sur la sigillée africaine* (Tunis: Institut National du Patrimoine, 1997), 141–42, fig. 77; Herrmann and van den Hoek, *Light*, cat. no. 37; Herrmann and van den Hoek, "Two Men," 293–318.

120. Grabar, *Christian Iconography*, 102, fig. 260.

121. Ibid., 114, 132, figs. 275, 319 (two angels); Herrmann and van den Hoek, "Two Men," 306–7, figs. 10–11.

122. Herrmann and van den Hoek, "Two Men," 307, fig. 11.

123. Volbach, *Early Christian Art*, pls. 133–35; R. F. Hoddinott, *Early Byzantine Churches in Macedonia and Southern Serbia* (London and New York: Macmillan, 1963), 173–79, pls. VI, VII,

who also stand on globes (figs. 2.6–7). While this relationship of angels and Lamb corresponds to nothing in biblical texts, the starry sky behind the Lamb makes it clear that this is a celestial apparition of God and, as Josef Engemann put it, alludes to the end of time, according to Revelation 21.[124]

In the mosaics of the Rotunda at Thessaloniki, probably datable between 424 and 436, Christ stood in a huge roundel supported by four gigantic angels at the apex of the dome.

Figure 2.40. Mosaic of Lamb of God and angels, chancel bay, 547 CE, S. Vitale, Ravenna.

Unfortunately only small fragments of the majestic mosaic survive.[125] Martyrs praying in golden colonnaded structures on a lower level, which is better preserved, are clearly located in the heavenly Jerusalem (and Bethlehem).[126] The whole vast composition represents a vision of heaven. Whether it is a static image of paradise or, as seems more likely, an active image of the second coming could be debated. In any case, it is an apocalyptic composition with only a loose relationship to textual sources.[127]

The Tetramorph in the East: A Creature with Four Heads and Four Wings

In the eastern Mediterranean, apocalyptic visions often show unmistakable signs of a source in Ezekiel rather than Revelation. The clearest evidence of the source is provided by the monsters that accompany the vision of God.

48; Deichmann, *Kommentar*, II *Teil*, 177–78; Jürgen Christern, in Brenk, *Spätantike*, cat. no. 159; Mathews, *Clash*, 115–21, figs. 112–13.

124. Engemann, "Images," 94–95, fig. 17–18.

125. Beautifully illustrated in E. Kourkoutidou-Nikolaïdou and A. Tourta, *Wandering in Byzantine Thessaloniki* (Athens: Kapon, 1997), 63–65. For the date, see Aristotle Mentzos, "Reflections on the Interpretation and the Dating of the Rotunda of Thessaloniki," *ΕΓΝΑΤΙΑ* 6 (2001–2): 76–79.

126. Volbach, *Early Christian Art*, pls. 122–27; Hoddinott, *Early Byzantine Churches*, 112–21; Christern, in Brenk, *Spätantike*, pls. 154b–155.

127. For recent interpretations, see Mentzos, "Reflections," 70–76; Hjalmar Torp, "Dogmatic Themes in the Mosaics of the Rotunda at Thessaloniki," *Arte medievale* n.s. 1.1 (2002): 11–34. For a review of these and other theories about the monument and a reading of the Rotunda in terms of local literary and historical traditions, see Laura Nasrallah, "Empire and Apocalypse in Thessaloniki: Interpreting the Early Christian Rotunda," *JECS* 13 (2005): 465–508.

In Revelation, the four living creatures each have three pairs of wings and each takes a different form: that of a winged lion, ox, man, and eagle (Rev. 4:6–8). In Ezekiel, on the other hand, each of the four living creatures has four faces, which are those of the same four species, and each has two pairs of wings (Ezek. 1:5–10). In several works of art from the eastern Mediterranean, single composite beasts have the four different faces and must have been inspired by Ezekiel.

One such tetramorph appears on the underside of the lintel of the Evangelists' Basilica at Alahan Monastery near the southeast coast of Turkey (about 450–550; fig. 2.37b).[128] The bust of a man forms the dominant central axis of the cluster, the forepart of a lion projects at his right, and a bull spills out at his left. As in Ezekiel, the lion is at the proper right and the bull at the left. In the text, the man was at the front and the eagle at the back, a situation resolved in the sculpture by placing a small eagle at the man's waist. Each face has one pair of wings rather than the two pairs for the entire tetramorph called for in Ezekiel's text. The tetramorph is probably to be read in connection with the bust of Christ on the front of the same lintel (fig. 2.37a); as in Ezekiel, the tetramorph appears below the "firmament" with the Lord.

On either side of the creature, a mantled figure stands beside a tree and gestures toward the apparition. These figures are puzzling, since Ezekiel's vision was a private one. They might allude to the multitude of prophets in the Hebrew Bible who at various times saw God. It is also possible that the two men were inspired by Revelation 11:3–12, where two witnesses prophesy for 1260 days and are murdered and resurrected.[129] At the beginning of the passage they are identified with the olive trees in the courtyard of the temple of God, perhaps explaining the trees seen on the lintel at Alahan.

Figure 2.41. Ascension, Rabbula Gospels, 586 CE, Bibloteca Medicea-Laurenziana, Florence, Ms. Plut. 1, 56.

128. Bakker, "Buildings at Alahan," 87–88, pl. 19; Herrmann and van den Hoek, "Two Men," 304, fig. 6.
129. An interpretation suggested by Margaret Butterworth.

A source in Ezekiel is strongly evident in an "apocalyptic ascension" in the Syriac Rabbula Gospels, made by the priest Rabbula at Zagba in 586 (fig. 2.41).[130] A true tetramorph with four faces and two pairs of wings supports Christ in his mandorla. This time the apparition has wheels, and fire bursts out around it, as in Ezekiel 1:4, 15. The sun and moon, symbols of eternity[131] and echoes of Luke 21:25, appear in the upper corners. Christ carries an unrolled scroll (Ezek. 2:9–10). Not mentioned in biblical texts are two angels that help to carry Christ in his mandorla. Two more angels with covered hands present wreaths, thereby alluding perhaps to the presentation of *aurum coronarium* (but they may also be mimicking the acts of veneration of the elders of Revelation). The lower zone of the miniature is an embellished version of the ascension according to Acts 1:2; the men in white are interpreted as angels, and each addresses a group of six apostles. The Virgin Mary is added at the center between the two groups.

Living Creatures Clustered around the Ring of Light: East and West

Flanked by Two Men in Mantles

There is yet another artistic tradition for representing the apparitions of Christ. The full figure of Christ holding an unrolled scroll or a book is enclosed in a ring or mandorla, and the foreparts of a winged lion, ox, man, and eagle emerge radially around the ring. The nature of and sources for this apparition are ambiguous, since the protomes can be interpreted either as four separate living creatures, as in Revelation, or as the four faces of a single creature, as described by Ezekiel. The creatures may be transporting the throne of Christ, as in Ezekiel 1, or simply surrounding it and giving praise, as in the book of Revelation.[132] Figures emerging from a mandorla appear in a variety of narrative contexts, including the second coming and the ascension. Although there are Western examples, the scheme is usually associated with the Greek-speaking East. In the East, Christ is enthroned, while in the sole Western example he stands.

An early and especially beautiful example appears in the mosaic of the fifth-century chapel of Hosios David in the Stonecutters' Monastery, Thessaloniki

130. Grabar, *Christian Iconography*, 35, pl. 1; Herbert Kessler, in Weitzmann, *Age of Spirituality*, 454–55, fig. 68; Herrmann and van den Hoek, "Two Men," 307, fig. 12; Luisa Musso, "Governare il tempo naturale, Provvedere alla *felicitas* terrena, Presiedere l'ordine celeste figurative," in Ensoli and La Rocca, *Aurea Roma*, 380–81.

131. Heads of the sun and moon are carried by Aeternitas on coins of Vespasian, Trajan, and Hadrian. See www.coinarchives.com/a/.

132. Ihm, *Programme*, 42–51, "Die liturgische Maiestas."

Figure 2.42. Apparition of Christ, fifth century, Hosios David, Stonecutters' Monastery, Thessaloniki.

(fig. 2.42).[133] The creatures have eyes on their wings, and Christ is seated on a rainbow and surrounded by a radiant disc of light. In a very general way, the image is compatible with Ezekiel's text (Ezek. 1:4–28). The rainbow on which Christ sits visually renders Isaiah's vision of God seated in heaven (Isa. 66:1).[134] Nonetheless the book of Revelation seems to be the dominant influence. The four creatures have books and symbolize the evangelists. They thereby represent four separate creatures with only one face, as in Revelation. Each head has three pairs of wings and different faces, as in Revelation 4:6, rather than the two pairs for the entire tetramorph, as in Ezekiel 1:6, 11.[135] Moreover, the springs of the rivers of Eden flow out from below Christ, evoking Mount Zion (Rev. 14:1) and the water of life (Rev. 22:1). As Christa Ihm has pointed out, the composition is a kind of synthesis of common features from Ezekiel, Isaiah, and Revelation; conspicuous and unique features of Revelation that are not included in the other prophetic works, such as the Lamb, the scroll with the seven seals, the elders, and the candelabra, have been omitted.[136] Ezekiel's wheels and flames do not appear either.

In the landscape on either side of the apparition are two dignified men in white mantles, who are usually identified as the prophets Ezekiel and either Habakkuk,[137] Isaiah, or Zacharias, to whom the monastery was dedicated. One crouches down in awe, while the other calmly consults his book.

133. Volbach, *Early Christian Art*, pls. 133–35; Hoddinott, *Early Byzantine Churches*, 173–79, pls. VI, VII, 48; Grabar, *Christian Iconography*, 44, fig. 117; Christern, in Brenk, *Spätantike*, cat. no. 159; Mathews, *Clash*, 115–21, fig. 88.

134. Ihm, *Programme*, 44.

135. Not one pair as in Ihm, *Programme*, 42. Triple pairs of wings are visible in Christern, in Brenk, *Spätantike*, cat. no. 159; Mathews, *Clash*, figs. 88–89; Kourkoutidou-Nikolaïdou and Tourta, *Wandering*, 92–93.

136. Ihm, *Programme*, 45.

137. In favor of Habakkuk, see Bissera V. Pentcheva, "Imagined Images: Visions of Salvation and Intercession in a Double-Sided Icon from Poganovo," *DOP* 54 (2000): 143–44.

Symmetrical prophets, saints, or angels are frequent complements to holy visions, as at Alahan (fig. 2.37b), on North African lamps (fig. 2.39), and in Marseille, where they represent Peter and Paul.[138] Pairs of witnesses or prophets might have been inspired by the two witnesses who prophesy for 1260 days and are murdered and resurrected in Revelation 11:3–12. Since the two prophets of Revelation were left nameless, it would have been tempting for the designers of works of art to have projected biblical names on them (fig. 2.42).

The scroll that Christ extends to Ezekiel in his vision contains "words of lamentation and mourning and woe" (Ezek. 2:10). This is typical of apocalyptic visions, which usually promise misery and suffering for the faithful before retribution strikes evildoers. Texts in mosaics, such as this one, however, make it clear that the message of early Christian works of apocalyptic art was far different and much more comforting. In the mosaic, Christ's scroll reads, "Behold, our God in whom we hope and we rejoiced over our salvation, for he will give rest to this house."[139] As Denis Feissel has pointed out, this text is a literal quotation from Isaiah 25:9–10, except for an additional verb and the last words.[140] Isaiah had God bestow eternal rest on Mount Zion, while the inscription substitutes the church ("this house"). The text in the seated prophet's book is equally positive: "This whole honorable house (is) a life-giving source that receives and nourishes faithful souls."[141] In this case there is no clear biblical background. The same thought is expressed more fully and clearly in the donor's dedication below the figures. The focus on this very church as a source for God's nurture is common to all three inscriptions. A similar reassuring tone and almost domestic perspective emerges in the inscription in Christ's codex in the mosaic of S. Pudenziana in Rome: "The Lord, conservator of the church of Pudens" (fig. 2.19). The passage from Isaiah quoted in Hosios David occurs in a context of an apocalyptic vision that promises peace. Visual imagery has been transferred from threatening biblical texts to dramatize prophecies of God's benevolent power and majesty. These and other works of apocalyptic art synthesize a variety of biblical visions to concentrate image and text on a promise of bliss rather than punishment.

138. On the sarcophagi of Marseille, see above, note 117.

139. ἰδοὺ ὁ θ(εὸ)ς ἡμῶν ἐφ' ᾧ ἐλπίζομεν κ(αὶ) ἠγαλλιώμεθα ἐπὶ τῇ σωτηρίᾳ ἡμῶν ὅτι ἀνάπαυσιν δώσει ἐπὶ τὸν οἶκον τοῦτον. For the text, see Feissel, *Recueil*, 97–99, no. 103B, pl. XXIII. For a slightly different translation, see Hoddinott, *Early Byzantine Churches*, 176.

140. Feissel, *Recueil*. Isa. 25:9–10: καὶ ἐροῦσιν τῇ ἡμέρᾳ ἐκείνῃ Ἰδοὺ ὁ θεὸς ἡμῶν, ἐφ' ᾧ ἠλπίζομεν καὶ ἠγαλλιώμεθα, καὶ εὐφρανθησόμεθα ἐπὶ τῇ σωτηρίᾳ ἡμῶν. ὅτι ἀνάπαυσιν δώσει ὁ θεὸς ἐπὶ τὸ ὄρος τοῦτο. . . . "On that day they will say 'behold, our God, in whom we hoped and rejoiced, and we will be joyful over our salvation, for God will give eternal rest on this mountain.'" The connection with Isaiah has also been discussed in Ihm, *Programme*, 42, 46.

141. πηγὴ ζωτική, δεκτ(ικ)ή, θρεπτικὴ ψυχῶν πιστοῦν [sic] ὁ <π> πανέν(τι)μος οἶ(κ)ος ο(ὗτ)ος.

Figure 2.43. Ascension, wooden door lintel from the church of Al-Mo'allaqa.

The Virgin Mary in an "Apocalyptic" Ascension

The ascension on a wooden door lintel in Cairo of the fifth or sixth century, has a "semi" or "implied" radial scheme; the winged lion and bull project obliquely from the lower part of Christ's mandorla, but the winged man and the eagle are not visible above (fig. 2.43).[142] This is undoubtedly because two large flying angels carry the mandorla, and their wings and hands cover the space beside and above it. Curtains pulled back at either side increase the sense of revelation, as in other Coptic theophanies (fig. 2.38). Bystanders appear beside the apparition rather than below it, the more usual position. Beyond the curtain to Christ's right is a woman (Mary?) and to his left is a man with long hair and a staff topped with a small crossbar (John the Baptist?). Beyond them are figures gesturing with great animation in front of a city wall with towers; clearly Jerusalem[143] and perhaps Bethlehem are intended. The architectural backdrop could well have been inspired by earlier theophanies in Italy, such as city-gate sarcophagi (fig. 2.9). In any case, the ascension has again been transformed through the influence of apocalyptic texts.

The Sun and Moon

The scheme of Christ in a ring with faces of the four living creatures on the diagonals appears in the Latin West at least as early as it does in the East. In the second coming on the wooden doors

Figure 2.44. Second coming, wooden doors, 422–432 CE, S. Sabina, Rome.

142. Severin, in Brenk, *Spätantike*, cat. no. 287; Gabra and Alcock, *Coptic Museum*, cat. no. 41; Herrmann and van den Hoek, "Two Men," 304, fig. 9.

143. Christ's entry into Jerusalem takes place at the far left of the lintel (from the observer's point of view).

of S. Sabina (of 422–432), Christ stands, holding a scroll with the letters ΙΧΥΘΣ (Ἰησοῦς Χριστὸς Υἱὸς Θεοῦ Σωτήρ; fig. 2.44).[144] The letters A and Ω flank him. The ring enclosing him is a victor's wreath—perhaps of laurel—not the oval mandorla of sixth-century works. The composition seems to draw on apocalyptic visions from the three major sources: Ezekiel, Revelation, and the Gospels. The tips of the wings of the four creatures touch, as in Ezekiel 1:11, but they are clearly separate creatures with single faces, as in Revelation. They are directed toward rather than emerging from behind Christ's wreath. Below is a hemisphere with the sun, moon, and stars, which evoke the "signs in the sun, the moon, and the stars" of Luke 21:25. As noted earlier, the sun and moon are Roman symbols of eternity.[145] Below this, Peter, Paul, and Mary look up, echoing Luke 21:28: "Now when these things begin to take place, stand up and raise your heads, because your redemption is drawing near." They hold up a wheel with a cross, perhaps displaying the sign of Christ to demonstrate that they are among the saved.

Figure 2.45a. Second coming, fresco from Bawit, Monastery of S. Apollo, Chapel 6, sixth or early seventh century.

Chariots of Fire

Four living creatures emerge radially around Christ's mandorla in apse paintings of the fifth to seventh centuries from the Monastery of S. Apollo at Bawit, Egypt.[146] A particularly fine example, now in the Coptic Museum, Cairo, comes from Chapel 6 (figs. 2.45a–c).[147] In these paintings, Christ is usually enthroned and carries a codex. The compositions are a mixture of influences from Revelation, Ezekiel, and Isaiah. The living creatures or seraphim each have six wings covered with eyes, as in Revelation 4:8 and Isaiah 6:2. Wheels appear below the mandorla, and flames burst out, as in Ezekiel 1:4, 15. In Christ's codex appear the words "hagios, hagios, hagios" a phrase that was not only a fixture in the Orthodox Christian liturgy since the first

144. Grabar, *Christian Iconography*, 76, fig. 195; Elisabetta Lucchesi-Palli, in Weitzmann, *Age of Spirituality*, cat. no. 438; Gisela Jeremias, *Die Holztür der Basilika S. Sabina in Rom* (Tübingen: Wasmuth, 1980), 80–88, pls. 68–69; Herrmann and van den Hoek, "Two Men," 302, fig. 5.

145. See above, note 130.

146. Ihm, *Programme*, 42–52, 198–205, pls. 13.2, 14.1, 18.1, 23.1, 24, 25; Grabar, *Christian Iconography*, 44, 134–35, figs. 84, 118–19, 323–27.

147. Severin, in Brenk, *Spätantike*, cat. no. 291a; Gabra and Alcock, *Coptic Museum*, cat. no. 9.

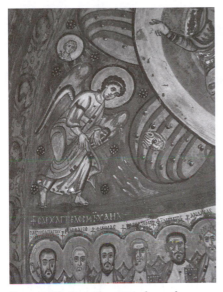

Figure 2.45b. Second coming, fresco from Bawit, Monastery of Apollo, Chapel VI, sixth or early seventh century.

Figure 2.45c. Second coming, fresco from Bawit, Monastery of Apollo, Chapel VI, sixth or early seventh century.

centuries but also in Talmudic and other Jewish prayer traditions of late antiquity.[148] This trishagion alludes to the angelic words in Isaiah 6:3 and possibly to the blessing of God's glory in Ezekiel 3:12 (in the Masoretic text and the Septuagint). It was sung by the seraphim (Isa. 6:3) and subsequently by the four creatures (Rev. 4:8). In extended form the hymn became a praise of the holy Trinity in the Byzantine liturgy.[149]

This hymn of praise was in all probability intoned in the liturgy performed in front of such pictures. Egyptian liturgies also describe Christ as seated on the cherubic, flaming throne or chariot. Such liturgical evocations of the majesty of God may have stimulated theologians and artists to create the syntheses of apocalyptic visions painted in the apses.[150]

The eternal sun and moon are regular components of these paintings, and angels usually flank the central apparition. In this case they are labeled as the archangels Michael and Gabriel. They bow toward Christ in veneration.

148. See, e.g., Esther G. Chazon (Hebrew University of Jerusalem), "Human and Angelic Prayer in Light of the Dead Sea Scrolls," http://orion.mscc.huji.ac.il/symposiums/5th/chazon00.html; Stefan C. Reif (Genizah Research Unit of the University of Cambridge), "Jewish Liturgy in the Fourth Century," www.liturgica.com/html/litJLitHist1.jsp?hostname=null#Fourth.

149. Ἅγιος ὁ θεός, Ἅγιος ἰσχυρός, Ἅγιος ἀθάνατος, ἐλέησον ἡμᾶς. See Andrew Louth, "Trishagion," *TRE* 34 (2002): 121–24.

150. Ihm, *Programme*, 48–50.

Below the apparition in the apse are the apostles, two local saints, and Mary, who is enthroned with the Christ child. This confident row of holy persons may be assembled to pass judgment at the second coming, as the apostles do in a Coptic homily of the sixth century.[151] Such apocalyptic scenes are nourished not only by biblical texts but also by pictorial traditions, liturgy, and evolving local beliefs about the heavenly realm.

Conclusions

Biblical apocalyptic texts provided material to enhance visionary experience of paradise in funerary art and in the minor arts. The process of enhancement took place in an evolutionary way and in different parallel traditions. In the second half of the fourth century, relatively unobtrusive borrowings are worked into traditional themes, such as Christ teaching his apostles, but in the fifth and sixth centuries borrowings from apocalyptic texts become more detailed, extensive, and conspicuous, and they set the stage for highly biblical presentations of paradise and the second coming. Apocalyptic material is also used to enhance presentations of Christ's ascension.

A variety of biblical writings provided material for artistic compositions. In the Latin West the book of Revelation was dominant. From this text came the alpha and omega, the Lamb of God on Mount Zion, the enthroned one in a rainbow ring, the scroll with seven seals, the seven candelabra, and the four living creatures with six wings.

Ezekiel's vision of the future temple with its palm trees was an important source: his vision helped to form the concepts of paradise and to transmit a new law to a Christian authority. Designers of Christian works of art interpreted Ezekiel's reception of God's *leges* before the temple of Jerusalem as a model for Christ's delegation of divine justice to Peter. Isaiah may have provided authority for placing Christ on the celestial globe.

The synoptic apocalypse was a source for artistic compositions throughout the Mediterranean world, although its influence may have been strongest in Italy. The sign in heaven before the second coming, Christ coming through the clouds, and the angels gathering the faithful were important themes inspired by Gospel texts.

In popular art, representations of rewards in heaven were inspired by Paul's vision of his heavenly crown (2 Tim. 4:7–8). On the model of rewards for athletic or military victory, Christ presents wreaths to apostles, martyrs, and happily married couples on gold-glass bowls, African lamps, and African red slip ware vessels.

151. Françoise Morard, "Homélie copte sur les apôtres," in Warren, *Early Christian Voices*, 417–30.

In the East, where the book of Revelation was often regarded with suspicion, Ezekiel had a more prominent role as source for apocalyptic works
of art. His distinctive tetramorph—one creature with four faces (lion, ox,
man, and eagle), four wings, wheels, and emitting flames—appears in several
eastern works. Four separate creatures with one face and six wings according to Revelation were popular in the West, where they became symbols for
the evangelists.

Revelation was a significant source in the East, but allusions to it were
often veiled. Unambiguous borrowings from Revelation, such as the Lamb
of God on Mount Zion or the twenty-four elders, are generally avoided. In
compositions with the four living creatures on the diagonals, unique features
from Ezekiel are also excluded, and the resulting apparition is a synthesis of
features common to several biblical apocalyptic visions.

Non-Christian pictorial sources also provide many models for formulating
otherworldly imagery. At times schemes of Roman origin are the bearer of
Christian apocalyptic messages in compositions that lack any biblical reference: the thrones with symbols in the Orthodox Baptistery of Ravenna and
busts or symbols of Christ in wreaths of victory carried by flying Victories are
the prime examples. Other motifs, such as the celestial globe, can be taken
over from Roman art with very little change in meaning.

Early Christian apocalyptic works tend to be flexible in their treatment
of sources. Biblical inspiration can at times be quite specific and literal, but
usually apocalyptic works of art display conspicuous divergences from the
texts. Contemporary political, social, esthetic, and theological concerns obviously lay behind many of these manipulations. The desire to translate biblical
visions into more specifically Christian terms led to the addition of apostles,
martyrs, and contemporary ecclesiastics where they were not called for in
the biblical texts. The desire to balance Gentile Christianity with Jewish
Christianity frequently led to innovations. The heavenly Jerusalem of biblical visions was balanced by a nontextual heavenly Bethlehem, possibly to
deal with the same ethnic concerns. Undignified details of texts are altered;
the twenty-four elders offer their crowns to Christ rather than throw them
down before him.

In these flexible compositions, biblical sources are often veiled. The characters of Revelation can be replaced by figures of greater contemporary or
local interest. Apostles and martyrs venerate Christ or offer their wreaths
of victory to him, taking the place of the twenty-four elders. The elect who
are gathered to Christ at his second coming are given specific identities as
local martyrs and bishops. Peter and Paul replace angels as the agents of
gathering. The details are changed—often radically—but the structure is still
apocalyptic in inspiration.

The designers of these visions of paradise and the second coming were extremely selective in their borrowings from apocalyptic texts. Artists omitted

some features that violated the canons of traditional Greco-Roman naturalism too flagrantly, such as the seven eyes and seven horns of the Lamb of God (Rev. 5:6). God does not appear as jasper and carnelian (Rev. 4:3).

Scenes of punishment and disaster were completely avoided. Biblical apocalyptic texts are terrifying and promise a dreadful fate to all but the most faithful and pure, but this frightening message is not what is communicated by apocalypses in early Christian art. The intention comes out explicitly in the inscriptions of mosaics at S. Pudenziana in Rome and the Monastery of the Stonecutters in Thessaloniki. The texts underline that God is there to be viewed, he is present in the building, and he brings salvation. The message could hardly be more comforting. Apparitions from threatening visions were used to illustrate prophecies of peace. Apocalyptic texts have been mined to extract material for images of a benevolent God in heaven and returning to earth. Apostles, saints, bishops, and churches are presented as parts of a system that mediates between heaven and earth and that offers safety, hope, and joy to the faithful individual. In the terrifying world of the late Roman Empire and the early Middle Ages, carefully crafted apocalyptic works of art were intended to provide the viewer with gratification and freedom from anxiety.

3

Turning Points in Early Christian Apocalypse Exegesis

Bernard McGinn

The Apocalypse of John was born in contention and has continued to be a subject of disagreement for almost two thousand years. Alfred North Whitehead, the child of an East Anglian parsonage, described the book "as one of the finest examples of imaginative literature," but also accused it of illustrating "the barbaric elements which have been retained to the undoing of Christian intuition." He found it shocking that the Apocalypse closed the Bible and suggested that it be replaced by "the imaginative account given by Thucydides of the Speech of Pericles to the Athenians."[1] (One may wonder what the readers of the Bibles found in countless hotel rooms might have thought had they discovered that the New Testament ended with Pericles' account of a free education for the orphans of those who die for the state.) Among other twentieth-century opponents of John's revelation, George Bernard Shaw stands out for the comment found in his ironic spoof of religion, *The Adventures of the Black Girl in Her Search for God* (1932). Shaw describes the Apocalypse as "a curious record of the visions of a drug addict which

---

1. Alfred North Whitehead, "The New Reformation," in *Adventures of Ideas* (New York: Macmillan, 1933), 170–71.

was absurdly admitted to the canon under the title of Revelation."[2] Shaw's contemporary in English letters, D. H. Lawrence, raised in what today we would call a fundamentalist family, also despised the Apocalypse, but could not dismiss it. His fascinating love-hate commentary on the book proclaims: "The Apocalypse of John is, as it stands, the work of a second-rate mind. It appeals intensely to second-rate minds in every country and every century."[3] For those who are fascinated with the Apocalypse, this criticism strikes home, but they can be consoled by the observation of the New England divine, Cotton Mather, who once remarked, "I confess Apocalyptic Studies are fittest for those Raised Souls, whose Heart Strings are made of a Little Nicer Clay than other men's."[4] Mather, to be sure, was as prejudiced on his side as Whitehead, Shaw, and Lawrence on theirs, but he does suggest that the conflict of interpretations over the Apocalypse has no end in sight. This clash supports the observation of the Romantic philosopher Johann Gottfried von Herder, who, like many others, could not refrain from writing a commentary on the Apocalypse under the title *Maranatha* (1779). Herder sagely noted: "Where a book, through thousands of years, stirs up the hearts and awakens the soul, and leaves neither friend nor foe indifferent, and scarcely has a lukewarm friend or enemy, in such a book there must be something substantial, whatever anyone may say."[5]

In this essay I will deal first with apocalyptic tensions in early Christianity, then with the Apocalypse in the second century CE, and finally with the emergence of spiritual readings of the Apocalypse.

Apocalyptic Tensions in Early Christianity

These modern contentions mirror those found in the early church. From roughly 150 CE, John's Apocalypse was the subject of debate, not only about how it should be read, but also whether it should be included in the list of authentic books, the developing canon of orthodox Christianity.[6] These two

2. George Bernard Shaw, *The Adventures of the Black Girl in Her Search for God* (London: Constable, 1932), 73.

3. D. H. Lawrence, *Apocalypse* (1931; repr., New York: Viking, 1960), 20; see also 187–89.

4. Cotton Mather, in a sermon given to an artillery company, cited by Stephen Stein, "Transatlantic Extensions: Apocalyptic in Early New England," in *The Apocalypse in English Renaissance Thought and Literature*, ed. C. A. Patrides and Joseph Wittreich (Manchester: Manchester University Press, 1984), 277.

5. Johann Gottfried von Herder, *Maranatha*. The English translation is that of Moses Stuart, *Commentary on the Apocalypse* (Andover: Allen, Morrill and Wardell, 1845), 2:501.

6. On the reception of the Apocalypse in general, see Judith Kovacs and Christopher Rowland, *Revelation*, BBC (Oxford: Blackwell, 2004.). A useful, if old, account of the role of the Apocalypse in early Christianity is Ned Bernard Stonehouse, *The Apocalypse in the Ancient Church: A Study of the History of the New Testament Canon* (Goes, Holland: Oosterbaan & Le Cointre, 1929). More detailed and up to date, but with omissions, is the first two parts of Gerhard Maier, *Die Johannesoffenbarung*

issues cannot be easily separated, because the emergence of readings of the Apocalypse that were judged fruitful for the life of the church was central to the arguments of those who insisted on its apostolic origin and canonicity.[7] Given the ongoing contention over the last book of the Bible, it may be useful to examine, once again, some of the key stages in the debate over the book during the second and third centuries. These early turning points in the reception of the Apocalypse set the stage for later debates about the book's usefulness and correct interpretation.

Every book of the Bible has been subject to diverse readings. Yet Jerome recognized that the Apocalypse had a special claim in this regard. As he put it: "The Apocalypse has as many mysteries as it does words."[8] Mysteries attract some, repel others. To readers like Jerome and those who followed him, the ambiguous symbolism, confusing structure, and strange character of the book as a new type of apocalypse (the first not cast in a pseudonymous form) all helped make John's revelation a conundrum. Though we often think that the early churches of Asia Minor to whom the book was directed immediately grasped its message, we cannot be sure. Perhaps the book needed interpretation right from the outset. What is clear is that, during the second century, aspects of the message of the Apocalypse, as well as the way in which it claimed authorization, emerged as flash points for critics. A look at these contentions and how they played out reveal some key aspects in the development of patristic apocalypticism.

Some students of the history of the early church have seen the crisis over the delay, or better, the nonappearance, of the parousia as a crucial moment in the development of the earliest Jesus communities into the nascent "great church."[9] Without denying that the failure of Jesus' return was a significant issue, interpretations that concentrate on the supposed abandonment of the apocalyptic sense of history in the second century overlook the fact that apocalypticism comes in many forms. One can argue that the second century showed an impressive amount of apocalyptic creativity, not the rejection of a supposedly "real" apocalyptic perspective. It

---

und die Kirche (Tübingen: Mohr, 1981). See also Georg Kretschmar, *Die Offenbarung des Johannes: Die Geschichte ihres Auslegung im 1. Jahrtausend* (Stuttgart: Calwer, 1985). Two recent histories of patristic eschatology offer much valuable information on the role of the Apocalypse: Brian E. Daley, *The Hope of the Early Church: A Handbook of Patristic Eschatology* (Cambridge: Cambridge University Press, 1991); and Charles E. Hill, *Regnum Caelorum: Patterns of Millennial Thought in Early Christianity*, 2nd ed. (Grand Rapids: Eerdmans, 2001).

7. For a general picture of the development of the canon, see John Barton, *Holy Writings, Sacred Text: The Canon in Early Christianity* (Louisville: Westminster John Knox, 1997).

8. Jerome, *Epistula* 53.8: "Apocalypsis Johannis tot habet sacramenta quot verba" (PL 22:548–49). Jerome continues with high praise for the book: "Parum dixi pro merito voluminis. Laus omnis inferior est: in verbis singulis multiplices latent intelligentiae."

9. This is the "consistent eschatological" interpretation of early Christianity, favored by Albert Schweitzer, Martin Werner, and their followers.

was during this century that the basic Christian picture of the last events, whether viewed as temporally imminent, or psychologically so, was created. The emergence of this grand scenario of the last times, evident in Irenaeus and Hippolytus, and to some extent in Tertullian, was an impressive theological achievement.[10] The development of the scenario, however, had less to do with John's Apocalypse than might be imagined. The standard picture of the end time events was a theological construction that sought to amalgamate many sources, both from the Bible and from other writings and oral traditions, some not readily recoverable today. This is evident, for example, in the emerging theology of the Antichrist, whose contours were shaped, at least in part, by developments in second-century Christology.[11] The fact that John's Apocalypse, after much debate, was accepted as canonical should not obscure the place of this larger body of traditions in the history of patristic apocalypticism. Nevertheless, John's Apocalypse did have an important role.

The debate over the Apocalypse has often been tied to the issue of chiliasm or millennialism, that is, belief in the thousand-year reign of Christ and the resurrected saints on earth after the defeat of the forces of evil but before the end, as found in chapter 20 of the Apocalypse.[12] The connection between chiliasm and the acceptance of the Apocalypse is important, but it too should not be exaggerated for several reasons.[13] The first is that we do not know how widespread chiliastic beliefs actually were among Christians of the first one hundred and fifty years of the church. Some apocalyptic texts, both scriptural, such as the Pauline letters, and quasi-scriptural, such

10. The full scenario of the last events constructed from diverse biblical and other sources is found in Irenaeus, *Adversus haereses*, Book 5 (hereafter *AH*); Hippolytus, *Commentarium in Danielem*, Book 4 (hereafter *Com. Dan.*); Hippolytus's treatise *De Antichristo* (hereafter *Ant.*), chaps. 5 and 64; and Tertullian, *De resurrectione carnis*, chap. 25. A general account of this emergence can be found in Bernard McGinn, *Antichrist: Two Thousand Years of the Human Fascination with Evil*, 2nd ed. (New York: Columbia University Press, 2000), chap. 3.

11. For more on the development of the Antichrist legend in early Christianity, see L. J. Liefert Peerbolte, *The Antecedents of Antichrist: A Traditio-Historical Study of the Earliest Christian Views on Eschatological Opponents* (Leiden: Brill, 1996). There is a helpful collection of texts on early patristic views of the Antichrist in Gian Luca Potestà and Marco Rizzi, eds., *L'Anticristo*, vol. 1, *Il Nemico dei Tempi Finali: Testi dal II al IV secolo* (Milan: Mondadori, 2005).

12. In this essay I will use chiliasm and millennialism synonymously as referring to the expected earthly reign of Christ and the saints, often, but not universally, conceived of as lasting a thousand years. Millenarianism will refer to the wider phenomenon of any hope for a better future earthly age.

13. The literature on millennialism is very large. A helpful overview can be found in Robert E. Lerner, "Millennialism," in *The Encyclopedia of Apocalypticism*, vol. 2, *Apocalypticism in Western History and Culture*, ed. Bernard McGinn (New York: Continuum, 1998), 326–60. For the period under review, see the summary by Clementina Mazzucco, "Il millenarismo cristiano delle origini (II–III sec.)," in *"Millennium": L'attesa della fine nei primi secoli cristiani. Atti delle III giornate patristiche torinesi*, ed. Renato Uglione (Turin: CELID Editrice, 2002), 145–82.

as the *Didache*, are free of chiliasm.[14] Significant second-century authors, such as Justin and Irenaeus, were millennial in outlook; others, like Clement, Ignatius of Antioch, and Hermas, were not. A key figure is Hippolytus, who accepted and helped develop the full-fledged apocalyptic scenario of the events of the end time partly under the influence of Irenaeus, but who did not share the bishop's chiliasm and broke with tradition by explicitly rejecting an imminent parousia.[15] As Charles Hill puts it: "A solidly entrenched, non-chiliastic eschatology was present in the Church to rival chiliasm from beginning to end."[16]

Second, we should note that there were a variety of forms of millennialism—it is not just whether there will be an earthly kingdom, but what form the kingdom is to take, especially how "materialistic" it will be.[17] John's description of the thousand-year reign in Apocalypse 20:1–6 is rather noninformative about the actual nature of the millennium. His account of the New Jerusalem that descends to earth in chapters 21 and 22 (especially 21:22–22:5), an eternal reign that comes after the Last Judgment (20:11–15), is more substantive, mentioning details such as the precious stones of the city's construction, as well as unfading illumination, untold wealth, and abundant fruitfulness. These characteristics are close to some of the physical descriptions of the thousand-year kingdom found in second-century authors.[18] Other accounts, especially those that project not only extravagant feasting but also sexual activity and bearing of children for the whole millennium, go further in a materialistic direction, reflecting the language found in some Jewish apocalyptic texts.[19] In sum, not only was there a variety of sources for early Christian chiliasm,[20]

14. The importance of non-chiliastic beliefs about the last things has been vindicated by Hill, *Regnum Caelorum*, who argues for two basic views. The first is the chiliastic position, defined as "belief in a temporary, earthly, Messianic kingdom to be realized sometime in the future" (5). Hill shows that this view logically involves belief that after death all souls, even of the just, go to Hades to await the resurrection of the body. The millennial kingdom, then, prepares the resurrected just for the vision of God in the eternal heavenly kingdom. Nonchiliastic eschatology holds that the souls of the just immediately go to heaven, thus obviating need for an earthly stage of preparation (16–20). See also his conclusion on pp. 249–53.

15. David G. Dunbar, "The Delay of the Parousia in Hippolytus," *VC* 37 (1983): 313–27.

16. Hill, *Regnum Caelorum*, 253. Mazzucco ("Millenarismo," 174–77) also stresses the coexistence of millennial and nonmillennial views throughout the early church.

17. This issue was recognized by Jean Daniélou, who argued for two basic types of millennialism: the materialistic Asiatic variety for which Papias and Cerinthus are witnesses, and the view found in Syria and Egypt where a more vague conception of the messianic reign was related to astrological calculations about the cosmic week of seven thousand years. Jean Daniélou claimed that Irenaeus fused the two streams; see Daniélou, *The Theology of Jewish Christianity* (Chicago: Regnery, 1964), 377–404.

18. On this point, Hill, *Regnum Caelorum*, 235–42.

19. The more materialistic elements in the picture of the coming millennium also involve extraordinary earthly fertility and the pacification of animals.

20. This point is discussed by Mazzucco, "Millenarismo," 155–62.

but it is also incorrect to claim that chiliasm was an integral feature of all early Christian apocalypticism. The relatively mild form of millennialism found in Apocalypse 20 was neutral enough to lend itself to both materialistic and more spiritualized readings.

The Apocalypse in the Second Century CE

Evidence for knowledge and use of the Apocalypse during the second century tells us much about the arguments for the book's apostolicity that was integral to its final canonical status.[21] Among the earliest witnesses to the use of the Apocalypse is that of Papias (d. ca. 130), bishop of Hieropolis in Asia Minor. Papias's strongly materialistic chiliasm, however, does not appear to be based on Apocalypse 20.[22] Although Papias's *Expositiones* is lost, Irenaeus cites the famous logion found in it concerning the fruitfulness of the millennium that the bishop claims he received from the elders, who in turn got it from John, who received it from the Lord.[23] Irenaeus accepted the dominical authenticity of this saying, but Eusebius's account of Papias's chiliasm ascribes it to the ignorant bishop's misunderstanding of the apostolic writings, while Jerome says that Papias advanced Jewish views.[24] So, Papias knew the Apocalypse and ascribed it to the apostle John, but his millennialism goes beyond what is found in the twentieth chapter of the book.

Justin Martyr's view of the millennium is unusual. The doctrine does not surface in his *Apologies*, possibly because of the intended audience, but it is featured prominently in his *Dialogus cum Tryphone*.[25] In chapters 80–81, on the basis of the authority of John, he supports both a double resurrection and a millennial reign to be enjoyed in a rebuilt Jerusalem: "A certain man among us, whose name was John, one of the apostles of Christ, prophesied

21. A claim to apostolic authorship, of course, was not automatic proof of the authenticity of any apocalypse, as we can see in the case of the Apocalypse of Peter and later the Apocalypse of Paul.

22. On the relation of second-century forms of chiliasm to the Apocalypse, besides Hill, see Clementina Mazzucco and Egidio Pietrella, "Il rapporto tra la concezione del millennio dei primi autori cristiani e l'Apocalisse di Giovanni," *Aug* 18 (1978): 29–45.

23. Irenaeus, *AH* 5.33.3–4. The closest parallels to Papias's logion occur in Jewish apocalyptic literature, such as *2 Bar.* 29, *1 En.* 10–11, and *Oracula Sibyllina* 3:744–61.

24. Eusebius, *Historia ecclesiastica* (hereafter *HE*) 3.39.12; Jerome, *De viris illustribus* (hereafter *De vir. ill.*) 18. Jerome's description of the adherents of millennialism here is well known: "Hic [Papias] dicitur annorum mille iudaicam edidisse δευτέρωσιν. Quem secuti sunt Irenaeus et Apollinaris et ceteri, qui post resurrectionem aiunt in carne cum sanctis Dominum regnaturum" (*Hieronymi De viris inlustribus liber*, ed. G. Herding [Leipzig: Teubner, 1879], 22). On Eusebius's view of Papias, see Robert M. Grant, "Papias in Eusebius's *Church History*," in *Mélanges d'histoire des religions offerts à Henri-Charles Puech* (Paris: Presses universitaires de France, 1974), 209–13.

25. Hill (*Regnum Caelorum*, 23–27) advances the argument that the *Dialogus* is an early work based on a real discussion with the Jew Trypho not long after Bar Kochba's revolt, perhaps ca. 140, while the *Apologies* reflect a later development in Justin's views.

in a revelation made to him, that those who believed in our Christ would dwell a thousand years in Jerusalem."[26] While Justin contends that this view was that of those who are "right-minded" on all issues of belief, he accepts that there are good Christians who think otherwise.[27]

Among the other second-century supporters of the authority of the Apocalypse we can list Melito of Sardis, who, according to Eusebius and Jerome, wrote something on the book perhaps about 170.[28] The major second-century witness to the scriptural authenticity of John's revelation and its teaching about the end time is Irenaeus, especially in the *Adversus haereses* written in the 180s. In his great work, Irenaeus includes the letter sent by the Gallic church to Asia Minor around 177 in which the Apocalypse is referred to as Scripture (*AH* 5.1.58). In the course of laying out his views of the last times in book five, he uses passages from sixteen of the twenty-two chapters of the Apocalypse. His defense of a literal view of the millennium makes considerable use of Apocalypse 20, but also of other chiliastic traditions.[29] From the period around 200 we find another possible witness to the apostolicity of the Apocalypse in the "Muratorian Canon," if it is indeed a product of the Roman Church from around 200 and not a late fourth-century work.[30] Finally, Tertullian, a witness to North African Christianity, considers the text apostolic, and also defends a mild form of chiliasm compatible with Apocalypse 20.[31]

Given the geographical spread of the early Christian writers who accepted the authority of the Apocalypse and ascribed it to the apostle John, we may be surprised at the opposition to the book that also became evident in the second century. But opposition there was. Marcion (ca. 140–150) rejected the book, as might be expected.[32] Gnostic Christians, such as Valentinus and his followers, used some of the symbols from the Apocalypse, but within the

26. *Iustini Martyris: Dialogus cum Tryphone*, ed. Miroslav Marcovich (Berlin: de Gruyter, 1997), chap. 81 (pp. 210–12).

27. Hill (*Regnum Caelorum*, 11–16) argues that Irenaeus *AH* 5.31–32.1 reflects the same two groups of orthodox, chiliastic and nonchiliastic, but that Irenaeus is more intent on showing nonchiliastic Christians the error of their views.

28. On Melito's lost work, see Eusebius, *HE* 4.26; and Jerome, *De vir. ill.* 24.

29. Irenaeus, *AH* 5.30–34. Stonehouse (*Apocalypse*, 80) notes the variety of sources. For accounts of Irenaeus's eschatological views, see Hill, *Regnum Caelorum*, 11–20; and Daley, *Hope of the Early Church*, 28–32. On Irenaeus's chiliasm, see also Marjorie O'Rourke Boyle, "Irenaeus's Millennial Hope: A Polemical Weapon," *RTAM* 36 (1969): 5–16.

30. On the debate over the Muratorian Canon, see Geoffrey Mark Hahneman, *The Muratorian Fragment and the Development of the Canon* (Oxford: Clarendon, 1992), who argues for the later date.

31. On Tertullian's defense of the apostolicity of the Apocalypse, see, e.g., *De resurrectione carnis* 38 and *De monogamia* 19. His nonmaterialistic chiliasm was in part polemical, being employed against the thought of Marcion and found in his *Adversus Marcionem* 3.24 and *De resurrectione carnis* 25.1 and 26.7–10. On Tertullian's chiliasm, consult Hill, *Regnum Caelorum*, 27–32.

32. Marcion appears to have taught that there would, indeed, be a coming Messiah (=Antichrist) who would restore Jewish rule at Jerusalem before the return of Christ, the true Messiah. See Hill,

context of a view of redemption that denied the bodily resurrection taught in the book.[33] Rejection of the Apocalypse in the late second century has often been tied to the reaction against Montanism. The Montanists emphasized the superiority of ecstatic prophecy to episcopal authority (as John seems to do in the letters to the churches in Rev. 1–3), and they believed in a new descent of the Paraclete as announced by Jesus in John 16. They may also have expected the end of the age and an imminent descent of the heavenly Jerusalem upon their centers in Asia Minor (see Rev. 21).[34] Given these views, some of the opponents of the "New Prophecy" appear to have attacked the authenticity of the Johannine texts that the Montanists used to support their beliefs.[35] This interpretation of the source of opposition to the Apocalypse has some weight, but there were doubtless a number of factors at work.

Another important source of the reaction against the Apocalypse was the church's relation to Rabbinic Judaism. During the course of the second and third centuries, nascent orthodox Christianity was engaged in a struggle to work out its own interpretation of the Old Testament (the first "Scripture") against its perceived opponents, especially the "hard-hearted and ignorant members of the circumcision" and the "members of the heretical sects," as Origen termed two groups of exegetical enemies in *De principiis* 4.2.1. John's Apocalypse has been called the most Jewish book of the New Testament, because of its language, imagery, and proximity to Jewish apocalyptic sources. Hence an important factor in the struggle over the Apocalypse was how such a "Jewish" book could be given a properly spiritual reading that made it useful for the church.[36] Just as Christians had vindicated Old Testament prophecies about the Messiah and his kingdom by reinterpreting them in spiritual fashion as pointing to Christ and the church, so too exegetes were called on to show how the Apocalypse could be read as a message about the

---

Regnum Caelorum, 71–73. From this perspective, John's Apocalypse would contain a false revelation of the evil God of the Old Testament.

33. See Daley, *Hope of the Early Church*, chap. 3, for gnostic eschatology.

34. For the debate over whether the Montanists really held that the heavenly Jerusalem had or would soon descend on their centers at Pepuza and Tymion, see Hill, *Regnum Caelorum*, 146–51.

35. For this argument, see Stonehouse, *Apocalypse*, 49; and Robert M. Grant, *Augustus to Constantine: The Thrust of the Christian Movement into the Roman World* (New York: Harper & Row, 1970), 139–40. The extent of the chiliasm of the original Montanists of Asia Minor, however, has recently become a contested issue. Hill (*Regnum Caelorum*, 143–59) sees no evidence for real chiliasm in the Montanists, while Christine Trevett (*Montanism: Gender, Authority and the New Prophecy* [Cambridge: Cambridge University Press, 2002], 95–105) admits a muted chiliasm and a strong interest in eschatology in general, but no apocalyptic sense of imminence. However, if the saying ascribed to the prophetess Maximilla by Epiphanius in *Panarion* 48.2.4 ("After me there will be no prophet, but the end" [συντέλεια]) is authentic, some sense of imminence of the end seems to have been present.

36. Mazzucco ("Millenarismo," 170–73) notes the anti-Jewish polemic found in many early Christian opponents to millennialism, suggesting that ongoing conflict with Jewish communities seen as religious competitors was a factor in the debates.

present life of the church as much as, or perhaps even more than, a prophecy about controversial events of the end time that should not be interpreted in "Judaistic" fashion.

The major late second-century opponents of the Apocalypse are generally described as *Alogoi* (Alogists), because they are said to have rejected not only the revelation ascribed to John but also the Johannine Gospel with its teaching about the Logos. Much about the group remains shadowy and controversial.[37] The *Alogoi* were found in Asia Minor and also in the West, specifically in the church at Rome. As noted above, they may have been, at least in part, a reaction to Montanism. We know the name of only one "Alogist" author, the Roman priest Gaius, active in the late second century.[38] Eusebius tells us that Gaius was an antichiliast who disputed with a Montanist named Proclus. According to the Father of Church History, Gaius held that the heretic Cerinthus was the true author of the Apocalypse and its chiliasm: "Cerinthus, who through revelations attributed to the great apostle, lyingly introduces portents to us as though shown him by angels, and says that after the resurrection the kingdom of Christ will be on earth and that humanity living in Jerusalem will again be a slave of lusts and pleasure."[39] (We have no direct evidence, however, that Gaius also rejected John's Gospel.) The problem of Gaius and his views has evoked debate in recent decades—not surprising for a lost text. It used to be thought that something of Gaius's views could be recovered from the fragments of his writings found in the refutation of Gaius by Hippolytus (the *Capitula adversus Gaium*, as they have been called). This text also no longer exists, and the later fragments that purport to reflect the debate between Gaius and Hippolytus have become the subject of controversy.

The Emergence of Spiritual Readings of the Apocalypse

The Roman presbyter Hippolytus (ca. 170–236), once an uncontroversial figure with a list of recognized writings and an important position as a theologian and exegete, has become the subject of much controversy.[40]

37. For an account of the Alogists, see Stuart G. Hall, "Aloger," in *TRE*, 2:290–95. Irenaeus (*AH* 3.11.9) seems to be referring to the Alogists without using the name when he speaks of some Christians who reject John's Gospel. There is a more complete, but possibly tendentious, picture of the heresy in Epiphanius, *Panarion* 51 (for an English translation, see Philip R. Amidon, SJ, *The Panarion of St. Epiphanius, Bishop of Salamis* [New York: Oxford University Press, 1990], 177–88). Epiphanius tells us that they ascribed the Apocalypse not to John, but to his opponent Cerinthus.

38. On Gaius, see especially Emanuela Prinzivalli, "Gaoi e gli alogi," *Studi storici religiosi* 5 (1981): 53–68; Maier, *Johannesoffenbarung*, 69–85; and Stonehouse, *Apocalypse*, 92–99.

39. Eusebius, *HE* 3.28.2.

40. For an introduction to Hippolytus, see Marcel Ricard, "Hippolyte de Rome (saint)," in *Dictionnaire de spiritualité* (Paris: Beauchesne, 1937–94), 7:531–71. Ricard's treatment of 1969 does not, of course, reflect recent disputes, on which see Allen Brent, *Hippolytus and the Roman Church:*

Newer research generally favors distinguishing two "Hippolytuses"—the writer of works such as the *Commentarium in Danielem* and the treatise *De Antichristo*,[41] and a second author of the chronographical and antiheretical writings formerly ascribed to "Hippolytus."[42] Nevertheless, the authentic writings, as well as the disputed fragments said to reflect the *Capitula adversus Gaium*,[43] provide us with evidence for the emergence of a new way to read the Apocalypse designed, at least in part, to counter the objections of the "Alogists." Although the treatise on the Antichrist and commentary on Daniel (both written shortly after 200 CE) were of great importance in the development of Christian eschatology, Hippolytus was not fundamentally apocalyptic, at least in the sense of expecting an imminent return of Christ. He not only recalibrated Christian eschatological expectations to show that the second coming was not to be expected for some three centuries,[44] but he also marked an important stage in the process of the reinterpretation of the Apocalypse.

Along with the *Capitula adversus Gaium*, Hippolytus is credited in several sources with an *Apologia*, or commentary, on John's Gospel and the Apocalypse.[45] Earlier scholars thought that some dialogical passages ascribed to "Gaius" and "Hippolytus" in the apocalypse commentary of Dionysius bar Salibi reflected the lost *Capitula*. Other fragments of readings of the Apocalypse

---

Communities in Tension before the Emergence of the Monarch-Bishop (Leiden: Brill, 1995). For treatments of Hippolytus's eschatology and view of the Apocalypse, see Stonehouse, *Apocalypse*, 99–109; Daley, *Hope of the Early Church*, 38–41; Hill, *Regnum Caelorum*, 160–70; David G. Dunbar, "The Eschatology of Hippolytus of Rome" (PhD diss., Drew University, 1979); Dunbar, "Delay of the Parousia"; and most recently, Enrico Norelli, "L'attesa della fine: 'Ippolito' e la sua tradizione," in Uglione, *"Millennium,"* 65–99. For a survey of Hippolytus's contribution to the Antichrist legend, see McGinn, *Antichrist*, 60–63.

41. Hippolytus's *Com. Dan.*, the earliest surviving free-standing Christian biblical commentary, was first edited by Georg Nathanael Bonwetsch, *Hippolyt Werke: Erster Band. Erster Teil. Kommentar zu Daniel*, GCS 7 (Leipzig: Hinrichs, 1897). I will use the second, improved edition of Marcel Ricard (Berlin: Akademie Verlag, 2000). For the *Ant.*, I will use the edition and commentary of Enrico Norelli, *Ippolito: L'Anticristo. De Antichristo*, Biblioteca Patristica (Florence: Nardini, 1987).

42. The unity of Hippolytus was first questioned by Pierre Nautin in 1947. For recent evaluations, see, Norelli, "L'attesa della fine," 67–68; and Brent, *Hippolytus*, chaps. 4 and 5.

43. The first edition, along with an English translation and discussion, of the purported fragments of the *Capitula adversus Gaium* found in the twelfth-century Apocalypse commentary of the Syriac author Dionysius bar Salibi, was published by Dr. Gwynn, "Hippolytus and His 'Heads against Caius,'" *Herm* 6 (1888): 397–418. Hans Achelis gave a German translation in his *Hippolyt Werke: Erster Band. Zweiter Teil. Hippolyt's kleinere exegetische und homilitische Schriften*, GCS 7 (Leipzig: Hinrichs, 1897), 241–47. Later discussions and translations will be noted below.

44. On the importance of Hippolytus's redating of the "World Week," i.e., the seven thousand-year pattern of history, see Dunbar, "Delay of the Parousia," esp. 313–19.

45. Among the sources that mention Hippolytus as the author of an *Apologia*, or *De Apocalypsi*, is Jerome, *De vir. ill.* 61. For a discussion of the authenticity of the *Capitula* and the *De Apocalypsi*, see Brent, *Hippolytus*, 144–84.

ascribed to Hippolytus are extant not only in Syriac but also in Greek, Coptic, Arabic, and Old Slavic.[46] Fragments continue to be discovered.[47] What are we to make of this confusing picture? Could some of these later texts reflect the lost commentary? The weight of opinion today is against the existence of a separate commentary on the Gospel and the Apocalypse.[48] Doubts have even been raised about the authenticity of the *Capitula adversus Gaium*.[49] "Hippolytus" has become a fruitful garden for the growth of many hypotheses difficult to prove. Nevertheless, when we investigate the use of the Apocalypse in the authentic Hippolytan exegetical texts, such as the work on Antichrist and the commentary on Daniel, as well as the fragmentary and doubtless much-edited excerpts that reflect, however distantly, his reactions to those who denied the authenticity of the Apocalypse ("Gaius"), we do get the sense of an original exegetical program, one that can be said to form a third-century alternative to the Alexandrian current soon to reach its crest in Origen.[50]

The debate between Gaius and Hippolytus preserves echoes of an important conflict at the end of the second century and in the early third. From the perspective of the history of Christian beliefs about the end, especially the role of John's Apocalypse, the antichiliasm of Gaius appears to be linked to a view that saw the book as a specimen of "Judaizing" literalism at odds with the true predictions of the end time found in Paul and the Synoptic Gospels. The dialogue between Gaius and Hippolytus found in Dionysius bar Salibi contains a series of objections to the Johannine view of the end based on the

46. A German translation of a set of twenty-two fragments, embracing twenty-one passages from an Arabic commentary on the Apocalypse (I–XXI) and one Old Slavic passage, was published by H. Achelis in *Hippolyt Werke: Erster Band. Zweiter Teil*, 229–38 (Achelis notes which Arabic fragments correspond to his translations of the Syriac fragments from Dionysius bar Salibi). Achelis studied the fragments in his *Hippolytstudien*, TUGAL 16.4 (Leipzig: Hinrichs, 1897), 169–88. The texts found in Dionysius bar Salibi were translated into French and given a detailed commentary by Pierre Prigent, "Hippolyte, commentateur de l'Apocalypse," *TZ* 28 (1972): 391–412. The Arabic fragments, as well as some citations of Hippolytus from the sixth-century Greek Apocalypse commentator Andreas of Caesarea, were translated and studied by Pierre Prigent and Ralph Stehly in "Les fragments du De Apocalypsi d'Hippolyte," *TZ* 29 (1973): 313–33. The two authors also produced a translation and study of two further Syriac fragments in their article, "Citations d'Hippolyte trouvées dans le ms. Bodl. Syr. 140," *TZ* 30 (1974): 82–85. The most recent discussions of the fragments can be found in Brent, *Hippolytus*, 144–84; and Norelli, "L'attesa della fine," 69–75.

47. Sebastian Brock has published sixth-century Syriac fragments of Hippolytus's reading of the Apocalypse from a manuscript at Mount Sinai. For an Italian translation and discussion of the fragments, see Alberto Camplani and Emanuela Prinzivalli, "Sul significato dei nuovi frammenti siriaci dei *Capitula adversus Caium* attribuiti a Ippolito," *Aug* 38 (1998): 49–82. This article also treats the relation between these fragments and those in Dionysius bar Salibi (63–82).

48. These doubts were first expressed by Prigent, "Hippolyte, commentateur," 411–12; and Prigent and Stehly, "Fragments," 332–33.

49. The case against the *Capitula* is put by Brent (*Hippolytus*, 149, 161, 171, 173–84), who argues that the Hippolytan dialogue found in Dionysius bar Salibi is a pseudonymous work that may contain elements from Hippolytus found in florilegia and catenae.

50. On the originality of Hippolytus's exegesis, see Camplani and Prinzivalli, "Sul significato," 76.

differences between what is found in the Apocalyse and the teaching about the end in Paul and the Synoptics. Hippolytus answers Gaius's objections by showing the conformity of John with the other New Testament predictions of the last times.[51] For example, commenting on the eschatological sign of the blowing of the trumpets in Apocalypse 8 and 9, Gaius claimed that these open predictions of the end contradict Paul's statement that the last things "will come like a thief in the night" (1 Thess. 5:2). Hippolytus responds by arguing that Paul's thief in the night does not refer to the suddenness of the end, but rather to the fact that the wicked will be surprised by the coming of the Lord because they dwell in the darkness of sin. Concerning the prediction in Apocalypse 9:14–15 about the sixth trumpet when the four angels bound at the Euphrates will be loosed to kill a third of the human race, Gaius (according to Dionysius bar Salibi) says, "It is not written that the angels will make war, nor is it written that 'a third of the human race will be destroyed,' but rather 'nation will rise against nation'" (Matt. 24:7)—thus pitting the Gospel view of the end against that found in the revelation ascribed to John. Hippolytus answers by identifying the angels with the nations that they oversee, a position found in Daniel and followed by a number of Christian writers.[52]

With regard to chiliasm, Gaius contrasts the promise of the binding of Satan at the time of the millennial kingdom (Rev. 20:2) with Matthew 12:29: "How can one enter a strong man's house, . . . without first tying up the strong man?" In other words, since Christ has already bound Satan during his time on earth, there can be no future binding and therefore no millennial kingdom. Hippolytus's refutation of Gaius provides evidence for an emerging nonliteral view of the predictions found in the Apocalypse. Against Gaius's interpretation of Apocalypse 20, he argues that it is evident that Satan is still at work in the world. He also contends that there is a place for the prediction of the millennial kingdom, at least when spiritually understood. Hippolytus insists that "the number of the years is not the number of the days, but it represents the space of one day, glorious and perfect, in which, when the King comes in glory with his slain, the creation is to shine. . . . Accordingly," he says, "when with the eye of the Spirit John saw the glory of that day [i.e., of the sabbath day], he likens it to the space of a thousand years; according to the saying, 'One day in the world of the righteous is as a thousand years' (Ps. 90:4). And by that number he shows that day to be perfect for those that are faithful."[53] This rather elliptical statement is scarcely a literal form

51. For a study of the objections, see Brent, *Hippolytus*, 150–69; and Camplani and Prinzivalli, "Sul significato," 66–72, who emphasize the attempt to harmonize John and Paul in the text.

52. Gwynn, "Heads against Caius," 402.

53. The discussion of Rev. 20:2–3 forms fragment 7 of Achelis's translation of the passages from Dionysius bar Salibi's commentary (Achelis, *Hippolytstudien*, 246–47). Brent (*Hippolytus*, 166–67) considers this passage doubtful because of the supposed quotation of 2 Pet. 3:8, but the use of Ps.

of chiliasm. In passages from the authentic works, Hippolytus gives an even more spiritualized reading, identifying the seventh age, or thousand-year period, with the kingdom of the saints (Dan. 7), the endless reward Christ bestows on the just after the general resurrection.[54]

Without attempting to solve all the problems about how far the later fragments are based on positions originating in Hippolytus, let alone how these views were passed down over the centuries, on the basis of a comparison of some of the fragments with the two major works acknowledged as Hippolytan we may be able to gain some perspective on this third-century figure's reading of John's enigmatic revelation.[55] The exercise is worthwhile, because one can argue that Hippolytus marks a real turning point in the history of Apocalypse exegesis.

Seven of the twenty-two Arabic fragments ascribed to Hippolytus and available in Achelis deal with chapter 12.[56] The same passage from the Apocalypse is also treated in chapters 60–62 of the *De Antichristo*,[57] thus allowing a comparison of two forms of "Hippolytan" texts. The emphasis given to Apocalypse 12, as well as the general conformity between the two treatments, suggest that Apocalypse 12 emerged in the third century as a key component of the new ecclesiological and tropological interpretation of John's book.[58] As Pierre Prigent has argued, Apocalypse 12 can be considered "the center and key to the whole book," at least in the new spiritual modes of interpretation.[59]

Hippolytus reads Apocalypse 12 in a basically ecclesiological and christological way.[60] The Arabic fragments contain an interpretation of most of the first part of the chapter, the confrontation between the woman and the dragon (Rev. 12:1–6). It begins with a detailed explanation of 12:1: "Hippoly-

---

90:4 in relation to the "World Week" scheme of history was widespread in many second-century Christian texts (e.g., *Barn.* 15.5).

54. For the view of the sabbath as a purely eternal kingdom based on Rev. 21–22, see *Com. Dan.* 2.37.4 (on the saints as already judging); 3.31.2–4; and 4.10–11, 23, 58 (Ricard, *Hippolyt Werke*, 128, 188–90, 214–20, 246, and 330). See also *Ant.* 65, which fuses the first and the second resurrections. There is a discussion of these texts in Hill, *Regnum Caelorum*, 162–69.

55. For a complete listing of the parallels between the fragments and *Com. Dan.* and *Ant.*, see Prigent, "Hippolyte, commentateur," 392–403; and Brent, *Hippolytus*, 159–60n158.

56. These are fragments 4–10 (Achelis, *Hippolytstudien*, 232–33).

57. *Ant.* 60–62 (Norelli, *Ippolito*, 140–46, with notes at 254–61).

58. According to the first three volumes of the *Biblia Patristica*, there are only fourteen references to Rev. 12 among second- and early third-century authors, but no less than seventy-three in the third and early fourth centuries (twenty-three by Hippolytus, twenty-four by Methodius, and thirteen by Victorinus). Origen refers to chap. 12 twenty-nine times, but this count is misleading, as will be seen below.

59. Pierre Prigent, *Apocalypse 12: Histoire de l'exégèse* (Tübingen: Mohr, 1959), 1. This useful volume gives an overview of the history of the interpretation of Apocalypse 12.

60. Ibid., 4–5, provides a helpful chart of the surviving traditions concerning Hippolytus's reading of the chapter.

tus, the Roman bishop, is of the view in his exposition of this verse that the 'woman' means the Church and the 'sun' with which she is clothed means our Lord Christ, because he is named the 'Sun of Justice' (Mal. 4:2). The 'moon' under her feet is John the Baptist, and the 'crown of twelve stars' on her head signifies the twelve apostles."[61] The exposition found in the fragments continues with the historical identification of the seven heads of the dragon (12:3–4) as seven kings, emissaries of the devil, who persecute the people of God, both in the time of the Old Testament and the New.[62] In the treatise on the Antichrist, Hippolytus provides a reading of verse 5 that emphasizes the church's continual role in bearing Christ in the world—"the Church, always bringing forth Christ, the perfect man child of God, who is declared God and man, becomes the instructor of all the nations. And the words, 'her child was caught up onto God and to his throne,' signify that he who is always born of her is a heavenly king and not an earthly."[63]

The second major part of Hippolytus's exegesis of the twelfth chapter of the Apocalypse concerns the meaning of the cosmic struggle between the dragon and the angelic host and its continuation on earth in the life of the church (Rev. 12:7–17).[64] This fits well with his concern for the interim life of the church, the time between Christ's first and second comings.[65] Chapter 61 of De Antichristo reads, verses 13–14, the dragon's pursuit of the heavenly woman and the two wings given her to fly off for "a time, times, and half a time" (v. 14), as the church's flight during the 1260 days of Antichrist when her faith in Christ's outstretched arms on the cross will be a protection for believers. Arabic Fragment 8, however, says that "Hippolytus explains the

61. Fragment 4. This reading is reflected, if more briefly, in the newly discovered Syriac fragments a/b; see Camplani and Prinzivalli, "Sul significato," 55–57, for the text in translation, and 73–75 for discussion. Ant. 61 (Norelli, Ippolito, 142–44) has a similar interpretation, save that the moon is given a generic reading as "heavenly glory." It is possible that the sun indicates Christ as the message of the New Testament, while the moon means John the Baptist as the representative of the Old Testament; see Prigent and Stehly, "Fragments," 322–23.

62. Fragment 6. The seven kings are Nebuchadnezzer, Kores the Mede (Cyrus), Darius, Alexander, the four successors of Alexander, the Roman Empire, and Antichrist. The ten horns are identified with the ten kings who precede Antichrist. These verses are not exegeted in Ant. 61. However, Com. Dan. 4.3–6 (Ricard, Hippolyt Werke, 198–206) interprets the vision of the four beasts in Dan. 7:2–12 with some distant parallels. See Prigent and Stehly, "Fragments," 323–24.

63. Hippolytus, Ant. 61 (Norelli, Ippolito, 142–44). There is no exegesis of Rev. 12:5 in the surviving fragments. There is a brief reference to Rev. 12:6 in a catenae on Matthew, which may go back to Hippolytus (see Achelis, Hippolytstudien, 207).

64. In this second part of Rev. 12 it must be admitted that we lack exegesis for important parts of the text, specifically vv. 7–9 and 11–12. Arabic Fragment 7 gives a brief reference to the "great voice from heaven" of v. 10 as coming from the angels. The passages that survive in the texts known to us deal with vv. 13–17. Presumably, Hippolytus commented on the other verses, but they have not survived.

65. Dunbar ("Delay of the Parousia," 318) notes, "The advance made by Hippolytus on earlier Christian thinkers is that he focuses attention on the time between the first and the second advents."

two wings as hope and love."[66] Arabic Fragments 9–10 contain an extended exegesis of verses 16 and 17 in which, after the river spit out by the dragon is swallowed by the earth, the dragon "went off to make war on the rest of her children, those who keep the commandments of God and hold the testimony of Jesus." The swallowing up of the river, the Arabic commentator says, can either be interpreted in an external way as predicting that the followers of Satan who persecute the church will actually be swallowed up the way Dathan and his group were at the time of the Exodus (Num. 16:32–35), or in an interior fashion as signifying that the wicked wander here and there and miss the goal of their journey, "as Hippolytus says." Finally, the Arab commentator insists that those who keep the commandments and adhere to Jesus' testimony (v. 17) do so not merely mentally, but by putting his example into practice. "The fact that they keep the testimony of Jesus consists in imitating him in patience, an effort in behalf of truth and of the acceptance of martyrdom." These people are stronger than those in the group who were swallowed up. Disagreeing with Hippolytus he goes on, "If they had retreated [from martyrdom] because of their riches and because of concern for their possessions, as Hippolytus says, they would not have remained firm before these calamities."[67]

From these rather extensive interpretations, both those in the authentic works and those in the debatable fragments, it is at least clear that Hippolytus had a coherent ecclesiological reading of chapter 12 of the Apocalypse, one that saw the text as a summary of salvation history—past (in relation to its foundation), present (in the ongoing life of the community), and to come (in relation to the final persecution). There also is some appeal to a moral, or tropological, appropriation of the symbolism of the cosmic and historical struggle portrayed by John, notably with regard to the virtues needed to resist persecution and be willing to submit to martyrdom.

When we come to the second great Apocalypse exegete of the third century, Hippolytus's younger contemporary, Origen (d. ca. 253), we find a use of John's revelation that goes even further in its spiritualizing emphasis. Among early Christian exegetes, Origen is noted for the way in which he directed his interpretation of Scripture toward the goal of deeper understanding of revealed truth in the service of an anagogic appropriation of the message of the Word hidden under the external letters of the sacred text.[68] Origen's deeply spiritual and antimaterialistic view of the Bible might have been thought to have led him to opposition to John's lurid revelation.

---

66. Fragment 8 (Achelis, *Hippolytstudien*, 233), and *Ant.* 61 (Norelli, *Ippolito*, 144).

67. Fragment 10 (Achelis, *Hippolytstudien*, 233). See the discussion and improved translations of Fragments 9–10 in Prigent and Stehly, "Fragments," 325–26.

68. For a good demonstration of the tropological and anagogical aspects of Origen's exegesis, see Karen Jo Torjesen, *Hermeneutical Procedure and Theological Method in Origen's Exegesis*, PTS 28 (Berlin: de Gruyter, 1986).

This was not the case. The Alexandrian considered the Apocalypse as canonical, and he cites it, implicitly or explicitly, quite often in his surviving
writings.[69] Unfortunately, Origen never got to write the commentary on
John's revelation that he apparently intended to compose.[70] His use of the
Apocalypse, as Adele Monaci has shown, concentrates on undermining
literal futuristic apocalyptic interpretations in the service of a realized
christological eschatology that adheres to a dogmatic, not historical, sense
of the biblical prophecies.[71] Somewhat surprisingly, Origen does not indulge
in much personal appropriation of the images of the book for moral and
mystical development. This dimension was to be taken up by those who
came after him.

Origen's comment on the "Little Apocalypse" in Matthew 24–25 provides
an example of what he might have done in a full commentary on the Apocalypse by showing how an internal reading of the images of resurrection and
final judgment in Matthew avoids the extremes of rejection of apocalypticism, on the one hand, and the literalism of some of his predecessors, on the
other.[72] Origen's understanding of the resurrection of the body, suggested
in Matthew 25:31–46 and endorsed in Apocalypse 20:11–15, has come in
for study in recent years.[73] His treatment of the Gospel predictions about
the second coming and the Last Judgment also demonstrate his concern for
reinterpreting the details of the scriptural picture of the last events in the
service of the dogmatic meaning of the symbols. For example, he argues that
the particulars of the judgment scene presented in Matthew should not be
taken as literal prophecies of what is to come, but rather as revealing various
aspects of how Christ will manifest himself spiritually to all humans at the
end of time—in glory to those who have been perfected in virtue, and in

69. According to the references compiled in the *Biblia Patristica*, vol. 3, *Origène* (Paris: CNRS,
1980), 466–69, Origen references the Apocalypse 416 times, but many of these citations are generic at best. On Origen's use of the Apocalypse, besides Stonehouse, *Apocalypse*, 117–123, see
esp. Manlio Simonetti, "Il millenarismo in Oriente da Origene a Metodio," in *Corona Gratiarum.
Miscellanea Patristica, Historica et Liturgica Eligio Dekkers O.S.B. XII Lustra complenti Oblata*
(Bruges: Sint Pietersabdij, 1975), 1:37–58; and Adele Monaci, "Apocalisse ed escatologia nell'opera
di Origene," *Aug* 18 (1978): 139–51. Origen seems to have been aware of the debates over the
authorship of the Apocalypse. In his late treatise, *Peri Pascha*, he refers to "the Apocalypse said
to be John's" (see O. Guéraud and P. Nautin, eds., *Origène sur la Paque* [Paris: Éditions du Cerf,
1979], 119).

70. See *Commentariorum Series in Matthaeum* 49 (GCS 11:105.8): "exponentur autem tempore
sui in Revelatione Iohannis."

71. Monaci, "Apocalisse ed escatologia," 142–43, 149–50.

72. For a sketch of Origen's rereading of scriptural apocalypticism, see Daley, *Hope of the Early
Church*, 47–60, who speaks of Origen's program as a form of demythologizing (48). Also see Hill,
Regnum Caelorum, 176–89, on his attitudes toward chiliasm and exegesis of Rev. 20.

73. See Daley, *Hope of the Early Church*, 51–55; and Caroline Walker Bynum, *The Resurrection of
the Body in Western Christianity, 200–1336* (New York: Columbia University Press, 1995), 63–71.

judgment to the wicked.[74] From this perspective, there could be no real millennium for the Alexandrian exegete. Origen attacked such a view as Jewish literalism in *De principiis* 2.11.2–3, as well as in many places in his writings, basing his argument on the exegetical principle set forth in book 4 that "in all the prophecies concerning Jerusalem . . . the scriptures are telling us about the heavenly city" (4.3.8).[75] For the Alexandrian, the thousand-year kingdom predicted in Apocalypse 20 is nothing else but the heavenly intermediate state in which the souls of the just await the last judgment and the final sabbath rest of the kingdom of heaven.[76]

Given the christological focus of Origen's interpretation of the Apocalypse, one in which the picture of the rider on the white horse of 19:11–16 takes a central role, it is strange that he made such little use of chapter 12, which Hippolytus had already developed in terms of the relation of Christ and the church. Although the Alexandrian references the chapter almost thirty times, his interest is marginal, centering on the activities of the seven-headed dragon, that is, Satan (e.g., *De prin.* 2.8.3). The dragon's tail that drags down a third of heaven's stars (vv. 3–4) is mentioned in the fragments of the Matthew commentary (Matt. 24:29–30), where Origen says he will not go into detail but affirms that the seven heads could either be seven evil princes (this like Hippolytus), or "such great sins as lead to death." The stars that are dragged down are read as those who at one time did actually shine like stars in following Christ, but who later lost their way and were brought down by the devil.[77] (Whether Origen has heretics, or perhaps apostatizing Christians, in mind is difficult to say.) Notices of verses 7, 9, and 10 also survive, but mostly as generic references to the role of "the devil and his angels" being cast down into this world (see, e.g., *De prin.* 1.6.3; *Contra Celsum* 7.17).[78]

Origen's rereading of chiliasm and his sporadic use of the Apocalypse did not mean that the book had clear sailing in the Christian East from the second half of the third century on. Literal millenarianism was alive and well in the time of Origen's pupil, Dionysius of Alexandria, as we can see from the bishop's letters that survive in Eusebius's *Historia ecclesiastica* 7.24–25. Dionysius's two books titled *De promissis* (significantly the same title as *De prin.* 2.11)

74. The most extensive discussion is in *Matt. Comm. Ser.* 32–73 (GCS 11:57–174). See also the *Commentarium in Evangelium Matthaei* 12.30–32 (GCS 10:133–43) and *Contra Celsum* 5.14–17 (GCS 2:15–19).

75. Origen, *De principiis* 2.11.2–3 and 4.3.8 (GCS 4:184–86, 333–35); see also *Contra Celsum* 7.28–29 (GCS 2:178–81). Origen's insistence that the eschatological Jerusalem is a heavenly, not an earthly, city runs directly counter to Irenaeus's claims that the prediction of the descent of the heavenly city to earth must be read literally (*AH* 5.35). Origen attacks literal readings of the millennium in many places; e.g., *Selecta in Psalmos* Ps 4:6 (PG 12:1149); *Commentarium in Cant. Canticorum*, prol. (GCS 8:66); and *Commentarium in Evangelium Matthaei* 17.35–36 (GCS 10:98–99).

76. See the discussion in Hill, *Regnum Caelorum*, esp. 176, 181, and 189.

77. Origen, *Matt. Comm. Ser.* 49 (GCS 11:105–6).

78. Verse 9 is the most frequently cited (sixteen times).

refuted the literal chiliasm of the deceased bishop Nepos whose followers had introduced "schisms and secessions of entire churches." By dint of long scriptural debates, Dionysius won back the schismatics. Eusebius quotes his argument proving that the apostle John cannot have been the author of the book, thus distinguishing the Gospel from the Apocalypse, but as Dionysius insists, "I myself would never dare to reject the book of which so many good Christians have a very high opinion, but realizing that my mental powers are inadequate to judge it properly, I take the view that the interpretation of the various sections is largely a mystery" (*HE* 7.25.6). This was a standard humility topos, however, because Eusebius notes that Dionysius went on to examine the whole Apocalypse, "proving the impossibility of understanding it in a literal sense."

Despite the efforts of Origen and Dionysius, the Apocalypse continued to be suspect in the East for some centuries, even among some of Origen's followers. Eusebius himself seems to have had two views of it—an early more favorable position, and a later suspicious one, although he never directly rejected the book (see *HE* 6.25.10).[79] But the story of the Apocalypse in the Christian East after ca. 300 will not be taken up here.

Origen never got to write his commentary on the Apocalypse. The more detailed examinations of the book by Hippolytus and Dionysius come down to us only in fragments. The earliest surviving attempts at extended exegeses of the Apocalypse, one partial, the other full, come from the second half the third century—the sections devoted to the Apocalypse in the *Symposion* of Methodius of Olympus and the Apocalypse commentary of Victorinus of Poetovio. These works constitute another major turning point in the history of the reception of John's revelation. In different ways they show how the images of the prophecy could be related not only to the understanding of the church, as we find in Hippolytus and Origen, but also to the lives of individual Christians in their daily struggle for virtue.

Methodius is something of a mystery man. He was not known to Eusebius, and therefore we have to go on fragmentary evidence aside from his own, not very informative, writings. Thought to be a bishop of Asia Minor in the later third century, he is said to have died a martyr in 311.[80] In the

79. For positive views of the apostolic authority of the Apocalypse, see, e.g., *HE* 3.18.1; 3.20.9; and 3.23.6. Later he followed Gaius in ascribing the work to Cerinthus; e.g., *HE* 3.28.2; 3.24.18; and 3.25.2, 4. For a discussion, see Robert M. Grant, *Eusebius as Church Historian* (Oxford: Clarendon, 1980), 130–36. The two different views parallel the divergent accounts of Papias found in the *HE*, as shown by Grant, "Papias."

80. Jerome, *De vir. ill.* 83. On Methodius, see L. G. Patterson, *Methodius of Olympus: Divine Sovereignty, Human Freedom, and Life in Christ* (Washington, DC: Catholic University Press, 1997); and Herbert Musirillo, "Introduction," in *St. Methodius: The Symposium. A Treatise on Charity* (Westminster: Newman, 1958), 3–37, whose translation will be used here. The standard edition is that of G. Nathanael Bonwetsch, *Methodius*, GCS 27 (Leipzig: Hinrichs, 1917). On Methodius's chiliasm, see Simonetti, "Millenarismo in Oriente," 54–58; Clementina Mazzucco, "Il millenarismo

late seventh century the most widely diffused of all postbiblical apocalypses, the *Revelationes Methodii*, was ascribed to him, though today we know it was originally composed in Syriac around 690.[81] Methodius wrote extensively, but little of his corpus remains. Among the authentic works, the *Symposion*, a philosophical dialogue in the style of Plato, occupies the central place. Methodius comes down to us as an opponent of Origen, due to his attack on the Alexandrian's conception of the preexistence of the soul and a purely spiritual resurrection, but his exegesis is deeply Origenistic in many ways. Of the eleven discourses praising virginity that constitute the *Symposion*, four treat three different sections from the Apocalypse. Two are fairly brief, the passages in *Discourses* 1.5 and 6.5 that take John's vision of the 144,000 virgins of Apocalypse 14:1–5 and 7:9 as predictive of the "very small number" of virgins found in the church.[82] A more extensive passage occurs in *Discourse* 9, the speech of the virgin Tusiane concerning the account in Leviticus of the Feast of Tabernacles (Lev. 23:39–43). This is seen as a type of the image of heavenly realities found in the earthly church, which are, in turn, types of what is to come, namely "the resurrection and building of our temple . . . in the Seventh Millennium [when] we shall celebrate the great feast of the true Tabernacle in that new creation where there will be no pain, when all the fruits of the earth will have been harvested, and men will no longer beget nor be begotten, and God will rest from the work of his creation."[83] In explaining this heavenly conception of the millennium, Methodius invokes texts both from the Apocalypse's account of the "first resurrection" (Rev. 20:6) and from its picture of life in the heavenly Jerusalem come to earth (22:1 and 13).[84] The discussion makes it clear that with Methodius we are scarcely talking about a real thousand-year kingdom, but rather, in the words of Emanuela Prinzivalli, "an almost evaporated millennialism."[85]

---

di Metodio di Olimpio di fronte a Origene: polemica o continuità?" *Aug* 26 (1986): 73–87; L. G. Patterson, "Methodius' Millenarianism," *StPatr* 24 (1993): 306–15; and Emanuela Prinzivalli, "Il millenarismo in Oriente da Metodio ad Apollinare," *Annali di Storia dell'Esegesi* 15 (1998): 125–51. See also Hill, *Regnum Caelorum*, 39–41; and Daley, *Hope of the Early Church*, 61–64.

81. On the *Revelationes Sancti Methodii*, see the new critical edition of the original Syriac text by G. J. Reinink, *Die Syrische Apokalypse des Pseudo-Methodius*, 2 vols. (Louvain: Peeters, 1993).

82. See *Symposium* 1.5 (ed., 13–14; trans., 47–48), and 6.5 (ed., 69–70; trans., 95).

83. *Symposium* 9.1 (ed., 114; trans., 132). For a survey of the ninth discourse, see Patterson, *Methodius of Olympus*, 105–13.

84. *Symposium* 9.3 (ed., 117; trans., 136).

85. Prinzivalli, "Millenarismo in Oriente," 127: "Si tratterebbe di un millenarismo quasi evaporato." Others agree. Hill summarizes: "Methodius's 'millennium' is no longer chiliastic in the important dogmatic sense of it being an interim reign on this earth prior to the last judgment" (*Regnum Caelorum*, 41). Patterson, noting the dependence on Clement and Origen, concludes: "While neither Clement nor Origen have any room for a 'millennium' of even Methodius' highly modified sort, and while Methodius is the first we know of to offer a millenarian interpretation of the Feast of the Tabernacles, it is plainly along the lines suggested by Clement and Origen that his interpretation of

If the ninth discourse gives us Methodius's picture of the church to come, the eighth discourse provides a view of the present church, also seen through the prism of the Apocalypse. This discourse, ascribed to the legendary virgin Thecla (supposedly a convert of Paul), centers on an extended exegesis of Apocalypse 12.[86] The reason for choosing this chapter of John's revelation for comment is that virgins, like the visionary John himself, are meant to soar aloft to heavenly visions (8.2), specifically the beholding of the ideal forms "of marvelously glorious and blessed beauty, and such as are difficult to describe" (8.3). While virgins often seem already to live in the "abundant light of the kingdom of heaven" (8.4), the afflictions and sorrows of the present life continue to trouble them. But, says Methodius, such clouds sent by the Evil One "will be blown away by the Spirit, if only, like your Mother the virgin who brought forth a man child in heaven, you will not be afraid of the Serpent" (8.4). Methodius's use of Apocalypse 12 is parenetic rather than predictive, an exercise in applying the mythic paradigms of John's vision to the life of the Christian virgin. There is little emphasis on salvation history, especially the past, but rather a call to direct our attention to the atemporal heavenly realities, the Christian version of Plato's vision of the forms.

Although Methodius admits the difficulty of John's revelation—what he speaks of as "the greatness of the mysteries of the text" (*to megethos tōn ainigmatōn tēs graphēs*)[87]—he constructs a seamless spiritual reading of the symbols of chapter 12.[88] The woman who appears in heaven clothed with the sun and crowned with twelve stars is our mother the church, who represents "virgins prepared for marriage" (8.5). She stands on the watery moon "as a tropological explanation for the faith of those who have been purified from corruption by baptism" (8.6). In answer to the objection that such a reading must be wrong because the woman of the Apocalypse brings forth "a man child," Methodius responds by laying out a fundamental principle of his spiritual exegesis: "Remember that the mystery of the Incarnation of the Word was fulfilled long before the Apocalypse, whereas John's prophetic message has to do with the present and the future" (8.7). Therefore, chapter 12 is no longer read about the past, but rather tropologically—a message about the present life of the church and her children. The child who is taken up to the throne of God to be protected against the dragon is not Christ himself, according to Methodius, but rather "all those who are baptized in Christ [and]

---

the feast becomes a vehicle for discussing the true significance of the restoration of souls to bodies in anticipation of their full perfection" (*Methodius of Olympus*, 113).

86. *Symposium* 8 (ed., 80–111; trans., 104–30). The eighth discourse forms the heart of the work and is discussed in detail by Patterson, *Methodius of Olympus*, 95–105. On the link between the spiritualized readings of Rev. 12 and 20 in the two chapters, see Mazzucco, "Millenarismo di Metodio," 82–83.

87. *Symposium* 8.9 (ed., 92.1; trans., 114).

88. For a summary of Methodius's spiritualizing reading of chap. 12, see Prigent, *Apocalypse 12*, 10–11.

become, as it were, other Christs by a communication of the Spirit; and here it is the Church that effects this transformation into the clear image of the Word" (8.8). Methodius concludes: "And thus it is that the Church is said to be ever forming and bringing forth *a man child*, the Word, in those who are sanctified" (8.9). Though the theme of the birth of the Word in the soul was already known to Origen, this part of Methodius's treatise is one of its most forceful expressions in patristic literature.[89]

The second part of Methodius's exegesis concerns the figure of the seven-headed dragon and the details of his pursuit of the woman and her child. The dragon, of course, is the devil; the third part of the stars he drags down with his tail is "the seditious group of heretics" who erred about the Trinity (8.10). The evisceration of all prophetic content in Methodius's immanentizing reading is most evident in the last part of his commentary. The wilderness into which the heavenly woman, or church, flees for 1260 days represents a paradoxical desert empty of what is evil and corruptible, but abounding in the fruit of virtues (8.11), while the 1260 days "signify the direct, clear, and perfect knowledge of the Father, Son, and Spirit, in which, as he grows, our Mother rejoices and exults during this time until the restoration of the new ages" (8.11)—a reference to Methodius's spiritual reading of the millennial kingdom. After a brief survey of the number symbolism underlying this interpretation (8.11–12), Methodius returns to the parenetic center of his reading, briefly commenting on how the defeat of the dragon signifies that the Christian virgin overcomes his seven heads or vices by practicing the opposing virtues, while she conquers his ten horns by combating sins against the ten commandments (8.13). Thus Methodius makes the symbols of Apocalypse 12 directly applicable to the moral life of the Christian virgin.

The same line of interpretation is continued in the *In Apocalypsin* by Bishop Victorinus of Poetovio in modern Slovenia. This text, written perhaps as early as 260, is the first full exposition of the book. Despite Jerome's aspersions on the intelligence of this martyr bishop, the commentary is a remarkable and original reading.[90] Perhaps Victorinus was able to provide a full commentary because he discovered a key aspect of the structure of the

89. On the birth of the Word in the soul, see Hugo Rahner, "Die Gottesgeburt: Die Lehre der Kirchenväter von der Geburt Christi aus den Herzen der Kirche und der Gläubigen," in *Symbole der Kirche: Die Ekklesiologie der Väter* (Salzburg: Müller, 1964), 7–87, who discusses Methodius on 35–40.

90. Our knowledge of Victorinus is largely dependent on Jerome, *De vir. ill.* 74. The most recent study is the detailed work of Martine Dulaey, *Victorin de Poetovio. Premier exégète latin*, 2 vols. (Paris: Institut d'Études Augustiniennes, 1993). Dulaey presents Victorinus's chiliasm in 1:255–70. Dulaey's view of Victorinus is summarized in her "Introduction," in *Victorin de Poetovio: Sur l'Apocalypse et autres écrits*, SC 423 (Paris: Éditions du Cerf, 1997), 15–41. See also Carmelo Curti, "Il regno millenario in Vittorino di Petovio," *Aug* 18 (1978): 419–33; Daley, *Hope of the Early Church*, 65–66; and Hill, *Regnum Caelorum*, 35–39. Victorinus is traditionally said to have died in the Great Persecution in 303. Dulaey (*Victorin de Poetovio*, 1:12) argues for a more likely date of ca. 283–284.

Apocalypse that has been revived by modern exegetes—*recapitulatio*, the notion that the work is organized according to repeating patterns of sevens. As he puts it in commenting on the relation of the seven trumpets to the seven vials (Rev. 8:6–9:21 and 16:1–21), "Do not regard the order of what is said, because the sevenfold Holy Spirit, when it has passed in review the events leading to the last times and the end, returns once again to the same events and completes what it had said more briefly. Do not seek the temporal order in the Apocalypse, but look for the inner meaning" (*Nec requirendus est ordo in Apocalypsi, sed intellectus requirendus*).[91] Victorinus's view of the recapitulation that provides the clue for the confusing repetitions of the Apocalypse was part of a wider theological agenda, inherited at least in part from Irenaeus, that made recapitulation the key to salvation history. Just as Christ recapitulates all ages and the stages of human life in himself, so too the Apocalypse, the final book of the Bible, gathers together all that had gone before it, both in the Old and the New Testaments. Victorinus's view of the Apocalypse as the master key to the Bible was to be renewed nine centuries later by the Calabrian abbot Joachim of Fiore, who once described the Apocalypse as "the key to things past, the knowledge of things to come, the opening of what is sealed, the uncovering of what is hidden."[92]

Victorinus is not only the first author to provide a synoptic reading of the Apocalypse, but he was also an innovator in how he used the book's symbols to reveal the unity of the revelation of the Word in both the Old and the New Testaments. Much of the symbolism that earlier and later interpreters regarded as prophetic of events to come Victorinus inteprets as revelations of the agreement between the preaching of the Old Law and that of the New, or as signs of Christ's fulfillment of prophecy. This is evident in the structure of his commentary, as Martine Dulaey has shown.[93] The comment on the first six chapters is fundamentally christological, a study of Christ's presence in the church. Apocalypse 1–3, the vision of the Son of Man who sends letters to the seven churches, is read as the manifestation of Jesus the God-man sending his sevenfold Spirit to the universal church manifested in seven forms (*In Apoc.* 1.7). The throne vision of chapters 4–5 signifies the unity of the preaching of the two Testaments. Speaking of the wings of the four living creatures in Apocalypse 4:8, for example, Victorinus says, "The wings are the testimonies of the books of the Old Testament, and that is why there are twenty-four, the same number as the Elders seated on the thrones. Just as an animal cannot fly without wings, so too the preaching of the New Testament is not trustworthy without the prior testimonies of the Old Testament by which it is lifted up

---

91. Victorinus, *In Apocalypsin* 8.2 (Dulaey, *Victorin de Poetovio*, 88).

92. Joachim of Fiore, *Expositio in Apocalypsim* (Venice: F. Bindoni and M. Passini, 1527; facsimile ed., Frankfurt am Main: Minerva, 1964), f.3rb.

93. See the discussion of the structure in Dulaey, *Victorin de Poetovio: Premier exégète latin*, 1:3. This discussion is summarized in the "Introduction" to *Victorin de Poetovio: Sur l'Apocalypse*, 30–35.

from the earth and flies."[94] In chapter six the Lamb opens the books sealed with seven seals, that is, Christ by his death and resurrection opens the inner meaning of the Old Testament.

The account of the seven seals in Apocalypse 6 to 9 is read both synchronically and diachronically, as Victorinus's exegesis begins to adopt a more historical stance. Although the seals were opened all at once in Christ's revelation of the meaning of the Old Testament, they also show the progress of the church through time. The first seal is the universal preaching of the Gospel, the second through fourth announce the persecutions of the church, while the fifth seal indicates the desire of the dead for the parousia.[95] The sixth seal represents the final persecution of Antichrist and the seventh seal is the "beginning of eternal rest," not its conclusion, as the recapitulation of the patterns of sevens in the rest of the book shows (*In Apoc.* 6.6). The later accounts of the seven trumpets and the seven vials Victorinus reads as filling in the details of the final persecution of the sixth seal. In the interpretation of chapters 10 and 11 Victorinus reprises his reading of the Apocalypse as the key to the Bible. The strong angel who descends to earth with the open book (Rev. 10:1–4) is Christ holding the Apocalypse, the revelation of all the mysteries of the Old Testament.

Victorinus's use of recapitulation enables him to read chapters 11 through 22 of the Apocalypse as a repeating, but incrementally increasing, revelation about the last persecution and the coming millennium predicted in chapters 20 and 21. The exception to this is his reading of chapter 12, a passage the bishop interprets as a special vision of the whole of history, past, present, and to come. The vision begins with the past because the woman crowned with the sun of verse 1 is identified as the "ancient Church of the patriarch, prophets and holy apostles," which groaned for Christ's coming.[96] The dragon is Satan who is not able to devour the woman's child because the devil had no power to hold Christ in death. The rapture of the child into heaven (v. 5) is the ascension. In unique fashion, Victorinus then turns to the present and future, reading the woman of verses 6–14 as referring to "the whole Catholic Church, in which the one hundred and forty-four thousand will come to

94. *In Apocalypsin* 4.5 (Dulaey, *Victorin de Poetovio: Sur l'Apocalypse*, 70).

95. Hill (*Regnum Caelorum*, 37–38, 245) notes Victorinus's exegetical ingenuity in maintaining the old chiliastic view that all souls, even those of the martyrs, have to wait in Hades until Christ's inauguration of the millennium. Victorinus achieves this by distinguishing between the golden altar of heaven and the bronze altar of the earth under which are the souls of those who died for Christ (Rev. 6:9). See *In Apocalypsin* 6.4 (Dulaey, *Victorin de Poetovio: Sur l'Apocalypse*, 80–82).

96. *In Apocalypsin* 12.1 (Dulaey, *Victorin de Poetovio: Sur l'Apocalypse*, 98–100). Victorinus's reading is unusual. The sun is the hope of resurrection and reward, the moon is the bodily death of the ancients, which nonetheless does not extinguish their hope in Christ, while the crown of twelve stars indicates the choir of patriarchs who are Christ's bodily ancestors. On Victorinus's reading of chap. 12, see Prigent, *Apocalypse 12*, 7–9.

believe in the last time under the preaching of Elijah."[97] This *populum binum*, a twofold people consisting of Gentiles and the Jews who will be converted at the end, is both the contemporary church subject to persecution by the dragon's seven heads, that is, Roman emperors, and the future church of the time of the final assault of the Antichrist, which will flee into the desert and be protected by God during the three and one-half years of his reign (*In Apoc.* 12.4–7).

After the defeat of the Antichrist, Victorinus, like many early Christians, believed that there would be a millennial reign of Christ and the saints as predicted in Apocalypse 20. Jerome, who reedited Victorinus's commentary around 380, was scandalized by this and replaced the bishop's discussion with his own exegesis of the passage.[98] Victorinus's chiliastic views are both archaic and innovative. He is old-fashioned in claiming two resurrections (*In Apoc.* 20.2) and in making use of many of the material descriptions and biblical passages found in earlier Christian chiliastic texts (e.g., *In Apoc.* 21.1–6). He also identifies the thousand-year reign promised in Apocalypse 20:1–6 with the descent of the heavenly Jerusalem described in chapter 21, as some earlier authors had.[99] But when it comes to the details of this final sabbath age, the bishop, in line with the Origenist view, provides allegorical and spiritual readings of the joys of the coming kingdom that make it often difficult to distinguish it from the eternal bliss of heaven.[100] Victorinus's moderate and spiritualized view of the millennium represents an attempt at a fusion between the literal chiliasm of many early Christians and the spiritualization of the millennium that emerged in the third century to help the last book of the Bible maintain its role for the faith of an increasingly established church.[101]

We may wonder if these old debates over how to read the Apocalypse have more than antiquarian interest today. Those who doubt that they can still provide food for thought, however, might want to look at the popular "Left Behind" series, or the numerous literal interpretations of biblical prophecy found on the shelves of fundamentalist bookstores. These contemporary works are more than just entertainment; they often help support misleading,

97. *In Apocalypsin* 12.4 (Dulaey, *Victorin de Poetovio: Sur l'Apocalypse*, 102): "Mulierem autem uolasse in deserto auxilio alarum magnae aquilae . . . ecclesiam omnem catholicam, in qua in nouissimo tempore creditura sunt centum quadraginta quattuor milia sub Helia propheta."

98. On the relation of Jerome to Victorinus, see Martine Dulaey, "Jérome 'éditeur' du *Commentaire sur l'Apocalypse* de Victorin de Poetovio," *REAug* 37 (1991): 199–236.

99. Conflating the thousand-year reign of Rev. 20:1–6 with the account of the descent of the heavenly Jerusalem of Rev. 21 can be found in such authors as Justin (*Dialogue* 81.1), Tertullian (*Adversus Marcionem* 3.24), and Commodianus (*Institutiones* 1.41 and 44).

100. For a study of these spiritualized readings, see Curti, "Regno millennario," 431–32.

101. Recent interpreters of Victorinus have stressed the moderate nature of his chiliasm. See Dulaey, *Victorin de Poetovio: Premier exégète latin*, 1:255–70, and "Introduction," in *Victorin de Poetovio: Sur l'Apocalypse*, 39–41; and Curti, "Regno millennario."

even dangerous, theological and political agendas. Literal readings of the Apocalypse are perhaps more widespread today than ever. The attacks against John's Apocalypse by thinkers such as Whitehead, Shaw, and Lawrence, noted at the outset, have a foundation in history—the often sad and destructive story of those who have read the last book of the Bible as a literal blueprint for what is to come, and sometimes as a scriptural warrant for violence in God's name.[102] The tension between literal and spiritual treatments of John's revelation that originated in the second and third centuries did not end in the fourth century with the triumph of spiritual readings in East and West. The reemergence of varying forms of literal reading is one of the most fascinating aspects of the later history of the Apocalypse and its reception—and, alas, often one of the most tragic. This may be why many contemporary Christians seem inclined just to try to forget about the Apocalypse—that dangerous text—and to leave it to the fundamentalists. Perhaps a study of the efforts of the great exegetes of the early church can suggest that this is not the only, or even the best, option.

102. On the complex relationship between apocalyptic beliefs and violence, see Bernard McGinn, "Apocalypticism and Violence: Aspects of Their Relation in Antiquity and the Middle Ages," in *Scripture and Pluralism: Reading the Bible in the Religiously Plural Worlds of the Middle Ages and Renaissance*, ed. Thomas J. Heffernan and Thomas E. Burman (Leiden/Boston: Brill, 2005), 209–29.

4

"FAITHFUL AND TRUE"

Early Christian Apocalyptic and the Person of Christ

BRIAN E. DALEY, SJ

Lo, he comes with clouds descending,
    Once for favored sinners slain;
Thousand, thousand saints attending
    Swell the triumph of his train;
Hallelujah, hallelujah!
    God appears, on earth to reign![1]

Charles Wesley's great hymn, linked in the minds of many Western Christians to the start of the Advent season, is but one of many evocations of what has remained, since the time of the earliest church, the centerpiece of Christian hope: the reappearance of Jesus on earth, still bearing on his body what Wesley calls "his glorious scars," "the dear tokens of his passion," yet resplendent now in divine power, triumphant over the enemies of faith, and surrounded by those who have faithfully endured persecution for his name. The scene, as Wesley paints it, is focused on Jesus: Jesus in glory, Jesus

---

1. From the 1870 Methodist *Hymnbook*, no. 66; see Frank Whaling, ed., *John and Charles Wesley: Selected Prayers, Hymns, Journal Notes, Sermons, Letters and Treatises* (New York: Paulist Press, 1981), 276.

106

bringing to a conclusion the story that began with the Gospel accounts of his resurrection and ascension, Jesus as Savior yet to come. Yet the colors of the scene are borrowed from that particular Jewish and Christian tradition we identify as apocalyptic: from the book of Revelation, the only full exemplar of the genre in the New Testament canon, and from its canonical and postcanonical Jewish sources and parallels. While this may not seem surprising at first glance, it suggests some important aspects of both classical Christology and Christian apocalyptic that I will explore further here, if only in summary and in a somewhat hypothetical way.

At the risk of saying the obvious, let me characterize what I understand as the principal features of the apocalyptic literary genre, since its form, significance, and history remains the subject of considerable debate.[2] In their classical guise, apocalyptic works are dramatic religious narratives, usually telling of journeys beyond the world of ordinary experience, in dream or vision, in which the narrator is permitted by the sovereign God to glimpse the underlying secrets of human history, past and future. They are normally pseudepigraphic works: the author conceals his or her identity under the name of some already-familiar personality from the biblical past, a strategy calculated both to give credibility to the work's message and to guarantee its continuity with received religious tradition. The scene of the seer's journey is normally set on a grand scale, offering a glimpse of the mechanics and dimensions of the world well beyond the screen of our daily experience. The characters in the drama are also usually fantastic, larger-than-life figures, embodying the forces of good and evil that struggle to control the world's history. Assuming that our present human situation, with all its dangers and ambiguities, is veiled in mystery, its outcome uncertain, the narrative offers a glimpse—a "revelation" or *apocalypsis*—of otherwise inaccessible meaning; and the message, in its simplest terms, is that God remains in control, that God is faithful to his promises, and that he will save his chosen ones from danger. Usually, this message of reassurance is interwoven with strong criticism of the dominant forces behind the social and political situation

2. See my remarks in "Apocalypticism in Early Christian Theology," in *Encyclopedia of Apocalypticism*, vol. 2, *Apocalypticism in Western History and Culture*, ed. Bernard McGinn (New York: Continuum, 1998), 3–6, as well as the discussions of the genre by other authors in the same work, esp. John J. Collins, "From Prophecy to Apocalypticism: the Expectation of the End," in *Encyclopedia of Apocalypticism*, vol. 1, *The Origins of Apocalypticism in Judaism and Christianity*, ed. John J. Collins (New York: Continuum, 1998), 129–61; Fiorentino García Martínez, "Apocalypticism in the Dead Sea Scrolls," in Collins, *Encyclopedia of Apocalypticism*, 1:162–92; James C. VanderKam, "Messianism and Apocalypticism," in Collins, *Encyclopedia of Apocalypticism*, 1:193–228; David Frankfurter, "Early Christian Apocalypticism: Literature and Social World," in Collins, *Encyclopedia of Apocalypticism*, 1:415–53. For a useful survey of the genre, see Christopher Rowland, *The Open Heaven: A Study of Apocalyptic in Judaism and Early Christianity* (New York: Crossroad, 1982); John J. Collins, *The Apocalyptic Imagination: An Introduction to the Jewish Matrix of Christianity* (New York: Crossroad, 1984).

of believers, and with an equally strong appeal to believers themselves to remain faithful to God and to the moral and religious obligations he has laid on them. Although we can only guess at the actual social context in which particular works in the genre were written, the intended audience was clearly people who felt themselves to be marginalized, under threat by the world's superpowers, struggling for survival; at the same time, apocalyptic works usually convey a sense of privilege, of election, of strong traditional bonding, in which both the personality of the pseudepigraphic speaker and the prophetic rhetoric of his message can be expected to deliver maximum impact. It is a literature that presumes a strong sense of religious boundaries and that seems calculated to reinforce them.

What I want to argue here is that the apocalyptic genre, in the hands of Christians in the patristic era, underwent a fairly rapid transformation, late in the second century, that robbed it of much of its original mystery, drama, and rhetorical tension, even as it wove apocalyptic imagery into a growing common Christian understanding of the identity and person of Jesus, the reality of the material world and its importance in God's plan of salvation, and the nature of the church as God's elect community.

It seems beyond question that both Jesus and his disciples, and Paul, Jesus' earliest written interpreter, were steeped in the motifs and images of Jewish apocalyptic literature.[3] The apocalyptic discourses of Jesus in the Synoptic Gospels, for instance (Matt. 24–25; Mark 13; Luke 17:20–37; Luke 21), suggest clearly that the earliest oral traditions placed his message of the coming kingdom within the context both of the final struggle of cosmic powers and of the accompanying exhortation to fidelity and trust that is characteristic of this late Jewish genre. Paul's earliest letter, 1 Thessalonians, describes the "coming of the Lord," Jesus who has died and is risen, as something to be expected soon, an event that will mean salvation for the faithful, dead or living, and judgment for all (1 Thess. 4:13–5:11). The book of Revelation or Apocalypse of John—the New Testament's only full example of the genre, and indeed the paradigm of later Christian apocalyptic thought[4]—brings us fully

3. See Dale C. Allison Jr., "The Eschatology of Jesus," in Collins, *Encyclopedia of Apocalypticism*, 1:267–302; Richard A. Horsley, "The Kingdom of God and the Renewal of Israel: Synoptic Gospels, Jesus Movements, and Apocalypticism," in Collins, *Encyclopedia of Apocalypticism*, 1:303–44; M. C. DeBoer, "Paul and Apocalyptic Eschatology," in Collins, *Encyclopedia of Apocalypticism*, 1:345–83. For apocalyptic elements in the Synoptic Gospels, see G. R. Beasley-Murray, *Jesus and the Last Days: The Interpretation of the Olivet Discourse* (Peabody, MA: Hendrickson, 1993). For Paul's use of apocalyptic themes, see J. C. Beker, *Paul the Apostle: the Triumph of God in Life and Thought* (Philadelphia: Fortress, 1980). For a discussion of modern scholarly debate about the apocalyptic dimension of Paul's theology, see R. Barry Matlock, *Unveiling the Apocalyptic Paul: Paul's Interpreters and the Rhetoric of Criticism* (Sheffield: Sheffield Academic Press, 1996).

4. See Richard Bauckham, *The Theology of the Book of Revelation* (Cambridge: Cambridge University Press, 1994); Adela Yarbro Collins, "The Book of Revelation," in Collins, *Encyclopedia of Apocalypticism*, 1:384–414. The most recent and thorough large-scale commentary on the book of

into the visionary world of enormous beasts and world-changing battles, of moral exhortation and urgent reassurance, characteristic of classical Jewish apocalyptic. It weaves into its narrative a multitude of texts and allusions from those sections of the earlier Jewish canon that paved the way for this form of literature, especially Daniel 7–12; Ezekiel 40–48; and sections of the book of Isaiah and the Psalter. This work is, in a sense, a pastiche of powerful apocalyptic images and warnings from earlier Jewish tradition; but here, as in 1 Thessalonians 4 and even, by implication, in the synoptic apocalyptic passages I have mentioned, the central figure of the vision is precisely the crucified and risen Jesus. It is "Jesus Christ, the faithful witness, the first-born of the dead, and the ruler of the kings on earth" (Rev. 1:5) who is the source of the moral exhortations that the seer sends to the seven churches of Asia; it is Jesus, who remains near to his disciples, "standing at the door, knocking" (Rev. 3:20), who promises them victory over the enemies that now threaten to distract or destroy them. And it is Jesus, "the Lamb that was slaughtered" (Rev. 5:6, 12; 13:8; cf. 7:14)—now standing in the place of honor before the gloriously enthroned God of Israel's prophetic visions (see, e.g., Exod. 24:9–11; Isa. 6:1–4; Ezek. 1:22–28)—who unseals the secrets of God's purpose in history, and who promises to defeat the forces of oppression. The apocalyptic form has become, overtly in these works and as a subtext in other New Testament passages, a central instrument for confessing Jesus as Messiah, enthroned with God, and as Lord of history.

My purpose here, however, is not to characterize the apocalypticism of the New Testament writings, but to survey the changing character of this powerful style of Jewish and Christian thought, and its use in the wider context of an emerging orthodox consensus on the interpretation of Christ's person and work, during the six or seven centuries that followed their composition. What I want to argue here is that even as the drama of Christian apocalyptic narrative lost much of its urgency, as Christian communities came to be more sure of themselves within the wider matrix of late Roman society, the apocalyptic image of the glorified Jesus—"the Lamb who was slain"—as judge to come, victor over the demonic powers of evil, and hidden companion of his church in what was assumed to be the continuing, final age of history, took on a formative, even a determining role for the development of doctrine. Christology, cosmology, ecclesiology—to use the distorting categories of modern academic theology—all became, in the course of the patristic period, East and West, "apocalypticized"; but it was an apocalypticism that had become a vehicle for acknowledging Jesus as Lord of history. Apocalyptic prophecy to communities under threat, beginning from what is found in the texts of the Bible and in early post-70 Jewish and Christian

---

Revelation in English is David E. Aune, *Revelation 1–5*, WBC 52a (Dallas: Word Books, 1997); idem, *Revelation 6–16* and *17–22*, WBC 52b–c (Nashville: Nelson, 1998).

works, was gradually transformed into a set of images for the glorified Christ, and a scenario for the present and future course of the age of the church.[5] In broad strokes, at least, let me try to fill out this very general scheme of theological development with some concrete examples.

Early Christian Apocalyptic

Undoubtedly the clearest example of a noncanonical early Christian document fully embodying the apocalyptic genre is the *Ascension of Isaiah*, a work generally thought to have been written in Syria between 112 and 138.[6] Although the language of its composition was probably Greek, only a few fragments of that original version remain; we do have a later Greek paraphrase, as well as partial translations in Latin, Slavonic, and Coptic, and an apparently complete version in Ethiopic, which serves as the foundation for most modern translations. For a long time the work was curiously neglected by students of earliest Christianity, although a spurt of interest, especially among Italian scholars, resulted in a ground-breaking conference in 1981, numerous articles and monographs since then, and a long-awaited critical edition.[7] Well before this trend began, however, Jean Daniélou identified the *Ascension* as the clearest literary example of what he called "Jewish Christianity":[8] an

5. For an exploration of the impact of apocalyptic imagery for Christ on the catechesis and church iconography of the fourth and fifth centuries, see Geir Hellemo, *Adventus Domini: Eschatological Thought in Fourth-Century Apses and Catecheses* (Leiden: Brill, 1989).

6. For a full discussion of the probable date and place of this work's origin, see esp. Michael A. Knibb, "The Ascension of Isaiah," in *OTP* 2:143–50; Jonathan Knight, *Disciples of the Beloved One: The Christology, Social Setting, and Theological Context of the Ascension of Isaiah* (Sheffield: Sheffield Academic Press, 1996), 33–39.

7. See esp. Mauro Pesce, ed., *Isaia, il Diletto e la Chiesa: Visione ed esegesi profetica cristiano-primitiva nell' Ascensione di Isaia*, Conference in Rome, 1981 (Brescia: Paideia, 1983), with important articles on the work's text, literary background, and theology; Antonio Acerbi, *Serra Lignea: Studi sulla Fortuna dell' Ascensione di Isaia* (Rome: Editrice AVE, 1984), on the literary and theological influence of the work; idem, *L'Ascensione di Isaia: Cristologia e profetismo in Siria nei primi decenni del II secolo* (Milan: Vita e Pensiero, 1989), offering a close exegesis of the text; Enrico Norelli, *L'Ascensione di Isaia: Studi su un apocrifo al crocevia dei cristianesimi* (Bologna: EDB, 1994), a collection of studies by the editor of the Greek versions of the text; Jonathan Knight, *The Ascension of Isaiah* (Sheffield: Sheffield Academic Press, 1995), a concise introduction to the work and analysis of its content; and idem, *Disciples of the Beloved One*, Knight's fuller discussion of the critical problems of the work as well as its theology. The new critical edition of the work, in its Ethiopic, Greek, Coptic, Latin, and Old Slavic or Paleo-Bulgarian versions, including a valuable synopsis of all the versions, has been produced by the first-rate team of Italian scholars originally gathered by Mauro Pesce, in Corpus Christianorum, Series Apocryphorum 7 (Turnhout: Brepols, 1995). This is now the basis for any serious translation or study of the work. There is now also a concordance of the Ethiopic version, which is the only witness to the complete text: Gianfrancesco Lusini, *Ascensione di Isaia: Concordanza della versione etiopica* (Wiesbaden: Harrasowitz, 2003).

8. Jean Daniélou, *The Theology of Jewish Christianity* (London: Darton, Longman and Todd, 1964), 12–14 and passim.

unambiguously Christian work that presents the gospel of Christ's coming and victory in the full trappings of Second Temple apocalyptic.

The *Ascension* is framed in a narrative of the persecution and martyrdom of the prophet Isaiah, due to the unrelenting enmity of Beliar or Sammael, the "great prince" (*Ascension* 4.2) and leader of the spirits opposed to God and his faithful people.[9] It offers two separate prophetic narratives embodying the Christian gospel of salvation through Christ, God's "Beloved,"[10] both of them presented as the record of an ecstatic vision granted the prophet Isaiah before he was arrested and sawn in two.[11] The first of these begins with a summary of the story of Jesus, as this work presents it:

> Through [Isaiah] the coming forth of the Beloved from the seventh heaven had been revealed, and his transformation, his descent and the likeness into which he was to be transformed, namely, the likeness of a man, and the persecution which he was to suffer. . . . and that he was to be crucified together with criminals, and that he would be buried in a sepulcher, and that the twelve who were with him would be offended because of him, and the watch of the guards of the grave, and the descent of the angel of the church which is in the heavens, whom he will summon in the last days; and that the angel of the Holy Spirit and Michael, the chief of the holy angels, would open his grave on the third day, and that the Beloved, sitting on their shoulders, will come forth and send out his twelve disciples, and that they will teach to all the nations and every tongue the resurrection of the Beloved, and that those who believe in his cross will be saved.[12]

This first prophetic narrative goes on to speak in vivid terms about the problems that will increasingly infect the community of disciples in the time after this first proclamation of Christ: conflicting expectations about his second coming, ambition, lack of holiness among community "shepherds," greed, "respect for persons," slander and boasting, all leading to the radical decline of the prophetic charism among them (*Ascension* 3.22–28). The document then sketches a picture of the final age soon to follow, in which Beliar will descend from heaven in the form of Nero returned from the grave, performing nature-miracles and daring to "speak in the name of the Beloved"

9. That this narrative seems most likely based on oral rather than written Jewish sources is argued by Mauro Pesce in "Presupposti per l'utilizzazione storica dell'Ascensione di Isaia: Formazione e tradizione del testo; genere letterario; cosmologia angelica," in *Isaia*, 13–76; cf. Knight, *Disciples of the Beloved One*, 13–14, 28–29, and further references there.

10. For the use of this title in the New Testament for Jesus, see Matt. 3:17 par; 12:18 par; Eph. 1:6. In the Old Testament, see Isa. 5:1; cf. Gen. 22:2, 12, 16.

11. For the prophet's death, see Matt. 5:11; this same tradition seems to be alluded to in Heb. 11:37.

12. *Ascension of Isaiah* 3.13–18 (trans. and ed. R. McLaren Wilson, based on the German translation of C. Detlef and G. Müller, in *New Testament Apocrypha*, ed. Edgar Hennecke and Wilhelm Schneemelcher, 2 vols., rev. ed. [Louisville: Westminster John Knox, 1992], 2:608).

(*Ascension* 4.6)—an Antichrist, in other words, who will seduce the faithful into apostasy. After 1,332 days, "the Lord will come with his angels and with the hosts of the saints from the seventh heaven" (*Ascension* 4.14), and will defeat the forces of Beliar; then, in a version of the "rapture" alluded to by Paul in 1 Thessalonians 4:17, the faithful "who are found in the body" will be caught upwards and clothed in the glorious "garments which are stored on high in the seventh heaven"—bodies of light apparently—while their material bodies remain on earth.[13] After this will come further conflict, resurrection and judgment, and in the end the "Beloved" will send forth fire to consume his enemies completely (*Ascension* 4.18).

The second part of the work presents the christological part of Isaiah's vision—his prophetic glimpse of Jesus' coming, passion, and resurrection as a narrative of "descent" and "ascent"—in new terms, and in much richer detail than the earlier summary given above. Here we are told of the prophet's ecstasy (*Ascension* 6); of his experience of being guided upwards by an unnamed angel through six heavens, each peopled with spirits formally arranged, each bathed in a greater degree of glory (7–8); of his entry into the seventh or uppermost heaven, where God dwells, by the permission of Christ himself (9.1–6); and of his vision there of the "garments" of glory reserved for the elect (9.7–12; cf. 8.26). There Isaiah is allowed to see "one whose glory surpassed that of all" (9.27), "my Lord Christ who shall be called Jesus" (10.7), and standing alongside him a "second angel, . . . the angel of the Holy Spirit" (9.35–36). The prophet is told to join the whole company of the seventh heaven in worshiping these two glorious figures, and is then invited by them to join with them in worshiping "the most high of the high ones, who dwells in the holy world and rests with the holy ones, who will be called by the Holy Spirit, through the mouth of the righteous, the Father of the Lord" (10.6).

This second part of the *Ascension*, then, presents us with an unmistakably trinitarian portrait of the divine power ruling the cosmos,[14] as well as with a vision of a highly structured cosmos, peopled with mighty invisible powers, that lies beyond the boundaries of normal human sensation. Within this monumental setting, the final two chapters of the document tell the story of the coming of God's Beloved, as Jesus, into the world: a descent in which the prophet is told that he will "become like you in appearance, and it will

13. *Ascension* 4.17. For a rich discussion of the Jewish and early Christian tradition, particularly in early Syriac literature and the ascetic literature of Egypt in the late fourth century, of God's "body of light" and of its implications for the future form of human disciples, see Alexander Golitzin, "Recovering the 'Glory of Adam': 'Divine Light' Traditions in the Dead Sea Scrolls and the Christian Ascetical Literature of Fourth-Century Syro-Mesopotamia," in *Dead Sea Scrolls as Background to Postbiblical Judaism and Early Christianity* (Leiden: Brill, 2003), 275–308; idem, "The Vision of God and the Form of Glory: More Reflections of the Anthropomorphite Controversy of A.D. 399," in *Abba*, ed. John Behr (Crestwood, NY: St. Vladimir's Seminary Press, 2003), 273–97.

14. For the Trinitarian scheme assumed by this work, see *Ascension* 7.7–8, 23; 9.27–42; 11.32–33.

be thought that he is flesh and a man" (9.13). Disguise, in fact, is central to the narrative's plot: as the Beloved, sent by the invisible Father, descends through the storied layers of the heavens to earth, his appearance changes to resemble that of each heaven's population; he is accepted by each group of angels as one of them, not singled out for special praise. Eventually he comes to the human world, and is born of the Virgin Mary, in a miraculously speedy and painless way, as a human child (11.2–14). Later on, as an adult, he "performs great signs and wonders in the land of Israel and in Jerusalem" (11.18), is crucified, descends into the underworld, and is raised after three days (11.19–21). And when he ascends then into glory, up through the six lower heavens, all the spirits now recognize him in his glorious form for who he is, and worship him in wonder, asking themselves, "How did our Lord remain hidden from us when he descended, and we perceived not?" (11.26). At the end of his ascent, he is enthroned "on the right hand of that great glory, whose glory . . . [the prophet confesses,] I was not able to behold," while "the angel of the Holy Spirit" is enthroned on the left (11.32). It is from there that his final path to judgment and victory presumably will begin.

Even more than the New Testament book of Revelation, this work (of almost equal antiquity) uses all the literary techniques of the apocalyptic imagination to present us with a carefully sketched portrait of Christ: as the Beloved of the mysterious, transcendent God, to whom both he and the Holy Spirit pay homage; as Lord of all angels, who himself is sent on a mission of revelation and of engagement with the forces of evil analogous to theirs, but climactic in its importance; as superior to the angels, just as he is superior to humans, yet as capable of assuming the form of all of them in order to disguise his identity. This emphasis on the Son's disguises, on his "appearing" to be like angels or human beings—what Jonathan Knight has called the work's "naïve docetism"[15]—is not to be taken as a denial of his body or his real human experiences; unlike the heavenly savior of Gnostic narratives, he is genuinely born in the flesh, and genuinely dies. It is, rather, a way to explain his mysterious, changing identity: though a divine being, he becomes like all the species of angels, and eventually like us as well, in order to win the worship and confidence of everyone ready to discover the mystery of his coming. Just as the saints may hope one day to put on the "robes" and "crowns" of glory now stored up for them in the upper heavens, the Beloved has put on a form similar to our own, to reveal and to achieve the saving plans of God.

Curiously, perhaps, this work from the earliest period of what is usually called "Judaeo-Christianity" is also the last work to make full use of this Second-Temple genre for entirely Christian purposes. Other early Christian works only partially qualify, at best. The first two and last two chapters of

---

15. Knight, *Disciples of the Beloved One*, 140.

the Latin Vulgate *4 Ezra* (a version of Hebrew *2 Ezra*), usually called *5* and *6 Ezra* respectively, are clearly Christian additions to a late Jewish apocalypse; similarly, a number of passages in the collection of the *Sybilline Oracles* seem to have a Judaeo-Christian origin, and use images borrowed from the apocalyptic tradition. The Coptic *Apocalypse of Elijah*, an Egyptian work probably put together in the late third century, seems to be a Christian reworking of older Jewish material about the final crisis of the world, but it lacks most of the classic literary features of apocalyptic literature.[16] The Nag Hammadi collection, too, contains a number of texts labeled "apocalypses," most of uncertain date,[17] but for the most part these revelation-discourses have little literary connection with the traditional apocalyptic form.

In the second half of the fourth century, it is true, and for roughly two centuries thereafter, Christian works were again composed with a number of strong apocalyptic features. Two other Nag Hammadi documents, for instance, which seem both to be late fourth-century products, draw on features of the Jewish and Christian apocalyptic traditions to present a dramatic vision of the coming end of material creation, in violence and conflict: *On the Origin of the World* (Nag Hammadi II, 5 and XIII, 2) and *The Concept [Ennoia] of Our Great Power* (Nag Hammadi VI, 4). The second of these describes an age of oppression led by the "Archon of the Western regions"—a kind of Antichrist figure who comes from the West to invade "that place where the Logos first appeared"[18]—and identifies the consummation of the present world with the return of Christ, who will lead purified souls into "the immeasurable light."[19] Neither of these brief works, however, could be called a fully developed apocalypse. Closer to classical apocalyptic form, but still somewhat underdeveloped, is the *Apocalypse of Thomas*, a fifth-century Latin work that may be based on a fourth-century Greek original, and that transforms a scenario for the end of the world and the resurrection of the saints into a new, angelic form that strongly echoes passages from the book of Revelation. The better-known *Apocalypse of Paul*—a Greek work probably composed in the first two decades of the fifth century—uses the narrative form of a visionary tour, granted to the apostle Paul, of regions beyond the present world, as a way to sketch out a picture of the fate of individuals after death, to reinforce moral and ascetical exhortation. All of these works, along

16. The best translation of this work, with an authoritative brief introduction, is that of O. S. Wintermute in *OTP* 1:735–53. For a discussion of the work's background and theology, see David Frankfurter, *Elijah in Upper Egypt: The Apocalypse of Elijah and Early Egyptian Christianity* (Minneapolis: Fortress, 1993).

17. The collection contains an *Apocalypse of Paul* (V, 2), not related to the fifth-century *Visio Pauli or Apocalypse of Paul*; two *Apocalypses of James* (V, 3 and V, 4); an *Apocalypse of Adam* (V, 5); and an *Apocalypse of Peter* (VII, 3).

18. *The Concept of Our Great Power* 44.1–2, trans. Frederik Wisse, in *The Nag Hammadi Library*, ed. James M. Robinson, 3rd ed. (San Francisco: Harper, 1990), 315.

19. Ibid. 46.9, p. 316.

with the later Byzantine "political apocalypses," like the fifth-century *Oracle of Baalbek*, which embody social critique within a vision of the coming end of history, make use of themes and narrative elements from earlier Jewish and Christian apocalyptic in order to underline the fragility of human life and the vulnerability of the material world, but (with the exception, perhaps, of the *Apocalypse of Thomas*) they do not attempt to revive the genre in its full literary form. Fascinating works, but marginal in terms of their lasting influence on Christian theology, they are partial heirs of the apocalyptic tradition, rather than its authentic representatives.[20]

The Transformation of Apocalyptic

The more central and lasting imprint of apocalyptic on Christian theology and worship, I suggest, is to be found in the presence of certain themes and images, taken especially from the book of Revelation, which from the mid-second century on continued to find their way into the efforts of Christian thinkers to express their understanding of the reality and importance of the material cosmos, the person of Christ and his ongoing role in history, and the status and hope of the church. All I can hope to do here is simply to point out a few striking examples of this doctrinal, openly christocentric transformation of apocalyptic themes—or perhaps better, the apocalyptic tinting of a developing Christian orthodoxy—as a kind of hybridization that would remain enormously influential in Christian thought.

Apocalyptic Cosmology

One of the first Christian theologians to rely heavily on the Christian apocalyptic tradition in support of a wider theological argument is Irenaeus of Lyons. Irenaeus's five books, *Against Heresies*, written in Gaul around 185, is above all a tortuous but relentless polemic against the Valentinian cosmogonic myth and its implications for Christian teaching and Christian community life: a plea for the importance of the flesh, the visible world, and our daily lives in the world on the grounds of Christ's involvement in all of them, his "recapitulation" of this visible cosmos and its history in his own person. The fifth book of *Against Heresies* is really Irenaeus's main engagement with the Christian apocalyptic tradition, the section of this massive work in which—by what may seem at first a curiously reversed argument—he looks ahead toward common Christian eschatological hope, and to the typically apocalyptic themes of resurrection, the coming of the Messiah, judgment and

---

20. For further discussion and bibliography concerning these later apocalyptic works, see Daley, "Apocalypticism in Early Christian Theology," 35–39; see also my *The Hope of the Early Church*, 2nd ed. (Peabody, MA: Hendrickson, 2003), 26–27, 120–22, 178–79.

a millennial kingdom for the just, precisely as a way to confirm the urgency of rejecting a Gnostic view of the material world.

Irenaeus begins book 5 by pointing out that our only source of knowledge for "the things of God" is Jesus, the Word who became human; because he spoke audible words and performed visible actions, we have communion with the God who is "beyond creation" (*Against Heresies* 5.1.1). His point here is that if we confess Jesus' death on the cross to be a saving act, and look on the Eucharist as our means to share in that saving act—two points of faith he seems to presume among his readers—then clearly both Jesus' flesh and blood and ours must be centrally involved in this act of salvation: Jesus cannot simply be a phantom savior of the inner person.

> If this [flesh] does not attain salvation, then neither did the Lord redeem us with his blood, nor is the cup of the Eucharist a communion in his blood, nor the bread which we break a communion in his body. For blood can only come from veins and flesh, and whatever else makes up the substance of a human person, such as the Word of God was actually made. . . . When, therefore, the mingled cup and manufactured bread receives the word of God, and the Eucharist becomes the body of Christ, and from them the substance of our flesh is increased and supported, how can they [the Gnostic Christians] affirm that flesh is incapable of receiving the gift of God, which is eternal life?[21]

For Irenaeus, the implication is that our bodies must undergo the same process of decay and revitalization that seems to take place in the grain made into bread:

> Just as a grain of wheat, falling into the earth and becoming decomposed, rises with manifold increase by the Spirit of God, who contains all things, and then, . . . having received the Word of God, becomes the Eucharist, which is the body and blood of Christ; so also our bodies, being nourished by it, and deposited in the earth, and suffering decomposition there, shall rise at their appointed time, the Word of God granting them resurrection to the glory of God. (*AH* 5.2.3)

As his argument develops, Irenaeus insists that the resurrection of the dead reveals God's transcendent power (*AH* 5.3.2), in a way fully commensurate with his power revealed in creating; just as our flesh was brought to life by his original touch, so flesh will receive life again after decomposition. Irenaeus then connects this hope for fleshly resurrection with the kerygma of Christ's resurrection: neither can be conceived by us simply as a spiritual event (*AH* 5.7.1). Christian faith confesses that "the Word has saved that which really was dead humanity, bringing about by means of himself that communion

---

21. *Against Heresies* 5.2.2–3, in *ANF* 1 (repr. Grand Rapids: Eerdmans, 1981), 528 (altered); hereafter *AH*.

(*koinonia*) which he needed to have with it, and seeking out its salvation" (*AH* 5.14.2). We must understand, then, that the Lord "had, himself, flesh and blood, recapitulating in Himself not some other, but that original handiwork of the Father, seeking out what had perished" (*AH* 5.14.2).

In the last eleven chapters of the book, Irenaeus turns from bodily resurrection to what were for him the other key aspects of the apocalyptic scenario: the coming of the Antichrist, Jesus' second coming and judgment, and between them the millennial kingdom of earthly blessedness promised to the just. Here he alludes frequently to the book of Revelation. Both the mysterious name of the Antichrist and the millennium are solidly witnessed to, he insists, by oral tradition as well as by apostolic text (*AH* 5.30.1; 5.33.4). In his view, too, the earthly millennium is not only required in justice as a reward for those who have suffered bodily persecution (*AH* 5.32.1), but is also the fulfillment of God's promise to Abraham, which was focused not simply on spiritual gifts but on a land (*AH* 5.32.1–2); it also makes intelligible Jesus' assurance at the Last Supper (Matt. 26:27) that he would share the "fruit of the vine" with his disciples in the kingdom of God. For Irenaeus, the earthly millennium is a transitional stage to a more comprehensive and mysterious salvation, allowing the righteous to "become accustomed to partake in the glory of God the Father" (*AH* 5.35.1). But because the flesh, created by God, is made for life, and because the Word took our flesh on himself to save it, the salvation of the flesh must be taken with utter seriousness, and the vision of the latter chapters of the book of Revelation not diluted by typological interpretation. "Since there are real human beings, so must there be a real establishment [*plantatio*], so that we might not vanish away among non-existent things, but progress among things that have an actual existence" (*AH* 5.36.1). The events promised in the book of Revelation must be part of the real future, if the mainstream Christian confession of the Word made flesh, and the highly physical, eucharistic practice of Christian worship, are not to be made empty gestures. Living as Christians in the present world requires apocalyptic hope if it is to be coherent at all.

Apocalyptic Christology

For Irenaeus, the key to this integration of apocalyptic themes and images into his antignostic apologetic is his understanding of Jesus, not only as Savior (which he also was, of course, for Valentinian theology) but as the Christ of the Judaeo-Christian apocalyptic tradition, ready to come in triumph to raise the bodies of his faithful ones and inaugurate the final drama of the world's judgment. This christological focus remained central to the Christian theological use of apocalyptic images, even as interest in the details of the final conflict and an emphasis on the millennium began, in many places, to wane, from the early third century on.

An important example is Hippolytus's *Commentary on Daniel* (hereafter *Com. Dan.*), usually assumed to have been written by a Greek-speaking presbyter of that name in Rome, around 204, but possibly the work of a theologian from western Asia Minor contemporary with Irenaeus.[22] This earliest Christian Scripture commentary interprets the book of Daniel in a homiletic, heavily moralizing way, and attempts straightforwardly to connect the narrative and visions of the book with subsequent history. Underlying Hippolytus's interpretive scheme, however, is an Irenaean sense of the shape of God's plan for redemption, in which the Logos, the agent of God's saving works through history, is revealed more and more clearly to humanity in understandable, human terms. The angel who comes to encourage the three young Jewish men in the furnace and teach them to join all creation in praising God, in Daniel 3, and whom King Nebuchadnezzar recognizes as "like a son of God" (Dan. 3:25 LXX), is clearly the Logos (*Com. Dan.* 2.33), who also submerged the Egyptians in the Red Sea, who rained fire on Sodom and who appeared to Isaiah and Ezekiel—the "angel of great counsel" (Isa. 9:6), whom the Father has appointed judge of the nations (*Com. Dan.* 2.32). Daniel's vision in chapter 7 of "one like a son of man" is a prophetic glimpse of the Logos's "complete humanization" (*tēn kath' holou enanthrōpēsin—Com. Dan.* 4.39) that Hippolytus has previously taken pains to date precisely at the midpoint of the fifth millennium of world history.[23] In interpreting the four beasts that precede this vision in Daniel 7, Hippolytus sees already a dramatic tableau of history's end:

> Then earthly things will cease and heavenly things will begin, so that the indestructible and eternal kingdom of the saints might be revealed, and the King of heaven, in addition, revealed openly to all—no longer seen by means of a

22. The first modern attempt to divide the works ascribed to Hippolytus between two authors was that of Pierre Nautin, *Hippolyte et Josipe* (Paris: Éditions du Cerf, 1947); see also his *Lettres et écrivains chrétiens des IIe et IIIe siècles* (Paris: Éditions du Cerf, 1961). The question was discussed at length in two symposia sponsored by the Institutum Patristicum Augustinianum in Rome: *Ricerche su Ippolito: Studia Ephemeridis "Augustinianum"* 13 (1977), and *Nuove Ricerche su Ippolito: Studia Ephemeridis "Augustinianum"* 30 (1989). Arguing for the unity of authorship of all the works ascribed to Hippolytus, with the exception of *Contra Noetum*, is Josef Frickel, *Das Dunkel um Hippolyt von Rom* (Graz: Grazer Theologische Studien, 1988); see also C. Scholten, "Hippolyt II von Rom," *RAC* 15:492–551, esp. 503–4. The most recent attempt to argue that the commentaries ascribed to Hippolytus, along with the treatise *On the Antichrist*, are the work of a second- or early-third-century Greek author, probably from western Asia Minor, is J. A. Cerrato, *Hippolytus between East and West: The Commentaries and the Provenance of the Corpus* (Oxford: Oxford University Press, 2002).

23. *Com. Dan.* 4.23: "The first coming (*parousia*) of our Lord, the fleshly coming which led him to be born at Bethlehem, took place the eighth day before the calends of January, a Wednesday, in the forty-third year of the reign of Augustus, five thousand five hundred years after Adam." Hippolytus goes on to give the precise date of Jesus' passion, as well, and suggests that at the end of the sixth millennium of creation—five hundred years after Christ's birth, the "kingdom of the saints" on earth will begin, with Jesus' second coming.

vision, as on Mount Sinai, nor revealed in a pillar of cloud on a mountaintop, but with the powers and hosts of angels, God enfleshed and a human being, Son of God and of Man, the judge come from heaven to be present in the world. (*Com. Dan.* 4.10)

The real content of this vision, Hippolytus goes on to explain, is really nothing less than a glimpse of God's own being: in Daniel's "ancient of days" (Dan. 7:9, 13), "the Lord of all things, God and King, who is Father of Christ"; and in the "one like a Son of Man," who is given "dominion and glory and kingly power," the incarnate Word still to come on earth, first as humble Son of Mary and then as victorious judge.

By subjecting all things to his own Son, the Father . . . has clearly shown that he is the first-born of all things: first-born of God, so that he might be revealed as second after the Father, since he is God's Son; first-born before the angels, so that he might appear as lord of angels; first-born from a virgin, so that he might be shown to re-shape in himself Adam, the first of creatures; "first-born from the dead" (Col. 1:18), so that he might himself be the "first-fruits" (1 Cor. 15:23) of our resurrection. (*Com. Dan.* 4.11)

In language echoing Irenaeus, Hippolytus finds in Daniel, especially in the chapters that became the model for later Jewish and Christian apocalyptic writing, a revelation not simply of future events, but of the person of Christ and of his ever more manifest role in history.[24] Put in modern terms, Christ's second coming, for Hippolytus, will really be a statement about Christology.

Hippolytus's Alexandrian contemporary, Origen, shares this tendency to read the Christian biblical apocalyptic tradition as primarily revealing Christ, in himself and in his relationship with the church. Origen refers frequently to the book of Revelation in his works, and assumes—unlike his admiring pupil Dionysius of Alexandria[25]—that it was written by the Beloved Disciple, who was also the author of the Fourth Gospel.[26] For Origen,

24. For very detailed discussion of the Christology of the works ascribed to Hippolytus, see Antonio Zani, *La cristologia di Ippolito* (Brescia: Morcelliana, 1984). A good overview of the literary and theological character of the *Commentary on Daniel* is still Gustave Bardy's introduction to the edition and translation of the work in SC 14 (Paris: Éditions du Cerf, 1947).

25. See Eusebius, *Historia ecclesiastica* (hereafter *HE*) 7.25, where Eusebius quotes Dionysius's arguments for a diversity of authorship at some length. Dionysius here expresses his reverence for the book, as containing "a certain concealed and wonderful meaning in every part," even though he finds that that meaning often escapes him (*HE* 7.25.4–5).

26. See, e.g., *Commentary on John* 1.22, 84; 2.45. For a good survey of Origen's use of the book of Revelation and his attitude toward it, see Clementina Mazzucco, "Apocalisse," in *Origene*, ed. Adele Monaci Castagno (Rome: Città Nuova, 2000), 22–24. Origen says, in the *Commentariorum Series in Matthaeum* 49, probably part of a commentary on Matthew written in the late 240s, that he intends to explain some difficult passages in the book of Revelation *tempore suo*. There is no evidence

however, despite the "deep obscurity" of the book's "unfathomable mysteries" (*On First Principles* 4.2.3), its real message is its vision of Christ; none of the other sacred authors, he remarks near the beginning of his commentary on the Gospel of John, "revealed his divinity so clearly as John," and he quotes both the Gospel and the Apocalypse to illustrate his point (*Commentary on John* 1.22; hereafer *Com. Jn.*). One of Origen's favorite passages, it seems, in this regard is the dramatic portrayal, in Revelation 19, of the risen Christ, seated on a white horse, returning at the head of a victorious heavenly army to judge the world for God. Although Origen alludes to this passage forty-seven times in his known works, his most extended exegesis of it is near the beginning of the second book of his *Commentary on John*. Here—having finally reached the Gospel's second verse—he is explaining in detail who and what the Word is, who "was in the beginning with God" (John 1:2). To underline the fact that he is not only "with" God, but God's own Word—the expressive, dynamic force that finds its "beginning" in the divine Wisdom—Origen suddenly turns from the Johannine Gospel to Revelation 19 (*Com. Jn.* 2.42–63). Origen notes that in this passage, the author tells us that the majestic rider is called not only "Faithful and True" (Rev. 19:11) but "Word of God" (Rev. 19:13) and that he bears on his blood-sprinkled robe a third name, "King of kings and Lord of lords" (Rev. 19:16). As Origen reads the text, the evangelist-prophet is offering us a kind of miniature treatise on the divine Logos. He is God's Word, the only Word in the universe—hence he is named without a definite article, so as not to suggest a multiplicity of intellectual mediators between the spiritual world and the world of creatures (*Com. Jn.* 2.43–44). He appears in an "open heaven" (Rev. 19:11) to suggest his role as the sole revealer of divine reality to those who have preserved in themselves something of the image of God (*Com. Jn.* 2.47). His "white horse" (Rev. 19:11) seems to represent his communication of knowledge to created minds, so that they, as members of his army, will eventually ride white horses of their own (*Com. Jn.* 2.62; see Rev. 19:14); he sits on it "firmly" and "royally," "on words that cannot be turned aside," a vehicle "sharper and more swift than any horse," which leaves all hostile simulations of revelatory language—he seems to be thinking of gnostic documents—behind in the dust (*Com. Jn.* 2.48). He is called

---

he ever attempted to write a commentary on the work. The fragments published by Constantine Diobouniotis and Adolf von Harnack in 1911, eagerly identified by Harnack as excerpts from such a commentary, are now recognized to come from a variety of authors and represent what A. de Boysson, in his review of their work, called "un Origène simplifié, assagi, . . . mais affaibli et énervé." See C. Diobouniotis and A. von Harnack, *Das Scholien-Kommentar des Origenes zur Apokalypse Johannis*, TU 38 (Leipzig: Hinrichs, 1911); A. de Boysson, "Avons-nous un commentaire d'Origène sur l'Apocalypse?" *RB* 10 (1913): 555–67. For a thoughtful recent discussion of the value and possible identity of these fragments, see Éric Junod, "À propos des soi-disant Scolies sur l'Apocalypse d'Origène," *Rivista di storia e letteratura religiosa* 20 (1984): 112–21.

"faithful and true," as Moses called Israel's God in Deuteronomy (Deut. 32:4 LXX): faithful "not because he believes but because he is believable—that is, worthy of being believed" (*Com. Jn.* 2.49), and true because he realizes God's justice in himself and embodies it for creatures (2.53). His role in the world, as Word of God, is to "make war" against deceit and lies in the heart of every would-be disciple (2.55–56); his eyes "are like a flame of fire," because they consume all the chaff of "gross material thoughts" in those on whom he gazes (2.57). The "many diadems" of the triumphant warrior signify his many victories over forms of false knowledge;[27] he also has "a name written which no one knows but himself," because there are mysteries now known only to God's Word, which may some day be shared at least partially with those who share in his life (2.60). And John emphasizes, as Origen says, that "the Word of God on his horse is not naked," but that he is "wrapped in a robe sprinkled with blood,"

> because the Word who became flesh, and who died because he had become flesh, so that his blood was spilled on the ground when the soldier pierced his side, is wrapped in the marks of that passion. For perhaps even when we come to be in the highest, ultimate stage of contemplating the Word and the Truth, we will not completely forget that our introduction to them took place through him, in this body of ours. (*Com. Jn.* 2.61)

For Origen, here as elsewhere, the real message of Scripture is not so much a key to future events in history as it is a pointer to that education and transformation that are the only really significant history any of us live through. So this scene from the Johannine apocalypse becomes a revelation not simply of future conflicts and victories for God's people, but of Christ, in and through whom victory is modeled and won. Similarly, in his comments on Jesus' apocalyptic discourse in Matthew 24, Origen suggests that the battles Jesus describes are most "worthily" interpreted as the inner battles of the disciple struggling to live by the Truth (*Comm. Ser. Matt.* 35; 38), and that the one who "sees his glorious coming" is the one who perceives "the coming of Wisdom into his soul" (38). Apocalyptic language, for Origen, is a central part of the Bible's way of revealing Christ to us, in symbols that clearly call forth figural interpretation; but the most important stage on which the drama is played out is the present life of faith, the inner apocalyptic of Christ's coming to conquer the warring spirits within us, and to heal and illumine the battleground of the fallen mind.

27. *Com. Jn.* 2.58. In his comments on Christ's conflict with the Antichrist, as represented in Jesus' apocalyptic discourse in Matthew, Origen also insists that what is referred to is really the continuing conflict between the truth taught by Christ and the specious imitations of it promoted by the evil spirits: *Commentariorum series in Matthaeum* 33, GCS 11 (Leipzig: Hinrichs, 1933), 62–63; hereafter *Comm. Ser. Matt.*

Apocalyptic Ecclesiology

In a way typical of his speculative, endlessly suggestive approach to biblical interpretation, Origen also provides us with a different emphasis in the Christian use of apocalyptic imagery that was to become more and more dominant from the third century on, especially as a strategy for interpreting the New Testament's book of Revelation: seeing the drama as referring principally to the present life of the church as she lives out the conflicts of the end time, awaiting Christ's second coming. In the second book of his *Commentary on the Song of Songs*, composed perhaps ten to fifteen years later than the first books of the *Commentary on John*,[28] Origen returns to the vision of the rider on the white horse of Revelation 19 to shed light on Song 1:9 (LXX): "I have compared you to my mare among the chariots of Pharaoh." Here Origen suggests that one might take the "white horse" in Revelation to stand for the body assumed by the Lord, or for his soul, or perhaps for both together; but one might also take it, he suggests, to refer to the church, "which is also called his body," and which "is 'without stain or wrinkle' because he has himself 'made it holy by the bath of water.'" Origen continues:

> To this white horse, then, on which he rides who is called Word of God, or else to this heavenly army that follows him on horses that are equally white, Christ compares his Church, and makes it similar. (*Commentary on Canticles* 2.6.9)

Later patristic exegetes of the book of Revelation attach themselves in varying degrees to Origen's exegetical strategy, seeing the work less as a revelation of unknown things to come than as an affirmation of the victory of Christ and a representation of the life of the church, his body, in its present time of struggle.[29] Such exegesis begins with Victorinus of Poetovio's Latin commentary, written around 300, and continues through the later Latin tradition in such authors as the African Donatist Tyconius, Victorinus's editor Jerome, the mid-sixth-century commentaries of Caesarius of Arles in Gaul,[30] Primasius of Hadrumetum in Africa,[31] Cassiodorus the

28. Luc Brésard and Henri Crouzel, the editors and translators of the *Commentary* in SC, suggest a date of composition around 240: see SC 375.11–12. The *Commentary on John* was begun in Alexandria in the late 220s, and Origen had probably completed the first five books before moving to Caesaraea in 231.

29. For brief expositions of the commentaries of these authors, see Daley, *Hope of the Early Church*, 65–66 (Victorinus); 127–31 (Tyconius); 210–11 (Primasius and Apringius); 179–83 (Oecumenius); 198–200 (Andrew). See also Daley, "Apocalypticism in Early Christian Theology," 17–18, 24–26, 40–41.

30. Dom Germain Morin, the editor of this *Expositio in Apocalypsin*, which was long attributed to Augustine, has called it an "undigested hash." He believes it was meant to serve as a set of homily notes rather than as a full-scale commentary. See *S. Caesarii Arelatensis Opera*, 3 vols. (Maredsous, Belgium: Abbaye de Maredsous, 1942), 2:210–77, with Dom Morin's brief introduction.

31. PL 68:793–934, with omissions supplied in PLS 4:1207–21.

Senator in southern Italy,[32] Apringius of Beja in the Iberian peninsula,[33] and the eighth-century compendium of the Spanish monk Beatus of Liébana.[34] The only Greek commentaries we possess from the patristic period—the early sixth-century commentary of Oecumenius[35] and that of Andrew of Caesaraea,[36] metropolitan of Cappadocia, from the end of the century—also follow Origen's exegetical strategy.

Jerome characterized Victorinus, for instance, as a follower of Origen in his exegesis, even though he was a millenarian—a position that Origen himself despised.[37] Although Victorinus does try to link individual figures and episodes in the work to historical events, his main interest is in the work's portrait of Christ. Tyconius, the fourth-century Donatist whose "keys" for unlocking the puzzling figures of Scripture Augustine adopts in *De Doctrina Christiana* 3, also left a commentary on the book of Revelation that exists in manuscript fragments, and that can to some extent be recovered from later commentaries that made use of it.[38] Here, as in the dependent works of Caesarius and Primasius, the drama of the Johannine Apocalypse is really being played out now in the life of the church. The Antichrist is already active, but held in check by the faith of Christians;[39] the millennial kingdom is already under way, in the church's present time of "rest," which extends "from the passion of the Lord to his second coming" (Beatus 11.5.9). The "first resurrection" referred to in Revelation 20:5 is accomplished now for the Christian in baptism—a notion that has antecedents in Origen (Beatus 11.5.3).[40]

32. This brief, little-known work of Cassiodorus's old age is an attempt to identify the cohesive thread of meaning in the work. So the author called it *Complexiones in Apocalypsi*. See the new critical edition by Roger Gryson, in *Commentaria Minora in Apocalypsin Johannis*, CCSL 107 (Turnhout: Brepols, 2003), 101–29.

33. Apringius's commentary, written as a series of homilies or *tractatus*, has also been critically edited by Gryson, *Commentaria*, 13–97.

34. Critical edition by E. Romero-Pose, *Beati in Apocalypsin libri duodecim* (Rome: Typis Officinae Polygraphicae, 1985).

35. This work has now been published in a new critical edition: *Oecumenii Commentarius in Apocalypsin*, ed. Marc De Groote (Leuven: Peeters, 1999).

36. The authoritative edition and textual study of this work is that of Josef Schmid, *Studien zur Geschichte des Griechischen Apokalypse-Textes. 1. Teil: Der Apokalypse-Kommentar des Andreas von Kaisareia*, text: Münchener theologische Studien, Ergänzungsband 1 (Munich: Zink, 1955); *Einleitung* (Munich: Zink, 1956).

37. For Victorinus's Origenism, see Jerome, *Epistles* 61.2; 84.7; *Apologia adversus libros Rufini* 3.14; *Commentarius in Ecclesiasten* 4.13.

38. For a thorough consideration of the issues involved in recovering Tyconius's commentary, as well as a very useful survey of Latin Patristic commentaries on this book, see Kenneth B. Steinhauser, *The Apocalypse Commentary of Tyconius: A History of Its Reception and Influence* (Frankfurt: Peter Lang, 1987).

39. See the probable comment of Tyconius in Beatus of Liébana's commentary, 2.6.82–83 (hereafter Beatus).

40. See Origen, *Com. Jn.* 10.243–45; *Hom. Luc.* Greek frag. 83.

The first extant Greek commentary on the book of Revelation, composed by a certain Oecumenius, probably in the first decade of the sixth century, also interprets the work mainly as a representation of the present spiritual struggles of the church, and the hope of Christians for a largely spiritual form of blessed union with God. Oecumenius interprets the vision of the mounted warrior, in Revelation 19, as a vision of the glorified Jesus, "making war with and for his holy ones, and commanding the forces against their enemies"[41] in the present age; the "white horse" on which he sits reminds us that "Christ rests on none other but the pure, on those not marked by any stain of sin."[42] The "thousand years" in which Satan is bound in the abyss (Rev. 20:2–3) signify, for Oecumenius, not a thousand-year interval of bliss for holy souls, before their own reincarnation, as Plato imagines, but this present age, in which the faithful live in the "daylight" of the Word made flesh:

> The incarnation of the Lord has become "day" and "morning" for us, since "the sun of justice" (Mal. 4:2) shines on us—for that is what Malachi calls him—providing us with "the light of knowledge" (Hos. 10:12 LXX); Zachary announced the coming of this divine light, when he said, "The dawn from on high has overshadowed us, to shine on those seated in darkness and the shadow of death" (Luke 1:78–79). . . . Since Scripture says that a day is counted "as a thousand years" with God (Ps. 90:4; 2 Pet. 3:8), and, in contrast, the Lord's presence on earth is called "day," the author calls this day "a thousand years," since there is no difference with God between one day and a thousand years. In this "day," the incarnation of the Lord, the devil has been bound, unable to struggle back against the divine revelation of the Savior.[43]

Although Andrew of Caesaraea, writing his own commentary at the end of the same century, seems intent on correcting some of the Origenist tendencies in Oecumenius's work, he also identifies the millennium in Revelation 20 with the present life of the church, and stresses the spiritual character of the rewards of the saints. Details of interpretation vary, of course, for particular passages, but in general these later commentators joined Origen's project of reading the book of Revelation, the only apocalypse in the Christian canon, as revealing principally Christ's present relationship to the believer and the community, rather than the shape of things to come.

Maximus the Confessor, the great—and ever-critical—seventh-century synthesizer of the theological and spiritual tradition that reaches back through the sixth-century christological controversialists to Dionysius, Evagrius, the Cappadocian Fathers, and Origen, offers us no direct commentary in his works on the book of Revelation. Apart from a number of allusions to familiar

41. *Commentary* 10.13 (De Groote, *Oecumenii Commentarius*, 241.255–57).
42. Ibid. (De Groote, *Oecumenii Commentarius*, 241.260–61).
43. Ibid. 10.16 (De Groote, *Oecumenii Commentarius*, 248.438–249.451).

phrases from the work—calling Jesus "alpha and omega" (Rev. 1:8; 21:6; 22:13) or "the fountain of the water of life" (Rev. 21:6)—he seldom averts to it. Yet Maximus, too, offers us a synthetic vision of the person of the glorified Christ, as the center of the life of the church and the guiding norm for the flow of time, that seems embedded in this same Origenist tradition of translating apocalyptic imagery into the present existence of the Christian believer, as he or she looks to the future. In *Replies to Thalassius*, Question 22, for instance, Maximus—writing in the early 630s—struggles with the relationship of future and present eschatology head on: "If God 'will reveal his riches in the ages to come,'" he asks, quoting Ephesians 2:7, "how has 'the end of the ages come upon us?'" (1 Cor. 10:11). Is the fulfillment of God's plan still ahead of us, or do we already live in its spell? Maximus answers by dividing the whole history of creation, in God's providential plan, into two great periods: the first, in which the Word has steadily involved himself more and more in human life, eventually becoming human himself in the Incarnation; and the second, in which human beings, incorporated into him by faith and the life of grace, are gradually allowed to become divine by participation.

> Let us . . . distinguish the ages in our thought, and allot some of them to the Mystery of God's becoming human (*enanthrōpēsis*), and others to the grace of humanity's becoming divine. We shall find that the first set of these (ages) have reached their proper goal, but that the others have not yet arrived. To put it concisely, some of the ages belong to God's descent towards humanity, the rest are part of humanity's ascent towards God. If we understand this, we will not flounder around in unclarity about the sacred words, thinking that the holy Apostle himself was also in the dark. Rather—since our Lord Jesus Christ is the beginning and middle and end of all ages, of those past and those present and those still to come—then the end of the ages really has come upon us in the power of our faith—that end that will be formally brought to realization, by grace, in the divinization of those who are worthy.[44]

We live already in the age of eschatological fulfillment, of the realization of the apocalyptic vision of Daniel and the book of Revelation: Jesus has come, "the Word became flesh . . . and we have seen his glory" (John 1:14). Yet the apocalyptic promise of salvation from the dangers of mortality still waits to be carried out in us, as individuals and as a church; the Messiah who has already come must come again—not alone and obscure this second time, but with "thousand, thousand saints attending," with humanity itself now looking on and sharing openly in his victory.[45] For Maximus and for most of the

---

44. *Replies to Thalassius*, Question 22, CCSG 7 (Turnhout: Brepols, 1980), 139–65.
45. Cyril of Alexandria emphasizes this contrast between the secrecy of Jesus' identity in his first coming, necessary in order that his enemies might "crucify the Lord of glory" (1 Cor. 2:8), and the

patristic tradition before him, the apocalyptic promise was really a promise of revelation and participation: the promise that God's faithful ones would not simply be rescued from oppression, but that they would see and share in God's own transformed humanity.

"illustrious and terrible" openness of his second coming; see *Homilies on Luke* 139, trans. Robert Payne Smith (Boston: Stoudion, 1983), 555.

5

PSEUDO-HIPPOLYTUS'S *IN SANCTUM PASCHA*

A Mystery Apocalypse

DRAGOŞ-ANDREI GIULEA

Scholars have noticed the presence of mystery terminology and imagery in the ancient paschal homily—a Greek anonymous document—that bears the title *Eis to hagion Pascha*. In this respect, the following passage pertaining to chapter 62 may be one of the most significant:[1]

> O mystical choir [*ō tēs chorēgias tēs mystikēs*]! O feast of the Spirit [*ō tēs pneumatikēs heortēs*]! O Pasch of God, who hast come down from heaven to earth, and from earth ascend again to the heavens. O feast common to all [*tōn holōn heortasma*], O universal joy, and honor of the universe, its nurture

---

1. *In sanctum Pascha* 62, in Adalbert-G. Hamman, ed., *The Paschal Mystery: Ancient Liturgies and Patristic Texts*, trans. Thomas Halton (Staten Island, NY: Alba House, 1969), 68. The first critical edition belongs to Pierre Nautin, *Homélies Paschales*, SC 27 (Paris: Éditions du Cerf, 1950). See also the critical edition made by Giuseppe Visonà, *Pseudo Ippolito: In sanctum Pascha: Studio, edizione, commento* (Milano: Vita e Pensiero, 1988). For the present study, I follow Visonà's numbers and the abbreviation *IP* for *In sanctum Pascha*. For mystery language, see Raniero Cantalamessa, *L'Omelia "In S. Pascha" dello Pseudo-Ippolito di Roma. Ricerche sulla teologia dell'Asia Minore nella seconda metà del II secolo* (Milano: Societa Editrice Vita e Pensiero, 1967), 104–8; and Visonà, *Pseudo Ippolito*, 345–47.

and its luxury,[2] by whom the darkness of death has been dissolved and life extended to all, by whom the gates of heaven have been opened [*aneōchthēsan*] as God has become man and man has become God. . . . An antiphonal choir has been formed on earth to respond to the choir above. O Pasch of God, no longer confined to the heavens and now united to us in spirit; through him the great marriage chamber has been filled. . . . O Pasch, illumination [*phōtisma*] of the new bright day [lit. "torch procession," *lampadouchia*]—the brightness [*aglaisma*] of the torches of the virgins, through which the lamps of the soul are no longer extinguished, but the divine fire of charity [lit. "the fire of grace," *tēs charitos . . . to pyr*] burns divinely and spiritually in all.

Cantalamessa regards the presence of mystery language in the paschal celebration as part of the general Christian polemical response to mystery religions, also manifest in Melito of Sardis or Clement of Alexandria.[3]

In addition to mystery terminology, it is also noticeable that this passage contains biblical imagery and language such as "pascha," "spirit," "angelic choir," "virgins," and "marriage chamber," and references to God's "descent" and "ascension." Nonetheless, in the present essay I would like to direct investigation toward a reading of the text under a different hermeneutical key, namely the Jewish apocalyptic traditions, and in this way to draw the conclusions that the presence of such traditions entails. Another pivotal passage (*IP* 1.1–12) of the text may be helpful for the opening of this new angle of investigation:

Now is it the time when the light of Christ sheds its rays;[4] the pure rays [*phōstēres*] of the pure Spirit rise and the heavenly treasures of divine glory [*doxa*] are opened up. Night's darkness and obscurity have been swallowed up, and the dense blackness dispersed in this light of day; crabbed death has been totally eclipsed. Life has been extended [*ephēplōthē*] to every creature and all things are diffused in brightness [*phōs*]. The dawn of dawn ascends over the earth [*anatolai anatolōn epechousi to pan*][5] and he who was before the morning star and before the other stars, the mighty [*megas*] Christ, immortal and mighty [*polys*], sheds light brighter than the sun on the universe.

2. Most likely, the Greek passage κοσμικὸν πανηγύρισμα, ὦ τοῦ παντὸς χαρὰ καὶ τιμὴ καὶ τροφὴ καὶ τρυφὴ might be rendered into English as "cosmic solemnity, the joy and honor, nurture and luxury of all."

3. Cantalamessa, *L'Omelia*, 104.

4. I would propose a minimal change in Halton's rendering of the expression ἱεραὶ μὲν ἤδη φωτὸς αὐγάζουσι Χριστοῦ ἀκτῖνες from "the blessed light of Christ sheds its rays" into "the light of Christ sheds its sacred rays." Compare with Nautin's solution ("les rayons sacrés de la lumière du Christ resplendissent"—*Homélies*, 116) and Visonà's ("brillano i sacri raggi della luce di Cristo"—*Pseudo Ippolito*, 231).

5. For the purpose of the present study, it would be significant to mention that Nautin translated the Greek word τὸ πᾶν through "l'univers" (*Homélies*, 116), while Visonà rendered it through "l'universo" (*Pseudo Ippolito*, 231).

Anticipating some of the key conclusions of the present study, one may affirm that *In sanctum Pascha* might be envisaged as a special sort of apocalypse, which I would call "mystery apocalypse." Since the divine temple extends its presence to the terrestrial world and the celestial king descends to earth, ascension becomes useless and the visionary's ascent sensibly changes into a mystagogy. Instead of ascension, the visionary needs to cross from the visible to the invisible, from the phanic to mystery, and from the sensible realm to the intelligible one. Pertaining to the same Asiatic tradition with Melito's homily yet more visible than in Melito, the homily of Pseudo-Hippolytus witnesses to a pivotal synthesis of two traditions in the Christian mind-set, namely mystery and apocalyptic. The application of synthesis to one of the central Christian celebrations—the festival of pascha—was so profound, that it would remain normative for the Christian liturgical life until the present day.

Scholarly Debates over the Origins of the Text

The document has crossed the centuries under the names of two famous Christian theologians: John Chrysostom and Hippolytus of Rome. It is preserved in eight manuscripts found in Greece and ascribed to John Chrysostom. Besides these, the palimpsest from Grottaferrata, the fragments from the Syrian *Florilegium Edessenum Anonymum*, and the *florilegium* added to the Acts of the Council of Lateran ascribe the homily to Hippolytus of Rome.[6] In modern times, scholars became suspicious of these paternities and proposed various substitute hypotheses. One of the most significant hypotheses came from Cantalamessa, who placed the homily in the second century Asia Minor. He advocated his position especially on internal theological and linguistic grounds (which Melito of Sardis would have shared as well in his *Peri Pascha*), and also on various theological positions typical for the second century.

To the contrary, Gribomont, Stuiber, and Visonà manifested caution in dating the homily, keeping open Nautin's possibility of the early fourth century. Nonetheless, one may respond to Visonà's argumentation in the following way: since the homily seems to have been used as a liturgical text as Visonà argues, historical-critical methods may be applied to the text and affirm that the rhetorical embellishments of the text might belong to a later period and come from the hands of a series of editors.

However, a large majority of scholars generally agreed with Cantalamessa's dating of the homily. Daniélou, Grillmeier, Botte, Simonetti, Hall, and Richardson embraced Cantalamessa's position; Kretschmar, in his turn, assumed that the homily had been written at the beginning of the third century. In

---

6. Cf. Claudio Moreschini and Enrico Norelli, *Histoire de la littérature chrétienne antique grecque et latine*, vol. 1, *De Paul à l'ère de Constantin* (Genève: Labor et fides, 2000), 175.

addition, Blanchetière, Mara, and Mazza used the homily as a second-century document in order to prove their theses about Ignatius of Antioch, Melito, the *Gospel of Peter*, or Hippolytus of Rome. Finally, for Gerlach, *IP* should be associated with the paschal tradition conveyed in the Asia Minor of the third century.[7] These scholars have emphasized several elements of similarity between *IP* and various writings pertaining to the first three centuries, such as the general mystery and Melitonean language, pneumatic Christology and binitarian theology, as well as the similarities with the *testimonia* used in scriptural exegesis and with the liturgical tradition of the first three centuries.

The Cosmic Extension of the Heavenly Temple

In a schematic phrase, John Collins tried to encompass some emblematic features of every apocalypse:[8]

> [A] genre of revelatory literature with [1] a narrative framework, in which [2] a revelation is mediated by [3] an otherworldly being to a [4] human recipient, disclosing [5] a transcendent reality which is both temporal, insofar as it envisages eschatological salvation, and spatial insofar as it involves another, supernatural world.

At the same time, one has to keep in mind E. J. C. Tigghelaar's following methodological observations: "[a] definition is not a prerequisite for historical studies, and might even prove to be an impediment," and "apocalyptic, too, is resistant to definition."[9] Likewise, Collins's perspective is usually called the "generic" approach to apocalypses and F. García Martínez affirms that sometimes this approach manifests the weakness of being too general and ahistorical.[10] In this way, I am aware that Collins's definition, while delineating some of the most frequent characteristics of the Jewish apocalyptic traditions, is not ahistorical and indispensable. However, it is useful and I will employ it merely as a helpful guideline as to which features do not have to be considered necessary and complete.

---

7. For bibliography on the history of the text and its interpretations, see, e.g.: Visonà, *Pseudo Ippolito*; Moreschini and Norelli, *Histoire*; and Karl Gerlach, *The Antenicene Pascha: A Rhetorical History* (Leuven: Peeters, 1998).

8. John J. Collins, *The Apocalyptic Imagination* (Grand Rapids: Eerdmans, 1998), 5.

9. See Eibert J. C. Tigghelaar, "More on Apocalyptic and Apocalypses," *JSJ* 18 (1987): 137–44. For the *religionsgeschichtlich* perspective on apocalypticism at the Uppsala colloquium, see *Apocalypticism in the Mediterranean World and the Near East: Proceedings of the International Colloquium on Apocalypticism, Uppsala, August 12–17, 1979*, ed. David Hellholm (Tübingen: Mohr Siebeck, 1983).

10. See Florentino García Martínez, "Encore l'Apocalyptique," *JSJ* 17 (1986): 224–32.

According to my hypothesis, all these features, with some modifications that I will mention below, can be identified in the Pseudo-Hippolytean work. First of all, regarding the role of a narrative framework, the homily encompasses a clear-cut two-step history of salvation that implies a divine economy developed in two stages: the era that precedes incarnation, a time of figures, types, and symbols, and the era of truth, when the divine king with his temple and light descend to earth. Nautin and Visonà, for instance, divided the whole text following this wide two-step framework.

Nautin		Visonà	
vv. 1–3	Exordium	vv. 1–3	Hymn of opening
vv. 4–8	Subject and plan	vv. 4–7	The plan of the homily plus the reproduction of the text of Exodus 12
vv. 9–42	The First Part: The Figures	vv. 8–42	The Pascha of the Law and its accomplishment/perfection [in Christ]
vv. 9–10	The Law	vv. 9–15	The paschal mystery in the light of the economy of the Law
vv. 11–42	The Pascha	vv. 16–42	[Typological] exegesis on Exodus 12
vv. 11–15	The First Pascha		
vv. 16–42	The Solemnity		
vv. 43–61	The Second Part: The Truth	vv. 43–61	The Pascha of the Logos in its actualization/realization
vv. 43–48	Christ's Coming	vv. 43–48	The Incarnation
vv. 48–61	The Passion	vv. 49–58	The Passion and Death
		vv. 59–61	The Glorification
vv. 62–63	The Peroration	vv. 62–63	Final Aretalogy and Peroration

Moreover, Melito's *Peri Pascha* follows the same framework.[11]

The passage 1.1–12 appears to depict the common apocalyptic image of the opened heavens, which recalls for example Ezekiel 1:1, especially if one observes the usage of the same verb that renders the English verb "to open," פתח/*pth*, *anoigō* (in LXX and *IP*). Thus the expression "the heaven opened" and other similar ones seem to be *termini technici* in biblical and apocalyptic literature, as ringing bells announcing a celestial vision.[12] Furthermore, the

---

11. Cf. Alistair Stewart-Sykes, *The Lamb's High Feast: Melito, Peri Pascha, and the Quartodeciman Paschal Liturgy at Sardis* (Leiden and Boston: Brill, 1998). For Ps.-Hippolytus, see Nautin, *Homélies*, 67; and Visonà, *Pseudo Ippolito*, 49.

12. See also Gen. 7:11; Ps. 78:23; Matt. 3:16; Mark 1:10 [σχίζω]; 7:34 [διανοίγω]; Luke 3:21; Acts 7:56; 10:11; Rev. 4:1; 19:11.

picture that describes the consequences that the opening of the heavens implies appears to enclose a special element: the heavenly light floods the universe, and its source—Christ—is envisioned in huge dimensions.

Pseudo-Hippolytus does not spend much time expounding on the earthly temple, the church, being instead more interested in the divine and mystical one, while the earthly and visible temple seems to represent the mere entrance or the lintel to the celestial Jerusalem. As shown in different studies, the heavenly temple represents a constant aspect in apocalyptic literature.[13] The visionary experiences rapture by being translated into the celestial temple where he is allowed to contemplate the heavenly king, the throne, and the myriads of angels glorifying the king.[14] In one of her articles, Martha Himmelfarb noticed an important distinction between prophetic and apocalyptic visions: the prophets are neither translated into, nor do they ascend into, the heavenly temple. "Ezekiel is the only one of all the classical prophets to record the experience of being physically transported by the spirit of God, but even Ezekiel does not ascend to heaven."[15] Isaiah, for instance (Isa. 6:1–3), receives the divine revelation inside the earthly temple in Jerusalem.

Nonetheless, Pseudo-Hippolytus's writing seems to be part of a different paradigm, since the heavenly glory descends to earth. Here Christ's coming (*epidēmia*) turns out to be the moment when the border between the celestial temple and the earth disappears, and the earth becomes flooded by the presence of the divine light. The homilist states in the opening phrase of the hymn: "the heavenly treasures of the divine glory [*doxa*] are opened up."[16] It should be also noticed that the tradition of the divine light/glory stored beyond the heavens has ancient biblical origins. Psalm 8:1, for example, reads "you have set your glory above the heavens."

The idea of a descended or extended celestial temple seems to manifest similarities with the biblical and extra-biblical literature. Second Chronicles 7:1–3 probably represents one of the most ancient witnesses to this paradigm.

> When Solomon had ended his prayer, fire came down from heaven [*to pyr katebē ek tou ouranou*] ... and the glory of the Lord filled the temple [*doxa kyriou eplēsen ton oikon*]. ... When the children of Israel saw the fire come

13. For an extended bibliography, see, e.g., Rachel Elior, *The Three Temples: On the Emergence of Jewish Mysticism* (Oxford and Portland, OR: Littman Library of Jewish Civilization, 2004).

14. See, e.g., *1 En.* 14; Dan. 7:9–14; *Songs of the Sabbath Sacrifice*; *Apoc. Zeph.* 8; *4 Bar.* 10; *2 En.* 3; 22; Rev. 4; *Ascen. Isa.* 7–10.

15. Martha Himmelfarb, "From Prophecy to Apocalypse: The Book of the Watchers and Tours of Heaven," in *Jewish Spirituality: From the Bible through the Middle Ages*, ed. Arthur Green (New York: Crossroad, 1986), 1:145–65, esp. 150.

16. *IP* 1.3: οὐράνιοι δὲ δόξης καὶ θεότητος ἀνεῴγασι θησαυροί. The word "glory" represents a well-known apocalyptic concept: כבוד/kvwd, God's glory; see, e.g., Jarl Fossum, "Glory," in *DDD*, 348–52.

down and the glory of the Lord upon the temple [*pantes hoi huioi Israēl heōrōn katabainon to pyr, kai hē doxa kyriou epi ton oikon*], they bowed down with their faces to the earth on the pavement.

Psalm 148 is also emblematic, since it depicts a cosmic glorification of Yahweh where both the heavenly realm (angels, hosts, sun and moon, stars, the highest heavens, and the waters above the heavens) and the terrestrial one (sea monsters and ocean depths, fire, hail and snow, smoke, storm, mountains and hills, trees, beasts, kings, and peoples) offer their particular praise. The thirteenth line ("Let them praise the name of the Lord, for his name alone is exalted: his glory (הוד/*hwd*) is above earth and heaven") is especially significant for disclosing the idea that the divine glory is stored beyond the heavens, although it is not obvious whether the glory descends. It might also be worth noting that the psalm is read or sung in the Eastern Church in the service during the paschal night. Likewise, in the *Paschal Canon* ascribed to John of Damascus the cosmic liturgy of light comes out as well, for example in the Ode 3, Troparia: "Now all things have been filled with light, both heaven and earth and those beneath the earth; so let all creation sing Christ's rising, by which it is established."

Furthermore, the theme of the descended glory or king of glory is also present in the New Testament writings and pseudepigraphic materials. The Gospels, for example, depict Christ's incarnation as the moment when the heavenly light descended to earth, as in the visions of Matthew (4:16–17) and Luke (1:78–79). In Luke 2:13–14, the angelic armies descend to earth and sing for their incarnated king. In addition, the eschaton, as described in Matthew 24:27 and Luke 17:24, seems to be the moment when the Son of Man will appear as lightning (*astrapē*, used in both cases) filling the whole world. For John, too, Christ was light (e.g., John 1:7–9; 1 John 1:1–3, 5, 7; 2:8–10), and his disciples have seen his glory (*doxa*; John 1:14).[17] Another argument for the deep Johannine influence on Pseudo-Hippolytus might be that the passage parallels in its emblematic images the prologue of the Gospel of John: Christ, who is the "light" and "life" come into the world. "Darkness" has been swallowed up, and the life has been "extended to every creature." The author is also indebted to John for other christological titles such as "manna" or "bread" that came down from heaven (*IP* 8.4; 25.11–12). Perhaps the most explicit text appears in the book of Revelation where one can read: "And in the spirit he carried me away to a great, high mountain and showed me the holy city Jerusalem coming down out of heaven from God.

17. For the idea that Jesus was conceived as temple in the writings of the New Testament, see, e.g., Bill Salier, "The Temple in the Gospel according to John," 121–34, and Steve Walton, "A Tale of Two Perspectives? The Place of the Temple in Acts?" 135–49, in *Heaven on Earth: The Temple in Biblical Theology*, ed. T. Desmond Alexander and Simon Gathercole (Carlisle, UK: Paternoster, 2004).

It has the glory [*doxa*] of God and a radiance [*phōstēr*] like a very rare jewel, like jasper, clear as crystal" (21:10–11).

An internalized version of the theme of descended glory may be encountered in 1 Corinthians 6:19, where the idea of a third temple emerged, namely the temple of the human body (*sōma*) deemed as the "temple of the Holy Spirit." There are also writings pertaining to the Second Temple, such as *Joseph and Aseneth* 6.5, which are significant for the idea of the descent of the heavenly temple or *hekhal*.[18] As for the New Testament pseudepigraphic materials, the *Gospel of Nazarenes* or the *Epistle of the Apostles* may constitute good examples. *In sanctum Pascha* and the *Epistle of the Apostles* display further common elements: (1) the descent of *light* and *life*, which are identical (*IP* 1; *EpApost.* 39); (2) Christ's coming is at the same time a descent (*EpApost.* 13.2; 39.11) followed by an ascension (*EpApost.* 13.8; 14.8; 18.4; 29.7), and also compared with the rising of the sun and employing the same verb *anatellō* (*IP* 1.2; *EpApost.* 16.3); (3) the two sources connect Christ's coming with the Pascha (*EpApost.* 16); (4) the two sources had strong Johannine influence.

The theme emerges in other important early Christian writings such as Melito's *Peri Pascha*, where, in 44 (289) for instance, Christ comes from above in opposition to the earthly temple. In 45 (290–300), comparing the Jerusalem from above with the terrestrial one, Melito reckons that the glory (*doxa*) of God is enthroned (*kathidrytai*) not in a single place (*eph heni topō*), but his grace (*charis*) overflows unto all the boundaries of the inhabited world (*epi panta ta perata tēs oikoumenēs*). The pivotal idea of the descended heavens will also appear in Tertullian's *De carne Christi* 3 (the episode of Epiphany), Cyprian's *On the Lord's Prayer* (Treatise IV), Clement's *Protreptikos* 11.114.1–2, and Origen's first *Homily on Ezekiel* 1.6–8. According to David J. Halperin, Origen's source of inspiration seemed to be the *Sinai Haggadot*.[19] However, all these sources and probably *IP* (if a pre-Origenian writing) give witness for a more ancient tradition.

18. See Frances Flannery-Dailey, "Calling Down Heaven: Descent of the Hekhal in Second Temple Judaism as a Window onto Ritual Experience" (paper presented at the SBL national conference, Washington, DC, November 2006). For the concept of mystery in apocalyptic writings, see, e.g., *1 En.* 41.1–7; 42.1–3; 48.1; 49.1; *Jos. Asen.* 16.1–8; 17.2–3, 6; for the theme of divine disclosures, see *T. Lev.* 1.2; 18.2; *T. Jos.* 6.6; *T. Benj.* 10.5; *Jos. Asen.* 16.7; *2 Bar.* 6.2; 10.5; 35.1; *3 Bar.* Prologue 1; 4.13; 11.7; 17.4; *1 En.* 9.6 (Gr); 10.7; 16.3; *L.A.B.* 25; 27.10; 34.2, *b. Yoma* 67b; *Ep. Arist.* 315. Cf. Michael E. Stone, "Lists of Revealed Things in Apocalyptic Literature," in *Magnalia Dei, the Mighty Acts of God: Essays on the Bible and Archaeology in Memory of G. Ernest Wright*, ed. Frank M. Cross, Werner E. Lemke, and Patrick D. Miller Jr. (Garden City, NY: Doubleday, 1976), 414–52; Christopher Rowland, *The Open Heaven: A Study of Apocalyptic in Judaism and Early Christianity* (New York: Crossroad, 1982), 14; Markus N. A. Bockmuehl, *Revelation and Mystery in Ancient Judaism and Pauline Christianity* (Tübingen: Mohr Siebeck, 1990), 24–41.

19. See David J. Halperin, *The Faces of the Chariot: Early Jewish Responses to Ezekiel's Vision* (Tübingen: Mohr Siebeck, 1988), esp. 327–35.

Pascha and Celestial Liturgy

At the same time, following Hebrews 8:1 ("we have such a high priest [*archiereus*], one who is seated at the right hand of the throne of the Majesty in the heavens"), *IP* becomes more complex through portraying Christ as a divine high priest. Pseudo-Hippolytus depicts Christ with certain apocalyptic titles such as the "eternal high priest" (*archiereus aiōnios*; 46.33, 36), "the true high priest of the heavens" (55.16–17), and especially the "King of the powers" (46.36), the "King of glory" (46.29–31; 61.9–14), the "eternal King" (46.3, 19), the "great King" (9.28), or the "Lord of the powers" (46.26, 30, 36).[20]

As for the visionary, one of the noticeable elements consists in the "democratization" of the accessibility to the hidden realm of heavens. Every human person can be initiated and become a visionary of the highest mystery of the universe, namely the luminous theophany of the Lord of powers. Angels, humans, stars, waters, and the whole earth are all present contemplating the King of glory in his various manifestations. In one of the central scenes (*IP* 55.5–25), they are terrified spectators at the divine passions of the King of the universe:

> Then the world was in amazement at his long endurance. The heavens were shocked, the powers were moved, the heavenly thrones and laws were moved at seeing the General of the great powers hanging on the cross; for a short time the stars of heaven were falling when they viewed stretched on the cross him who was before the morning star. For a time the sun's fire was extinguished, the great Light of the world suffered eclipse. Then the earth's rocks were rent . . . the veil of the temple was rent in sympathy, bearing witness to the High priest of the heavens, and the world would have been dissolved in confusion and fear at the passion if the great Jesus had not expired saying: Father, into your hands I commit my spirit (Luke 23:46). The whole universe trembled and quaked with fear, and everything was in a state of agitation, but when the Divine Spirit rose again the universe returned to life and regained its vitality.

The next scene (*IP* 3.1–15) depicts the whole creation glorifying the victory and resurrection of the King of glory:

> Exult, ye heavens of heavens, which as the Spirit exclaims, *proclaim the glory of God* (Ps. 18:1 LXX) in that they are first to receive the paternal light of the Divine Spirit. Exult, angels and archangels of the heavens, and all you people, and the whole heavenly host as you look upon your heavenly King come down in bodily form to earth. Exult, you choir of stars pointing out him who rises

---

20. Divine priest represents a central apocalyptic theme as one can find, e.g., in Philip G. Davis, "Divine Agents, Mediators, and New Testament Christology," *JTS* 45 (1994): 479–503; or Crispin H. T. Fletcher-Louis, "God's Image, His Cosmic Temple and the High Priest," in Alexander and Gathercole, *Heaven on Earth*, 78–99. See further bibliography in these articles.

before the morning star. Exult, air, which extends over the abysses and intermi-
nable spaces. Exult, briny water of the sea, honored by the sacred traces of his
footsteps. Exult, earth washed by the divine blood. Exult, every soul of man,
reanimated by the resurrection to a new birth.[21]

This language reveals the liturgical background of the homily.[22] The last three
chapters of the booklet, in particular, depict a mystic choral chanting (*chorēgia
hē mystikē*), a spiritual feast, and an antiphonal choir where angels and humans
sing and respond to each other.[23] There are also images associated with the
liturgical experience such as the marriage chamber, the wedding garments,
certain interior lamps of the human souls, and "the divine fire of grace (*charis*)
that burns divinely and spiritually in all, in soul and body, nurtured by the
oil of Christ" (*entheōs dē kai pneumatikōs en pasi tēs charitos dadoucheitai
to pyr, sōmati kai pneumati, kai elaiō Christou chorēgoumenon*).[24]

Mystery Language and *Visio Dei*

While the paschal event seems to convert into a visionary moment—into
an apocalyptic incidence—our author does not seem to offer a traditional
apocalyptical treatment in terms of preparation for the access to this luminous vision through ascension, but develops a mystagogy instead. The fact
that Christ, the king of angels descends himself to the initiand and gradually
reveals himself—from the stage of the human form that he put on to the final
epiphany of the huge incandescent divine body—also adds a new element to
the mystery dimension of the homily.

Pseudo-Hippolytus manifestly affirms in a short methodological exposition
in chapters 4–7 that the divine temple and its light are not visible in the way
we see the sensible things, but they are rather hidden and mysterious and
part of the veiled side of the world, where the mysteries of the truth can be
found.[25] Similar to Philo's *Questions and Answers on Exodus* and Melito's *Peri
Pascha*, the homilist connects this mystagogy with a typological exegesis of
Exodus 12.[26] While the types or figures (*typoi*) of the book of Exodus could
be seen through the bodily eyes, the prototypes or paradigms (*prōtotypoi
kai paradeigmata*) are not visible, but hidden (*mystika*), and able to be seen

21. See also *IP* 62.
22. Visonà, *Pseudo Ippolito*, 149–57.
23. *IP* 62.16–19.
24. *IP* 62.30–32.
25. *IP* 7.5: τὰ τῆς ἀληθείας μυστήρια.
26. It seems that a hermeneutical tradition of interpreting Exod. 12 within the paschal context
may be traced from Philo's *Questions and Answers on Exodus* to Melito, Ps.-Hippolytus, and Origen.
While Philo interpreted Exod. 12 allegorically, the Christian theologians changed the allegorical
interpretation into a typological one.

only through intellection or intuition (*nous*; *IP* 6.10). Since the glory is not located exclusively within the upper realm but present everywhere on earth, the heavenly ascension becomes utterly meaningless. For this reason the author logically changed the *ascension* into a *mystagogy*, a penetration into the mystery realm, which exists on the earth as well, not solely in heaven. Therefore the visionary, namely the Christian initiand, has to seek to acquire a mystical knowledge (*IP* 4.2; 50.5) by pursuing the itinerary of contemplating with acerbity the mysteries hidden within the types.[27] Since the light of Christ and the Spirit spread in the universe cannot be seen with the unaided eye, the participants in the liturgy need to be initiated (*IP* 4.2). Within this context, the paschal celebration does not take place within the visible world; it is not so much *cosmic*, but rather *mystical*, or a *mystery*.

Carrying on the same logic, Pseudo-Hippolytus claims that the sacrifice and even the Lamb that "has come down from the heaven" (*IP* 2.15) are mystical.[28] The Lamb is then a "sacred sacrifice" (*to thyma to hieron*; 18.1), and "perfect" (*teleion*; 19.1), while the pascha is also mystical (1.15). Thus the same combination of mystery and apocalypticism emerges here again. It is a well-known aspect that pascha is connected with the apocalyptic theme of resurrection and the heavenly Lamb represents an apocalyptic image, which appears in the book of Revelation, first as the slaughtered or sacrificed Lamb, then as the Lamb sitting on the heavenly throne among the angels who glorify him.[29] The mystery adjective *hieros* (sacred) qualifies in *IP* everything connected with Christ and his temple: rays (1.1), church (63.3), pascha (16.4), feast (6.1; 8.1), solemnity (3.28), knowledge (4.2), victim (18.1), lamb (23.2), body (41.4; 49.6), head (53.2), rib (53.9), blood and water (53.9–10), spirit (47.6–7), word (59.4), resurrection (60.1–2).

The recurring usage of such terms as *hieros, mystikos, pneumatikos, theios*, and *megas* might not be the "mania for hyperbole of a mediocre orator,"[30] but rather the effort to suggest that those realities of the temple and especially its

---

27. *IP* 6.5–6: τὴν δὲ ἀκρίβειαν τῶν μυστηρίων διὰ τῶν τυπῶν θεωροῦντες. Asia Minor has a particular tendency toward apocalyptic literature, due to its special connection with the book of Revelation and the Johaninne tradition. See, e.g., Adela Y. Collins, "The Revelation of John: An Apocalyptic Response to a Social Crisis," *CurTM* 8 (1981): 4–12; Larry V. Crutchfield, "The Apostle John and Asia Minor as a Source of Premillennialism in the Early Church Fathers," *JETS* 31 (1988): 411–27; Thomas B. Slater, "On the Social Setting of the Revelation to John," *NTS* 44 (1998): 232–56; Roland H. Worth, *The Seven Cities of the Apocalypse and Greco-Asian Culture* (New York: Paulist, 1999); Philip A. Harland, "Honouring the Emperor or Assailing the Beast: Participation in Civic Life among Associations (Jewish, Christian and Other) in Asia Minor and the Apocalypse of John," *JSNT* 77 (2000): 99–121; Collin J. Hemer, *The Letters to the Seven Churches of Asia in Their Local Setting*, The Biblical Resource Series (Grand Rapids: Eerdmans, 2001).

28. *IP* 20.4–5: τὸ πρόβατον ἔρχεται τὸ μυστικὸν τὸ ἐκ τῶν οὐρανῶν.

29. Rev. 5:6, 9, 12–13. Cf. John 1:29, 36; Acts 8:32; 1 Cor. 5:7; 1 Pet. 1:19; 2:24. For the roots of this image, see Gen. 22:7–8, 13; Exod. 12:21; Lev. 4:35; 5:6; 9:3. For the image of the suffering righteous connected to the lamb, see Isa. 52:13–53:7; Jer. 11:19.

30. Nautin, *Homélies*, 46. See for instance the repeated adjective μέγας in Ezekiel the Tragedian.

king—the preexisting Christ—do not belong to the sensible realm, but to the invisible, noetic, or mysterious one. It can also be noticed that the attribute *megas* is used as well, particularly in connection to the divine temple and Christ's body: *megas Christos* (*IP* 1.11); *megalē megalou basileōs epidēmia* (2.3); *megalou basileōs* (9.28); *tō megalō sōmati* (32.3); *to megethos pan tēs theotētos* and *pan to plērōma tēs theotētos* (45.10; cf. Col. 2:9); *tōn ektatheisōn cheirōn Iēsou* (15.14); *cheiras exetainas patrikas ekalypsas hēmas entos tōn patrikōn* (38.3–4); *tas cheiras tas megalas* (63.2–3). Consequently, rather than being a note of grandiloquence,[31] it might be the Jewish biblical and pseudepigraphical theme of divine body, as I will illustrate a few pages further. In this way, all these adjectives might constitute the linguistic instrumentarium of a theologian expressing old apocalyptic ideas pertaining to the early Jewish-Christian mindset rather than the rhetorical artifices of a fourth- or fifth-century orator.

The Nature of Christ's Luminous Body

The initiatory process of revealing mysteries reaches its completion with the highest revelation, which is the light that fills the whole creation or the huge luminous body of Christ. A significant aspect of the nature of this light is that of being manifested as a body not of material, but of pneumatic or spiritual nature. With the idea of a humanlike form or body of God one encounters the Jewish theme, both scriptural and apocryphal, of the divine luminous form contemplated by the prophets and apocalyptic visionaries alike. Some of the most famous passages are Exodus 24:9–11, Ezekiel 1:26 (where on the throne sits a "figure [דמות/*dmwt*] with the appearance [מראה/*mr'h*] of a man [אדם/ *'dm*]"; cf. LXX: *homoiōma hōs eidos anthrōpou*), Daniel 7, or Philippians 2:6 ("in the form of God" [*en morphē theou*]). While there is no textual evidence, it is plausible that Pseudo-Hippolytus would have taken over this theme from a Jewish context, given the considerable Jewish presence in Asia Minor at the time, the author's Quartodeciman position, and his mention of a "secret" Hebrew tradition about creation.[32] At the same time, it is also plausible that he adapted the theme of God's form through the mediation of his Christian community where the theme was popular in the second century. The idea of the image or form of glory, or of the huge body of Christ, also appears, for example, in Matthew 17:2; Mark 9:2; Luke 9:29; 1 Corinthians 11:7; Philippians 2:6; 3:21; *2 Clement* 17.5; *Gospel of Philip* 57.30–58; and in Herakleon of Alexandria who, in his commentary to John 1:27—as Origen testifies in *Commentary on John* 6.39—reads: "The whole world is the shoe of Jesus."

Pseudo-Hippolytus speaks about a body that touches the heavens and makes the earth fast by its feet, while the huge hands embrace the winds

31. Nautin, *Homélies*, 43.
32. *IP* 17.4.

between the heaven and earth.[33] The metaphor of the "hand of God" is one of the most ancient Jewish anthropomorphic expressions for the Spirit of God, present, for example, in Exodus 15:16; 32:11; Deuteronomy 6:21; 7:8, 19; 9:26; Isaiah 25:10; and Ezekiel 37:1 where the hand of God is identified with the Spirit of God. It can be also found in 1 Peter 5:6. Actually, the Hebrew word ד' / *'d* denotes simultaneously "hand" and "power," the latter term being a well-known synonym for the Spirit (e.g., Mic. 3:8). The idea is present as well in Irenaeus of Lyon, for whom the Son and the Holy Spirit are the hands of God operating in the universe, and in Theophilus of Antioch, for whom the Holy Spirit is identical with the "Hand of God."[34]

At the same time, the luminous body in the Pseudo-Hippolytean text is identical with the celestial tree, the tree of paradise, the pillar of the universe, the Spirit that permeates all things, and the "ladder of Jacob, the way of angels, at the summit of which the Lord is truly established."[35] One should also observe that none of these realities is visible and sensible, but all are mystical and pneumatic. For Pseudo-Hippolytus, such titles as "divine" (*theios*), "pneumatic/spiritual" (*pneumatikos*), perfect (*teleios*), or "separated" (*aprositos*) refer to something completely different from the things of the universe, namely to the divine. Being separated, the effusions or emanations (*embolai*) of the Spirit/Christ remain unmixed (*akratos, amiges*) with the sensible things.[36] Although echoing the following pneumatological fragment from Philo, the Pseudo-Hippolytean pneumatology employs some different terminologies:

> But as it is, the spirit which is on him [Moses] is the wise [*to sophon*], the divine [*to theion*], the excellent spirit, susceptible of neither severance [*to atmēton*] nor division [*to adiaireton*], diffused in its fullness everywhere and through all things [*to pantē di' holōn ekpeplērōmenon*], the spirit which helps, but suffers no hurt, which though it be shared with others or added to others suffers no diminution [*elattoutai*] in understanding and knowledge and wisdom.[37]

It is noteworthy that among the expressions related to the huge body of Christ, scattered among different parts of the text, some regard the fiery constitution of his body. Passage 1.1–12 avers that the mighty (*megas*) Christ, immortal and immense (*polys*), sheds light brighter than that of the sun. At 55.11 the Johannine christological title "the light of the world" also receives the attribute of "mighty" (*to mega tou kosmou phōs*). Furthermore, comment-

---

33. *IP* 51. Cf. *IP* 63, for the hands of God.

34. E.g., Irenaeus, *AH* 4.20.1; and Theophilus, *To Autolycus* 5.

35. *IP* 51.

36. *IP* 45.7–9. Cf. 1 Tim. 6:16, where God is called φῶς ἀπρόσιτος. The same title also appears in Athenagoras's *Legatio* 16.3, along with πνεῦμα, δύναμις, and λόγος.

37. Philo, *Gig.* 6.27 (LCL, *Philo* 2:459).

ing on Exodus 12:8 ("They shall eat the lamb that same night; they shall eat it roasted over the fire") the author makes the following cryptic affirmation:

> This is the night on which the flesh is eaten, for the light of the world has set on the great body of Christ: *Take and eat; this is my body.*[38]

Since the liturgical or eucharistic context is noticeable here, the interpretation needs to be done from a liturgical perspective. My reading would be that Pseudo-Hippolytus refers to the Christian Eucharist, which is taken or received without the vision of Christ's glory; in translation, it is taken "in the night." This night does not refer to the incapacity of seeing the visible light, but to the incapacity of perceiving the invisible, mystical, or pneumatic glory.

The Eucharist is identified then with the "great body of Christ" on which the "light of the world" is set (*edy*). A series of analogies may provide a better understanding of these expressions:

The visible sun—parallels the *light of the world* (a comparison frequently used in the Christian literature; see *IP* 1.12), which is Christ.

The night—parallels the *mystery* of the visible elements of the Eucharist, which covers the divine light of Jesus' glorious body.

The earth—parallels the *bread of the Eucharist*, the visible realm, which veils the divine light.

One chapter further (*IP* 27.1–2), while commenting on Luke 12:49 ("I came to cast fire upon the earth"), he straightforwardly affirms that the "flesh is roasted with fire, for the spiritual or rational body of Christ is on fire" (*ta de krea opta pyri empyron gar logikon sōma tou Christou*).

This christological conception also implies a particular understanding of the incarnation. Pseudo-Hippolytus does not employ such verbs as *sarkoō*, *ensōmatoō*, or *enanthrōpeō*, but renders various aspects of the mystery of the incarnation through different vocabulary. He uses, for instance, *apostolē* (sending; *IP* 3.21) to underline the fact that the Father sent the Son into the world. A correlative term for "sending" is *epidēmia* (2.3; 7.6; 21.3; 43.2–3; 44.1; 47.10; 56.9)—"arriving," "coming" on (*epi*)—either on earth (43.2) or into the body (*sōma*; 47.10). Another noun—*anatolē* (dawn; 3.4; 17.14; 45.23)—renders the light of Christ that fills the universe (cf. Matt. 2:2; Luke 1:78). This dawn or Orient is spiritual (*pneumatikē*; 45.23) as well and therefore mystical, not visible. The huge light, according to the author, was set (*edy*), contracted (*systeilas*), collected (*synathroisas*), and compressed (*synagagōn*)[39] in

---

38. *IP* 26.1: Ἐν νυκτὶ δὲ τὰ κρέα ἐσθίεται.

39. For ἔδυ, see *IP* 26.1; for the other three attributes, see *IP* 45.10–11. The idea is not new in Christian context; cf. Phil. 2:6; *Odes Sol.* 7.3–6; *Acts Thom.* 15.80.

Christ's body, while the immenseness of his whole divinity (*to megethos pan tēs theotētos*) remained unchanged.

> He willingly confined himself to himself and collecting and, compressing in himself all the greatness of the divinity, came in the dimensions of his own choice in no way diminished or lessened in himself, nor inferior in glory [*ou meioumenos en heatō oude elattoumenos oude tē doxē dapanōmenos*].[40]

In order to discover the divine body of light veiled and enveloped by Christ's visible body, namely the visible elements of the Eucharist, Christians need to be initiated.

Conclusion

Coming back to Collins's definition, one might state that the homily displays (1) a large framework, which is the history of salvation, where (2) the paschal celebration inserts itself as a privileged opportunity of accessing the divine temple extended into the whole universe, and of seeing (3) the divine king in a mystical way. This transcendent reality is not especially placed in an upper realm, but present in a deeper, hidden *here*. (4) Participants are human initiands in a mystery rite, while (5) the homilist represents the initiated mystagogue divulging one by one the sacred mysteries. *In sanctum Pascha*, therefore, seems to reflect similar features with some of the most representative categories of apocalyptic literature; it is a revelation of the heavenly and divine king, of his throne, glory, and angelic choirs, but it is an apocalypse of a different nature, namely a mystery apocalypse.

The preceding discussion uncovers three elements: paschal celebration, apocalyptic language, and mystery language. The first two elements appear to be a common idea in first-century Christian writings.[41] The last element is slightly suggested in Melito, but clearly developed by Pseudo-Hippolytus in a mystery apocalypse. One can thus suppose that all these ideas were present within the intellectual atmosphere of the Christian communities in second- and third-century Asia Minor, and Pseudo-Hippolytus articulated

---

40. *IP* 45.10–13. Cf. Melito of Sardis, *Frg.* 14. For a more detailed analysis in the context of the second century, see Cantalamessa, *L'Omelia*, 187–273.

41. See, e.g., Massey Shepherd's research on the existence of a paschal liturgy in John's apocalypse: *The Paschal Liturgy and the Apocalypse* (London: Lutterworth, 1960). For the similar eschatological expectation of the glorious coming of the Messiah on the paschal night in Christian and rabbinic traditions, see Brian Daley, "Seeking to See Him at the Festival of Pascha: The Expectation of the Divine Glory in Early Rabbinic and Christian Paschal Materials," in *The Theophaneia School: Jewish Roots of Eastern Christian Mysticism*, ed. Andrei Orlov and Gregory Lurie, Scrinium 3 (St. Petersburg: Byzantinorossika, 2007), 30–48.

them in a more unitary way, adding as well the theme of Christ's divine body, which does not occur in Melito.

Asia Minor in the second to fourth centuries was consequently the place of a decisive synthesis of two traditions—apocalypse and mystery—a synthesis that would come to dominate the liturgical life of the church until today. Pseudo-Hippolytus's *IP* witnesses to the application of this synthesis in the paschal celebration or, putting it differently, to a development of the paschal language toward this mystery-apocalyptic vocabulary. In addition, the homily may put in a new light such writings as Philo's *Questions and Answers on Exodus* and Melito's *Peri Pascha*, writings that can be envisaged as the roots of this application. With time, important debates of the church such as the anthropomorphic quarrel eliminated anthropomorphic tendencies, while the christological and pneumatological debates, along with more Greek rhetoric, led to the intricate paschal homilies of the famous Cappadocians, Gregory of Nazianzus and Gregory of Nyssa.

Pseudo-Hippolytus's homily is consequently important as a pool of testimonies; it displays an affluent terminological and ideological treasury for the Christian theology of the second, third, or perhaps even the early fourth century. The synthesis of Jewish apocalyptic images and Greek mystery terminology definitely witnesses to a period of syncretism, as well as to a Christian community in search of the language to express, and give shape to, its own identity.

6

THE DIVINE FACE AND THE ANGELS OF THE FACE

Jewish Apocalyptic Themes in Early Christology and Pneumatology

BOGDAN G. BUCUR

The divine "Face" and the select group of angels conducting their liturgy before the divine throne are themes quite central to the apocalyptic literature of Second Temple Judaism.[1] Leaving aside the Mesopotamian roots

Several months after giving my paper at the First Pappas Conference, I discovered that some of its essential elements had been sketched out three decades earlier by Gilles Quispel ("Genius and Spirit," in *Essays on the Nag Hammadi Texts in Honour of Pahor Lahib*, ed. M. Krause [Leiden: Brill, 1975], 155–69). I take this opportunity to dedicate this essay to the memory of the recently departed master.

1. For a presentation of Jewish traditions centering on the vision of God's "Face" and "Glory," their Mesopotamian roots and later development from the Second Temple to later Rabbinic Judaism, see Friedrich Nötscher, *"Das Angesicht Gottes schauen" nach biblischer und babylonischer Auffassung* (1924; repr., Darmstadt: Wissenschaftliche Buchgesellschaft, 1969); C. L. Seow, "Face," and Jarl Fossum, "Glory," in *DDD*, 322–25, 348–52; Andrei Orlov, *The Enoch-Metatron Tradition*, TSAJ 107 (Tübingen: Mohr Siebeck, 2005); idem, "The Face as the Heavenly Counterpart of the Visionary in the Slavonic *Ladder of Jacob*," in *Of Scribes and Sages: Early Jewish Interpretation and Transmission of Scripture*, ed. C. A. Evans (London and New York: T&T Clark, 2004), 59–76. For "angels of the Face," see *Jub.* 2.2, 18; 15.27; 31.14; *T. Jud.* 25.2; *T. Levi* 3.5; *1 QH* 6.13.

of both courtly and visionary language, the scriptural roots of this imagery are to be found in such throne-theophanies as Exodus 33:18–20, Ezekiel 1:26, and Isaiah 6:1–5. Here "God's form remains hidden behind His light. The hidden *Kavod* (Glory) is revealed through this light, which serves as the luminous screen, 'the face' of this anthropomorphic extent . . . a radiant *façade* of His anthropomorphic 'form.'"[2]

The prominence of these themes in the apocalyptic literature of Second Temple Judaism was only amplified with the emergence of Christianity. In the following pages I shall discuss some of the ways in which early Christian writers—whether so-called Jewish Christians,[3] Valentinians, or members of the "great church," writing in Greek, Latin, or Syriac—used these fundamental concepts as building blocks in the construction of their doctrines of Christ and the Holy Spirit.

The Divine "Face" and the "Angels of the Face" in Clement of Alexandria[4]

Clement of Alexandria "Celestial Hierarchy"[5]

On the basis of a theological tradition inherited from primitive Jewish Christian circles, Clement furnishes, especially in his *Excerpta ex Theodoto* and *Eclogae propheticae*, a detailed description of the spiritual universe.[6]

2. Andrei Orlov, "Ex 33 on God's Face: A Lesson from the Enochic Tradition," *SBLSP* 39 (2000): 135.

3. Throughout this essay, the term "Jewish Christian" will be taken in the sense described by Jean Daniélou in his classic work *The Theology of Jewish Christianity* (London: Darton, Longman and Todd, 1964). As long as the narrative of an early and radical parting of the ways between "Christianity" and "Judaism" remains normative, despite its inability to explain a great deal of textual evidence from the first four centuries, the term "Jewish Christianity" remains useful as a description of "Christianity" itself. For more recent treatments of this problem, see the essays collected in *The Ways That Never Parted*, ed. A. H. Becker, and A. Y. Reed, TSAJ 95 (Tübingen: Mohr Siebeck, 2003); Daniel Boyarin, *Border Lines: The Partition of Judaeo-Christianity* (Philadelphia: University of Pennsylvania Press, 2004).

4. The Greek text is that of the GCS critical edition (*Clemens Alexandrinus*, ed. O. Stählin, L. Früchtel, and U. Treu, 3 vols., 4th ed. (Berlin: Akademie Verlag, 1985–). For the *Stromateis*, I am using the text available in the Ante-Nicene Fathers collection, with slight modifications (indicated as such); references to the *Stromateis* indicate book, chapter, and section. The passages from the *Excerpta ex Theodoto*, *Eclogae propheticae*, and the *Adumbrationes* are my own translations.

5. For an expanded version of this section, see Bogdan G. Bucur, "The Other Clement: Cosmic Hierarchy and Interiorized Apocalypticism," *VC* 60 (2006): 251–68.

6. Clement's strictly hierarchical universe goes back to earlier tradition. See in this respect Paul Collomp, "Une source de Clément d'Alexandrie et des Homélies Pseudo-Clémentines," *RevPhil* 37 (1913): 19–46; Wilhelm Bousset, *Jüdisch-christlicher Schulbetrieb in Alexandria und Rom: Literarische Untersuchungen zu Philo und Clemens von Alexandria, Justin und Irenäus* (Göttingen: Vandenhoeck & Ruprecht, 1915); Jean Daniélou, "Les traditions secrètes des Apôtres," *ErJb* 31 (1962): 199–215. Despite the pertinent critique of some of Bousset's conclusions (see Johannes Munck, *Untersuchungen*

This "celestial hierarchy"—if the anachronism is acceptable—features, in descending order, the Face, the seven angels "first created" (*prōtoktistoi*), the archangels, and finally the angels.[7]

For Clement, "the Face of God is the Son."[8] The first level of celestial entities contemplating the Face are the angels "first created" (*prōtoktistoi*). These *protoctists* are seven, but they are simultaneously characterized by unity and multiplicity. "Among the seven," Clement explains, "there has not been given more to the one and less to the other; . . . [they] have received perfection from the beginning, at the first [moment of their] coming into being, from God through the Son." Although distinct in number, the *protoctists* are equal, and have the same activity: "their liturgy," says Clement, "is common and undivided."[9] They mark the turning point, where divine unity passes into multiplicity, and conversely, the multiplicity of the world is reassembled into the unity of the Logos.

The *protoctists* fulfill multiple functions: in relation to Christ, they present the prayers ascending from below; on the other hand, they function as "high priests" with regard to the archangels, just as the archangels are "high priests" to the angels.[10] In their unceasing contemplation of the Face of God, they represent the model (*prokentēma*) of perfected souls. These *protoctists* are identified successively with the "seven eyes of the Lord" (Zech. 4:10; Rev. 5:6), the "angels of the little ones" (Matt. 18:10), the "thrones" (Col. 1:16).[11] Here we find a definite echo of the Jewish and Jewish-Christian traditions about the highest angelic company.[12]

über Klemens von Alexandria [Stuttgart: Kohlhammer, 1933], 127–204), the thesis of a Jewish and Jewish-Christian literary source behind Clement remains solidly established (see Georg Kretschmar, *Studien zur frühchristlichen Trinitätstheologie* [Tübingen: Mohr, 1956], 68n3).

7. The term "hierarchy" was coined centuries later by the anonymous Pseudo-Areopagite. Nevertheless, the multistoried cosmos of apocalyptic writings such as the *Ascension of Isaiah*, *2 Enoch*, or the *Epistula Apostolorum* can also be labeled "hierarchical." Moreover, there are some surprising similarities between the Clementinian and Dionysian "hierarchies" (see the brief note by Alexander Golitzin, in his *Et introibo ad altare Dei: The Mystagogy of Dionysius Areopagita, with Special Reference to Its Predecessors in the Eastern Christian Tradition*, AV 59 [Thessalonica: Patriarchal Institute of Patristic Studies, 1994], 265).

8. *Excerpta* 10.6; 12.1. It is certainly true that "the image of the Son as the Father's Face may have played a significant role in Valentinian theologies" (April DeConick, "Heavenly Temple Traditions and Valentinian Worship: A Case for First-Century Christology in the Second Century," in *The Jewish Roots of Christological Monotheism*, ed. C. C. Newman, J. R. Davila, and G. S. Lewis, JSJSup 63 [Leiden: Brill, 1999], 325). Nevertheless, the repeated occurrence of the same designation in Clement of Alexandria (*Paed.* 1.57; 1.124.4; *Strom.* 7.58) and Tertullian (*Adv. Prax.* 14) indicates that "Face" as a christological title was at least as popular in mainstream Christianity as it was in Valentinian tradition.

9. *Excerpta* 10.4; 11.4.

10. Ibid. 27.2; 10.6; 11.1.

11. *Strom.* 5.6.35; *Eclogae* 57.1; *Excerpta* 10.

12. For the group of seven angels, see Ezek. 9:2–3; Tob. 12:15; *1 En.* 20; 90.21; *Prayer of Joseph*. The notion of "first created" is important to the author of *Jubilees* (*Jub.* 2.2; 15.27). Among Christian texts, Revelation mentions seven spirits/angels before the divine throne (1:4; 3:1; 4:5; 5:6; 8:2), and

As I already mentioned, the divine "Face" is used as a christological designation. Quite naturally, then, Clement identifies the *prosōpon* of Matthew 18:10, the *charaktēr* of Hebrews 1:3, and the *eikōn* of Colossians 1:15 with the Son or Logos of God.[13]

The second element under discussion, the angels of the Face, occupies an area of confluence between Clement's angelology and pneumatology. The cosmological scheme described in *Stromateis* 5.6 or in the *Excerpta* features, in descending order, the Father, the Son, and the *protoctists*; it seems to reserve no place for the Holy Spirit. Such is not the case, however. Following an older study by Christian Oeyen, which retains its exceptional value even today, I submit that Clement of Alexandria is heir to an archaic *Engelpneumatologie*, for which the seven *protoctists* "are" the Holy Spirit.[14]

Clement's Theory of Prophetic Inspiration

Clement is aware of the two major functions traditionally ascribed to the Holy Spirit, namely the inspiration of Old Testament prophets and the indwelling of Christian believers.[15] However, he often ascribes the same functions to the Logos, even while maintaining some role for the Holy Spirit. He affirms, for instance, that the Logos "tunes" the world—the great cosmos, as well as the human microcosm—through (or by means of) the Holy Spirit, (*hagiō pneumati*; *Protr.* 1.5.3). "The Logos through the Spirit": this expression is given a precise explanation in Clement's account of prophecy.

According to *Eclogae* 51–52, prophecy occurs when the Logos moves the first rank of the *protoctists*, and this movement is transmitted from one level of the angelic hierarchy down to the next. The lowest angelic rank, and, by consequence, the one closest to the human world, will transmit the "movement" to the prophet.[16] Following the logic of the text, one could say

---

the *Shepherd of Hermas* knows of a group of seven consisting of the six "first created ones" (πρῶτοι κτισθέντες), who accompany the Son of God as their seventh (*Vis.* 3.4.1; *Sim.* 5.5.3). Among later Jewish writings, see *3 En.* 10.2–6 ("eight great princes"), *Pirkē de Rabbi Eliezer* (4.23).

13. *Strom.* 7.58.3–6; *Excerpta* 19.4.

14. Christian Oeyen, *Eine frühchristliche Engelpneumatologie bei Klemens von Alexandrien* (Bern: Internationalen Kirchlichen Zeitschrift, 1966). See also Bogdan G. Bucur, "Revisiting Christian Oeyen: 'The Other Clement' on Father, Son, and the Angelomorphic Spirit," *VC* 61 (2007): 381–413.

15. E.g., *Paed.* 2.1.8; 2.2.30; 2.12.126, 129. In *Excerpta* 24.2, Clement affirms the perfect identity between the Paraclete working (ἐνεργῶν) in the church and the Paraclete formerly active (ἐνεργήσαντι) in the prophets.

16. "*The heavens proclaim the glory of God* [Ps. 18:2 LXX]. By 'heavens' are designated in manifold ways both 'the heavens' pertaining to distance and cycle [= the sky], and the proximate operation [ἐνέργεια προσεχής] of the first-created angels, which pertains to covenant. For the covenants were wrought [ἐνηργήθησαν] by the visitation of angels, namely those upon Adam, Noah, Abraham, and Moses. For moved by the Lord, the first-created angels worked in [ἐνήργουν εἰς] the angels that are close to the prophets, as they are telling the 'glory of God,' [namely] the covenants. But the works accomplished by the angels on earth also came about for 'the glory of God,' through the first-created

that the prophet represents the highest level in the human hierarchy. A few centuries later, the Pseudo-Areopagite will assign this position to the bishop. Clement, instead, seems much closer on this issue to the *Shepherd of Hermas* (*Mand.* 11.9), for whom the point of contact between the inspiring angel and the community of believers is the prophet, or to the book of Revelation, where the prophet is *twice* described as "a fellow servant" with the angels (Rev. 19:10; 22:8–9).[17] I note, however, Clement's conviction, anticipatory of Pseudo-Dionysius, that "the grades . . . in Church, of bishop, presbyter and deacons, are imitations of the angelic glory."[18]

Through a sort of telescoping effect, the first mover—the Logos—is simultaneously far removed from the effect of prophecy and immediately present. This principle of "mediated immediacy" becomes evident when Clement says that Jude refers the action of a lower angel ("an angel near us") to a superior angelic entity, the archangel Michael;[19] similarly, "Moses calls on the power of the angel Michael through an angel near to himself and of the lowest degree (*vicinum sibi et infimum*)."[20] Ultimately, the action of inspiration must be referred to the original mover, the Logos, since Clement also applies the outlined theory of angelic mediation to the prophetic call of Samuel (1 Sam. 3), where the text repeatedly mentions the Lord or the voice of the Lord.[21]

In this light it becomes clear how Clement understands the traditional statements about the Logos speaking to the prophets *hagiō pneumati*, as in *Protreptikos* 1.5.3, quoted above: Christ is "casting light, 'at sundry times and diverse manners,' on those who believe . . . through the ministry of the *protoctists* [*dia tēs tōn prōtoktistōn diakonias*]" (*Strom.* 5.6.35), and the prophet experiences the presence and message of the Logos "channeled" as it were through the "energy" of the proximate angel.

---

angels. So, [the following] are called 'heavens': in a primary sense, the Lord; but then also the first-created [angels]; and with them also the holy persons [that lived] before the Law, as well as the patriarchs, and Moses and the prophets, and finally the apostles" (*Eclogae* 51–52).

17. The statements about the angel being "a fellow servant" with the prophet may serve, on the one hand, to correct any angelolatric tendencies; on the other hand, however, "John's purpose was . . . perhaps, to claim for his brothers a certain primacy in the affairs of churches" (Martin Kiddle, *The Revelation of St. John* [London: Hodder and Stoughton, 1963], 449).

18. *Strom.* 7.13.107.

19. "'When the archangel Michael, disputing with the devil, was arguing over the body of Moses.' This confirms the *Assumption of Moses*. 'Michael' here designates the one who argued with the devil through an angel close to us" (*Adumbrationes* in Jude 9).

20. *Adumbrationes* in 1 John 2:1. This principle of "mediated immediacy," by which Clement explains away biblical passages in which a higher angelic being (e.g., the archangel Michael) is said to interact with humans, instead of an angel of "lower" degree, is strikingly similar to how Ps.-Dionysius will explain why Isa. 6:1 affirms that Isaiah was "initiated" by a seraph (*Celestial Hierarchy* 13.1, 300B).

21. *Adumbrationes* in 1 John 2:1. The same idea occurs in the *Stromateis* in a more veiled manner. See my analysis of *Strom.* 6.3.34 in "Revisiting Oeyen," 401–2n74.

It is thereby made clear that the prophets conversed with Wisdom, and that there was in them the "Spirit of Christ," in the sense of "possession by Christ," and "subjection to Christ" (*secundum possessionem et subiectionem Christi*); for the Lord works through archangels and through angels that are close (*per . . . propinquos angelos*), who are called "the Spirit of Christ" (*qui Christi vocantur spiritus*). . . . He says, "Blessed are you, because there rests upon you that which is of his glory, and of God's honor and power, and who is His Spirit." This "his" is possessive, and designates the angelic spirit (*Hic possessivum est "eius" et angelicum spiritum significat*).[22]

Once again, the "telescopic" view of the hierarchy is presupposed, so as to convey the presence of Christ through (*per*, presumably rendering *dia)* the work of the lowest angelic level.[23] The Spirit of Christ is treated, in a way that could hardly be more explicit, as a designation for angelic beings: "archangels and kindred angels . . . are called *Spirit of Christ*";[24] "*his* Spirit" is "the *angelic* spirit." It is fitting to note at this point that Clement identifies the *protoctists* not only with various types of angels, but also with the "seven spirits resting on the rod that springs from the root of Jesse" in Isaiah 11:1–3, and "the heptad of the Spirit."[25] In other words, the seven *protoctists* also carry a definite pneumatological content.

Is there a tradition in early Christianity that is reworking Jewish apocalyptic traditions about the highest angelic company to speak about the Holy Spirit? The answer, I believe, is affirmative.

The Angels of the Face in Aphrahat the Persian Sage

Aphrahat's[26] *Demonstrations*, although written during the second quarter of the fourth century, are, by virtue of their noted "archaism" or "traditionalism," a unique treasure trove of older exegetical and doctrinal traditions. Indeed, unlike his younger contemporary Ephrem of Nisibe, Aphrahat can

22. *Adumbrationes* in 1 Pet. 2:3; *Adumbrationes* in 1 Pet. 4:14.

23. Oeyen (*Engelpneumatologie*, 27–28) and Wolf-Dieter Hauschild (*Gottes Geist und der Mensch: Studien zur frühchristlichen Pneumatologie* [München: Kaiser, 1972], 79) identify the "angeli propinqui" with the *protoctists*. This interpretation appears to miss half of Clement's intention: the prophetic inspiration is, indeed, worked out through the *protoctists*, who are "close" to the Son; yet the movement is further transmitted in the same way to the archangels, who are "close" to the *protoctists*, and the angels, who are "close" to the archangels. Finally, the lowest angelic rank is the last element in the chain of prophetic inspiration. This is, for Clement, the "spirit" that rests on the prophets.

24. *Spiritus Christi* could, in theory, be translated as a plural ("spirits of Christ"), but Clement is here expanding on 1 Pet. 4:14, τὸ τοῦ Θεοῦ πνεῦμα ἐφ᾽ ἡμᾶς ἀναπαύεται.

25. *Strom.* 5.6.35; *Paed.* 3.12.87.

26. For details on Aphrahat, see the introductory studies by Marie-Joseph Pierre in *Aphraate, "Les Exposés,"* SC 349 (Paris: Éditions du Cerf, 1988), 33–199; and Peter Bruns, in *Aphrahat: Unterweisungen*, Fontes christiani 5.1 (New York and Freiburg: Herder, 1991), 35–71.

be described as "entirely traditional, that is, he transmits the teaching that he received, lays out the *testimonia* pertaining to each topic, in order to convince or reassure a reader whose intelligence functions according to this logic of faith."[27] Most important for my argument is that "there is next to nothing in his writings to suggest that he had much of any contact at all with . . . the earlier writings of the Greek Church Fathers."[28]

The following quotes are drawn from Aphrahat's first and sixth *Demonstrations*:

> And whatever man there is that receives the Spirit from the water (of baptism) and grieves it, it departs from him until he dies, and returns according to its nature to Christ, and accuses that man of having grieved it. . . . This is the Spirit, my beloved, that the Prophets received, and thus also have we received. And it is not at every time found with those that receive it, but sometimes it returns to Him that sent it, and sometimes it goes to him that receives it. Hearken to that which our Lord said, *Despise not one of these little ones that believe on Me, for their angels in heaven do always behold the face of My Father.* This Spirit then goes frequently and stands before God and beholds His face, and whosoever injures the temple in which it dwells, it will accuse him before God.[29]

> And definitely did He show concerning this stone:—Lo! *on this stone will I open seven eyes* (Zech. 3:9). And what then are the seven eyes that were opened on the stone? Clearly the Spirit of God that abode on Christ with seven operations, as Isaiah the Prophet said, *The Spirit of God shall rest and dwell upon Him*, (a spirit) *of wisdom and understanding, of counsel and of courage, of knowledge and of the fear of the Lord* (Isa. 11:2–3). These were the seven eyes that were opened upon the Stone, and *these are the seven eyes of the Lord which look upon all the earth* (Zech. 4:10).[30]

Aphrahat argues here one of the axioms of his ascetic theory: the Holy Spirit departs from a sinful person, and goes to accuse that person before the throne of God. It is quite striking that the work of the Holy Spirit is presented in unmistakably angelic imagery (the Spirit "goes frequently," stands before the divine throne, and beholds the Face of God) and supported by recourse to Matthew 18:10. If the two passages from the *Demonstrations* are

27. Pierre, "Introduction," in *Aphraate*, 66. For the difference between Aphrahat and Ephrem on the issue of "traditionalism," see Robert Murray, "Some Rhetorical Patterns in Early Syriac Literature," in *A Tribute to Arthur Vööbus*, ed. R. H. Fischer (Chicago: The Lutheran School of Theology at Chicago, 1977), 110.

28. Alexander Golitzin, "The Place of the Presence of God: Aphrahat of Persia's Portrait of the Christian Holy Man," in *ΣΥΝΑΞΙΣ ΕΥΧΑΡΙΣΤΙΑΣ: Studies in Honor of Archimandrite Aimilianos of Simonos Petras, Mount Athos* (Athens: Indiktos, 2003), 401.

29. Aphrahat, *Dem.* 6.14–15. For the Syriac text, see J. Parisot, *Aphraatis Sapientis Persae Demonstrationes*, PS 1–2 (Paris, 1894, 1907). The English translation is that of J. Gwynn, in the Nicene and Post-Nicene Fathers series.

30. Aphrahat, *Dem.* 1.9.

combined—and it is certainly legitimate to do so, given the common theme (the Holy Spirit), and the formal structure (evidence from the Scriptures for the activity of the Spirit)—it becomes apparent that Aphrahat uses the same cluster of biblical verses that we encountered earlier in Clement: "the seven eyes of the Lord" (Zech. 3:9; 4:10); "the seven gifts of the Spirit" (Isa. 11:2–3); and the "angels of the face" (Matt. 18:10). I submit, therefore, that, just as in the case of Clement, we have here an echo of the tradition about the highest angelic company, combined with a definite pneumatological content.

Yet the use of Matthew 18:10 as a pneumatological proof text should not be taken as evidence that Aphrahat himself consciously and actively promoted an angelomorphic pneumatology. It should be noted that this is neither the only way in which Aphrahat interprets Matthew 18:10,[31] nor the only image he uses for the Holy Spirit.[32] Moreover, it is quite obvious, from the way he writes, that Aphrahat does not see himself as proposing anything new or unusual. He is most likely transmitting an older tradition.

It is certain, however, that no direct literary connection exists between Aphrahat and Clement of Alexandria.[33] Quispel was convinced that the tradition behind both Clement and Aphrahat goes back to Jewish Christian missionaries "who brought the new religion to Mesopotamia," and were also "the founding fathers of the church in Alexandria."[34] If one were to speculate about a common source for the cluster of biblical passages and pneumatological exegesis of Matthew 18:10 that occurs in both authors, a possible candidate would be the source(s) used by Pseudo-Clement *Homily* 17.[35]

The Seven Spirits in the Book of Revelation[36]

In between Matthew 18:10 and Clement's "elders," perhaps at the same time as the Jewish apocalyptic *2 Enoch*, one finds the seven "angels of the face" in the canonical Apocalypse of John. Four times in this text (Rev. 1:4; 3:1;

---

31. See the simple quote in *Dem.* 2.20.

32. Aphrahat also views the Spirit as God's "spouse," as "mother" of the Son and of all creation, as "medicine," and as the "breath" that constitutes the divine image imparted to Adam. For more details, see Winfrid Cramer, *Der Geist Gottes und des Menschen in frühsyricher Theologie*, MBT 46 (Münster: Aschendorff, 1979), 59–85.

33. Among Greek patristic writings available in Syriac translation, "Hermas, Justin, Irenaeus, Clement of Alexandria and Origen are conspicuous by their absence" (Sebastian P. Brock, "The Syriac Background to the World of Theodore of Tarsus," in his volume *From Ephrem to Romanos* (Aldershot, Brookfield, Singapore, and Sydney: Ashgate Variorum, 1999), 37.

34. Quispel, "Genius and Spirit," 160, 164.

35. For details, see Bogdan G. Bucur, "Matt. 18:10 in Early Christology and Pneumatology: A Contribution to the Study of Matthean *Wirkungsgeschichte*," *NovT* 49 (2007): 209–31.

36. For an expanded version of this section, see Bogdan G. Bucur, "Hierarchy, Prophecy, and the Angelomorphic Spirit: A Contribution to the Study of the Book of Revelation's *Wirkungsgeschichte*," *Journal of Biblical Literature* 127 (2008): 173–94.

4:5; 5:6), one reads about "the seven spirits of the Lord." The first of these references, which occurs in the opening blessing (Rev. 1:4–5), is notoriously difficult to understand.

Revelation 1:4 invokes "grace and peace" from God upon the recipient. The blessing seems to be given by three coordinated entities: God, the seven spirits, and Jesus Christ. Since the source of "grace and peace" can only be divine, the three must, in some way, stand for the divinity (cf. "the grace of the Lord Jesus Christ, the love of God, and the communion of the Holy Spirit" in 2 Cor. 13:13).[37] This is why it seems most likely that the mention of the "seven spirits" corresponds to the expected reference to the Holy Spirit. In other words, the author's expression "seven spirits" would designate what the early church more often referred to as the Holy Spirit.

On the other hand, the angelic traits of the seven spirits are quite obvious. Revelation brings together "the seven spirits before his throne" (Rev. 1:4) and "the seven angels before the throne" (Rev. 8:2) in Revelation 3:1, where we read of the one who "has" (*ho echōn*) "the seven spirits and the seven stars." "The seven stars" are explicitly said to represent "the seven angels" (Rev. 1:20). This well-defined group of seven—*the* seven stars, *the* seven angels, *the* seven spirits—is placed before the divine throne, clearly subordinated to Christ (seven eyes of the Lord, seven stars in his hand, seven horns of the Lamb), ever contemplating the divine Face, offering up the prayers mounting from below and passing on the illumination that descends from above. These are standard elements in the depiction of angelic intercession, contemplation, and service. The simplest solution is to admit that we have here symbolic references to the same reality, which the author conveyed by recourse to the language of angelic worship before the divine throne.

Patristic exegesis—as well as modern-day commentators—has outlined the following exegetical alternatives: (1) Revelation connects the seven spirits/eyes/lamps of the Lord (Zech. 3:9; 4:10) with the rest/tabernacling of the seven spiritual gifts (Isa. 11:2; Prov. 8:12–16); (2) Revelation connects the seven spirits/eyes/lamps of the Lord (Zech. 3:9; 4:10) with the seven angels of the presence (Tob. 12:15; *1 En.* 90.20–21).[38] The exegetical impasse is evident. Patristic authors from the fifth century onward are overcautious, given the potentially dangerous character of the passage, and tend to appeal to the well-established tradition of combining Isaiah 11:1 and Zechariah

37. See also the list of passages illustrating Paul's "soteriological trinitarianism" in Gordon Fee, "Christology and Pneumatology in Romans 8:9–11 and Elsewhere: Some Reflections on Paul as a Trinitarian," in *Jesus of Nazareth: Lord and Christ: Essays in the Historical Jesus and New Testament Christology*, ed. M. Turner and J. B. Green (Grand Rapids: Eerdmans, 1994), 329–30.

38. The first position is held by the vast majority of scholars, patristic and modern. The second is defended by Joseph Michl, *Die Engelvorstellungen in der Apokalypse des hl. Johannes* (Munich: Max Hueber, 1937), and David E. Aune, *Revelation 1–5*, WBC 52 (Dallas: Word Books, 1997), 33–35.

3:9.[39] Modern exegetes tend to juxtapose the two solutions, rarely daring to eliminate either possibility.[40]

I suggest that both solutions (equating the seven *protoctists* either with the seven gifts of the Spirit, or with seven supreme angels) are partially correct, and can be fused by appealing to a new descriptive category: "angelomorphic pneumatology."

Angelic or Angelomorphic Pneumatology?

The following question imposes itself: is "holy spirit" a designation for the seven "angels of the Face," or is "seven *protoctists*" a designation for the Holy Spirit? Briefly put: "angel" pneumatology or "pneuma" angelology?[41]

The angelic traits are undeniable. On the one hand, the seven spirits of Revelation and Clement's seven *protoctists* are depicted before the divine throne, contemplating the divine Face, offering up the prayers mounting from below and passing on the illumination that descends from above. On the other hand, the pneumatological content is also quite clear: the *protoctists* appear in instances where one would expect the Holy Spirit, they carry out functions usually asociated with the Holy Spirit, and exegesis fuses the passages suggestive of angelic beings (Zech. 3:9; 4:10; Matt. 18:10) with those implicitly identifying the seven as a "gift" of the Holy Spirit.

These observations amount to a distinction between "angelic" and "angelomorphic" pneumatology. Here I follow the convention of using the term "angelomorphic" to denote the angelic *characteristics* of an individual or community, whereas the latter's *identity* cannot be reduced to that of an angel or angels. Thus God or humans can be depicted in an "angelomorphic"

39. I rely on the fragments from patristic commentaries provided by Henry B. Swete, *The Apocalypse of St. John: The Greek Text with Introduction, Notes, and Indices* (Grand Rapids: Eerdmans, 1909), 5–6, and Michl, *Engelvorstellungen*, 113–34. For the combination of Isa. 11:1 and Zech. 3:9, see Karl Schlütz, *Isaias 11:2 (Die sieben Gaben des Heiligen Geistes) in den ersten vier christlichen Jahrhunderten* (Münster: Aschendorff, 1932), 34.

40. Aune (*Revelation 1–5*, 34), e.g., is exhaustive in his references but very reserved in advocating the identification between the seven spirits and the principal angels.

41. Far from being a Christian invention, the use of πνεῦμα to designate an angelic being is widespread in pre- and post-exilic Judaism, witnessed by the LXX and authors of the diaspora, and also prominent at Qumran. See John Levinson, "The Angelic Spirit in Early Judaism," *SBLSP* 34 (1995): 464–93; idem, "The Prophetic Spirit as an Angel according to Philo," *HTR* 88 (1995): 189–207; idem, *The Spirit in First Century Judaism*, AGJU 29 (Leiden, New York, and Cologne: Brill, 1997); and Arthur E. Sekki, *The Meaning of Ruach at Qumran*, SBLDS 110 (Atlanta: Scholars Press, 1989), 145–71. In the Old Testament, the *locus classicus* is Isa. 63:9–10, where the angel of the Lord is referred to as "holy spirit"; in the New Testament, aside from the designation of *evil* angels as (impure) "spirits," the equivalence of "spirit" and "angel" is implicit in Heb. 12:9 ("Father of spirits"), and Acts 8:26, 29, 39, where Philip's guide is successively described as "angel of the Lord," "spirit," and "spirit of the Lord."

manner.[42] The virtue of this definition is that it signals the use of angelic *characteristics* in descriptions of God or humans, while not necessarily implying that the latter are angels *stricto sensu*.[43] In other words, the seven spirits of Revelation, or Clement's *protoctists*, or even "the angels of little ones" (according to the reading of Matt. 18:10 echoed by both Clement and Aphrahat) *are* the sevenfold Spirit in archaic "angelomorphic" language.

Conclusion

In this chapter, I have discussed the ways in which the apocalyptic themes of the divine Face and the angels before the Face, inherited from Second Temple Judaism, were appropriated in early Christianity. I have limited myself to passages in the only canonical apocalypse, the book of Revelation, a Syriac writer, Aphrahat, characteristically inclined to preserve archaic traditions of Scripture exegesis and theology, and certain writings by Clement in which the Alexandrian master echoes the doctrines and practices of earlier Christian teachers.

These texts and writers illustrate a larger phenomenon in early Christianity: the apocalyptic themes of the divine Face and the angels of the Face, which were part of the matrix of Christian thought, are taken over and used in an effort to account for the Christian faith in Father, Son, and Holy Spirit. The resulting Christology, and its correlative angelomorphic pneumatology, were both perfectly acceptable in the early centuries.

Face Christology never became a major player in classic definitions of faith. Like "Name" Christology, "Wisdom" Christology, or "Glory" Christology, once crucial categories in the age of Jewish Christianity, this concept went out of fashion, giving way to a more precise vocabulary shaped by the christological controversies of the third and fourth centuries. Angelomorphic pneumatology, however, and the associated exegesis of Matthew 18:10 illustrated by Clement and Aphrahat, became problematic with the advent of the Arian and Pneumatomachian confrontations, and were eventually discarded.[44]

In a larger religio-historical perspective, the use of apocalyptic themes such as the divine Face and the angels of the Face as building blocks for an emerging Christian doctrine of Christ and the Holy Spirit illustrates a larger phenomenon, namely the indebtedness of pre-Nicene theology (and, by reaction, also of later Christian thought) to the categories inherited from Jewish apocalyptic literature.

42. Crispin H. T. Fletcher-Louis, *Luke-Acts: Angels, Christology, and Soteriology*, WUNT 2.94 (Tübingen: Mohr Siebeck, 1997), 14–15.

43. Cf. Daniélou, *Jewish Christianity*, 118.

44. For the polemical counter-exegesis of Matt. 18:10 in the Cappadocians, see Bucur, "Matt. 18:10."

7

HIPPOLYTUS AND CYRIL OF JERUSALEM ON THE ANTICHRIST

When Did an Antichrist Theology First Emerge in Early Christian Baptismal Catechesis?

J. A. CERRATO

A cursory survey of the Antichrist literature of the early Christian world demonstrates that several genres were employed in the textualization and dissemination of this concept. A primary one, familiar to biblical and patristic scholars, is apocalypse. A second is the tractate, or treatise (*tractatus*), as exemplified in Irenaeus's multivolume *Adversus haereses*. A third is biblical commentary, such as Hippolytus's *Commentary on Daniel* or, much later, Oecumenius's *Commentary on the Apocalypse*. The Christian homily and letter were also used, as in the case of Augustine. These genres have all received varying degrees of attention in recent years.[1]

But another genre (if we may call it that) was also employed, perhaps one not quite so clearly noticed. This was a particular form of baptismal catechetical instruction, the baptismal catechetical homily (i.e., the sermon

---

1. See especially Bernard McGinn, *Antichrist* (San Franciso: Harper, 1994), and Gregory C. Jenks, *The Origins and Early Development of the Antichrist Myth*, BZNW 59 (New York: de Gruyter, 1991).

or lecture delivered to those about to receive or having recently received baptism). A principal example is Cyril of Jerusalem's *Catecheses*, including his *Procatechesis* and perhaps the *Mystagogical Catecheses* (if we accept, as many scholars do, Cyril's authorship). The Cyrillian *catecheses* proper were composed, delivered, and recorded in mid-fourth-century Jerusalem.

The Greek text of Cyril's work is proof positive that the Antichrist theology was, at least by the fourth century, part of the baptismal training of early Christians. Somewhere in the course of its development the doctrine was incorporated into baptismal instruction and constituted a substantial feature of it, certainly in Jerusalem. Cyril's *Lecture* 15 is dedicated largely, although not exclusively, to an elaboration of the Antichrist teaching, given under the broader christological-eschatological heading "he will come in glory to judge the living and the dead, and his kingdom will have no end," a piece of the Apostles' Creed, which served as Cyril's guideline in his lectures.

So, under this particular eschatological portion of the creed, Cyril imports a great deal of extra-creedal language on the rise of an evil world-ruler that will deceive the Jewish people and the nations, ravaging the church and signaling the parousia of Christ.

It is sensible to suppose that the setting of his lectures, Jerusalem itself, demanded some statement of such a doctrine. It is not difficult to imagine how pious pilgrims, arriving from across the empire in the holy city, brought with them a diversity of notions of apocalyptic expectation, some highlighting the role of Jerusalem in the end times.

The laity of Cyril's communities, whom he was catechizing, would have found it necessary to live out their faith in an atmosphere of such speculation. They needed rudimentary preparation allowing them to understand the church tradition, not only on the parousia of Christ, as the creed stated, but also on the precursor Antichrist, and on the role of Jerusalem, especially its ancient temple site.

Cyril's assessment of the needs of his laity goes even deeper. In the *Procatechesis* he explicitly states that the purpose of his catechism is the "arming" of his auditors for defense against encroachments from opponents in the heresies, Judaism, paganism, and, as only a Palestinian bishop could say, the Samaritans. With reference to what these various groups would have to say to neophytes about the Christian doctrine of Antichrist we can only guess. Yet it is clear that Cyril saw himself as preparing those about to be baptized to understand misunderstandings of apocalyptic evil.

We can rightfully ask, when did the Antichrist theology of the early church make its way into Christian catechesis? Was Cyril a pioneer in his approach to teaching the parousia portion of the baptismal creed by adding material on the Antichrist, or are there prior hints about the beginning of this inclusion?

The aim of this brief study is to suggest that in the text of Hippolytus titled *On the Antichrist* (or *On Christ and Antichrist*), produced about a century and a half before Cyril, we have a window into just such a beginning.

The Greek treatise of Hippolytus cannot, like the work of Cyril, be classified as a series of catechetical lectures, but it does exhibit evidence of design for a baptismal catechetical setting. Generally speaking, it is a compendium of biblical texts, several quoted at length, accompanied by introductory and interlaced commentary on those texts, sent from one teacher to another for the purpose of instruction. Hence it can be viewed as biblical commentary. But specifically, the introductory statements of the author support the supposition that it had been composed to provide teaching on the figure of the Antichrist for someone in charge of training others, most likely a catechist or catechists.

The author Hippolytus is a self-acknowledged expert in the field of Christian apocalyptic interpretation and describes himself as such. Another teacher, probably a bishop, by the name of Theophilus has written to him for help on the Antichrist doctrine. He has sent headings, or topic-heads, to Hippolytus outlining what he wishes him to treat. This is clear from Hippolytus's mention of the prior communication in the first sentence, as well as his listing of the inquiry headings later in the text. This is sufficient to establish that the Hippolytean work was not a treatise written for a general readership, but was the response of one instructor to another. In all likelihood, as I have suggested elsewhere, both were bishops.[2]

But there is evidence of an even more specific purpose. In the introductory section Hippolytus explicitly warns that the teaching he is about to impart should not be allowed to fall into the hands of the *apistoi* (generally translatable as "unbelievers"). He goes on to quote 1 Timothy 6:20–21 and 2 Timothy 2:1–2. Around these he says of his own treatise:

> But do not give these words to faithless and blasphemous babblers,[3] for this is no ordinary danger. Rather impart them to pious and believing persons who wish to live a "holy and just" (1 Thess. 2:10) life with fear. For not without cause the blessed apostle[4] urges Timothy, writing: "O Timothy, guard what has been given to your care, turning away from profane, empty talk and the conflicts of knowledge falsely so-called, which some profess. They have wandered concerning the faith" (1 Tim. 6:20–21). And again he writes: "You then, my

---

2. J. A. Cerrato, *Hippolytus between East and West: The Commentaries and the Provenance of the Corpus*, OTM (Oxford: Oxford University Press, 2002), 147–52.

3. Literally "tongues," taken here as a sarcastic synecdoche for speaking human beings.

4. Saint Paul the Apostle, the first century missionary, writer, and martyr, whom Hippolytus takes to be the author of the New Testament epistles bearing his name. He immediately cites two passages from the Pastoral Epistles, in order to focus on false *gnosis* and reiterate the need to guard the tradition. Hippolytus's application of these texts to the situation of Theophilus is especially germane, given the growth of the gnostic movements in his day (the end of the second century, or the outset of the third).

child, be strong in the grace that is in Christ Jesus and what you heard from me through many witnesses, these things entrust to faithful persons, who will also be able to teach others" (2 Tim. 2:1–2). If then the blessed apostle handed down these things with a sense of godly fear—things that were not well known—foreseeing by the Spirit that "the faith does not belong to all" (2 Thess. 3:2), how much more should we ourselves be in danger, if we were to give over, carelessly and thoughtlessly, the words of God to impious and unworthy men?

Here I believe we are looking into a mind-set focused astutely on the *disciplina arcani*,[5] the intentional reservation and sense of secrecy surrounding early Christian baptismal teachings. In these statements Hippolytus reflects that anxiety characteristic of baptismal instructors in the first centuries of the Christian era.

Such a concern is evident in other early sources, especially in Cyril. In the *Catecheses*, Cyril warns in several loci against sharing the teachings he is unfolding with the unenlisted, even with catechumens, that is, with those in the first stages of baptismal catechesis. In a "note to the reader" attached to the end of the *Procatechesis* he is particularly explicit. He says:

> You may give these catechetical lectures to *photizomenoi*, in preparation for baptism, to read, and to believers who have already received the sacrament of the font. Do not give them, under any circumstances, to catechumens or any other persons not actually Christian, as you shall answer to the Lord. And, as in the sight of the Lord, you shall transcribe this note before any copy that you make of the lectures.[6]

Hippolytus also, in the middle of his treatise, turns aside a second time to warn his readers:

> Beloved, we impart these things to you with fear and yet readily because of the love of Christ that surpasses all. For if the blessed prophets who preceded us did not choose to proclaim these things openly and boldly, although they knew them, lest they disquiet the souls of men, but recounted them mystically in parables and dark sayings, speaking thus, "Here is the mind that has wisdom" (Rev. 17:9), how much greater risk will we run in venturing to declare openly the things spoken by them in obscure terms.[7]

---

5. For the general background on this early Christian practice, see esp. Vincenzo Recchia, "Disciplina Arcani," in *EECh* 1:242; and P. Vacandard, "Arcane," in *Dictionnaire d'Histoire et de géographie ecclésiastiques*, ed. Alfred Baudrillart, Albert de Meyer, and Roger Aubert (Paris: Letouzey et Ané, 1912–), 3:1497–1513.

6. English translation of William Telfer, *Cyril of Jerusalem and Nemesius of Emesa*, LCC 4 (Philadelphia: Westminster, 1955), 76–77.

7. Hippolytus, *Antichrist* 29.

This fear factor in the Hippolytean Antichrist compendium points to a practice, or perhaps better, to the beginnings of a practice at the outset of the third century, similar to Cyril's in the fourth. The task of the recipient is to be twofold: (1) to refute heresies out of a proper understanding of apocalyptic eschatology, and (2) to guard the biblical texts provided, as well as their commentary.

The crucial questions that remain are: What is the evidence that the catechesis Hippolytus is urging ("impart them to pious and believing persons") is actually baptismal, that is, related directly to the baptismal catechumenate of his generation? Was there not a general catechesis carried on apart from preparation for baptism?

The second question first: certainly there was a general catechesis. But what I would like to suggest, at the very least, regarding the first question, is that the provision of such texts and commentary to a bishop, or even to a teacher of other teachers, assumes that the texts could be used for baptismal instruction. Although the terms "catechesis" and "baptism" do not appear in the Hippolytean treatise, the supposition of its use in formal, textual instruction is clearly present. And a subset of this in the early third century was the baptismal catechetical process, by then coming under the umbrella of a *disciplina arcani*.

It is this combination of factors gleaned from the text that suggests a catechetical context, that is, specifically baptismal preparation. It was mainly in the educational process leading to and from baptism that Christian anxieties developed to the point of requiring a secret course. When compared with similar language in later instructors, such as Cyril, Ambrose, and Theodore, the Hippolytean Antichrist treatise makes sense as a baptismal catechetical document. It was composed in the age when the *disciplina arcani* was coming into its own and when the primary external threats to the Christian communities engaged in baptismal catechesis were the gnosticisms.

To reiterate, then, the following combination of data can be adduced to show Hippolytus's purpose as baptismal catechesis:

1. The Antichrist treatise of Hippolytus was written as a response to the request of a church leader named Theophilus, probably a bishop who supervised catechism in his community. This accounts in part for why Theophilus needs to know more about the Antichrist doctrine in the first place. Hippolytus, in his introduction, assumes him to be such by asking him first to use the information in the treatise to combat the teachings of heretics and second to pass on its doctrine to "the faithful" only, not to those who would misuse it. This is the context of baptismal catechesis.

2. In the preface of the treatise Hippolytus warns against giving the teachings to the *apistoi*. While this term can mean "unbelievers" generally, it

is also known to signify the unbaptized in later catechetical literature. This is the language of baptismal catechesis.

3. In the same passage of the preface, Hippolytus cites the Pastoral Epistles where they warn the missioner Timothy to guard the received traditions, particularly keeping them from those who profess *gnosis* (falsely so-called), and where they instruct him to hand on the teachings to "faithful persons, who will also be able to teach others." This is the language of catechesis.

4. Later, toward the middle of the work, Hippolytus again warns against the open publication of the doctrines he is handing on to Theophilus. This reflects the caution of the *disciplina arcani*.

In conclusion, perhaps the most persuasive element in the text is the fear itself. Where else in early Christian literature do we see the Christian sense of anxiety about openness of instruction other than in the baptismal catechumenate? In this one treatise Hippolytus is eminently cautious about the Antichrist doctrine. He will not be so again in the remainder of his corpus. Even the Daniel Commentary, so rich in its exegesis of the Antichrist theology, contains little by the way of warnings against openness. Irenaeus before him was not cautious either.[8] This treatise, then, seems to have been geared specifically for use among those who were being prepared to become Christians in the most guarded of ways.

---

8. Irenaeus discusses the Antichrist most thoroughly, and apparently without reservation, in his *Adversus haereses* 5.

8

EXPECTATIONS OF THE END IN EARLY SYRIAC CHRISTIANITY

UTE POSSEKEL

Apocalypses and apocalyptic images are widespread in the Greek and Latin patristic literature, as the contributions to this volume illustrate.[1] In this essay I shall ask whether these apocalyptic traditions played a similarly prominent role for the earliest Syriac-speaking Christians. Early Syriac Christianity was diverse, and one site of multiple early Christianities was the city of Edessa in Mesopotamia, later to become one of the great centers of Syriac Christian theology and spirituality. By the late second century various Christian groups existed here side by side: Gnostics, Marcionites, Bardaisanites, and the so-called Palutians, predecessors of the later nor-

This chapter originally appeared in *Hugoye: Journal of Syriac Studies* 11, no. 1 (2008) and is published here with permission. For a full, annotated version, please consult the online publication of this essay at http://syrcom.cua.edu/Hugoye/Vol11No1/HV11N1Possekel.html.

1. On the subject of apocalyptic literature in early Christianity, see, e.g., Brian E. Daley, "Apocalypticism in Early Christian Theology," in *The Encyclopedia of Apocalypticism*, ed. Bernard McGinn (New York: Continuum, 1998), 2:3–47 (with further literature). On the subject of patristic eschatology more generally, see Brian E. Daley, *The Hope of the Early Church: A Handbook of Patristic Eschatology* (Cambridge: Cambridge University Press, 1991).

mative church.[2] Of the earliest Edessan Christian communities, it was the group around Bardaisan (d. 222) that has left the most extensive—although still rather fragmentary—written record. I shall first ask how Bardaisan and his community envisioned the end, and then interpret their eschatological expectations within the social context of the early Bardaisanite community. In addition, two further bodies of early Syriac Christian literature shall be examined here with regard to their imagination of the end, namely the *Odes of Solomon* and the *Acts of Thomas*, composed most likely in the second and early third centuries, respectively. Both the *Odes* and the *Acts of Thomas* originated in approximately the same era in which Bardaisan flourished, but they cannot easily be associated with a particular locality, so that it becomes much more difficult to interpret them within their social contexts. How did these early Syriac Christians envision the end? What expectations did they hold concerning the Last Judgment and the world to come? Did they employ apocalyptic imagery to describe the end? And if not, why not? We shall begin this survey with Bardaisan, the theologian from Edessa.

Bardaisan

While the *Odes* and the *Acts of Thomas* are of unknown provenance, it is quite certain that Bardaisan flourished in the city of Edessa in northern Mesopotamia, for not only is he named after the river Daisan that flows through the city, but an eyewitness account of his activity at the king's court has come down to us from the pen of Julius Africanus.[3] Bardaisan's thought is preserved in fragments of his own writings, in refutations by later opponents, and in the *Book of the Laws of the Countries*—the only contiguous text from Bardaisan's community that has come down to us—compiled by a disciple in the early third century.[4] Although Bardaisan's later followers came to be regarded as heretical on account of their inability to adapt to the emerging doctrinal consensus, Bardaisan in his time was regarded as a champion of

2. The Marcionite presence in Syriac-speaking regions is addressed by David Bundy, "Marcion and the Marcionites in Early Syriac Apologetics," *Mus* 101 (1988): 21–32. In the fourth century, Ephrem still much polemicized against Marcionite Christians in his *Prose Refutations*, in Charles W. Mitchell, Anthony A. Bevan, and Francis C. Burkitt, eds., *S. Ephraim's Prose Refutations of Mani, Marcion, and Bardaisan*, 2 vols. (London: Williams and Norgate, 1912–21), hereafter *PR*.

3. Sextus Julius Africanus, *Cesti* I, 20.39–53, in *Les "Cestes" de Julius Africanus*, ed. Jean-René Vieillefond (Paris: Didier, 1970), 185.

4. Han J. W. Drijvers, ed., *The Book of the Laws of Countries: Dialogue on Fate of Bardaiṣan of Edessa* (Assen: Van Gorcum, 1965; repr., Piscataway, NJ: Gorgias, 2007), hereafter *BLC*, cited from Drijvers's edition by page and line number; translations are mine.

The most important witness for Bardaisan's theology, besides the *BLC*, is Ephrem, who repeatedly refers to Bardaisan's ideas and occasionally quotes short fragments of Bardaisan's writings in his *Prose Refutations* (see n. 2 of this chapter) and his *Hymns against Heresies* (hereafter *CH*), ed. Edmund Beck, CSCO 169–70, Syr. 76–77 (Louvain: Peeters, 1957).

orthodoxy[5] and made significant contributions to theological discourse among Syriac-speaking Christians.[6] Bardaisan, a philosopher, former astrologer, and adult convert to Christianity, formulated his theology in the culturally and religiously diverse Edessan milieu.[7]

Scholars of apocalyptic literature, such as Hultgård in his work on Persian apocalypticism, have stressed that there is a coherence between an author's theology of the end of the world and his theology of its beginning, his cosmogony.[8] A similar coherence should be observable between an author's theology of the end of an individual and his theology of human nature, his anthropology. This connection is clearly evident in Bardaisan. Just as Bardaisan's cosmogony informed his cosmic eschatology, so did his anthropology form the basis of his individual eschatology. It is the latter, his individual eschatology, to which I shall turn first.

The Individual Resurrection

Bardaisan upheld the Christian teaching of the resurrection of the individual, yet he believed that only the human soul, not the body, would rise from death. In my previous research I have shown that Bardaisan's belief about the resurrection of the soul alone is rooted in his anthropology, which was principally intended to refute fatalism.[9] To summarize the argument briefly, Bardaisan held that human beings, created by God, are charged to follow the divine commandments,[10] and as beings endowed with free will they are capable of choosing the good and right behavior. Indeed, acting rightly is natural to humankind, Bardaisan argued, for when a person acts rightly, feelings of joy and gladness arise, whereas evil deeds result in feelings of anger and shame[11]—an interesting precursor to the Ignatian "discernment of spirits"! Yet many challenged Bardaisan's doctrine of free will, arguing instead that human behavior is conditioned by fate. Bardaisan therefore needed to formulate an anthropology that on the one hand maintained human freedom, and on the other hand could explain the misfortunes of life that

5. Eusebius praises Bardaisan's defense of Christian doctrine in *Ecclesiastical History* 4.30.1, in *Eusebius, Werke II*, ed. Eduard Schwartz and Theodor Mommsen, GCS 6 (Berlin: Akademie Verlag, 1999), 392.19–20.

6. In particular, Bardaisan's arguments against fatalism had a *Nachleben* in the Syriac Christian communities. Ephrem draws on them in *CH* 4.15.

7. On Edessa in late antiquity, see the classic study by Judah B. Segal, *Edessa "The Blessed City"* (Oxford: Oxford University Press, 1970).

8. Anders Hultgård, "Persian Apocalypticism," in *The Encyclopedia of Apocalypticism*, vol. 1, *The Origins of Apocalypticism in Judaism and Christianity*, ed. John J. Collins (New York: Continuum, 1998), 39–83, esp. 44.

9. Ute Possekel, "Bardaisan of Edessa on the Resurrection: Early Syriac Eschatology in Its Religious-Historical Context," *OrChr* 88 (2004): 1–28.

10. *BLC* 14.24–16.4.

11. *BLC* 18.5–7, 21–24; 20.2–9.

inevitably befall some people, but are generally undesired, such as illness, poverty, or breakdown in human relationships.[12] Bardaisan's anthropological solution was to concede that the body—but only the body—may be subject to disturbing planetary influences, which are understood to be the cause of life's uncontrollable misfortunes.[13] Human freedom, however, is not subject to fate, and in order to uphold this position, Bardaisan had to posit that free will, the ability to fulfill the divine commandments, must be independent of one's bodily constitution.[14] Consequently he located human identity in the mind or soul—the seat of free will—drawing on Greek philosophy rather than on the biblical notion of a human being as a psychosomatic unity. Bardaisan regarded the human body as only a secondary constituent of human nature, which "even without the sin of Adam would turn to its dust."[15] Out of this anthropology, which locates personhood in the human soul, arose his conviction that only the soul would rise at the resurrection.

Bardaisan substantiated his view of the resurrection of the soul by means of exegetical arguments. Unfortunately, these are only very partially preserved in Ephrem's later refutation of Bardaisan, which exists only in the form of a palimpsest. The exegetical fragments that were thus preserved address the fall of humankind, words spoken by Jesus, and the story of Christ's descent into Sheol.

With regard to the fall, Bardaisan noted that according to the Genesis account the consequence of Adam's sin would be death (Gen. 2:17). Yet it was not Adam, but Abel killed by Cain who was the first to die, and hence Bardaisan concluded that the death that would be the recompense of sin (Rom. 6:23) must be the death not of the body, but of the soul.[16] Among Jesus' words recorded in the Gospel, Bardaisan found confirmation of his resurrection theology in the text of John 8:51, in which Jesus promises: "Everyone who keeps my word will not taste death forever."[17] Bardaisan observed that, despite this promise of immortality, Jesus' followers had physically died. Therefore, Jesus must have used the word "death" to refer to the death of the soul. Third, Bardaisan pointed to the story of Christ's descent to Sheol to support his belief that only the soul will be resurrected. Had the consequence of Adam's sin been death of the body, he reasoned, Christ ought to have brought back from Sheol the bodies, which evidently was not the case.

---

12. He gives divorce or estranged children as examples for the latter. *BLC* 30.4–24; 34.17–21.

13. *BLC* 30.3–38.7.

14. He emphasizes that neither physical strength, nor social status, nor professional skill are required to obey the Golden Rule, to follow the commandments, and to avoid stealing, lying, adultery, or hate (*BLC* 16.4–18.5). Doing good is possible and it is easy, and thus each person is able to "live according to his own (free) will, and to do everything that he is able to do, if he wishes it, or if he does not wish, not to do it. And he may justify himself or become guilty" (*BLC* 12.13–15).

15. Ephrem, *PR* 2:143.1–4 (no. 1).

16. Ephrem, *PR* 2:151.11–152.2 (nos. 32–34); *PR* 2:153.20–154.2 (nos. 40–41).

17. Ephrem, *PR* 2:164.20–22 (no. 80) and 2:165.10–12 (no. 83).

Bardaisan wondered: "Our Lord, who was raised, why did he not raise all their bodies, so that as their destruction was by Adam, so their resurrection should be by our Lord?"[18]

Bardaisan's individual eschatology was thus shaped by two major conceptions. The first was an understanding of human nature that locates personhood exclusively in the soul, an anthropology that he formulated with the apologetic purpose of rejecting the astrologers' claim that planetary constellations determine human actions, a position that he himself had formerly embraced.[19] The second major component of Bardaisan's individual eschatology was a salvation-historical approach: the consequence of Adam's sin was death—understood as death of the soul, the essential part of human nature; death was overcome by Christ, whose teachings enabled the soul, hitherto condemned to Sheol, to rise up and pass over into the kingdom.[20]

Bardaisan's Cosmogony

Bardaisan's general eschatology, as has been mentioned above, is rooted in his cosmogony. For Bardaisan, the cosmos is the work of God the creator, but he does not consider this a creation from nothing. The concept of a *creatio ex nihilo* was just emerging as normative Christian doctrine in his time, and Bardaisan was not alone in assuming the existence of primordial matter.[21] Bardaisan assumed the preexistence of several elements, which possessed some kind of power.[22] Out of these God fashioned the world. The elements now occur in a mixture, not in their originally pure state, yet they retain some of their primeval power. In particular, the heavenly bodies retain some of this power—which for Bardaisan constitutes fate—but at the same time, they are subject to the laws imposed by God the creator.

It should be emphasized that this cosmogony is not a dualistic creation myth as can be found among some Gnostic groups or in the Iranian apocalyptic tradition.[23] To be sure, Bardaisan acknowledges the existence of evil,

---

18. Ephrem, *PR* 2:162.32–39 (no. 74). The *Diatessaron*, which presumably was available to Bardaisan, in its earliest versions did not include the canonical text of Matt. 27:52; cf. William L. Petersen, *Tatian's Diatessaron: Its Creation, Dissemination, Significance, and History in Scholarship* (Leiden: Brill, 1994), 404–14.

19. *BLC* 26.19–22.

20. Ephrem, *PR* 2:164.41–165.8 (no. 82), cf. nos. 81, 83.

21. Gerhard May, *Creatio ex nihilo: The Doctrine of 'Creation out of Nothing' in Early Christian Thought*, trans. A. S. Worrall (Edinburgh: T&T Clark, 1994). Justin refers to a creation out of unformed matter, ἐξ ἀμόρφου ὕλης—*1 Apol.* 10.2 (*Iustini Martyris Apologiae pro Christianis*, ed. Miroslav Marcovich, PTS 38 [Berlin: de Gruyter, 1994]); cf. *1 Apol.* 59.

22. *BLC* 14.13–18; 62.9–13.

23. Gnostic texts often regard the created world as negative, as work of the demiurge. An overview of gnostic apocalyptic texts is given by Francis T. Fallon, "The Gnostic Apocalypses," *Semeia* 14 (1979): 123–58. On Zoroastrian apocalypticism, see, e.g., Hultgård, "Persian Apocalypticism," 39–83.

which is the work of the enemy.[24] Evil occurs when a person does not act rightly, does not follow his or her natural inclination to do good, or is perturbed or unwell in his or her nature.[25] In Bardaisan's thought, however, evil clearly is not a cosmic force, battling with the good God on the level of equals. Indeed, throughout the *Book of the Laws of the Countries*, Bardaisan strongly emphasizes the goodness and oneness of God the creator, thereby taking an explicitly anti-Marcionite position, as has been argued by Han Drijvers.[26] The anti-Marcionite orientation of Bardaisan's theology is of significance for his eschatology, and I will come back to it below.

The Last Judgment

Repeatedly Bardaisan in the *Book of the Laws of the Countries* refers to the end of the world and to the judgment to be held on the last day.[27] History, then, is regarded neither as infinite—although Bardaisan postulates the preexistence of elements—nor as cyclic; rather, it is conceived as having a beginning and an end in time. On the last day, judgment will be made of all based on whether they used their free will, a gift from God, to act according to the divine commandments.[28] Bardaisan stated: "And it is given to (a human being) that he should live according to his own (free) will, and to do everything that he is able to do, if he wishes it, or if he does not wish, not to do it. And he may justify himself or become guilty."[29] This emphasis on the freedom of the human will and its ability to perform good deeds worthy of eternal life, although rejected by the Protestant Reformers in the sixteenth century, was shared by many other early theologians who, like Bardaisan, wished to refute the fatalism so widespread in late antique society. It is not a harmful native horoscope nor the influence of maleficent stars that leads people to sin, they maintained, but a person's free will. Justin Martyr, for instance, argued that "punishments and good rewards are given according to the quality of each man's actions. If this were not so, but all things happened in accordance with destiny, nothing at all would be left up to us. . . . And if the human race does not have the power by free choice to avoid what is shameful and to choose what is right, then there is no responsibility for actions of any kind."[30]

24. *BLC* 14.22–24; 18.22–23.

25. *BLC* 18.20–24.

26. Han J. W. Drijvers, *Bardaisan of Edessa* (Assen: Van Gorcum, 1966), 75f., 82f., and passim; idem, "Bardaisan's Doctrine of Free Will, the Pseudo-Clementines, and Marcionism in Syria," in *Liberté chrétienne et libre arbitre. Textes de l'enseignement de troisième cycle des facultés romandes de théologie*, ed. Guy Bedouelle and Olivier Fatio (Fribourg: Éditions Universitaires, 1994), 13–30.

27. *BLC* 14.10–11, 16–18.

28. Bardaisan does not develop a doctrine of atonement. By following Christ's commandments, one can obtain justification and salvation.

29. *BLC* 12.12–15.

30. Justin Martyr, *1 Apol.* 43, in Marcovich, *Iustini Martyris*, 92.5–11; trans. Cyril Richardson, *The Early Christian Fathers* (New York: Macmillan, 1970), 269.

Whereas Bardaisan's understanding of a Last Judgment of people, based on their deeds, was within the mainstream of early Christianity, another aspect of his eschatology was not. According to the theologian from Edessa, not only human beings but also some elements of the cosmos will be subjected to judgment. Although he continually emphasized God's sovereignty over all creation, he conceded that the elements and heavenly bodies did not lose all of their power due to the mixture of creation. To be sure, whatever power they still have is granted to them by God, but on account of this remaining freedom they, too, will be judged, as Bardaisan explained to his somewhat puzzled disciples.

> But know that those things [ṣebwatha, i.e., heavenly bodies], which I said were subject to the commandments, are not completely deprived of all freedom. And therefore they will all be subjected to judgment on the Last Day.[31]

One of his followers immediately wondered how those that lie under determination could be judged, to which the teacher responded:

> Not for that in which they are fixed . . . will the elements ['estokse][32] be judged, but for that over which they have power. For the heavenly bodies ['itye] were not deprived of their own nature when they were created, but the energy of their essence was lessened through the conjunction of one with the other, and they were subjected to the power of their creator. For that in which they are subjected they are not judged, but for that which is their own.[33]

The Last Judgment is thus envisioned as a cosmic event that involves all creatures with any kind of freedom.

A New World

As was noted earlier, Bardaisan understood world history as a process with a clear beginning and an end. This universe was ordered in a particular way by divine decree, and this order was to remain "until the course is completed and measure and number have been fulfilled, as it was ordained beforehand by him who commanded what the course should be and the completion of all creatures and the constitution of all elements ('itye) and natures (kyane)."[34] World history is thus aimed at perfection, at completion of its prescribed course. It does not depend on human action, but will occur according to the divine decree.[35] At the end of time, according to Bardaisan, there will be a new

---

31. BLC 14.8–11.
32. The word 'estokse here refers to the heavenly bodies.
33. BLC 14.13–18.
34. BLC 38.3–7.
35. Thereby Bardaisan's thought is more in conformity with the biblical tradition that we do not know the day and hour of the parousia (cf. Mark 13:32) than with the gnostic concept that human beings by their actions can contribute to the destruction of the cosmos.

world, which will be perfect and free of strife. Again, as in his cosmogony, the metaphor of mixture plays a prominent role in his description of the world to come. The new world will be founded upon a different intermixture, in which even the remaining freedom of the elements, which potentially could cause harm, will disappear. There will be, Bardaisan explained, different planetary conjunctions that will no longer produce strife and misery. In the world to come, there will be no place for inequalities, misfortunes, and even foolishness. Bardaisan described this peacefulness and perfection of the eschatological aeon in the conclusion of the *Book of the Laws of the Countries*: "In the constitution of that new world all evil impulses will have ceased and all rebellions will have ended, and the foolish will be convinced and (every) want filled, and there will be tranquility and peace through the gift of the Lord of all natures."[36]

Bardaisan's expectations of the end thus form a coherent system of thought that is based on his anthropology and his cosmogony. Perhaps somewhat surprisingly, we find little detail in the remaining literature of the Bardaisanites about the end of time. There are no references to a cosmic battle, to natural catastrophes, or other images typical of apocalyptic literature. Yet we may assume that Bardaisan, a bilingual man and an educated philosopher, was familiar with some form of apocalypticism, for it was widely spread across linguistic and cultural boundaries, as is evident from Jewish apocalypses, Greco-Roman oracles, and the Sibyllines.[37] The thirteenth chapter of Mark presents a picture of the end times, and this text was at least partially included in the *Diatessaron* and thus available to Syriac-speaking Christians. In the second century, a number of apocalyptic writings were produced by Christian communities in the Roman Empire, and several early Christian writings, even if they were not apocalypses per se, made use of apocalyptic ideas and images.[38] Moreover, other systems of thought prevalent in Mesopotamia, such as Zoroastrianism, have produced elaborate apocalyptic treatises.[39] Why then, we are led to wonder, did Bardaisan refrain from employing apocalyptic imagery?

36. *BLC* 62.15–18.

37. Jewish apocalypses from the first two centuries of the common era include *4 Ezra* and *2 Baruch*. A survey of Jewish apocalyptic literature is given by John J. Collins, *The Apocalyptic Imagination: An Introduction to Jewish Apocalyptic Literature*, 2nd ed. (Grand Rapids: Eerdmans, 1998).

38. The *Apocalypse of Peter* and the *Ascension of Isaiah* are both productions of Christian communities in the second century. They are translated with introductions by C. Detlef and G. Müller, in *New Testament Apocrypha*, ed. Edgar Hennecke and Wilhelm Schneemelcher, vol. 2 (Louisville: Westminster John Knox, 1992), 603–38. Apocalyptic themes also occur in the visions of Perpetua and in the writings of Tertullian and Hippolytus. Cf. Daley, "Apocalypticism in Early Christian Theology," 10–13.

39. See for example Hultgård, "Persian Apocalypticism," with further literature.

Theological and Social Context

Bardaisan's omission of apocalyptic language was, I think, a deliberate decision on his part. Two reasons—one theological, the other sociological—suggest that this was the case. First, apocalyptic images often present the rising up of evil powers that challenge the existing order, and are finally overcome by God, who establishes a new creation.[40] This type of imagery is dualistic in spirit, even if it does not picture the opposition of two nearly equal divine figures, such as Ahura Mazda and Angra Mainyu in Persian apocalypticism. Bardaisan, it seems, would have avoided at all costs the introduction of such imagery into his theological discourse, for one of his major goals was to refute the Marcionite claim of the existence of two gods. His anti-Marcionite stance, which earned him praise from Eusebius, would have been reason enough to avoid images of a final cosmic battle.

The second reason why Bardaisan might not have been inclined to employ apocalyptic elements in his theology pertains to the social setting, the *Sitz im Leben*, of apocalypticism. Scholars such as Isenberg, Hanson, Nickelsburg, and Frankfurter have studied the cultural setting of Jewish and Christian apocalyptic movements and have suggested that apocalyptic literature often arises in communities that feel marginalized by the social or religious majority. Nickelsburg sums up Hanson's approach:

> Ancient apocalyptic movements have a common *social setting* in which a group experiences alienation due to the disintegration of the life-sustaining socio-religious structures and their supporting myths. Institutional structures may be physically destroyed or a community may find itself excluded from the dominant society and its symbolic universe.[41]

What then, was the situation in Edessa in the time of Bardaisan? Our reconstruction of the Edessan milieu in the early third century must rely largely on material remains, reports by Roman historians, and later literary sources, for indigenous literary productions from this era are lacking (apart from the remains of Bardaisan's corpus). Nonetheless, careful interpretation of the sources gives much insight into Edessan culture in late antiquity. By the end of the second century, Edessa had been an independent kingdom for more than three hundred years,[42] striving to balance alliances with the adjacent

40. Perpetua, for instance, has a vision of fighting with and winning over an Egyptian man, who is later identified as Satan, in *Passion de Perpétue et de Félicité, suivi des Actes*, ed. Jacqueline Amat, SC 417 (Paris: Éditions du Cerf, 1996).

41. George W. E. Nickelsburg, "Social Aspects of Palestinian Jewish Apocalypticism," in *Apocalypticism in the Mediterranean World and the Near East* (Tübingen: Mohr Siebeck, 1989), 645. See also David Frankfurter, "Early Christian Apocalypticism: Literature and Social World," in Collins, *Encyclopedia of Apocalypticism*, 1:415–53, esp. 432–34.

42. Since 132 BCE; on Edessa's early history, cf. Segal, *Edessa*, 1–15.

"superpowers," Rome and Parthia. During Bardaisan's adulthood in the 190s, King Abgar VIII attempted to regain independence, but Septimius Severus (193–211) occupied the region and established Osrhoene as a Roman province in 195. Thereafter, the Edessan king adopted an attitude of greater loyalty to Rome. He took a Roman name, sent his sons as political hostages to Rome, offered the emperor the services of his world-renowned archers, and personally visited the imperial capital.[43] Edessa became a Roman *colonia* under Caracalla (in 213), but the kingship continued, at least nominally, until the 240s. This political turmoil, and the disastrous flooding of the city in 201, however, does not appear to have destabilized Edessan society, for many of Edessa's physical remains, in particular the astonishing mosaics, date from the early third century and indicate a flourishing city, self-confident in its artistic and cultural expressions. Moreover, Bardaisan's group was far from being a marginalized community in search of a symbolic universe. Bardaisan was a nobleman, prominent at the Edessan court, a superb archer (as Julius Africanus relates), a musician, and a capable disputant. He believed that he defended Christian orthodoxy in his apologies against Marcionites, Gnostics, and astrologers. His group stood at the center of early third-century Syriac Christianity, not at its margins. Bardaisan's expectations of the end, the judgment, resurrection, and the world to come are shaped by his cosmogony and his anthropology. The remaining fragments of his writings do not suggest use of apocalyptic imagery, which can at least be partially explained by his opposition to Marcionite dualism and by his prominent position in early Edessan society.

The *Odes of Solomon*

Let us now turn to a very different literary production of the early Syriac church, the *Odes of Solomon*, and the eschatological expectations expressed therein.[44] Unlike Bardaisan's writings, this poetic collection cannot easily be associated with a particular Christian community. Although efforts have been made to locate the *Odes* in the early Edessan church, no specific internal or external evidence supports this hypothesis.

Space here does not permit an exhaustive treatment of the eschatology of the *Odes*, and it must suffice to highlight some of the major themes.[45] The odist repeatedly expresses the joy that he feels for being united to the Lord,

---

43. Herodian, *History* 3.9.2; cf. 6.7.8, ed. C. R. Whittaker, *Herodian*, 2 vols., LCL (London: Heinemann, 1969–70). Abgar's visit to Rome, where he was lavishly received, is noted by Cassius Dio, *History* 80.16.2 (*Dio's Roman History*, ed. Earnest Cary, LCL [London: Heinemann, 1914]).

44. *The Odes of Solomon*, ed. and trans. in *OTP* 2:725–71; hereafter *Odes Sol.*

45. A brief discussion of the *Odes'* eschatology can be found in Daley, *Hope of the Early Church*, 15–16; a more detailed examination is David E. Aune, *The Cultic Setting of Realized Eschatology in Early Christianity* (Leiden: Brill, 1972), 166–94.

whom he has "put on."[46] He extols the eternal life that he has acquired by joining himself to the Immortal One.[47] He knows himself already crowned with the Lord,[48] a crown that brings salvation.[49] The Lord has already given him eternal rest.[50] The Lord has rescued the poet from the "depth of Sheol" and has freed him from the "mouth of death."[51] The odist is certain that he will not die,[52] for he is now already justified.[53] Already he has received salvation by leaving the way of error.[54] It is thus a realized eschatology that we find expressed in the *Odes of Solomon*, one in which apocalyptic imagery, such as details of the coming judgment, or frightful descriptions of the disasters and crises that will accompany the end times, are lacking. There is no apocalyptic tour of hell, but there is a visionary glimpse of paradise with its abundance of vegetation, a land irrigated by the river of gladness.[55] Themes of joy, comfort, and trust dominate in these poems.

As dissimilar as the eschatology of the *Odes* is from that of Bardaisan, neither one takes recourse to apocalyptic imagery. Moreover, they both employ the same striking image of crossing over into eternal life. Bardaisan teaches that the souls, previously unable to enter paradise—for they were hindered "at the crossing-place" (*ma 'barta*) by the sin of Adam—are now able, on account of Christ's work, to cross at the crossing-place and to enter the bridal chamber of light.[56] Ephrem summarizes Bardaisan's doctrine:

> "And the life," [Bardaisan said,] "that our Lord brought in is that he taught truth and ascended, and allowed them to pass over into the kingdom."[57]

While for Bardaisan it is only the soul that crosses over into eternity, for the author of the *Odes* the entire human person is able, through faith in the Lord, to cross the "raging rivers." The odist's poetic language does not spell out that this crossing takes the person from this world into the next, but the eschatological subtext of the hymn seems evident.

46. *Odes Sol.* 3.1; 7.4; 15.1; 23.1; 28.2.
47. Ibid. 3.8; 28.7.
48. Ibid. 1.1; 17.1.
49. Ibid. 1.5.
50. Ibid. 11.12; 38.3.
51. Ibid. 29.4.
52. Ibid. 5.14.
53. Ibid. 17.2.
54. Ibid. 15.6; cf. 15.8.
55. Ibid. 11.16–24. In his *Hymns on Paradise*, Ephrem gives a visionary description of paradise. Sebastian Brock, trans., *St. Ephrem the Syrian: Hymns on Paradise* (Crestwood, NY: St Vladimir's Seminary Press, 1990).
56. Ephrem, *PR* 2:164.33–165.19 (nos. 81–83).
57. Ephrem, *PR* 2:164.41–165.8 (no. 82); cf. *PR* 2:165.9–19 (no. 83).

But those who cross them [i.e., the raging rivers] in faith
Shall not be disturbed.

And those who walk on them faultlessly
Shall not be shaken.

Because the sign on them is the Lord,
And the sign is the way for those who cross in the name of the Lord.

Therefore, put on the name of the most high and know him,
And you shall cross without danger,
Because rivers shall be obedient to you.

The Lord has bridged them by his word,
And he walked and crossed them on foot.

And his footsteps stand firm upon the waters and were not destroyed,
But they are like a beam of wood that is constructed on truth. . . .

And the way has been appointed for those who cross over after him,
And for those who adhere to the path of his faith
And who adore his name.[58]

Imagery drawn from the Hebrew Bible and the New Testament is woven into this hymn to emphasize that faith in the Lord will enable the Christian to cross at the "crossing-places" (*ma'barta*).[59] This may refer to overcoming obstacles and being persistent in the faith in this world, but the hymn also has an eschatological dimension.

The *Acts of Thomas*

The *Acts of Thomas*, written in the form of an ancient novel, relate the missionary journeys of the apostle Thomas to India.[60] The *Acts* as a whole do not constitute apocalyptic literature,[61] but one element commonly found in apocalyptic treatises does occur in the *Acts of Thomas*, namely a visionary description of the punishments of hell. While the details of the account in the sixth act differ in the Greek and Syriac versions, the main story line is the

58. *Odes Sol.* 39.5–10, 13 (adapted).
59. Ibid. 39.2.
60. The *Acts of Thomas* (hereafter *Acts Thom.*) are preserved in both a Syriac and a Greek version. English translation of the Greek text by Han J. W. Drijvers in *The New Testament Apocrypha*, ed. Edgar Hennecke and Wilhelm Schneemelcher, 2 vols. (Louisville: Westminster John Knox, 1991–92), 2:339–411.
61. On the question of genre, see Collins, *Apocalyptic Imagination*, 2–21.

same. Upon hearing Thomas preach a life of *enkrateia*, a young man strove to persuade the woman he loved to become his "consort in chastity and pure conduct."[62] Much to his chagrin, the woman refused, and lest she have intercourse with others, the young man killed her. His crime was revealed when his hands withered up as he received the Eucharist. He related the events to Thomas the apostle, who first healed the man's disease and then accompanied him, followed by a great throng of people, to the woman's house. Upon being raised to life, she told of her extraordinary tour of hell and the punishments there to be suffered for various kinds of sins. The woman then converted, as did the multitude of onlookers.[63]

The dead woman's vision of hell functions in the *Acts of Thomas* to instill in the audience fear of future punishments in order to enforce a certain moral code. Similar stories are preserved from other eras of Christian history, and they usually serve the same parenetic function. Bede, for example, relates that the medieval Englishman Drythelm chose to enter the monastic life after his tour of heaven and hell during a near-death experience revealed to him what was at stake.[64] The inclusion of this apocalyptic episode in the *Acts of Thomas* shows that Syriac Christians were aware of apocalyptic literature and occasionally availed themselves of such themes,[65] but it remains a somewhat isolated example among the literature of the early Syriac church.

Conclusion

Among the earliest Syriac-speaking Christians, the traditions surrounding both Bardaisan and the *Odes of Solomon* show a marked absence of apocalyptic imagery, a somewhat surprising result considering the relative popularity of apocalyptic themes in the second century. For Bardaisan, the Edessan theologian about whose social setting we are fairly well informed, I have suggested specific theological and sociological reasons as to why he might have avoided apocalyptic symbols. Such considerations are impossible for the *Odes*, for their provenance remains unknown. The attribution of this collection of poems to Solomon, however, indicates that the author was more attuned to the themes of wisdom literature than to those of apocalyptic writing. The *Acts of Thomas* include a visionary description of the punishments of hell, one element often found in apocalyptic literature, but as a whole they do not belong to the genre of apocalyptic. The *Acts* thereby support our claim that

---

62. *Acts Thom.* 51, in Hennecke and Schneemelcher, *New Testament Apocrypha*, 2:361.

63. *Acts Thom.* 51–59, in Hennecke and Schneemelcher, *New Testament Apocrypha*, 2:360–64.

64. Bede, *Ecclesiastical History* 5.12, in *Bede's Ecclesiastical History of the English People*, ed. Bertram Colgrave and Roger A. B. Mynors, OMT (Oxford: Clarendon, 1992).

65. The vision of hell in the *Acts Thom.* bears certain resemblances to *Apocalypse of Peter* 7–12.

early Syriac Christians were familiar with apocalyptic themes, but generally chose not to convey their theologies through the medium of apocalyptic.

Even in a social context of severe distress, some early Syriac Christians counseled wisdom and patience, rather than casting their situation into an apocalyptic framework. Mara bar Serapion, a prisoner of war en route to his exile in a foreign land, writes to his son with parental advice and admonition.[66] In his letter, probably composed in the third century, he counsels his son to pursue wisdom and to meditate upon learning. The youth is to avoid the vanities of life, for worldly riches, fame, and beauty all may vanish. Wisdom, however, cannot so easily be taken away, and can become for him a father and mother.

Why are apocalyptic images so sparse in the early Syriac Christian literature? It is difficult to make generalizations, and any number of cultural factors might explain why the early Syriac Christians felt more drawn to wisdom traditions, as was the anonymous author of the *Odes of Solomon*, or to a philosophical approach, as were Bardaisan and Mara bar Serapion. It may be attributable to their residence in a region constantly embattled by two empires, neither of which could easily be associated with good or evil. Such a geopolitical situation may have made them less inclined to develop a symbolic universe in which good and evil forces engage in a cosmic battle. It was only in later centuries that the Syriac-speaking communities availed themselves of apocalyptic imagery, when more clearly defined hostile empires threatened their very existence. In the fourth century, Aphrahat, the Persian sage, drew on the apocalyptic passages in the book of Daniel and intimated the eventual demise of the Sassanian Empire.[67] And in the seventh century, in the context of the Arab conquests of the Near East, anonymous Syriac authors ascribed full-fledged apocalyptic sermons to the authority of two ancient and venerated figures, Ephrem and Methodius.[68]

66. Mara bar Serapion, *Letter to His Son*, ed. William Cureton, *Spicilegium syriacum* (London: Rivingtons, 1855).

67. Aphrahat, *Demonstration 5*, ed. Jean Parisot, PS 1.1 (Paris: Didot, 1894).

68. In the seventh century, apocalyptic treatises by Ps.-Ephrem and Ps.-Methodius refer to the Arab invasion in prophecies that are *vaticinia ex eventu*. Ps.-Ephrem's *Sermon on the End of the World* is available, with German translation, in *Des heiligen Ephraem des Syrers Sermones III*, ed. Edmund Beck, CSCO 320–21, Syr. 138–39 (Louvain, 1970), 60–71 (text) and 79–94 (trans.). Ps.-Methodius: *Die syrische Apokalypse des Pseudo-Methodius*, ed. Gerrit J. Reinink, CSCO 540–41, Syr. 220–21 (Louvain: Peeters, 1993).

9

Heavenly Mysteries

Themes from Apocalyptic Literature
in the Macarian Homilies and Selected Other
Fourth-Century Ascetical Writers

Hieromonk Alexander Golitzin

Introductory Remarks: Apocalyptic Literature, Ascents to Heaven, and the Monks

In Job 28 there is a hymn in praise of divine wisdom. After dwelling briefly on things that are earthly, and so knowable, a pair of questions and a statement of inaccessibility begin the section on wisdom itself: "But where shall wisdom be found? And where is the place of understanding? Mortals do not know the way to it, and it is not found in the land of the living." God alone, we are told a few verses later, "understands the way to it, and he knows its place" (Job 28:12–13, 23). This is surely the point, or one of them, that is underscored in the closing chapters of the book, when God appears to Job out of the whirlwind in order to pose to him the series of questions that begins with, "Where were you when I laid the foundation of the earth?" (Job 38:4), and continues in like manner with the limits of the sea, the home of light, the storehouses of wind and snow and rain, and so on—in short, all the mysteries of the created order, its origins and its maintenance. Understood throughout, of course, is that Job was not there at the beginning and does not, and cannot, know the mysteries that depend on it. According to the author of Job, these are beyond mortal ken, and the proper human response to them as well as to the mysteries of God's judgments, as chapter 28 concludes and as Job acknowledges—repenting "in dust and ashes" (Job 42:6) at book's end—is the reverent fear of God and avoidance of evil.

My purposes here do not include an analysis of this most profound and moving book, but I begin with it for a couple of reasons. The first is that sometime before 200 BCE, perhaps not long after the composition of Job itself (depending on the notoriously difficult matter of dating it), works begin to appear in the ambient of Second Temple Judaism that effectively lay claim to the very thing that the book of Job had reserved for God alone, that is, that there are some rare individuals who do know "the place of wisdom" and its mysteries. The opening thirty-six chapters of *1 Enoch*, dating from at least a couple of generations before the book of Daniel, describe the patriarch's ascent to heaven, which includes his coming before the divine throne itself; this is followed by an extended tour of the heavenly precincts, which feature more or less exactly the mysteries that God's questioning of Job had assumed were not in the latter's power to know: the place of the heavenly luminaries, the storehouses of wind and rain, and the divine judgments regarding the righteous and the reprobate. Indeed, according to *1 Enoch*, the patriarch, a human being, is even given a quasi-divine (or at least archangelic) assignment: he is required by God, "the Great Glory" on the throne, to act as a mediator of the divine judgment to the fallen angels of Genesis 6, the sons of heaven who had had intercourse with the daughters of men. This note, that of the visionary being accorded a heavenly status (implicit here in the very fact of Enoch's mission to the fallen "Watchers"), will appear with greater and more explicit force in a number of later apocalypses. We arrive thus at a definition of the genre of apocalypse offered by Christopher Rowland: "To speak of apocalyptic [literature] . . . is to concentrate on the direct revelation of heavenly mysteries." It also includes, to quote again from Rowland a little later on in his book *The Open Heaven*, the belief "that certain individuals have been given to understand the mysteries of God, man, and the universe."[1] I do not therefore

---

1. Christopher Rowland, *The Open Heaven: A Study of Apocalyptic in Judaism and Early Christianity* (London: SPCK, 1982), 14, 76. The bibliography on apocalyptic literature just for recent scholarship is vast, let alone the addition of the work I understand as relevant to it on early Jewish mysticism, the Qumran Scrolls, Christian origins, and early Christian ascetical and monastic literature. Let it suffice here to list some of the studies most important for my own work: John J. Collins, *The Apocalyptic Imagination: An Introduction to Jewish Apocalyptic Literature*, 2nd ed. (Grand Rapids: Eerdmans, 1998); Jarl E. Fossum, *The Name of God and the Angel of the Lord: Samaritan and Jewish Concepts of Intermediation and the Origin of Gnosticism*, WUNT 36 (Tübingen: Mohr Siebeck, 1985); idem, *The Image of the Invisible God: Essays on the Influence of Jewish Mysticism on Early Christology*, NTOA 30 (Göttingen: Vandenhoeck & Ruprecht, 1995); Gershom Scholem, *Major Trends in Jewish Mysticism* (Jerusalem: Schocken, 1941); idem, *Jewish Gnosticism, Merkabah Mysticism, and Talmudic Tradition* (New York: Jewish Theological Seminary of America, 1965); Ithamar Gruenwald, *Apocalyptic and*

think it hard to understand why generations of monks, especially Eastern monks, preserved this literature (for the great bulk of it, after all, is uncanonical), not infrequently in quiet defiance of their bishops. Surely the monks must have seen in this literature something of the prototypes of both the experience of God and God's kingdom that they themselves sought and of the illumined elder who plays so great a role in monastic literature from the very beginnings of the movement.[2] A late fourth-century monastic work, such as the *Historia monachorum in Aegypto*, is chock full of the themes of the ancient apocalypses: ascents to heaven, converse with angels, transformations into light or fire, and the like.[3] Even the markedly sober *Apophthegmata Patrum*, or *Gerontikon*, is occasionally leavened by such reminiscences, as in the following story about Abba Silvanus, in which we find a classical account of apocalyptic-type ascent: "[The Abba's disciple] . . . says to him: 'What happened to you today, Father?' And the other said: 'I was sick today, child.' But he, seizing the other's feet, said: 'I won't let you go until you tell me what you saw!' The old man says to him: 'I was caught up [cf. 2 Cor. 12:1–4] into heaven, and I saw the Glory of God, and I was standing there until now, and now I have been sent away.'"[4]

Aphrahat (together with an Occasional Desert Father) on the Perfected Christian

This brings me to my second reason for quoting the lines from Job 28, and, with it, to the most important—at least for my purposes here—of the select, other ascetical writers mentioned in my title. His name is Aphrahat, and he

---

Merkavah Mysticism, AGJU 14 (Leiden: Brill, 1980); Crispin H. T. Fletcher-Louis, *Luke-Acts: Angels, Christology, and Soteriology*, WUNT 2/94 (Tübingen: Mohr Siebeck, 1997); Alan F. Segal, *Two Powers in Heaven: Early Rabbinic Reports about Christianity and Gnosticism*, SJLA 25 (Leiden: Brill, 1977); idem, *Paul the Convert: The Apostolate and Apostasy of Saul the Pharisee* (New Haven and London: Yale University Press, 1990); Martha Himmelfarb, *Ascent to Heaven in Jewish and Christian Apocalypses* (Oxford and New York: Oxford University Press, 1993); Andrei A. Orlov, *The Enoch-Metatron Tradition*, TSAJ 107 (Tübingen: Mohr Siebeck, 2005); idem, *From Apocalypticism to Merkabah Mysticism: Studies in the Slavonic Pseudepigrapha*, SJSJ 114 (Leiden: Brill, 2006); Rachel Elior, *The Three Temples: On the Emergence of Jewish Mysticism in Late Antiquity* (Oxford and Portland: Littman Library of Jewish Civilization, 2005); Christopher R. A. Morray-Jones, "Transformational Mysticism in the Apocalyptic-Merkabah Tradition," *JJS* 43 (1992): 1–31; idem, "The Temple Within: The Embodied Divine Image and Its Worship in the Dead Sea Scrolls and Other Jewish and Christian Sources," *SBLSP* 37 (1998): 400–431.

2. For a more extensive discussion, see Alexander Golitzin, "*Earthly Angels and Heavenly Men*: The Old Testament Pseudepigrapha, Niketas Stethatos, and the Tradition of 'Interiorized Apocalyptic' in Eastern Christian Ascetical and Mystical Literature," *DOP* 55 (2001): 125–53.

3. See Alexander Golitzin, "The Demons Suggest an Illusion of God's Glory in a Form: Controversy over the Divine Body and Vision of Glory," *StudMon* 44 (2002): 13–43.

4. *Silvanus* 3, PG 65:409A (223) I have placed in parentheses the page reference to the English translation by Benedicta Ward, *The Desert Christian: The Sayings of the Desert Fathers* (New York: MacMillan, 1975).

lived in the Mesopotamia of the Persian Empire. In the years 337, 344, and 345 (we know these dates because he gives them to us himself), he wrote in Syriac a collection of twenty-three discourses, or *Demonstrations* as they are usually translated, devoted to the ascetical life. With one exception, the *Demonstrations* are addressed to "the sons of the covenant," believers who had, it seems, taken a vow of celibacy on the occasion of their baptism. These "proto-monks" antedate the rise of organized monasticism in Egypt and hence have been the source of most of the scholarly literature devoted to Aphrahat over the past century. But before 1894, which saw the publication of his works in the *Patrologia syriaca*, nothing is heard about him.[5] In late antiquity, only the Armenians ever bothered to translate him. He was effectively unknown in the Greek and Latin (or indeed Coptic) West, and the ignorance was largely reciprocal. While Aphrahat knows a few things about his coreligionists in the Roman Empire—he mentions, for example, Diocletian's persecutions as well as Constantine's conversion—there is no evidence that he knew the writings of any of the Greek Fathers of the pre-Nicene (let alone post-Nicene) era. It is this fact, I think, that makes him such an important witness to elements he holds in common with the better-known Christian literature of the Roman West.

The Portrait of the Sage

Aphrahat's *Demonstration* 14 is a "catholic epistle" addressed to the entire Persian Church, written to confront the severe difficulties, both internal and external, afflicting Christianity in the Persian Empire at the time. Those troubles do not concern us here. Suffice it to say that Aphrahat takes time in the middle of his diatribe to provide a positive example of the Christian hope, which he understands to be embodied in the perfected ascetic, whom he calls "the sage." The passage in question opens with a deliberate echo of the questions from Job 28:12–13 with which I began:

> Who has perceived the place of knowledge?
> Who has attained to the roots of wisdom? And who
> has insight into the place of understanding? The latter is hidden
> from the thoughts of every fleshly being,
> nor can the obstinate purchase it with gold. [Yet] its treasure
> is open and permitted to those who ask [for it]. Its light
> is greater than the sun, and its radiance more comely and beautiful
> than the moon. The innermost chambers of the intellect may touch it,
> and the perceptions of thought may attain to it, and fullness of mind
>   may

---

5. Jean Parisot, ed. *Aphraatis Sapientis Persae Demonstrationes*, PS 1, vols. 1–2 (Paris: Firmin-Didot, 1894, 1907).

inherit it. Whoever has opened the door of his heart
finds it, and whoever unfolds the wings of his intellect
possesses it. It dwells in the man who is diligent,
and is implanted in the heart of the sage,
whose nerves are set firmly in their sources, and [so]
in it [i.e., his heart] he possesses a hidden treasure. His thought flies
to all the heights, and his pondering
descends to all the depths. She [i.e., Wisdom] depicts
wondrous things in his heart, and the eyes of his perceptions
take in the bounds of the seas. All things created
are enclosed within his thought, and he
becomes vast so as to receive still more. He becomes
the great temple of his Creator. Indeed, the King of the heights
enters and dwells in him, and lifts his intellect up to the heights,
and causes his thought to fly to His holy house,
and He shows him the treasure of color within [it].
His mind is absorbed in the visions, and his heart
is enraptured by all its perceptions. He [i.e., the King] shows
him a thing that he never knew. He gazes on that place,
and contemplates it, and his mind is stupefied by everything
that it sees: all the watchers [i.e., angels] hastening to his ministry,
the seraphim chanting the thrice-holy to his glory,
flying swiftly with their wings, their vestments
white and shining; their faces are covered at
his radiance; their courses are swifter than the wind.
There is the throne of the kingdom established, [where]
the Judge makes ready the place of judgment;
[and] the chairs of the righteous are set out in order for them to judge
     the wicked
on the Day of Judgment. When the sage sees
in his mind the place of many treasures,
his thought is henceforth elevated, and his heart
conceives and gives birth to every good thing, and he meditates
on everything he had sought. While his form
and appearance are on the earth, the senses of [his] intellect are at
     once
above and below. His thought is swifter than the sun,
and its rays fly quicker than the wind,
swift as wings in every direction.
The sage grows strong in his thought. Though his appearance is small,
and [he makes himself] still smaller, yet he is infused and filled with a
     mighty treasure.
The darkness at night is made light [for him], and he sends
his thoughts out in all directions. His intellect touches
all the foundations and brings him a treasure of knowledge.
He has seen what his "ears have not heard," and he has perceived
what his "eyes have not seen." His interests traverse the seas,

> though he bothers not with their mighty
> billows, and his intellect is without a ship
> or a sailor, yet his commerce is great and exceptional.
> When he gives from what is his, he is no whit the less, and the poor
> are made wealthy from his treasure. There is no limit
> to his mind, which is gathered up and lodged in his inner being.
> The place where the King dwells and is ministered to, who
> could calculate its treasure for you? Many
> Are its affairs and expenses, as with a king for whom
> nothing lacks.[6]

This has to be one of the most extraordinary witnesses extant in fourth-century literature to the doctrine of salvation that Greek Christian writers were calling *theosis*, though neither Aphrahat nor any of his Syriac-speaking contemporaries seem to have known that word. Here a grammatical detail emerges: the third-person singular, pronominal, masculine suffixes in the climactic vision at the center of the passage—"the watchers hastening to *his* ministry" and the seraphim singing the *qedusha* to "*his* glory" and hiding their faces from "*his* radiance"—all have not God but the sage as their closest antecedent.[7] This is transformation with a vengeance because the holy man thus stands in the place of God himself, receiving angelic praise and glorious with divine light.[8] The sage becomes, in sum, the *locus dei*, "that place," theophany. In the larger context of Aphrahat's work, it is clear that he understands this transfiguration as the recovery of the image of God lost in Adam and restored in Christ.

Some of these same elements emerge in a story about Abba Pambo found in the *Gerontikon*. It is worth quoting: "They used to say that, just as Moses received the image of the glory of Adam when his countenance was glorified [Exod. 34:29–35], so too with Abba Pambo; that his face shone like lightning, and he was as a king seated upon his throne. And the same thing

---

6. *Dem.* 14.35, PS 1.1:660.23–665.9.

7. This was pointed out fifteen years ago by Robert Murray, "Some Themes and Problems of Early Syriac Angelology," *OrChrAn* 236 (1990): 143–53, at 150.

8. It is noteworthy that the words Aphrahat uses for "glory" and "radiance"—*iqara* and *ziwa*, respectively—verge on being technical terms for divine manifestation in both the Christian and Jewish literature of the era. *Iqara* serves in the Syriac Bible, the *Peshitta*, as the regular rendering of the Hebrew *kavod*, the theophanic term *par excellence* in the Hebrew Bible. It also appears regularly in the Palestinian Targumim, the Aramaic paraphrases of the Hebrew Bible read in the synagogues of late antiquity (see in this respect Domingo Muñoz-Leon, *La Gloria de la Shekinta en los Targumim del Penteteuco* [Madrid: Consejo Superior de Investigaciones Científicas, Instituto "Francisco Suárez," 1977]). The term *ziwa*, denoting the brilliance of the divine Presence, occurs in the Rabbinic phrase, *ziv haShekinah*, the blessed light of divinity on which the blessed "feed" in the age to come, and on which the *hekalot* mystics hope to "gaze" even in this life (see Ira Chernus, *Mysticism in Rabbinic Judaism*, SJ 9 [Berlin: de Gruyter, 1982], esp. the chapter, "Nourished by the Light of the Shekinah," 74–87).

applied as well to Abba Silvanus and to Abba Sisoes."[9] "All the glory of Adam," to recall a phrase from the Dead Sea Scrolls, is made available to us again in the Second Adam. I should like to focus on a few details in Aphrahat's account of the sage's transformation, details that will all, save the first, feature in my concluding discussion of the *Macarian Homilies*.

The Place of God

The first is his use of the word *place*. This is not a term or theme specific to apocalyptic literature for it belongs rather and first of all to the Hebrew Scriptures generally. It is, if anything, accentuated in the Septuagint (at least in one famous instance), and continues to be important in Rabbinic tradition and, perhaps less markedly but still genuinely so, in Christian ascetical literature as well. In a number of instances it signals the locus of divine manifestation, for example in Jacob's vision at Bethel (Gen. 28:17, "How awesome is this place!") or Moses before the burning bush (Exod. 3:5, "the place on which you are standing is holy ground"). Jeremiah uses the phrase "this place" some thirty times, all in reference to the Temple and, perhaps not inappropriately, the NRSV chooses on at least one such occasion (Jer. 17:12) to render the Hebrew word for place, *maqom*, simply as "shrine." It can also mean, and here we do venture into a keynote of those later apocalypses that interest me, the heavenly original of the earthly temple. In the canonical Scriptures, this appears at least once, namely, in the hymn of the cherubim recorded in Ezekiel 3:12, "Blessed is the Glory of God from his place."[10] The later, rabbinic-era apocalypse *3 Enoch*, and *hekhalot* literature in general (of which more anon), quotes this phrase repeatedly.[11] The rabbis themselves use the word *maqom* often as simply a divine name, such that "the Place," like "the Name" and "the Holy [One]," serves as a circumlocution for God.[12] This is more than a little reminiscent of that passage in the Septuagint I alluded to just now, Exodus 24:10. In the Hebrew, the elders went up the mountain with Moses and "saw

9. *Pambo* 12, PG 65:327A (197); *Sisoes* 14, PG 65:396BC (215); *Silvanus* 12, PG 65:412C (224).

10. Scholars argue that a scribal mistake in the Hebrew changed the original *b^erum kevod YHWH mimmeqomo* into *barukh kevod YHWH mimmeqomo*. The emendation of *barukh* to *b^erum*—for which there is no manuscript basis!—has resulted in the new translation, "the glory of the LORD rose from its place." If David J. Halperin is right (*The Faces of the Chariot: Early Jewish Responses to Ezekiel's Vision*, TSAJ 16 [Tübingen: Mohr Siebeck, 1988], 44–45), the move from *barukh* to *b^erum*—which must have happened early enough to be picked up by the LXX—was not due to scribal error but rather to the fact that the copyist, "perhaps unconsciously," brought Ezekiel's vision in line with the throne-theophany of Isa. 6; indeed, "once *barukh* has replaced *b^erum*, the resemblance of Ezekiel 3:12–13 to this passage in Isaiah is almost eerie" (45).

11. Peter Schäfer (*Konkordanz zur Hekhalot Literatur*, 2 vols., TSAJ 12, 13 [Tübingen: Mohr, 1986–68], 1:432) counts one hundred and twenty five occurrences of *maqom*, two dozen of which are citations or paraphrases of Ezek. 3:12.

12. See Ephraim E. Urbach, *The Sages: Their Concepts and Beliefs* (Jerusalem: Magnes, 1975), 69, on *maqom*, under the heading of "the omnipresent."

the God of Israel," but in the Greek, perhaps to allay the stark anthropomorphism implicit in the original (which is the usual explanation), "they saw the place where the God of Israel was standing." Finally, in the passage from Job with which we began, wisdom's "place" obviously refers to the heavenly realm, or simply to God, or, in any case, to that which is proper to divinity on high and which is emphatically not available to mortals here below.

Aphrahat obviously disagrees, and I read his use of Job here as underlining what he understands to be the changed situation brought about in Christ, through whom "that place" is both in heaven and within the Christian saint, fully present in all its fire and light. It has become accessible, as in the apocalypses that feature a heavenly ascent. Unlike them, the going up to heaven has become simultaneously a journey *ad intra*. In this use of "the place," our Persian ascetic echoes an unlikely figure in the Roman West who plays on the same word in near identical fashion. Evagrius of Pontus was the most learned of the Desert Fathers and perhaps in consequence the most "Greek," and hence stands in apparently direct opposition to the very semitic Aphrahat. His mysticism has most often been analyzed, with some notable exceptions, as exemplary of Neoplatonism. While I have no particular difficulty agreeing that he had probably read Plotinus, it is not the latter, nor any other philosopher of the classical or Greco-Roman era, who is his primary informant in the following passage:

> If then, by the grace of God, the intellect both turns away from these [the passions], and puts off the old man, then it will see its own constitution at the time of prayer like a sapphire or the color of heaven, which recalls as well what the Scripture calls "the place of God" seen by the elders on Mount Sinai [Exod. 24:10 LXX]. It calls this "place," and the vision "the peace" [cf. Ps. 75:3 LXX] by which one sees in oneself that peace which surpasses every intellect and which guards our heart. For another heaven is imprinted in a pure heart, the vision of which is both light and the spiritual "places" [i.e., angels].[13]

As with Aphrahat, and deploying the same word with its several resonances in biblical and post-biblical tradition, Evagrius arrives at the same result: heaven, its angels, and the divine presence are accessible within the illumined heart. There can be no question, so far as I know, of any influence from one to

---

13. *Epistle* 39, my translation of the Greek retroversion from Syriac found in Wilhelm Frankenberg, *Evagrius Ponticus* (Berlin: Weidmannsche Buchhandlung, 1912), 593. For other echoes of the "place" and Exod. 24:10, see the "Chapters" supplementary to the *Kephalaia Gnostica*: 2 (Frankenberg, 425), 4 (427), 21 (441), and 25 (449). See also Columba Stewart, "Imageless Prayer and the Theological Vision of Evagrius Ponticus," *JECS* 9 (2001): 173–204, for a sensitive exploration of Evagrius's exegetical and theological use of "the place of God"—though regrettably without any attention to the phrase's resonances in extra-canonical traditions, let alone its importance in Jewish rabbinical and Christian monastic literature (see in contrast the article by Nicholas Séd, "La shekinta et ses amis araméens," *COr* 20 (1988): 233–42.

the other. They lived several hundred miles, three generations, two empires, and at least one language apart from each other. I think that this argues for a common dependence on traditions that long antedate them both, and I would myself—though not here at length—argue that the sources of the traditions they share, and which they also share in good measure with then contemporary Jewish *merkavah* mystics, lie in Second Temple traditions, particularly (though not exclusively) as these appear in apocalyptic literature.

Aphrahat and the Sefer Hekhalot: *Parallels with Jewish Merkavah Mysticism with Some Important Differences*

Second, there is the matter of *merkavah* mysticism itself. *Merkavah* means "chariot" in Hebrew, and the chariot in question is the wheeled divine throne. This throne is carried by the four "living creatures" and bears in its turn the divine Glory, or the *kevod Adonai* that is "in appearance like a human being," that calls the prophet Ezekiel to his ministry in Ezekiel 1–3. The *kevod Adonai* also appears on two other occasions: departing the defiled Temple in Ezekiel 9–11, and reentering the restored Temple of the eschaton described with otherwise numbing (though not insignificant) detail in Ezekiel 40–48. The importance of these chapters for subsequent apocalyptic literature has come under increased scrutiny in recent decades, an interest stimulated in part by research into Jewish mysticism of the era of the *Talmud*'s composition, that is, roughly from the third through sixth centuries CE, though surely going on both well before and, definitely, after those centuries.[14] There are hints of this mysticism in the *Talmud* itself, but the main source is the collection of *Hekhalot* texts recently assembled and translated by the German scholar Peter Schäfer.[15] *Hekhalot* is the plural of *hekhal*, meaning "temple" or "palace," and the temples/palaces in question are those of the seven heavens through which the mystic ascends in order to arrive, in the seventh and highest heaven, at the vision of the divine Glory enthroned on the *merkavah*. Christian literature offers parallels to this schema, from St. Paul's ascent to "the third heaven" in 2 Corinthians 12:1–4 to the early second-century *Martyrdom and Ascension of Isaiah* (which does feature seven heavens) on down to Aphrahat and, as we shall see rather spectacularly, to the *Macarian Homilies*. Indeed, it is to one of the *hekhalot* texts, namely, *Sefer Hekhalot* or *3 Enoch*, that Robert

---

14. Among the more recent studies, see Elior, *Three Temples*; James R. Davila, *Descenders to the Chariot: The People behind the Hekhalot Literature*, JSJSup 70 (Leiden: Brill, 2001); Christopher R. A. Morray-Jones, *The Dangerous Vision of Water in Hekhalot Mysticism: A Source-Critical and Tradition-Historical Inquiry*, JSJSup 59 (Leiden: Brill, 2002).

15. Peter Schäfer, *Synopse zur Hekhalot-Literatur*, TSAJ 2 (Tübingen: Mohr Siebeck, 1981); idem, *Übersetzung der Hekhalot-Literatur*, 4 vols, TSAJ 17, 22, 29, 46 (Tübingen, Mohr Siebeck, 1987–95).

Murray appeals, in the article I cited above, for a standard of comparison with Aphrahat's extraordinary portrait of the transfigured sage.[16]

Chapters 7–15 in *3 Enoch* describe the ascent to heaven and transformation of the patriarch. It is an apocalypse that is obviously indebted to earlier versions of the Enoch myth, *1* and *2 Enoch*, but it goes well beyond them in the wealth of detail describing its hero's metamorphosis into a heavenly being—indeed, into the very greatest of the angels, Metatron, the "Prince of the Presence" (*Sar haPanim*, lit. "Prince of the Face"). The patriarch goes up to heaven "on the wings of the *Shekinah*" in order to "serve the throne of glory" together with the fiery company of the highest angels.[17] God reveals to him "all the mysteries of wisdom, all the depths of perfect Torah, and all the thoughts of mens' hearts," such that, as he declares, "there is nothing in heaven above or the deep beneath concealed from me."[18] His body becomes huge: "I was enlarged," he says, "and increased in size [lit. "measure," *shi'ur*] until I matched the universe in length and breadth."[19] He is given "a throne like the throne of glory," and likewise a cloak of glory and "a crown bearing the letters of the divine Name."[20] He is himself in fact called "the lesser YHWH," God Jr., as it were.[21] Before him "all the princes who are in the height . . . all the legions [of angels] . . . trembled and shrank," and "all fell prostrate."[22] In short, just as we saw with Aphrahat's sage, the angels worship him, and no wonder, for he has become the likeness of the Glory, changed entirely into divine fire. The passage concludes with Enoch describing his change: "My flesh turned at once to flame, my sinews to blazing fire, my bones to juniper coals, my eyelashes to hot flames, my eyeballs to fiery torches, the hairs of my head to hot flames, all my limbs to wings of burning fire, and the limbs of my body to blazing fire."[23] The parallels with Aphrahat's account of the transfigured sage are several, including: (1) the "flight" to heaven; (2) the acquisition of wisdom, specifically the divine wisdom informing the created universe (that we saw forbidden to poor Job); (3) mystical enlargement in order to receive that gift (recall that the sage, too, becomes "vast" enough for the world, and even for God); (4) transformation, expressed in terms of fire or light; (5) the presence of the throne; (6) angelic worship of the transfigured man; (7) the motifs of robe and crown, admittedly absent in the passage on the sage, but present elsewhere in Aphrahat's oeuvre in a way similar to what we find in

---

16. See Murray, "Themes and Problems of Early Syriac Angelology."
17. *3 En.* 7; Hebrew in Schäfer, *Synopse zur Hekhalot Literatur* 10; English in *OTP* 1:262.
18. *3 En.* 11.1, 3; *Synopse* 14; *OTP* 1:264.
19. *3 En.* 9.2; *Synopse* 12; *OTP* 1:263.
20. *3 En.* 10.1; *Synopse* 13; *OTP* 1:263–64.
21. *3 En.* 12.5; *Synopse* 15; *OTP* 1:265.
22. *3 En.* 14.1, 5; *Synopse* 17; *OTP* 1:266–67.
23. *3 En.* 15; *Synopse* 19; *OTP* 1:267.

3 Enoch;[24] and (8) arguably present in the background of both accounts are those traditions that portrayed Adam as enormous in size and as the recipient of angelic worship.[25]

There are also, however, a couple of significant differences. First and most notably, Aphrahat's is emphatically an effort to interiorize these motifs. It is the sage's inner man that is the abode of God and his angels, the "place" of the King. As we see toward the end of the pericope quoted above, the heart, or inner being, of the saint is infinite, "without limit," possessing the wealth of divinity in order to "make the poor wealthy" (*Dem.* 14.35, PS 1.1:665.3–4). Second, with respect to his outer, physical appearance and demeanor, however, "he makes himself small" (*Dem.* 14.35, PS 1.1:664.14–15, 19). This little phrase carries a very considerable freight. It is first of all christological, an echo of the *kenosis* of Philippians 2:7 found in Christian Syriac well before Aphrahat in the *Odes of Solomon* and after him in Ephrem and, indeed, in Greek in the *Macarian Homilies*.[26] Because Christ Jesus is our exemplar, however, the phrase also applies to the Christian life, specifically to the cultivation of humility, to which Aphrahat continually comes back throughout his work. Making oneself small allows the Majesty—literally, the "bigness" (*rabbuta*)—of God to enter.[27] Nor is this entry a matter for the sage's solitary delectation, but, as we

24. For being clothed (*lbš*) in Aphrahat, and for the "robe" or "garment" (*lebuša*), see *Dem.* 6.1, PS 1.1:240.12; 248.4–5 (the "wedding garment"); *Dem.* 6.6, PS 1.1:268.6–7 ("the robe not made with hands"); *Dem.* 6.18, PS 1.1:308.1–13 (being "clothed with the image of the heavenly Adam," an allusion to 1 Cor. 15:44–45, 49); and *Dem.* 14.39, PS 1.1:681.21 ("the robe of Glory," identified with Christ).

25. The traditions presupposed in various pseudepigrapha present Adam as very much the *divine* image, indeed as a heavenly being. For discussion of Adamic speculation among the Rabbis and related materials, see Jarl E. Fossum, "The Adorable Adam of the Mystics and the Rebuttals of the Rabbis," in *Geschichte—Tradition—Reflexion: FS Martin Hengel. Vol. 1: Judentum*, ed. Hubert Cancik et al. (Tübingen: Mohr Siebeck, 1996), 529–39; Alon Goshen-Gottstein, "The Body as Image of God in Rabbinic Literature," *HTR* 87 (1994): 171–95. In some Jewish sources, the angels mistake the first man for God himself because of his huge size and the brilliance of his body (*Gen. Rab.* 8.10; *Pirqe R. El.* 11, cited in Fossum, "Adorable Adam," 532). According to one text, "the apple of Adam's heel outshone the globe of the sun, how much more so the brightness of his face!" (*Lev. Rab.* 20.2, cited in Goshen-Gottstein, "Body as Image," 178–79). The angels mistake Adam for the heavenly original, the divine "body of Glory" and source of the *shi'ur qomah* tradition; hence the Rabbinic warning against the worship of the first man as demiurge, and their caution about the angels' worship (thus the meat of Fossum's argument in "Adorable Adam," 532–38). That worship of the first man tendered him by the angelic hosts, however, fits neatly into what we find in *3 Enoch* and in Aphrahat's *Dem.* 14.35. Both Enoch and the sage are said to have recovered the *imago* that Adam lost, the likeness of God's Glory and Majesty.

26. "In his kindness, he has made his greatness [*rabbuta*] small" (*Odes of Solomon* 7.3), where *rabbuta* answers to the cosmic size of the Glory, Christ. Cf. *Gospel of Philip* 58.5–10, *Acts of Philip* 142, and the similar expressions, though clearly treated as metaphorical, in the *Macarian Homilies*, e.g., 2.4.9–11 (*esmikrynen heauton*).

27. *Dem.* 23.59, PS 1.2:120.21–121.20, which begins by dwelling on God's immensity, echoing Isa. 66:1, in order to stress the paradox of the entry of His *rabbuta* into the Christian's "little heart." Note also the eucharistic resonance of 121.9–11: "You made Your Greatness small, sufficient for our tongue. Our mouth is capable of receiving You, and You have dwelt within us."

saw, the sage receives in order to pass the divine wealth on to others, just as Christ did: "he gives from what is his . . . and the poor are made wealthy from his treasure" (*Dem.* 14.35, PS 1.1:665.3–4). Aphrahat's saint is an embodiment of his Master: theophany, indeed, but more specifically, christophany.

The Macarian Homilist

A Singularly Important Writer

A generation or two after Aphrahat, somewhere on the Roman side of the border with Persia, an unknown ascetic began writing the materials—letters of advice, homilies, question-and-answer lists—that were later gathered into several collections and usually ascribed to Macarius the Great of Scete. For the sake of convenience, I will continue to refer to the author as "Macarius," but the fact is that we know nothing of his real name, nor when or where or by whom the four extant and somewhat differing collections of his works were assembled. All the Greek MSS we possess are medieval, rather like the *hekhalot* materials, though there are a few earlier MS witnesses to him in Syriac and Arabic translation.[28] We do know that he wrote in pretty good Greek, that his writings were controversial by the end of the fourth century and to a degree during his lifetime, and we can also, I think, assume that the name "Macarius" was posthumously given him as a sort of protective coloration, in much the same way that several of Evagrius's works were preserved in Greek under the name of St. Nilus of Sinai. The monks who cherished him—and they must have been very many—were not about to surrender him to an inspection team from diocesan headquarters.[29] So many, indeed, were

28. Of the four medieval Byzantine collections, three (including the best known *Fifty Spiritual Homilies*) exist in critical editions. Collection I appears in *Makarios/Symeon. Reden und Briefe: Die Sammlung I des Vaticanus Graecus 694 (B)*, ed. Heinz Berthold, 2 vols, GCS (Berlin: Akademie-Verlag, 1973); Collection II in *Die 50 geistlichen Homilien des Makarios*, ed. Hermann Dörries, Erich Klostermann, and Matthias Kröger, PTS 4 (Berlin: Akademie-Verlag, 1964); and Collection III in *Neue Homilien des Makarios/ Symeon. Aus Typus III*, ed. Erich Klostermann and Heinz Berthold, TU 72 (Berlin: Akademie-Verlag, 1961). The last has also been more recently edited and supplied with a French translation by Vincent Desprez: *Pseudo-Macaire, Oeuvres spirituelles. Vol. 1: Homélies propres à la Collection III*, SC 275 (Paris: Éditions du Cerf, 1980). When referring to or quoting from Macarius below, citations in the notes will begin with uppercase Roman numerals for the Collections, followed by Arabic numerals for the specific homily and its subsections.

29. The author of the Macarian Homilies was certainly not Macarius the Great of Egypt, though it was under the latter's name that his writings were eventually to find a safe haven. The name "Symeon of Mesopotamia" is often attached (particularly by German scholars) to "Macarius," owing to the appearance of that name, a leader in the Messalian movement, in a few of the ancient MSS. Hermann Dörries was the first to raise the possibility of Symeon in *Symeon von Mesopotamien: Die Überlieferung des messalianischen Makarios-Schriften*, TU 55 (Leipzig: Hinrichs, 1941), and was followed by many thereafter. For the question of Macarius's identity, see Desprez, "Introduction," SC 275:32–37.

the monks who knew and valued the *Homilies* that we can safely say that, together with Evagrius, Macarius was the most important monastic writer of the fourth century. It would not be exaggerating very much to hold that the two of them together, as Father Vincent Desprez observed some years ago, determined the subsequent shape of Eastern monastic spirituality—which is to say, of Eastern Christian spirituality—to the present day.[30]

Part of Macarius's importance, and perhaps of his power to sway the reader—aside, of course, from the little matters of his being a man of mystical experience, great insight, and capable of expressing himself in cascades of (for the most part) powerful imagery taken from the worlds of Scripture, nature, and human politics—lies in the fact that he represents a confluence of traditions. On the one hand, he read and wrote Greek. It is at least arguable that, like Evagrius, he knew something of Origen (though Evagrius, of course, knew a very great deal of Origen) or certainly of Origen-influenced Alexandrian spiritual exegesis, and it seems to be clear that, again like Evagrius, he was under some influence from the Cappadocians, though in his case the influence appears to have been reciprocal.[31] On the other hand, he also knew and was shaped by the traditions and vocabulary of Syriac-speaking Christianity. In him, we can say to a certain extent that the semitic Christianity of Aphrahat enters permanently into the bloodstream of the Byzantine Christian world. Indeed, this is exactly what seems to have been at the root of much of the controversy around the *Homilies*: a kind of culture clash, resulting from the transposition of terms and concepts perfectly familiar in one linguistic and cultural sphere into another where they appeared strange and even heretical.[32]

30. V. Desprez, "Macaire (Pseudo-Macaire; Macaire-Symeon)," *DS* 10:39.

31. The first item in Collection I, Macarius's *Great Letter*, is not included in Berthold's edition as it was edited previously by Werner Jaeger, *Two Rediscovered Works of Ancient Christian Literature: Gregory of Nyssa and Macarius* (Leiden: Brill, 1954). It was Jaeger's thesis that Macarius had based this treatise on Gregory's shorter work, *On Christian Perfection*. More recently, however, Reinhard Staats (*Makarios–Symeon: Epistola Magna. Eine messalianische Mönchsregel und ihre Umschrift in Gregors von Nyssa "De instituto christiano"* [Göttingen: Vandenhoeck & Ruprecht, 1984]) demonstrated convincingly that the relationship was in fact the reverse, i.e., that Gregory edited Macarius.

32. Columba Stewart, *"Working the Earth of the Heart": The Messalian Controversy in History, Texts, and Language to A.D. 431* (Oxford/New York: 1991), 69, 234–40; Desprez, "Introduction," SC 275: 38–56. The modern literature on Macarius as "Messalian" begins with Louis Villecourt ("La date et l'origine des 'Homélies spirituelles' attribuées à Macaire," in *Comptes rendus des séances de l'Académie des Inscriptions et Belles-Lettres* [Paris: Auguste Picard, 1920], 250–58), and reaches perhaps its most virulent expression in Irénée Hausherr's "L'erreur fondamentale et la logique du Messalianisme," *OCP* 1 (1935): 328–60, where Macarius emerges as a virtual compendium of heresies. For the "Messalian" dossier, see Michel Kmosko, ed., *Liber Graduum*, in PS 3 (Paris: Firmin-Didot, 1926), clxxii–ccxciii; and for discussion of the lists of errors and evolution of the controversy, Stewart, *Working the Earth*, 12–69. As Staats remarked, with perhaps a little exaggeration: "Messalianism is originally no more and no less than an obvious irruption of Syrian Christianity, and it could have been taken as heterodox only from the narrow perspective of an imperial orthodoxy" ("Messalianer-forschung und Ostkirchenkunde," in *Makarios-Symposium über das Böse*, ed. Werner Strothmann, GO 24 [Wiesbaden: Harrassowitz, 1983], 53).

The story of that controversy, and the confusions of much of the twentieth-century scholarship that has attended it, are not—thank God!—our concern in this article. In the space remaining to me, I should like to touch on the points I listed above in common between Aphrahat and *3 Enoch*, together with Aphrahat's adjustments, since these several themes are almost all present in Macarius as well.

"Interiorized Apocalypse," or the "Adjusted Merkavah" of the Macarian Homilist

Let me begin somewhat out of sequence with the matter of the throne, specifically of the chariot throne of Ezekiel 1. Macarius provides the clearest example I know of an "adjusted," Christian, *merkavah* mysticism. It opens the best-known collection of the *Macariana, The Fifty Spiritual Homilies*, where the author begins with an extended paraphrase of the biblical passage and then continues:

> The prophet truly and assuredly saw what he saw, but [his vision] also suggested something else. It depicted beforehand something secret and divine, a mystery truly hidden from eternity and, after generations, made manifest in the last days with the appearance [lit. "epiphany"] of Christ. For Ezekiel beheld the mystery of the soul that is going to receive its Lord and become his throne [*thronos*] of glory, since the soul which has been made worthy of fellowship with the Spirit of his [Christ's] light, and which has been illumined by the beauty of his ineffable glory after having prepared itself for him as a throne [*kathedra*] and dwelling-place [*katoikētērion*], becomes all light, and all face, and all eye. (II.1.2)

The mystical use of Ezekiel is not unique in early monastic literature. Abba Bessarion, for example, hints at something like this in the *Gerontikon*, as does Abba Ammonas in one of his letters preserved in Syriac, but Macarius does so more explicitly and extensively than either. This may be because he, as I think is also the case with Aphrahat, is directing his remarks to a monastic readership that was fascinated with the *merkavah*, that is, with throne visions, and that was quite likely hoping for an out-of-the-body experience along the lines of that in *3 Enoch*. In other words, they were hoping for a classically "apocalyptic" journey to heaven, such as we saw Abba Silvanus enjoy, or like that in one of my favorite stories from the *Historia monachorum in Aegypto* that features Abba Patermuthis going up to heaven and returning with a shopping basket full of heavenly produce (from the trees of Paradise) in order to prove his claims.[33]

---

33. In the *Historia monachorum in Aegypto*, see *Patermuthis* 21–22, *Sourous* 5–7, and *Macarius* 5–12 for trips to Paradise and, in Sourous's case, to the heavenly court. On converse with angels, see

Unlike Evagrius in, say, his hugely influential little treatise *On Prayer*, Macarius does not confront this desire for heavenly visions head on. He is quite matter of fact about the possibility of angelic visitations elsewhere in his works,[34] and here he has no trouble according the prophet full credit: Ezekiel did see what he saw. Then comes his little "but": but something greater is available here and now than even what happened to the great prophet. "With Christ," as he writes elsewhere, "everything is within" (III.8.1). The particular context for that remark is the salvation history of Israel, which Macarius is arguing has become in the new dispensation the history of the soul—an argument familiar to anyone who has read Origen. We may also take it as applying here and thus including in its scope that which the heroes of the ancient apocalypses were granted and for which contemporary Jewish (and Christian) visionaries were striving. It is the soul, the "inner man," or the "heart"—all three terms tending to overlap (as they do in Aphrahat as well)—that the Creator intended to be the true theater of revelation and bearer of his Presence. Put another way, the Christian soul is called to become itself the *merkavah*, as Macarius puts it a little later in the same homily: "The four living creatures which carry the chariot were also carrying a type of the four governing faculties [lit. "thoughts," *logismoi*] of the soul . . . I mean the will, the conscience, the intellect, and the power to love, for through them the chariot of the soul is steered, and upon them God takes his rest" (II.1.2). This is clearly at once a stunning marriage of Ezekiel with Plato's *Phaedrus*, whose imagery it is evident Macarius knows since he deploys it more or less straight elsewhere in the *Homilies*, and a reworking of both the prophet and the philosopher.[35] The former's vision is interiorized while the latter's schema of the soul is, so to speak, theologized, that is, subordinated to the divine Presence. The rational faculty, the *logistikon*, has been bumped out of the driver's seat, and replaced by the Glory of God, Christ.

This "interiorized apocalyptic," the contrast between inner and outer, with preference always being accorded the former, together with the motifs of the soul as throne, temple, tabernacle, church, altar, dwelling-place, house, and even, on a couple of occasions, "palace" (*palation*, and so recall *hekhal*)—all imagery and language deriving from the traditions of Temple and Zion, from the Scriptures to post-biblical Israel and Christianity—runs throughout the *Homilies* and comprises what is perhaps their single most important thread,

---

Apollo 5–6, 16–17, 38–41, 44–47; *Helle* 1–4, 14–15; *Sourous* 8; and *Paphnutius* 23–24. For a more detailed discussion, see Golitzin, "*Earthly Angels and Heavenly Men.*"

34. See the relevant texts with extensive discussion in Alexander Golitzin, "A Testimony to Christianity as Transfiguration: The Macarian Homilies and Orthodox Spirituality," in *Orthodox and Wesleyan Spirituality*, ed. S T Kimbrough (Crestwood, NY: St. Vladimir's Seminary Press, 2002), 129–56.

35. A similar combination of Ezekiel and the *Phaedrus* occurs in II.2.3, 9; II.33.2. For the *Phaedrus* taken straight, as it were, with the *nous* as charioteer, see II.40.5.

their signature tune. Macarius seems never to tire of repeating that the soul appears as temple. This very repetition, this frequency, suggests to me that he was struggling to communicate his message. It must have been hard to compete with stories like Abba Silvanus's ascent, or Abba Patermuthis's shopping basket. Even Abba Ammonas, whose intriguing if cryptic reference to a spiritual exegesis conflating Jacob's Bethel with Ezekiel's "living creatures" seems to be in the same ballpark as Macarius and thus deserves more attention than it has received. Yet even Abba Ammonas quotes approvingly the apocryphal *Martyrdom and Ascension of Isaiah* 8.21 (the prophet's ascent to the seventh heaven), and then adds: "There are some in this generation who have attained to this measure."[36] And the monks? They continued to cherish and copy both, Macarius (and Evagrius), on the one hand, and, on the other, the various apocrypha and pseudepigrapha that spoke, *inter alia*, of heavenly ascent and transformation.

If Interiorized, the Vision Is yet Real and Transforming: The Light Uncreated

Yet I would be very wrong if I gave the impression that Macarius is not, as it were, apocalyptically minded. He is fully as intent on the *visio dei*, and on the foretaste of the eschaton, as any of his correspondents. In fact, he and Aphrahat are the only writers I know of among Eastern Christian ascetics of the era, or indeed until Symeon the New Theologian six hundred years later, to speak in the first person singular of their own visions. Macarius only does so once, as does Aphrahat, but that once is enough to establish the fact that he is quite, quite serious when he repeatedly insists that the direct encounter with God and the things of heaven is open to us starting "right now" (*apo tou nyn*), as he puts it in one of his signature phrases.[37] Another signature phrase, "with all perception and assurance" (*en pasei aisthesei kai plerophoriai*), not repeated quite as often, underlines the reality of the experience he is holding out to his readers (and it also caused quite a stir among the authorities—but, happily, I am not telling that story here).[38] He repeatedly insists on these things, moreover, in terms and images that echo the eight themes I listed above that Aphrahat and *3 Enoch* have in common: entry into heaven, acquisition of supernal mysteries, mystical enlargement, transformation in divine light or fire, the throne of God (which we have seen already), angelic fellowship (though admittedly in the *Homilies* not quite worship), robes and crowns of glory, and the recollection—quite specific and frequent in Macarius—of the

---

36. *Letters of Ammonas*, in PO 10:594.
37. See, e.g., I.33.3.6; I.34.1; I.50.2.3, I.54.4.6, I.58.2.5.
38. For an analysis of the phrase, together with the related term *peira* ("experience"), see esp. Stewart, *Working the Earth*, 96–168.

glory of Adam.[39] At the same time, Macarius incorporates more or less the exact same qualifications, and for the exact same reasons, as does Aphrahat. Thus, aside from the interiority I labored to emphasize above, there are the motifs of smallness and humility, with all their christological resonance, and the human being as called to be the revelation of Christ.

I shall not provide quoted instances of all of these. To my knowledge, nowhere in the *Homilies* do we have quite so conveniently complete an assembly as in the long passage from *Demonstration* 14, and it would be tiresome to repeat eight or nine different passages. Allow me instead to cite three texts that cover ground Aphrahat does not specifically mention, at least in his description of the sage (though he does elsewhere): the model of Christ, the nature of the light of transformation, and the glory of Adam reflected in Moses on the mountain that foreshadows the greater glory brought by the Lord Jesus. I begin with Macarius on the humility of God the Word:

> The infinite God made himself small, and clothed himself with the members of this body, and withdrew himself from the unapproachable glory, and out of kindness and love for humanity, is transformed, embodying himself, and mingling himself with, and embracing holy and well-pleasing and faithful souls, and becomes with them one spirit . . . so that the soul might be enabled to live and to perceive in divinity, and become a partaker of immortal glory. (II.4.9.)

On the nature of that glory or fire or, as in the following, light, Macarius can be quite fiercely specific. While on several occasions he calls the crowns or robes of glory "uncreated," he twice expands on what he means by that, carefully ruling out an interpretation that might read the "light" of illumination as a phenomenon of the human intellect—a kind of illumination received through the study of the Scriptures and certainly a grace—but not God. Rather, Macarius insists in *Homilies* 17 and 58 of Collection I that this light is not a *noēma*, a product of our intellect. As he writes in *Homily* 17: "While we acknowledge ourselves that revelation also takes place in the Spirit when interpreting [Scripture], let them in their turn admit that it may also be a divine light, shining essentially and substantially [*en ousiai kai hypostasei*] in the hearts of the faithful . . . [the] divine and essential [*ousiōdēs*] light which is that which appears and shines in souls more than the light of the sun.[40]

He follows this up with a catena of proof texts, including 2 Corinthians 3:18 and 4:6; Psalms 118:18 and 42:3; Acts 9 and 22 (on the light at St. Paul's con-

---

39. See Alexander Golitzin, "Recovering the 'Glory of Adam': 'Divine Light' Traditions in the Dead Sea Scrolls and the Christian Ascetical Literature of Fourth-Century Syro-Mesopotamia," in *The Dead Sea Scrolls as Background to Postbiblical Judaism and Early Christianity: Papers from an International Conference at St. Andrews in 2001*, ed. James R. Davila, STDJ 46 (Leiden: Brill, 2003), 275–308.

40. I.17.1.3.

version); 1 Corinthians 15:49 ("the image of the heavenly man"); Philippians 3:21 ("the body of [Christ's] glory"); 1 Corinthians 2:9–10 ("what eye has not seen," which we also saw Aphrahat use for the sage's experience); and Romans 8:11 (the indwelling Spirit).[41] I cannot resist observing that many of these texts appear in like context in the argument that Alan Segal made ten years ago in his book *Paul the Convert* for St. Paul as a *merkavah* mystic. They are, in short, at least according to his reading, glory texts. A fourth-century Christian ascetic and a twentieth-century Jewish scholar of rabbinica find the same thing in the Apostle. This in turn is the light that shone from Moses's face when he came down from the mountain in Exodus 34, on which Macarius remarks:

> But I think that when he saw the glory of Adam on the face of Moses, the Enemy was wounded . . . [for] with Christ, it [i.e., the kingdom of Satan] was truly abolished. . . . [Exalted at the right hand, Christ] is full of glory, not only just in his face, like Moses, but throughout his entire body and being . . . and from that time true Christians carry in their inner man that glory, and thus within [them] death is abolished . . . [and] the glory of the Spirit shines perfectly in their souls. And so, at the Resurrection, death shall also be done away with completely from the bodies themselves of those who are glorified in the light.[42]

The whole drama of salvation, of the divine plan, is worked out here in terms of the *kevod YHWH* and the examples and potentialities of the presence of its radiance in human beings. As we saw in the story about Abba Pambo—he of the shining face "like a king sitting on his throne"—this was not an understanding limited to ascetics in Syria. It was, rather, shared across borders and languages by people who, although they did not know each other, would have recognized these traditions as their own. As I noted above, but it is worth repeating, I think that we are here in the presence of currents that go back to Christian origins in the era of the Second Temple.

Concluding Remarks: The Continuing Relevance of the Apocalypses

It has been rightly and often observed that apocalyptic literature is difficult for moderns to approach, let alone understand. All too often our American television and radio preachers make that truth abundantly clear, however unwittingly. Yet we can agree even with them on at least the one point that this literature is extremely important, after which, of course, our respective paths immediately diverge. It is or should be important for us, who make our

41. I.58.1–2; cf. the shorter catenae in I.17.1; 21; and 29.2.
42. I.3.13–15.

living studying and teaching Christian theology, because in it we confront our origins or, at the least, much of the stuff out of which the Gospel was made. To be sure, there was a divergence then, too, between the nascent church and the majority of Israel, and this happened because the former believed that a new thing had appeared and the latter did not. But that new thing, by which I mean the proclamation of Jesus Messiah risen from the dead and seated at the right hand of the Father, acted on materials, traditions, expectations, conceptions, and the such, already fully formed and, as it were, merely awaiting the opportunity to coalesce. I am doubtless not original in this, but I like to think of the late Second Temple era as a kind of super-saturate solution in which the ideas associated with the apocalypses played a considerable role. The Gospel of the Risen Jesus provided a catalyst, and what crystallized out as a result—and did so very quickly, at least as people like Martin Hengel and Larry Hurtado have argued—was Christianity substantially as we have it today: complete with the fundamentals of our theology, Christology, ecclesiology, soteriology, and, to use a word I do not much like, spirituality.[43] If therefore in a Macarius or an Evagrius or an Aphrahat we are reading our fathers in God, in the ancient apocalypses we meet our grandfathers, or in any case one particular set of grandfathers; and if we read both fathers and grandfathers, we can begin to discern the connections and maybe even something of the tradition itself. This is, perhaps, what the little monks knew who continued to copy those documents, even in the face of thundering denunciations from the likes of no less that St. Athanasius of Alexandria.[44]

So, I am grateful for the renewal of studies in apocalyptic literature over the past generation and more. They help me see who I am and where I come from, and they illumine—in the sense of the light that Macarius rejected—the liturgy I celebrate, its hymns, its architecture and form, as well as the saints it commemorates, a couple of whom took pride of place in this essay. I can only hope that I have made some return on that gift.

43. See Alexander Golitzin, "Theophaneia: Forum on the Jewish Roots of Orthodox Spirituality" and "Christian Mysticism over Two Millennia," in *The Theophaneia School: Jewish Roots of Christian Mysticism*, ed. Andrei Orlov and Basil Lurie (St. Petersburg: Byzantinorossica, 2007), 17–33.

44. Recall, e.g., Athanasius's *39th Festal Epistle* of 367, where the great archbishop provides a list of authoritative books for the sole purpose of excluding apocalyptic texts like the Enochic books and the *Ascension of Isaiah*, about which he tells us certain overly enthusiastic ascetics, "the wretched Meletians" in this case, "have been boasting." We might also bear in mind the fact that Athanasius was markedly unsuccessful. Old Testament Pseudepigrapha and related literature did not disappear immediately even in Egypt, let alone in other regions. We would have none of the OT Pseudepigrapha today were it not for Greek, Coptic, Syrian, Ethiopian, Armenian, and even Latin monks. On the continued interest in these materials, see Robert A. Kraft, "The Pseudepigrapha in Christianity," in *Tracing the Threads: Studies in the Vitality of Jewish Pseudepigrapha*, ed. John C. Reeves (Atlanta: Scholars Press, 1994), 55–86.

10

ESCHATOLOGICAL HORIZONS
IN THE CAPPADOCIAN FATHERS

JOHN A. MCGUCKIN

A Brief Prelude on the Significance and Classification of Eschatology

The first thing to note in any study of patristic eschatology is that there is no such thing. I suppose a "qualification" is called for at this juncture, that perennial spoilsport of academic discourse. What I mean by "no such thing," of course, is that the concept is a modern scholastic notion that would have passed without recognition before the eyes of the ancient fathers. For them the two all-embracing divisions of religious discourse were *theologia* and *economia*. If it was a reflection on the divine life of God that was at issue in the church, this was *theologia*. If it concerned an issue of how the divine life was communicated through the creation, or how it ordered the cosmos— namely, soteriology, anthropology, ecclesiology, ethics—it was *economia*. It was thus impossible to have a patristic "theology of work," or a "theology" of prayer, labor, sex, or liberation, for that matter. All of these matters were *economia* and could sensibly be understood and discussed only economi- cally (*oikonomikōs*—we might translate that as "tentatively yet openly, and with a number of intellectual trajectories at our disposal"); while all that was *theologia* could be understood only with difficulty, with a sense that all we discussed was not within the grasp of our basic concepts or language. Gregory of Nyssa's fundamental concept of *epektasis*,[1] for example, is obscured when it is rendered as "reaching out"[2]—it means more accurately "straining out" in the light of a deep instinct for "the better," a striving for the increasing grasp of the Good, and one that is inspired by the progressive revelations of God according to the capacity of responsiveness to earlier revelations. To that extent the striving after *theologia* was "mystical instinct," we might say today, and any resultant insight could be expressed only apophatically. All of which meant, as the fathers never tired of repeating, that one only engaged in *theologia* with great circumspection, and in the specific context of celebrating a *mysterion*. Such remains the context of the best, and most authentic, Orthodox theological statements to this day, even though the word has been weakened from its patristic sense to include now most of what the fathers would have regarded as predominantly economic discourse. Not that *economia* is not important; far from it. One of the corollaries of the understanding of "theology" is that we who call ourselves theologians ought actually to be primarily engaged in *economia*. Be that as it may, then, what we now call eschatology, a relatively modern (and highly problematized) schematization, the fathers would have described as *oikonomia tēs sōtērias*—soteriology.

An Even Briefer Prelude on Biblical Eschatological Idioms

Sometimes patristic theologians can have an impact on wider philosophical and theological issues, and here it might be pertinent to mention one of our Orthodox luminaries, Archpriest Georges Florovsky, who heavily influenced the semantic transition among New Testament writers of the mid-twentieth century from the impasse of "futurist eschatology" versus "realized eschatology," to the progressive adoption of the term "inaugurated eschatology." This was also partly determinative of the rise of the concept of Hope as a twentieth-century medium for reassessing ancient eschatology among the theologians, notably Moltmann.

The recent-past reception of the doctrinal nexus "eschatology" has been highly varied, but in twentieth-century New Testament study it has all been overshadowed by the remarkably unbalanced yet dramatic assessment of Schweitzer,[3] who brought the issue back into the forefront of theological

---

1. *Hom. 6 In Cant.*, PG 44:888A; idem, *Hom. 9 In Cant.*, PG 44:997.

2. It can mean expansion—beginning life as a simple term for semantic lengthening of vowels. In religious discourse it first appears as a technical credal term of the Valentinian Gnostics, whereby the "Heavenly Christ" transdimensionally stretches himself out in correlation to the lower cosmos by means of the archetype "Cross/Stauros." Cf. Irenaeus, *AH* 1.4.1; 1.7.2; 1.8.2.

3. In Albert Schweitzer, *The Quest for the Historical Jesus* (New York: Macmillan, 1910). See Thomas Francis Glasson, "Schweitzer's Influence: Blessing or Bane?" in *The Kingdom of God in the Teaching of Jesus*, ed. Bruce Chilton (London: SPCK, 1984), 107–20.

discussion, rescuing it from the scholastic category of the "last things" (the *eschata*): death, judgment, heaven, and hell. When Schweitzer published his study, R. H. Charles, then the greatest living expert on intertestamental literature, wrote the following review: "Schweitzer's eschatological studies show no knowledge of original documents, and hardly any of first hand works on the documents."[4] One is reminded of the dictum "Why let the evidence cloud the argument?" Schweitzer's lurid depiction of Jesus' eschatology in the *Quest for the Historical Jesus* does no justice either to the complexity of late Jewish apocalyptic writing before him (a literary context in which Jesus does not comfortably fit anyway), or the subtle overlayers of the message of Jesus, which quite evidently includes haggadic, halakic, and sophic materials in and alongside apocalyptic elements of the earliest kerygma. But Schweitzer, both for professional and lay enthusiast alike, tended to popularize eschatology as a metaphysical concept, and to judge from the large number of Web sites currently available on the theme, the mentality of eschatological language being a "Da Vinci code" for a secret kind of *mappa mundi* is thriving.[5]

Notwithstanding, intertestamental apocalypticism is best understood as a genre that renews the prophetic-moral impulse of Israelite preaching. This, in the end, is the purpose of all the visions, historical judgments, and metaphysical descriptions: all is subordinated to one overwhelming conception of the purifying power of the God of the covenant, who is taking into his hands in this decisive moment, the destiny of his people Israel. Central to that act of "taking the destiny" is the reform of the elect people, and central to that message is the conscious self-centering of the prophet-seer in the dynamic of the restoration of covenant. We should regard the mediator-dynamic as being quintessential to late apocalyptic thought and not (as in much contemporary Neo-Testamentica) separate the preached message of the Master from the titular acclamations of the disciples, as something allegedly disconnected and secondary. This is not the place to develop it here, but the overwhelming prophetic vision of Jesus (as enacted in all his parables of the kingdom feast, as well as the great sign of the "cleansing of the temple") is surely the sense of "pressing in" of the end of the time envisaged as "Covenant sustained by Temple sacrifice," and the conscious structuring of a new covenantal celebration, that will allow Israel, a New Israel, to continue in a renewed life after the doom he sensed the Romans will (and soon did) inflict. Of course this is not a popular notion in contemporary New Testament christological writing, either to assert that Jesus had prophetic charism (or other religious power), or apparently that he had any coherent notion whatsoever of anything he was doing; but it is, nonetheless, my reading of the evidence after many years

---

4. Preface to the 2nd ed. of his study *Eschatology* (1913), cited in Glasson, "Schweitzer's Influence," 113.

5. Most of the sites combine this with a Reformationist twist on the gleeful sermons on hellfire that were popular in medieval culture.

involvement as a New Testament exegete as well as a patristics student, and I have elaborated some of the arguments correlative to that understanding elsewhere.[6] But, if Jesus is above all else the prophet of the new meal, while John was the prophet of the new *mikvah*, it is not surprising that the church, understanding this, took the symbolic eucharistic meal as the sign par excellence of the "covenant establishing New Israel," even while elaborating its ancient theology that this was the function of the ritual of baptism. They, of course, stand apart in a historically bounded analysis, but concur in an eschatological relation as two different instances of the same continuum.

In the early Christian redaction of this apocalyptic metaframe (in other words throughout most of what we now designate as the core New Testament literature), the concept of Jesus' prophetic and halakic teachings are "re-set" and amplified in the light of the governing notions of the Lord's glorification (*anastasis, anabasis, analēpsis, doxa, hypsōsis*—it is important not to limit the scriptural array of metaphors and images by which it conveys the kaleidoscopic reality)[7] and his parousia (a further aspect of that same series, not an "additional afterthought"). The Gospels are extended narratives on how the prophetic ministry, the call to the covenant people, can be related to the experience of the glorification, through that mediating gateway of the prophetic absorption, to the point of death, in the vocation to be the faithful Servant. In other words, the tradition of the glorification is set as the resolving lens through which the prophetic ministry is reconsidered by the apostles and evangelists in the construction of the New Testament. Just as the glorification is not the annulment of the cross, therefore, or its compensation, rather its integral fulfilment and the manifestation of its significance in the true kingdom, so too the parousia, and what it reveals theologically, is not to be understood apart from the prophetic preaching and the sufferings of the Lord, but is rather their new epiphany in the light of the kingdom.

All too often, however, the eschatological and timeless unity of the total vision of the mysteries of the kingdom has been de-eschatologized, rolled out in time-bounded categories (and thereby falsified) for the ostensible purposes of making the theological constructs better understood in a linear taxonomy. One early example was St. Luke's horizontally sequential narrative of the eschatological events of the glorification in terms of linearly historicized events, such as resurrection, ascension, visionary appearances, descent of the Spirit, and final return of the Lord of Glory—a system that

6. See John A. McGuckin, "Jesus' Self-Designation as a Prophet," *ScrB* 19, no. 1 (Winter 1988): 8–11, 35–40; idem, "Sacrifice and Atonement: An Investigation into the Attitude of Jesus of Nazareth towards Cultic Sacrifice," in *Remembering for the Future*, 2 vols. (Oxford: Pergamon, 1988), 1:648–61; idem, "The Sign of the Prophet: The Significance of Meals in the Doctrine of Jesus," *ScrB* 16, no. 2 (Summer 1986): 35–40.

7. Such a limitation of eschatological horizon is unfortunately evoked by condensing all of the above notions into the term *anastasis*—resurrection.

had profound impact on the creation of the liturgical year mirroring those mysteries and thus forcing a taxonomic ordering of a non-linear reality. Here, perhaps more than anywhere else in the evangelical tradition, translation of the Semitic idiom of the first apostles into Greek falters. The Hellenistic sense of history as progressive events on a horizontal plane, touched by moments of the intervening activity of the gods, fails lamentably to embrace the biblical drama of the heavenly reality passing through the earthly surface that reflects it[8] at moments of decisive covenantal action, so that the mirror reflection of earthly history passes at a time of *krisis* into the reality of the other world, which constantly shapes it. This is why the "other dimension" constantly shapes and determines the New Testament structure. The ministry of Jesus is presented in terms of encounters with demons, raising of the dead, and finally *anastasis* and *anabasis*. When we compare the Johannine account of the *anastasis* with the Lukan version we see the compactly telescopic way John retains the unity of the mystery of *anabasis* in all its varied facets. Here the *anastasis*, *analépsis*, *horamata* (visions of the risen Lord), and gift of the Spirit are all synchronous events (not paschal "events" as Luke has them) of the selfsame momentous "Day of the Lord." The church at large retains this deeper sense of the non-linearity of the eschatological drama when it knows that all days are one day, that every Eucharist is the pascha, and that all time is the *kairos* of redemption—when it looks, that is, with the eye of the illumined heart. Consequently the church uses its annual cycle of feasts merely as an aid to weak imaginations that, inescapably sequential and rooted entirely in image-analogy, cannot easily sustain reflection on the timeless order of the kingdom and the transdimensionality of which it speaks.

This de-eschatologized translation of early Christian thought on "new *kairos*" into the doctrine of the "last things" can be seen to be progressively advancing after the fifth century. Earlier patristic eschatology, while it has this tendency, especially a desire to clarify and regularize differing traditions of the "heavenly life" (which remain relatively open-ended in Christian dogma as compared, for example, to Christology), nevertheless remains conscious of the deeper meaning of the eschatological dimension of Christianity. In this sense the early church preserves a deep awareness that eschatology cannot be explained within temporal categories but only symbolically sketched and hinted at.

The Cappadocians and Origen of Alexandria—A Pervasive Context

If we turn to ground this in a particular study of some of the fathers, the Cappadocians provide a good example. To understand them, we need to

8. The events of the heavenly court, being echoed and mirrored on the earth, as its fortunes wax and wane.

begin with Origen. Origen is the core thinker for all the Cappadocians. His eschatological agenda determines all their thinking—whether they are explicitly correcting him or following him on any given instance.[9] His scheme of *anabasis* and *katabasis* renders the coming of the Logos to earth part of a vast scheme of soteriology. Fallen noetic beings are caught up in a great cycle of renewal and repristination, which only begins in this present age and is consummated in the perfection of a great ascent back to communion with the Logos. Origen's radical transcendentalism was widely regarded as both magnificent in scope, as well as troubling in its implications, for it seemed to undermine the permanent value of the sacramental enfleshment of the Logos.

Gregory of Nazianzus—Shifting the Horizons of Origenianism

Gregory of Nazianzus has much to say about such a scheme of salvation as a time-transcendent transection of the divine life with human history. But fitted into the modality of eschatological analysis as it was defined by mid-century conceptions of that term, he is surprisingly alleged to have had nothing to say. Mossay, in a 1964 article titled "Eschatological Perspectives of Gregory of Nazianzus," concluded with a statement that has had a determinative effect on much later speculation in this area of Gregorian study—that is, shutting it off rather than encouraging it. He says, "One is only able to discover in our author's works what one could call a systematic thanatology."[10] While this might be technically correct, it is, nevertheless, an utterly misleading analysis of the Theologian. Brian Daley's more careful listing and scholarly discussion of Gregory's eschatological passages in his monograph on patristic eschatology,[11] which has established itself as the standard study of the subject, argues, in turn, that a "lack of systematic development is noticeable in Gregory's treatment of eschatology." What has struck Daley from his careful collation of several evidences in the primary texts is how Gregory apparently

9. Typically the Cappadocians (especially the two Gregories), accepted Origen's views that hell could not be eternally punitive, but divine punishments had to be pedagogically reformative in purpose. They also corrected his understanding of pretemporal fall of spirits to earth, softening it to the notion of the angelic metamorphosis of human creatures in the next age. Gregory Nazianzen is more circumspect on the idea of the *apokatastasis*, though he quietly advocates it, while Gregory of Nyssa is an open champion of the idea, both releasing it from its place in Origen's system in the idea of the pretemporal fall. For a synopsis see Brian E. Daley, "Eschatology," in *The Westminster Handbook to Origen*, ed. John A. McGuckin (Louisville: Westminster John Knox, 2004), 95–96.

10. Justin Mossay, "Perspectives eschatologiques de S. Gregoire de Nazianze," *Les Questions Liturgiques et Paroissales* 45 (1964): 328; see also Claudio Moreschini, "La meditatio mortis e la spiritualità di Gregorio Nazianzeno," in *Morte e immortalità nella catechesi dei padri del 3–4 secolo*, ed. S. Felici (Rome: Pontificium Institutum Altioris Latinitatis, 1984).

11. Brian E. Daley, *The Hope of the Early Church* (Cambridge: Cambridge University Press, 1991), 83–85, at 83.

has two doctrines of the "afterlife" that he does not seem too worried about reconciling. One is the "traditional" biblical motif of the "gloomy judgment" of Hades that awaits souls after death,[12] and the other is the vision of the transcendent soul rising to the eternal clarity of the vision of God.

The gloomy idea of death hanging over all earthly joy is a concept that dominates many of his *Carmina moralia*. Here his poems of lamentation take up the second sophistic theme of the bewailing of human existence. Several commentators on his poetry have wondered how this squares with the theme of Christian anthropological hope, and have often taken recourse to pseudological justifications of Gregory's senile psychology to explain it. In fact we have no good reason to think that the Sophic poems are the product of his advanced age, but rather were surely a product of many years of philosophical *symposia* we know he conducted for the ascetics and litterateurs of his home region in Cappadocia. Given this context and the manner in which the poems carefully and evidently demonstrate mastery of every genre and style and a broad array of classical allusions (not least an extensive set of references to the verses of Sappho—another unlikely inspiration for our ascetic father),[13] it is clear that the poetic reflections are a careful elaboration of classical Hellenistic themes in the sophistic manner for an audience of litterateurs and sophist ascetics. This audience would have recognized in the neo-Stoic doctrine of *apatheia* and the common philosophical topos of world-weariness a train of thought that provided commonalities of theme and judgment between the classical tradition of their literary paideia and their "specialist" interpretation of Christianity through ascetic modalities. In the poems the concept of the afterlife awaiting the soul as it ends its earthly journey as enfleshed being is more often than not added on as yet one more thing in the series of the "sorrowful trials of existence" that the human must endure, and through enduring, learn wisdom. In other words, the classical concept of Hades is brought in to be the Christian version of the last of the "series of the sorrows of this life"—not the "ending of the sorrows" as is found in several other classical sophistic musings on the topos of the pains of life.

Here, as in so many other aspects of his inner structure of thought, Gregory relies on Origen,[14] who precedes him in being the first to harmonize the classical doctrine of Hades and the biblical doctrines of gehenna. For Origen, the gates of Hades could serve as a highly plastic symbol. At one moment it referred to the arch-heresiarchs, and their construction of pedagogical gateways

---

12. *Carmina moralia* 2.141–44.

13. See Quintiliano Cataudella, "Derivazioni da Saffo in Gregorio Nazianzeno," *Bolletino di Filologia Classica* 33 (1926–27): 282–84; Willem J. W. Koster, "Sappho apud Gregorium Nazianzenum," *Mnemosyne* 17 (1964): 374 (vv. 5–6.10 of 1.2.14 [PG 37:755]); idem, "Sappho apud Gregorium Nazianzenum bis detecta," *Mnemosyne* 18 (1965): 75.

14. See Claudio Moreschini, "Influenze di Origene su Gregorio di Nazianzo," *Atti e memorie dell'Accademia Toscana la Colombaria* 44 (1979): 33–57.

to hell,[15] at another moment it referred to the fires of purgative punishment that awaited the souls of those who died and had not been entirely purified through noetic regeneration in the course of this life.[16] We can note as significant for the Cappadocians, too, that the fundamental purpose of life, for Origen, was the progressive purification of the *nous*, or spiritual existent—the new creature—by the "ascent" the Logos gave to it in myriad ways through the revelation of the *epinoiai*, the manners in which the Logos revealed itself and in so doing enlightened, purified, and radically spiritualized the noetic levels of creation.[17] For Origen all of life was seen teleologically, and the ultimate purpose of noetic being was return to ascentive communion with God in the Logos. This was partly why Origen got into such trouble, for if the fires of hell are purgative in nature, as befits a God who constantly seeks the advancement of his creation, it is impossible that they can be understood simply as punitive and eternal, a notion that precludes regenerative scope. Origen explained to his readers that the Scriptures themselves contained several views about the afterlife in imagistic form.[18]

The common notion among the less educated was that the "eternal fires" meant exactly that, unending flames of punishment. But, Origen points out, the biblical word "eternal" (*aiōnios*) does not mean "unending" (a sequential notion) but rather "of the next age"—"eschatological" if one prefers[19]—and eternity itself (the manner of transition and metamorphosis from this age to the next age, which he has set as the destiny of noetic creation) is God's overarching scheme of the restorative salvation of the cosmos.[20] When Origen describes his "intuition" of *apokatastasis*, how all manner of noetic being

---

15. Origen, *Commentary on Matthew* 12.12.54. For a fuller analysis, see Jason M. Scarborough, "Hades," in McGuckin, *Westminster Handbook to Origen*, 118–20. See also Constantine Tsirpanlis, "Origen on Free Will, Grace, Predestination, Apocatastasis, and Their Ecclesiological Implications," *PBR* 9 (1990): 95–121.

16. Cf. Origen, *On First Principles* 2.10.4.5.

17. See Claudio Moreschini, "Luce e purificazione nella dottrine di Gregorio Nazianzeno," *Aug* 13 (1973): 534–49.

18. Scarborough puts it succinctly: "In later Jewish thought, as in the New Testament, the term came to be read apocalyptically. It is the fiery abyss of Matt. 13:42 and the lake of fire in Rev. 20:10. It was the place of punishment after the last judgment. The canonical authors, however, were far from systematic in their use of the term. Luke 16:23, e.g., suggests that all souls proceed to the underworld, while Hades is exclusively the place of punishment. Other passages, such as 1 Pet. 3:19, suggest that only the souls of the ungodly reside in the underworld, while the larger apocalyptic tradition retained the view of Hades as an intermediate stage, destined eschatologically to be followed by the fires of Gehenna. For the canonical authors, Gehenna was pre-existent (that fire 'prepared from the beginning of the world'). Origen inherited this tradition, subtly adding to and extending it. With him, as with most early Christian writers, the existence of the underworld was seldom questioned, rather it was a question of the duration, purpose, and cause of humanity's stay in such a place" ("Hades," 118–19).

19. Origen, *Commentary on Romans* 6.5.

20. Cf. the elaboration of the ascentive scheme as the root meaning of "salvation" in Origen, *On First Principles* 1.6.3.

will be brought back into spiritual communion with the God of all, in an ultimate vision of the triumphant kingdom of God, he is notoriously unwilling to come down on either side of the doctrinal fence: that is, whether or not all things would be saved, and if so how this could be reconciled with the simpler biblical tradition of unending punishment of the damned. Many have seen him as inherently contradictory, or at best unsystematic. But the fact is, he is entirely systematic, as Fred Norris has recently argued.[21] What he wishes to do is to set a "deeper intuition" against a commonly recognized aspect of doctrine, not to deny the one by replacing it with the other, but to run the two simultaneously as mutual correctives. One is brought forward by apostolic tradition and commented on by the learned biblical interpreter who thus clarifies inner meanings such as the correct significance of *aionial* when referred to the gehenna fires, the other, the intuition that God's punishments are entirely therapeutic, not vindictive, is offered by himself as the inspired theologian, an office Origen regards as continuing the church's prophetic and apostolic tradition in serving as a "high priesthood" of the initiated seers.[22] What strikes the modern reader as lack of systematization, therefore, is a systematization of a very subtle order. It is explained by Origen's very common theme of pedagogy as necessarily tailored to the spiritual stature of the recipient,[23] which he describes as the threefold state of hearing truth on the mountaintop with the elite, on the plains with the common crowd, or down in the valleys among the defectives and the demoniacs. This deliberate juxtaposed parallelism of Origenian doctrine[24] is thus part of his consistent method to offer theological insights to his inner circle, and other kinds of teaching to his larger audiences.

It is the same with Gregory of Nazianzus. The coexistence of two conceptions of the afterlife, one as ascentive purgation of the soul, and the other as the fires of hell threatening the ungodly, is a deliberate following of Origen's lead. The larger crowd, not skilled in the subtleties of Logos-discourse, need

---

21. Frederick W. Norris, "Apokatastasis," in McGuckin, *Westminster Handbook to Origen*, 59–62.

22. Further see John A. McGuckin, "Origen's Doctrine of the Priesthood," *Clergy Review* 70, no. 8 (August 1985): 277–86; ibid., no. 9 (September 1985): 318–25; synopsis appears in *TD* 33, no. 3 (1986): 334–36.

23. He thus long predates Aquinas's basic dictum of pedagogy that *quidquid recipitur, secundum modum recipientis recipitur* (whatever is understood is understood according to the modality of the one understanding it).

24. See, e.g., Elizabeth A. Dively-Lauro, "Universalism," in McGuckin, *Westminster Handbook to Origen*, 211–14: "A modified Universalism was clearly Origen's fundamental soteriological belief, and though he manifested several internal doubts and qualifications in his exposition, probably because the common opinion of the Church of his day was against him on many aspects of the idea, he nevertheless presents a coherent theological narrative, though one that was not wholly consistent at every instance, and which gave his friends and critics in later ages room for further controversy on the subject."

the spice of a fiery threat to amend their lives. The more elect, those already on the road to progressive refinement, through the exaltation of their noetic capacities, can understand that spiritual motivation (or at least advanced acceleration) in the ways of God, is not provided by threats, but rather driven by love and the soul's burning desire for communion and purgation, that it might encounter the vision of God.

In Gregory's philosophical poems, which at first sight would appear to be exactly the material he would have composed for an inner-circle audience, one finds the same mix of Hellenistic and Christian notions of the afterlife state of the soul: on the one hand a spirit of light making its way into the inner sanctum of the divine Temple (what he likes to describe as the soul's passing from one level of the sanctuary to a higher state, as after death the enlightened soul is allowed to enter the holy of holies from which it was debarred while still in the flesh),[25] and on the other hand much material about the soul's wandering in the gloomy halls of Hades,[26] or the fires and gloom of hell that threaten the unworthy conscience.[27] The inner circle of his *symposia* guests regularly contained litterateurs as well as Christian ascetics (the kind of audience one finds throughout all his many letters, where he switches from Christian contexts of analogy to pagan contexts depending on the recipient of the text). The presumption of Gregory using the poetic material among his literary friends is that his many references will be readily understood, but that even so, there is probably a mixture of Hellenists and Christians in his intellectual community, and the imagery, accordingly, is mixed. By contrast, in his public preaching as a bishop in Cappadocia and Constantinople, he is not giving a message to an inner circle, but to the larger body of believers. We might expect this to be a medium where his doctrine is consistently reserved to the simpler Origenian teaching for the "common folk" that the fires of hell will chastise the unworthy. One does find such reference in his *Orations*,[28] but the overall thrust of his teaching is that the soul is meant to ascend progressively to God, from whom and in whom it receives no less than *theōsis*—deification.[29] It is almost as if he challenged his audience in the church to respond to the higher doctrine for initiates— such as they claimed to be by the mere fact of standing in church listening to his episcopal discourses. Gregory's theosis doctrine is also consciously

25. Further on this, see John A. McGuckin, "The Vision of God in St. Gregory Nazianzen," *StPatr* 32, ed. Elizabeth A. Livingstone (Leuven: Peeters, 1996), 145–52.

26. E.g., *Carmina moralia* 2.141–44.

27. *Carmina moralia* 15.98–100.

28. *Orat.* 3.7; 16.7–9; 39.19.

29. See Vladimir Kharlamov, "Rhetorical Application of *Theosis* in Greek Patristic Theology," in *Partakers of the Divine Nature: The History and Development of Deification in the Christian Traditions*, ed. Michael J. Christensen and Jeffery A. Wittung (Madison, NJ: Fairleigh Dickinson University Press, 2007; Grand Rapids: Baker Academic, 2008), 123–28; also John A. McGuckin, "The Strategic Adaptation of Deification in the Cappadocians," in Christensen and Wittung, *Partakers*, 95–114.

developing that of Athanasius, and in a poem possibly deliberately titled *De incarnatione* he polished up Athanasius's famous syllogism, rendering it as: "And since, therefore, God is made man, so man is thereby perfected as God, and such is my glory."[30]

In his *Fourth Theological Oration* Gregory makes a deliberate reference to the Origenian concept of the *apokatastasis*,[31] when God will be all in all in a perfectly restored communion of noetic life. Although this logically demands he accepts the Origenian correlative, that all punishment is purgative, he still does not feel the need to push that point home exclusively. In his *Oration on the Holy Lights* delivered to the catechumens of Constantinople at the Feast of Theophany in 381, he attacks the Novatians for their rigorism, and says that this will not be rewarded at the end, but will rather attract a punishment of God's purifying fire (a baptism of fire as he calls it).[32] In his *Oration on Baptism*, given in the same liturgical triduum of January that year, he takes up again this theme of the fire that Christ said he would cast down on the earth (Luke 12:49), concluding that many take this passage as an authority for the doctrine of the eternal fires of hell, "though some," he goes on (he does not state who but makes it clear he is in their number), "may prefer, even on this point, to take a more merciful view of this fire, one that is more worthy of the One who chastises [viz. God]." With supreme discretion he avers that the Origenian notion of cosmic redemption is preferable, but not something that can be dogmatically asserted, perhaps for fear of scandalizing the simple. Brian Daley has summarized his overall position succinctly when he says that in Gregory we find "the unitive, spiritualizing hope of Origen and his followers, expressed with the balance and pathos of the classical artist."[33]

Master of style he certainly is; recent work on Gregory of Nazianzus, however, has been consistently arguing that the old cliché—that he was correspond-

---

30. *Carmina dogmatica* 10.5–9; See also *Orat.* 21.2. Throughout his *Orations* and poetry, Gregory is very enthusiastic about the language describing the soul's "kinship" or "affinity" with the divine nature. He regularly describes the soul as a "breath of God" (*Carm. dogmatica* 8.1–3; *Carm. moralia* 1.156) or as a "spirit emanating from the invisible deity" or an "offshoot of the divine" (*Carm. dogmatica* 8.70–77; *Carm. moralia* 10.135). Adam was deified, he says, by his inborn propensity toward God (*Orat.* 38.11, 13), and it is that natural kinship that is at the root of our return to God and the deified life, but understood as a gift of God the creator, not the reassertion of any divine element innate within creaturely nature.

31. "God will be all in all in that time of restoration [*apokatastasis*]. I do not mean the Father alone, as if the Son were to be dissolved in him, like a torch that has been separated for a while from a great fire and then is rejoined to it [a notion of Marcellus of Ancyra] nor should the Sabellians be corrupted by this passage either [1 Cor. 15:28]. No, what I mean is God as a whole, at the time when we ourselves are no longer many, as we now are in our movements and passivities, bearing in ourselves little of God, or even nothing at all. On that day we shall be wholly like God, receptive of God as a whole, and God only. This, after all, is the perfection [*teleiōsis*] towards which we strive" (*Orat.* 30.6).

32. Ibid., 39.19.

33. Daley, *Hope of the Early Church*, 85.

ingly thin on substance—is no longer sustainable. In fact, Gregory's entire corpus is an extended meditation on the soteriological ascent of the New Adam to a transfigured destiny. His soteriology is eschatological throughout, except that it is an eschatology that is so pervasively rooted in his incarnationalism that it refuses to be detached in a separatist taxonomy. For him the doctrine of the three creations (angelicals, animal and insensate life, and humanity) is a critical context. The first two creations are absolutely coherent in their ontological structure. No shadow of faltering can be found within their essential makeup. In other words, angels, animals, and trees are perfectly balanced beings. Only the third creation is in a state of lament, torn constantly between two polarities of being: the sensory (doomed to die) and the spiritual (doomed to the incessant distraction of its wailing infant of the flesh). The third creation, however, will finally, in the *eschaton*, be rendered peaceful in its metamorphosis to the status of first creation—angelicals.[34] Here on earth the life of the philosopher can prefigure that acquisition of peace and *stasis*. To live the life of a true sophist[35] is, par excellence, the life lived in God. Already on this earth it is a deification, but for Gregory this transformation begun is only a harbinger of a greater glory to come when we are transfigured after this life.[36] In *Oration* 21 he presses the point home with great eloquence:

> Whoever has been permitted to escape from matter, and from the fleshly cloud (or should we call it a veil?) by means of reason and contemplation, so as to hold communion with God, and be associated with the purest light (in so far as human nature can attain to it): such a man is truly blessed: both in terms of his ascent from here, and in terms of his deification there, a deification which is conferred by true philosophy, and by virtue of his rising above all the duality of matter through that unity which is perceived in the Trinity.[37]

Ascesis, for him, is a historical embodiment of the *eschaton*, a transcendental evocation of the pure kingdom. Failure to connect the incarnationalist doctrine[38] with the concept of the three creations, and the pervasive encomia of the ascetical refinement given by the life of the mind[39] renders our

34. Further, see John A. McGuckin, *St. Gregory of Nazianzus: An Intellectual Biography* (New York: St. Vladimir's Seminary Press, 2004), 336–39, exegeting *Orat.* 38.

35. Which means primarily as a Christian; he constantly refers to Christianity as *philosophia imon.*

36. *Carmina dogmatica* 10.140–43.

37. *Orat.* 21.2.

38. Widely understood to have been highly significant, by earlier scholarship, but largely restricted to a mere moment in the anti-Apollinarist movement (see *Ep.* 101 to Cledonius). Gregory's "most famous" phrase, "What was not assumed, was not saved," in *Ep.* 101 (one might ironically observe) was not his at all but was his citation of the text of Origen of Alexandria.

39. See esp. the *First Theological Oration* on this score (*Orat.* 27), which argues that theology can only be attempted by those who have purified the *nous* by long preparatory mental and moral ascesis.

understanding of Gregory's eschatological subtlety somewhat ineffective. Unfortunately, little of the existing Gregorian scholarship has ever tried to connect these three fundamental axes of his systematic, constantly preferring to dismiss him (without much firsthand textual engagement to back it up, one might add) as an "inspired popularizer," to cite the words of that less inspired popularizer, G. L. Prestige.[40] In many ways, however, this nexus of Gregory's thought is clearly very similar to that of Gregory of Nyssa, whom he mentored over many years, and to whom we shall now turn.

Gregory of Nyssa as Eschatological Visionary

Gregory of Nyssa's deep significance for modern commentators on patristic eschatology can be readily gauged from Brian Daley's representative bibliography of the chief secondary literature on the theme, which is conveniently set out in the format of lists peculiar to the main writers of the period.[41] The section for Gregory Nazianzen, for example, has a lonely article by Justin Mossay, which gave the gist of his doctoral thesis, concluding that there was no eschatology as such, more a problematic *thanatology*. But that paucity is not untypical in relation to most of the other eschatological entries, three or four lines of twentieth-century bibliography in most cases, and then Ping! A jackpot with a few writers. The contrast for secondary literature on Irenaeus, Origen, Lactantius, and Gregory the Great, is quite remarkable; but the outright winner is, of course, Augustine of Hippo, who, as with most other things he handled, brought an elegant narratological order to a certain disarray he always tended to see in evidence around him.[42]

But our concern here is with Gregory of Nyssa. In this respect it is perhaps significant to record my memory of the initial shock on turning the relevant page in Brian Daley's bibliography[43] and seeing so graphically displayed there that Gregory of Nyssa personally receives more than the sum total of eschatological analyses of all other fourth-century Greek theologians combined.

40. George Leonard Prestige, *God in Patristic Thought* (London: SPCK, 1952), 234.

41. Daley, *Hope of the Early Church*, 266–87, esp. 270 onward.

42. He was, we should never forget, a controversial figure in his time, in a highly conflicted ecclesial environment, in what was commonly regarded as a remote and tendentious province of the church. In relation to "eschatology," as with much else in Augustine, peculiar stresses of the *theologoumena* of the North African littoral were brought with a bang (courtesy of Gregory the Great) into the main discourse of Latin Christianity after him. One chief reason for this was simply that he did the job of synthesis so well. His blend of traditional themes within an overarching schema prioritizing the soul's ascent to the vision of God in beatitude was masterful. His taxonomic ordering of the earlier eschatological traditions of the *Adventus Domini* was so persuasive and coherently structured that the medieval schematization of "eschatology" as we know it was thereby launched and endured, and would have no serious challenge until twentieth-century biblical scholars reopened the agenda.

43. Daley, *Hope of the Early Church*, 278.

Looking more closely at the date of those studies, however, things become a little more understandable, for a major rehabilitation of Gregory Nyssen has, as we know, been under way in the postwar decades of the twentieth century, and that movement itself (led by scholars who were also deeply learned in biblical literature) was quite clearly influenced by the explosion of interest in eschatology concurrently taking pace in European biblical departments. One evidently fed the other.

The Nyssen's doctrine of the *Epektasis* dominated scholarly imagination, and focused analysis on the manner in which the learned Cappadocian revitalized Origen's eschatological scheme of metamorphosized ascent, while more overtly connecting it with a Nicene doctrine of the incarnation. The synthesis is clearly witnessed in this passage from the *Treatise on 1 Cor. 15.28*.[44] Here (and it is typical of the Gregorian approach elsewhere) the incarnation is not merely an individual assumption of flesh, considered as a historical moment but is rather an eschatological process, a timeless moment of a soteriological "re-principling" (*anakephalaiōsis*) of the race, and as such designed as a healing of the major wound apparent in the cosmos, as it begins to suffer within time-gone-astray-in-alienation. Following Paul (and like him using a bewildering array of mixed metaphors), Gregory argues out how the incarnation constitutes "new man" or the New Adam, and sets the entire race on a new progress[45] to the parousia. In this instance it is not something that passes by the learned rhetorician that parousia semantically means the longed-for event of the *adventus*, and simultaneously the "presence" of the risen Lord. This "future-presence," a wittily rhetorical time-paradox, is very much at the heart of what the Cappadocian means to connote by the moral imperative of the *eschaton*. This is what he says:

> From the entirety of human nature to which the divinity is mixed, the Man-constituted-according-to-Christ is a kind of first fruits of the common dough. It is through this [divinized] man that all mankind is joined to the divinity. . . . Christ assumed from death both the beginning of evil's destruction and the dissolution of death; then, as it were, a certain order was consequently added. Decrease of the good always results by straying from its principle, while the good is found closer to us insofar as it lies in each one's dignity and power; thus, a result follows from the action preceding it. Therefore, after the Man-in-Christ, who became the first fruits of our human nature, received in himself the divinity, He became the first fruits of those who have fallen asleep and the first born from the dead once the pangs of death have been loosened. So then, after this person has completely separated himself from sin and has utterly denied in himself the power of death and destroyed its lordship and authority

44. *On the Subjection of the Son.*
45. *Prokopē*: the motion of progressive extension and developmental advancement—so favored a twin term of Gregory's when he discusses the dynamic principle of *epektasis*, not least in a moral and ontological context.

and might. . . . If anyone like Paul may be found who became a mighty imitator of Christ in his rejection of evil . . . such a person will fall in behind the first fruits at Christ's coming Parousia.[46]

Here Gregory of Nyssa shows himself a clear disciple of Irenaeus, Origen, Athanasius, and his mentor the elder Gregory, not to mention his brother Basil, though with a far more Origenian flavor than his brother witnessed in his later works. But it is the doctrine of the *epektasis* that is more widely known than this aspect of the christological summation of the cosmos. This is because it is more distinctly particular to Gregory, and mid-century scholarship also was dominated by "source critical" models where particularity was given an emphatic prominence, a trend that often continues methodologically unexamined today, or worse, methodologically justified, as an alleged part of a "hermeneutic of suspicion" in several contemporary early Christian studies.[47]

Gregory's doctrine of *epektasis*, which has been extensively discussed,[48] finds its dynamic coherence in a change Nyssan makes to Origen's soteriology on several key points. Let us begin with a passage that introduces the idea.[49] He offers it to his catechumens in the *Great Catechetical Oration*, that remarkably complex work that supposedly "does duty" as a theological primer. Gregory evidently expected his neophytes to be a rather learned sort, and to recognize in his image of the radiant eye a deliberate allusion to Plato's *Timaeus*.[50] Here in this famous text the point is to describe humankind's destiny as that of a creature rising to communion with the divine, in an eschatological mystery of the overcoming of time (the *diastasis* between the eternal and the mortal) and of creaturely limitation (the *diastasis* between the creator and the creature). His eschatology at this juncture becomes a theology of spiritual communion, one that turns on the notion of *metousia theou* (the impossible paradox of creaturely participation in the divine):

> Since he was created to take part [*metochos*] in divine blessings, man must have a natural affinity [*kataskeuazetai*] with that object in which he has participation [*metousia*]. It is just like an eye which, thanks to the luminous rays which

46. The translation is that of Rev. Casimir McCambley, OCSO, from his Gregory of Nyssa Web page: www.bhsu.edu/artssciences/asfaculty/dsalomon/nyssa/1corinth.html.

47. Scholars of early Christianity in the present, who, in a postmodern environment, are sometimes unsure of what tradition they represent, or if they represent one at all, are very prone to latch on to particularity and dissidence (selectively passing over the extensive evidence that both Christian and non-Christian rhetor-philosophers certainly knew themselves to be in a tradition of discourse, and related to it as carefully developmental exegetes). While this may be a useful corrective to earlier methods that passed over peculiarities in favor of tradition history, it is nonetheless a suspect and biased methodology that urgently needs correction.

48. The key work is David Balas, *Metousia Theou: Man's Participation in God's Perfections according to S. Gregory of Nyssa* (Rome: Pontificio Istituto San Anselmo, 1966).

49. *Catechetical Oration* 5; hereafter *Cat. Or.*

50. *Timaeus* 45bd.

nature provides it, is enabled to have communion [*koinōnia*] in the light. . . .
It is just so with man, who since he was created to enjoy the divine blessings
must have some affinity with that in which he has been called to participate.
And so he has been endowed with life, reason, wisdom, and all those truly
divine advantages so that each one of them should cause that innate desire of
his to be demonstrated within him. Since immortality is one of those benefits
that are appropriate to deity, it follows that our nature cannot be deprived
even of this in its constitution, but must possess within itself the disposition
to immortality in order that (thanks to this innate capacity) it might be able to
recognise that which is transcendent far beyond it [*hyperkeimenon*] and might
thus experience the desire for divine eternity. (*Cat. Or.* 5)

It is quite evident that here he has been influenced in his reading of the
Timaeus, by Origen, who took from that source a starting point for his
whole doctrine of the *apokatastasis* on which his own eschatology hangs
suspended. Though he affirms the concept of *apokatastasis*,[51] Gregory is
not a simple repetiteur. He makes two key departures from Origen. First,
while Origen taught that the physical body and the spiritual body of the
just saints after death were two different somata, Gregory insisted that
they were two different states of the same body.[52] Second, he replaces the
latter's concept of perfection as a conditional stasis[53] with his own dynamic
notion of perfection as an endless progress (*prokopē*) into the divine life.
This theology of the endless progress of a limited creature into the bound-
less infinity of God, and the resultant dynamic tension of the creaturely
"stretching out" (*epektasis*) in the authentic but paradoxical experience of
the limited directly knowing the illimitable, is motivated by his desire to
supersede the Platonic term of assimilation and replace it with the Chris-
tianized[54] keyword "participation" (*metousia theou*). One of Gregory's
distinctive emphases in theology was to identify goodness as one of the
essential perfections of God. From this it followed that participation in
sanctity was, in fact, participation in true being. At a stroke the distinction
between morality and ontology in the case of a divinely graced creature
became a false one. It was an illumined insight the Christian ascetic tradition did not fail to take to heart, as well as one that modern theology is in
great need of rediscovering.

51. *De anima* 69.
52. *On the Dead* (PG 46:109).
53. The purified *noes* of the elect are reconstituted in the first circle of heaven around the Logos,
contemplating God with rapt attention. But he still wonders aloud in the *De principiis* if their attention will again lapse from that attentiveness, resulting in another cosmic fall from true being.
54. It is central to Balas's thesis, for example, that although the notion of participation in the divine
by means of the praxis of the philosophic life was a common motif in much late Platonic theory of
the fourth century, Gregory's unique synthesis represents the most thoroughgoing Christianization
of the idea attempted since Origen. Cf. Balas, *Metousia Theou*, 164.

The Gregorian concepts of *metousia* and *theōsis* are the same thing seen from different viewpoints: moral and ontological. In the *Contra Eunomium* Gregory explicitly combines the two ideas, showing their essential synonymity by saying that, while deity does not participate in anything as of itself, since it transcends all other realities, nevertheless in Christ the humanity was indeed "brought to participate in the very deity itself."[55] In his treatise *De perfectione hominis*[56] he goes further and explicitly says that Christ did not merely unite his own nature to Godhead but through the dynamic of the incarnation will also admit human beings to participation in deity (*pros metousian tēs theotētos*), at least if we are purified of sin. If both doctrines, though distinct, are basically the same thing, it is because he is fundamentally theorizing about a fully manifested eschatological condition wherein time and spatial boundary, in fact all comprehensible *diastasis*, falls away.

Conclusions

The thought of these two very "close" Cappadocian theologians on the subject of eschatological metamorphosis shows essential similarities of structure, but there is also one clear line of differentiation. Gregory of Nazianzus regularly presumes that the post-death transfiguration of the deified saint-philosopher-ascete, will be comparable to a "promotion" to the higher *stasis* of the angelic order. He imagines the heavenly metamorphosis as an eventual "clarification" of the peculiar problem of human nature in its earth-bound condition as third creation, namely that it is *nous* "mixed with" clay. In the day of deified glory all will be light. The spiritual body will not be one of clay (as Paul also taught in 1 Corinthians) but will have the same harmony and focus as the first creation—the angelicals. His emphasis, in short, is to use the strong idioms of a poet to highlight Origen's sense of the profound metamorphosis involved in glorification. On the part of Gregory of Nyssa, however, we see a concern to clarify what metamorphosis involves. The eschatological new *kairos* of deification, he suggests, will not be a posthumous supercession of human nature, rather a passing beyond the current limits of human nature, by and in the same nature, whose metamorphosized transcendence is coterminous with its glorification in a bounded infinity. The restricting limitations that were once imposed on human nature by long ages of its common experience as a "nature that was separated from God," will be lifted, in Gregory of Nyssa's understanding, by the admission of the creature into the radiant fullness of the very purpose of creaturely human being, which is intimate communion with the endless mystery of the life-giving Presence.

55. *Eis tēn tēs theotētos metousian* (*Contra Eunomium* 3.4.22).
56. *De perfectione hominis* 8.1.

It is a small correction of an esteemed mentor but one that is revealing. It leads me to two conclusions that might on first hearing seem surprising. First, Gregory of Nazianzus is, in fact, much more Origenian than his younger colleague. Second—perhaps more importantly—both theologians are equally eschatological in the fundamental dynamics of their theological systems. If we have not sufficiently appreciated the pervasive matrix of the eschatological dimension in their thought, it may be partly because of our own preset limitations on what might constitute eschatological discourse, and partly because both writers, through a refined rhetorical and philosophical unraveling of familiar concepts, are strenuously attempting to resist the reification of eschatology in their time as a fixed dogma and preserve its vitality as a luminous "dissolver" of categories and, as such, an authentic vehicle for the language of *theologia* which can only (impossibly) be spoken of apophatically. In this the Cappadocians are far from being Hellenistic betrayers of biblical eschatological modes of thought; on the contrary they show themselves as their legitimate heirs and commentators.

11

CHRIST'S DESCENT TO THE UNDERWORLD IN ANCIENT RITUAL AND LEGEND

GEORGIA FRANK

For Christians and Jews in antiquity, apocalyptic storytelling opened up new worlds, whether inaugurated by cataclysmic events in the future or hidden far above or beneath the earth. Some visionaries raced into the eschatological future as others found themselves catapulted into the stacked heavens and plunged deep below the earth's surface. Jesus himself stands among these visionaries. According to early Christian legend, he journeyed to hell during the interlude between his death and resurrection. There the Savior preached to the dead, baptized them, defeated Death, and liberated the just, including Adam and the patriarchs. The harrowing of hell, as the legend is sometimes called, was the subject of numerous sermons and legends in late antiquity and survived well into the Middle Ages. With roots in Greco-Roman myth as well as early Jewish apocalypses, the legend of Christ's descent remained alive in Christian storytelling and ritual.

I thank Kirsti Copeland, David Frankfurter, and Karen King for their helpful comments on earlier versions of this essay. This essay went to press before the publication of an important article on the subject of Hades in Byzantium: Professor Emma Maayan-Fanar's "Visiting Hades: A Transformation of the Ancient God in the Ninth-Century Byzantine Psalters," *ByzZ* 99 (2006): 93–108. I have the opportunity to explore the relation between this iconographic evidence and Romanos's depiction of Hades in a forthcoming article in *Looking Beyond: Visions, Dreams and Insights in Medieval Art and History*, ed. Colum Hourihane, Occasional Papers from the Index of Christian Art 11.

Unlike apocalypses with graphic punishments of the wicked dead,[1] the dead whom Jesus visits endure no bodily torment. Instead, their suffering is temporal in nature: the misfortune of having lived before the coming of Christ into the world. And so these righteous ones remain captive in hell's dark abode until their liberation by Christ, less punished than detained. With Christ's descent, the punished would no longer be the dead so much as Death or Hades personified. This chapter explores the relation between ritually simulated descent in ancient Mediterranean religions and how early Christian legends about Christ's descent transferred this spectacle of punishment to the figure of Hades.

Underworld Journeys in Greco-Roman Religions

Christ's descent to hell belongs to a vast body of tales about journeys to the underworld. Among the most wondrous deeds recounted in Greek and Roman myth were those about the living who dared to visit the dead. Hermes visited Hades to plea for the release of the abducted Persephone. Orpheus descended there in search of his departed wife, Eurydice. For his twelfth and final labor, Herakles entered the underworld to fetch the many-headed hound of hell, Kerberos. Following the enchantress Circe's careful directions, Odysseus consulted the shades of the blind seer Teiresias, his heartbroken mother, and the despondent Achilles.[2] The list is much longer, but these examples suffice to show the quest for either a beloved, a beast, or simply knowledge.

In time, however, such journeys were no longer the special privilege of gods and heroes. Cult and healing centers around the Mediterranean held the promise of symbolic descents to Hades.[3] One famous site was the Greek oracle of Trophonius at Lebadea in Boeotia, where visitors spent days in

1. On whether the dead are already punished or anticipate future punishment, see Richard Bauckham, *The Fate of the Dead: Studies on the Jewish and Christian Apocalypses* (Leiden: Brill, 1998), esp. 49–80.

2. Persephone: *Homeric Hymn to Demeter*; useful syntheses and bibliography available in Timothy Gantz, *Early Greek Myth: A Guide to Literary and Artistic Sources*, 2 vols. (Baltimore: Johns Hopkins University Press, 1993), 1:65 (Persephone); 1:291–95 (Theseus); 2:721–25 (Orpheus); 1:413 (Kerberos); cf. the myth of Er in Plato, *Republic* 614b–621a; Homer, *Odyssey* 11.13–635; Virgil, *Aeneid* book 6.

3. Cataloged in Richard Ganschinietz, "Katabasis," in *Real-Encyclopädie der classischen Altertumswissenschaft*, ed. A. Pauly, G. Wissowa, and W. Kroll (1894), 10:2359–2449. On sites associated with Hades' descent at the abduction of Persephone, see: Pausanias, *Description of Greece* 1.38.5; 2.36.7; cf. 2.35.10 (on the chasm where Herakles emerged with Kerberos, the hound from hell). On the village of Henna in Sicily as the site of Persephone's abduction, see Diodorus Siculus 5.2.3; Ovid, *Metam.* 5.412–24; *Homeric Hymn to Demeter*, ed. Nicholas James Richardson (Oxford: Clarendon, 1974), 148–50. On the Plutonium at Hierapolis, see Larry J. Kreitzer, "The Plutonium of Hierapolis and the Descent of Christ into the 'Lowermost Parts of the Earth' (Ephesians 4:9)," *Bib* 79 (1998): 381–93, esp. 382–87. Cf. Ernest Benz, "Die heilige Höhle in der alten Christenheit und in der östlich-orthodoxen Kirche," *ErJb* 22 (1953): 365–432.

preparation for their descent to the underworld. According to the second-century CE travel-writer Pausanias,[4] the *Trophonion* included an incubation center, where suppliants underwent a strict regimen of river bathing and meat sacrificed to Trophonius and other gods, drank the "water of forgetfulness" from a sacred fountain, and spent several nights. The culminating event was the viewing of a sacred image of Trophonius, followed by entrance to a subterranean shrine, entered through a narrow opening, that required the devotee to enter feet first. With honeycakes in hand, a common food offering for the dead, the initiand learned the future and reemerged, once again feet first, from the "mouth" of the enclosure. Priests led these devotees one by one to the "chair of memory" upon which the inquirer narrated what took place underground, leaving a written testimonial to the events. The entire ritual drama repeated the underworld journey, or *katabasis*, of Trophonius.

Festivals were also occasions for subterranean journeys. The Roman Senate's crack-down on Bacchic cults in 186 BCE was fueled by allegations that male bacchants were "carried off by the gods who had been bound to a machine and borne away out of sight to hidden caves."[5] Towns like Eleusis in Greece, as well as Hierapolis in central Asia Minor, or Henna in Sicily, boasted the presence of a Plutonium, a small subterranean cavern, commonly regarded by locals and visitors as a passageway to the underworld, where visitors could reenact Persephone's annual return from the realm of the dead.[6]

Underworld journeys also played a role in the rites of groups referred to today as "mystery cults." Lucius, the hero of Apuleius's *Metamorphoses* (or *Golden Ass*), recounts his experiences of "pass[ing] down to the underworld" during his initiations into the mysteries of Isis: "I approached the boundary of death and treading on Proserpine's threshold, I was carried through all the elements after which I returned" (*Metam.* 11.6, 23).[7] In graves as far removed as south Italy and northern Greece, archaeologists have found tablets placed on the dead's chest, near a hand, or in the mouth, with instructions for the

4. Pausanias, *Description of Greece* 9.39.5–14 (trans. William H. S. Jones, LCL 4:348–55); cf. Strabo 9.2.38 (= C414; trans. Horace L. Jones, LCL 4:332–33). An extensive study now appears by Pierre Bonnechère, *Trophonios de Lébadée: Cultes et mythes d'une cité béotienne au miroir de la mentalité antique*, Religions in the Greco-Roman World 150 (Leiden: Brill, 2003), esp. 221–71. See also idem, "Trophonius of Lebadea: Mystery Aspects of an Oracular Cult in Boeotia," in *Greek Mysteries: The Archaeology and Ritual of Ancient Greek Secret Cults*, ed. Michael B. Cosmopoulos (London and New York: Routledge, 2003), 169–92.

5. Livy, *Ab Urbe Condita* 39.13.13: *Raptos a diis homines dici quos machinae inligatos ex conspectu in abditos specus abripiant*, trans. Evan T. Sage, LCL 11:254–55. On other caves, see Robert Turcan, *Liturgies de l'initiation bacchique à l'époque romaine (Liber)* (Paris: Boccard, 2003), 6–8. On the polemical context of this passage, see Mary Beard et al., *Religions of Rome*, 2 vols. (Cambridge: Cambridge University Press, 1998), 1:91–96. Even if the truth of Livy's account is dubious, the notion of underground transportation was not far-fetched for Roman audiences.

6. Kreitzer, "Plutonium of Hierapolis," 381–93.

7. Apuleius, *Metamorphoses (Asinus aureus)* 11.6, 23, trans. J. Arthur Hanson, LCL 453.

underworld journey, including passwords, greetings, and ritual formulae.[8] That sense of approach is captured in a Greek magical papyrus from the late third or early fourth century, which lists protective spells and passwords necessary for safe passage to the underworld. If a demon comes too close, travelers are advised to utter the names of the underworld goddess Ereschigal. If that spell fails, they are to recount previous underworld journeys, with these words: "I have been initiated and I went down into the (underground) chamber of the Dactyls, and I saw the other things down below" (*P. Mich.* inv. 7 = *PGM* 70, ll.13–15).[9] From this network of holy sites and sacred texts ancients learned that, with the help of a guide,[10] the underworld was within reach.

Ancient Jewish storytellers also recounted the exploits of biblical heroes who "crossed over," as they say now, and then returned to tell the tale.[11] Visionaries encountered hell as part of their sweeping tours of the cosmos. Some encountered the dead in detention awaiting the day of judgment (as in *1 Enoch*), whereas later apocalypses, such as the *Apocalypse of Elijah*, would focus their underworld tours on punishments.[12] Christians would eventually adapt apocalypses ascribed to Baruch, Ezra, Isaiah, and Zephaniah, which described the underworld and the postmortem punishments—when, for what, and to whom—that both horrified and warned the living.[13] For our present purposes, it is worth noting how well trodden the paths to the underworld had become in antiquity. Through simulated descents, visionary accounts, spells for the dead, and dialogues with the dead, ancient men and women acquired a vivid sense of this subterranean geography within easy and proximate reach.

Jesus' Descent in Early Christianity

The story of Jesus' descent to the underworld took shape over many centuries, yet several features remained constant. Unlike Greek heroes or Jewish or

---

8. Susan G. Cole, "Landscapes of Dionysos and Elysian Fields," in Cosmopoulos, *Greek Mysteries*, 193–217.

9. Discussed in Hans Dieter Betz, "Fragments from a Catabasis Ritual in a Greek Magical Papyrus," *HR* 19 (1980): 287–95, esp. 292.

10. On the guide, see Martha Himmelfarb, *Tours of Hell: An Apocalyptic Form in Jewish and Christian Literature* (Philadelphia: Fortress, 1983), 45–50.

11. On descent (*katabasis*) in antiquity, see Ganschinietz, "Katabasis," 10:2359–2449. Richard Bauckham's magisterial survey of the myths appears in *Fate of the Dead*, 19–38, with an extensive bibliography at 44–48. On visitors to the underworld, see also Guy Stroumsa, "Mystical Descents," in *Death, Ecstasy, and Other Worldly Journeys*, ed. John J. Collins and Michael Fishbane (Albany: State University of New York Press, 1995), 137–54; Sarah Iles Johnston, *Restless Dead: Encounters between the Living and the Dead in Ancient Greece* (Berkeley: University of California Press, 1999). For psychological implications of this myth, see David L. Miller, "The Two Sandals of Christ: Descent into History and into Hell," *ErJb* 50 (1981): 147–221.

12. Discussed in Bauckham, *Fate of the Dead*, 81–90.

13. Helpful analyses of this genre appear in Himmelfarb, *Tours of Hell*, 8–40, and Bauckham, *Fate of the Dead*, 49–93.

Christian apocalyptic travelers, Jesus undertook his journey after death and without a guide. The New Testament is quite terse in its mention of Jesus' descent. The apostle Paul alluded to Christ's underworld sojourn in Romans 10:7, and the idea was picked up by later Pauline communities, as in the reference to Christ's descent "into the lower parts of the earth" (Eph. 4:9). His purpose for the journey appears in 1 Peter, which states that Christ "went and made a proclamation to the spirits in prison" (1 Pet. 3:19; cf. 4:6).[14] The *Gospel of Peter*, considered Scripture in some Christian communities in the second century, includes in the tale of Jesus' death and resurrection an episode in which Roman guards at the tomb were struck dumb when two men descended from heaven and entered the tomb. When these celestial figures emerged from the tomb, they escorted a third man whose head "reached beyond the heavens," and were followed by a cross. A voice from the heavens stopped them to ask, "Have you preached to those who sleep?" To which the cross replied, "Yes" (*Gos. Pet.* 41–42).[15] Long before the descent was to be included in their creeds, starting in the mid-fourth century,[16] Christian storytellers populated the tale with voices, erupting from the heavens, from the below ground, and from a cross. Even the pagan critic Celsus mocked Christians for this belief.[17] As the legend developed in the following three centuries, Christians added new voices and new players to that of the speaking cross.

Already in the second century, the Syrian *Odes of Solomon* recount the events from Christ's perspective. Central to this account is Death's response to Christ's coming into Hades. As Christ describes it:

14. Rémi Gounelle, *La descente du Christ aux enfers: Institutionnalisation d'une croyance* (Paris: Institut d'études augustiniennes, 2000). Also useful, John A. MacCulloch, *The Harrowing of Hell: A Comparative Study of an Early Christian Doctrine* (Edinburgh: T&T Clark, 1930); Daniel Sheerin, "St. John the Baptist in the Lower World," *VC* 30 (1976): 1–22. Charles Perrot, "La descente aux enfers et la prédication aux morts," in *Études sur la première lettre de Pierre*, Congrès de l'ACFEB, Paris 1979, ed. Charles Perrot (Paris: Éditions du Cerf, 1980), 231–46 (I thank Prof. François Bovon for this reference). On allusions to the descent of Christ in Heb. 2:10–18, see Harold W. Attridge, "Liberating Death's Captives: Reconsideration of an Early Christian Myth," in *Gnosticism and the Early Christian World: In Honor of James M. Robinson*, ed. James E. Goehring et al. (Sonoma, CA: Polebridge, 1990), 103–15. On descriptions of Paul's descent to hell, postharrowing, see *Acts of Paul and Andrew*, ed. Xavier Jacques, *Or* 38 (1969): 187–213, cited in Gonnie van den Berg-Onstwedder, "The Apocryphon of Bartholomew the Apostle," in *Acts of the Fifth International Congress of Coptic Studies* (1992), vol. 2, *Papers from the Sections, part 2*, ed. David W. Johnson (Rome: CIM, 1993), 491–96, esp. 493–94.

15. *The Apocryphal New Testament*, ed. and trans. James Keith Elliott (Oxford: Clarendon, 1993), 156–57, hereafter Elliot.

16. The phrase, "and he descended into hell and on the third day rose again from the dead," remains part of the Apostles' Creed today. On its origins in creed, see J. N. D. Kelly, *Early Christian Creeds* (London: Longmans, Green, and Co., 1950), 378–79; Rémi Gounelle, "Le frémissement des portiers de l'Enfer à la vue du Christ: Jb 38,17b et trois symboles de foi des années 359–60," in *Le Livre de Job chez les Pères*, ed. Centre d'analyse et de documentation patristiques, Cahiers de Biblia patristica 5 (Strasbourg: Centre d'analyse et de documentation patristiques, 1996), 177–214.

17. Origen, *Against Celsus* 2.43 (SC 132:382–83); cf. 2.55 (SC 132:414–15); Gounelle, *Descente du Christ*, 36–37.

> Sheol saw me and was shattered
> and Death ejected me and many with me . . .
> and I went down with it as far as its depth . . .
> And I made a congregation of living among his dead;
> and I spoke with them by living lips.[18]

Another Syrian work, the *Acts of Thomas*, addresses Christ as a "messenger, sent from on high, who went down even to Hades; who also, having opened the doors, brought out from there those who had been shut in for many ages in the treasuries of darkness, and showed them the way that leads up on high."[19] The same work also includes the story of a young woman who, after being murdered and then restored to life, described her tour of hell. Her foul guide explained to her the punishments she witnessed. She also encountered there a nameless figure who both resembled Thomas and handed her over to Thomas. Audiences would have recognized in this enigmatic figure an underworld traveler, who, as Thomas's twin, might also be recognized as Jesus in Hades.[20]

In the centuries following the legalization of Christianity under the Emperor Constantine in 312, Christians took great interest in Jesus' descent to hell. Catechumens were reminded of these stories in fourth-century sermons delivered at Jerusalem. On the Monday of Holy Week, Cyril reminded catechumens as their baptism day approached that Jesus "descended alone into the netherworld, but ascended therefrom with numerous company, for he went down to death." "Death," he reminded them, "was panic-stricken on seeing a new visitant descending into the nether world, One not subject to the bonds of the place" (*Cat.* 14.19).[21] For Cyril, Christ's descent both resembled and reversed the prophet Jonah's. Just as Jonah spent three days and three nights in the belly of the fish, Jesus spent as long in the "heart of the earth."[22] Thus Death would "disgorge those it had swallowed up" (*Cat.* 14.17).[23] Cyril

---

18. *Odes Sol.* 42.11–20, esp. 11–15; *OTP* 2:771.

19. *Acts of Thomas* 10; Elliott, 451, cf. 143. Cf. Judas's appeal to Jesus as "shelter and haven of those who travel through dark countries" (*Acts of Thomas* 156; Elliott, 504).

20. On Thomas as twin, see John 11:16; 20:24; 21:2.

21. In *The Works of Cyril of Jerusalem*, trans. Leo McCauley and Anthony Stephenson, 2 vols., FC 61, 64 (Washington, DC: Catholic University of America Press, 1969–70), 64:43, hereafter designated by FC vol. no.; cf. *Cat.* 4.11–12; 11.23.

22. *Cat.* 14.17 (FC 64:43). Like other Christian writers, Cyril contrasted Christ's willingness with Jonah's flight: Jonah being cast into the belly and Christ voluntarily "descend[ing] to the abode of the invisible fish of death." On Jesus-Jonah, see Yvonne Sherwood, *A Biblical Text and Its Afterlives: The Survival of Jonah in Western Culture* (Cambridge: Cambridge University Press, 2000), 11–21. Cf. Lucian, *Ver. hist.* 1.30–2.2, cited in István Czachesz, "The Grotesque Body in the *Apocalypse of Peter*" in *The Apocalypse of Peter*, ed. István Czachesz and Jan N. Bremmer (Leuven: Peeters, 2003), 108–26, esp. 125.

23. On the personification of Death in earlier Greek poetry, see Diana Burton, "The Gender of Death," in *Personification in the Greek World: From Antiquity to Byzantium*, ed. Emma Stafford and Judith Herrin (Aldershot, UK/Burlington, VT: Ashgate, 2005), 45–68.

went on to puzzle how these visitants withstood the airless heat of the belly, so intense that even bones decomposed. Cyril's converts would have been struck less by the personification of Death than by Cyril's excursus on Death's digestive system, at once hot, putrid, and now disgorged.

By the fifth century the story was woven into the celebration of Easter, as the long hours of the all-night vigils inspired meditations on hell. Lectionaries indicate that Christians in many parts of the empire would have listened to scriptural readings containing strong intimations of hell. On Good Friday, Christians heard Psalm 88: "Like those forsaken among the dead, like the slain that lie in the grave, like those whom you remember no more, for they are cut off from your hand. You have put me in the depths of the Pit, in the regions dark and deep" (Ps. 88:5–6). The following night they heard the haunting lamentation of Job 38:2–28: "Have the gates of death been revealed to you, or have you seen the gates of deep darkness?" (Job 38:17).[24] Those undergoing baptism on that long night were instructed by one bishop that each immersion into the waist-deep font's waters corresponded to each of Christ's three days in the tomb. With each plunge downward, the initiate experienced a sightless moment in Hades.[25]

Witnesses to the Descent

One enduring description of Jesus' descent to hell appears in a work known as the *Gospel of Nicodemus*, a fifth-century composition that circulated as part of the *Acts of Pilate*, in which the Roman governor describes Jesus' trial, death, and resurrection.[26] In *Nicodemus*, twins named Karinus and Leucius recount the story of Jesus' arrival in the underworld. Sons of a Jew named Simeon, known from Luke's infancy account (cf. Luke 2:25–34), the twins had died and been restored to life during Christ's descent to hell. The bulk of *Nicodemus* comprises their testimony to Jewish leaders who demanded a

24. These two readings became deeply connected in Jerusalem Easter celebrations well into the fifth century. See Gounelle, *Descente du Christ*, 216–17. See also Robert F. Taft, "In the Bridegroom's Absence: The Paschal Triduum in the Byzantine Church," in *La celebrazione del Triduo pasquale: Anamnesis e mimesis. Atti del III Congresso Internazionale di Liturgia, Roma, Pontificio Istituto Liturgico, 9–13 maggio 1988*, AL 14 = SA 102 (Rome: Pontificio Ateneo S. Anselmo, 1990), 71–97; repr. in Robert F. Taft, *Liturgy in Byzantium and Beyond*, Variorum Collected Studies Series 494 (Aldershot: Ashgate, 1995).

25. Cyril of Jerusalem, *Catecheses mystagogicae* 2.4.4, in Auguste Piédagnel, ed., *Cyrille de Jéru-salem: Catéchèses mystagogiques*, SC 126 (Paris: Éditions du Cerf, 1966), 110–13. On baptismal allusions in tours of hell, see Kirsti B. Copeland, "Sinners and Post-Mortem 'Baptism' in the Acherusian Lake," in Czachesz and Bremmer, *Apocalypse of Peter*, 91–107.

26. A useful overview of the composition and transmission of the *Acts of Pilate* appears in Zbigniew Izydorczyk and Jean-Daniel Dubois, "Nicodemus's Gospel before and beyond the Medieval West," in *The Medieval Gospel of Nicodemus: Texts, Intertexts, and Contexts in Western Europe*, ed. Zbigniew Izydorczyk, MRTS 158 (Tempe, AZ: Medieval and Renaissance Texts and Studies, 1997), 21–41.

written account of these events. The making of that testimony is a story unto itself, as the framing narrative describes how the twins were sequestered and wrote what proved to be identical accounts, verbatim.

The testimony, according to the oldest extant version, preserved in Latin, depicts hell as a dark echo chamber, where voices carry and ignite others. The twins recall how a purple light flooded the underworld, prompting Adam to rejoice, then Isaiah, followed by the twins' father, Simeon. This cascade of testimonia continued with John the Baptist, who remembered Jesus' baptism, then Adam, followed by Seth. Word-of-mouth quickly turned to dialogue, as Satan and Hell (now personified) debated what to do. Satan commanded the gates to be secured, yet Hell hesitated, giving in to his own doubts and confusion. How would Satan expect to resist one who is so powerful? They argued bitterly until Jesus' thunderous voice cut them off: "Lift up your gates, O rulers, and be lifted up, O everlasting doors, and the King of Glory shall come in" (cf. Ps. 24:7). The thunderous voice unleashed the outcry of David, Isaiah, then all the saints against Satan. So virulent was the rebuke against Satan that even Hades joined in. Amid this outcry, Jesus "stretched out his right hand" and raised up Adam and then summoned the crowd to follow him to paradise. Upon completing their testimonia, each twin handed over the sheet to Jewish authorities. Their authors then became transfigured into a bright light and disappeared. Only then, we are told, were their writings discovered to be identical, to the letter.

There is neither landscape nor marked path in either account. Jesus simply arrives alone. He follows no guide except perhaps the traces of distant voices. Yet the narrative generates a sense of mnemonic topography, less a landscape than a sequence of recollections. As each prophet recalls an event from Christ's life above ground, the narrative presents the underworld as an active witness to the events of the Savior's life. Prophets and eventually Hades narrate the events of Jesus' infancy, baptism, and death. Thus even when plunged in darkness the patriarchs and prophets followed Jesus' events above ground with great excitement.

The tale of Jesus' descent would not remain confined to his opponents, whether Roman soldiers in the *Gospel of Peter* or Jewish leaders in the *Gospel of Nicodemus*. A series of apocrypha associated with the disciple Bartholomew shifted the narrative voice to one of Jesus' followers. *The Questions of Bartholomew* (hereafter *QB*), which survives in Greek, Latin, and Slavonic, is difficult to date precisely, although it may include traditions from as far back as the third or fourth century. Here Bartholomew recalls how he saw Christ hanging from the cross with angels descending from heaven to worship him. But when all went dark, presumably at the moment Christ died and an eclipse darkened the land, Bartholomew recalled only the silence above ground and the noises below. There was "only a voice in the parts under the earth, and great wailing and gnashing of teeth." Where, then, did

Jesus go? The narrative shifts below ground as Jesus offers his version of events. He tells how he descended the five hundred steps, while an anguished Hades trembled as he sensed a "great fragrance" and "hear[d] the breath of God."[27] He describes to Bartholomew how he freed Adam along with those around him and recalls Hades' lament to the satanic Beliar. After this discourse, Bartholomew demanded to see Beliar for himself. So Christ led the apostles down the Mount of Olives to the mouth of hell. Michael's trumpet summoned Beliar, a wild stinking behemoth, whose horrifying proportions sent all apostles down with their faces to the ground. Jesus then instructed Bartholomew to trample his feet on Beliar's neck and "pressed down his face into the earth as far as his ears" (QB 4.22). Crushed underfoot, Beliar confessed his demonic genealogy and rehearsed the catalog of punishments meted out to sinners of all types.

A later Coptic work featuring Bartholomew, titled *The Book of the Resurrection of Jesus Christ*,[28] points to even further elaboration of Christ's descent. As in the *Questions*, there are narrators on two levels. Yet here Death ascended into Christ's tomb in search of the Savior's soul, which had not arrived in Hades as expected. In the tomb Death interrogated and scolded the corpse, "Who are you? What are you? You have disturbed me exceedingly." His complaints were cut short, however, when the corpse suddenly sat up, ripped off the linens covering its face, and laughed in Death's face.[29] The legends associated with Bartholomew vary greatly and span several centuries, yet viewed in their entirety they illustrate new narrative directions, further voices, more vistas. Interestingly, one finds more pathways between earthly and underworld locations such that the tomb and Mount of Olives lead to Hades.

This brief survey of legends about the descent is a reminder that the descent to hell was narrated obliquely, in retrospect, from odd angles, and by casual observers. Without landscape, rivers, mountains, pits, or chasms, the tour of hell is remembered as an audiotour, as eyewitnesses and eavesdroppers narrated Christ's journey more often than Christ himself described it. Their knowledge remained partial, incomplete. Some saw, some only heard, some

---

27. QB Lat. 2, Gk. 13–15 (Elliott, 656). The mention of stairs is striking in a legend that typically omits mention of any route to hell. Cf. Fritz Graf, "The Bridge and the Ladder: Narrow Passages in Late Antique Visions," in *Heavenly Realms and Earthly Realities*, ed. Ra'anan Boustan and Annette Yoshiko Reed (Cambridge: Cambridge University Press, 2004), 19–33.

28. *Coptic Apocrypha in the Dialect of Upper Egypt*, ed. Ernest A. W. Wallis Budge (London: British Museum, 1913; repr., New York: AMS Press, 1977), 1–48, trans. 179–230. A work dated to the fifth or sixth century by Jean-Daniel Kaestli and Pierre Cherix, *L'Evangile de Barthelemy d'après deux écrits apocryphes*, Apocryphes 3 (Turnhout: Brepols, 1993): 145–73, esp. 172. Disputed by Matthias Westerhoff, who argues for an eighth- or ninth-century date in *Auferstehung und Jenseits im koptischen "Buch der Auferstehung Jesu Christi, unseres Herrn"* (Weisbaden: Harrassowitz, 1999), 226–27. I thank Dr. Kirsti Copeland for this reference.

29. Cf. Romanos in SC 45.

even surmised after the fact, yet none was entirely unaware of the event. Bartholomew stands out in this regard. Neither compelled to testify nor satisfied by what he is told, he demands his own descent as a way to reenact Christ's. This time, however, no doors or gates must be smashed. Bartholomew's interrogation has an important narrative function: to allow Satan to suffer physically *and* recount his own defeat and demise. For Bartholomew that union of physical agony and narrative voice took place on the threshold of hell. Others moved that drama to the underworld, to which I now turn.

Voices Below

Death's slow and tragic realization of his demise is at the center of several chanted homilies the hymnographer Romanos composed in the first half of the sixth century. Like the Syrian poems of Ephrem of Nisibis (ca. 306–373), Romanos imagines what Death personified said to Satan.[30] Striking in this dialogue is the participation of the audience, who gathered in churches on the outskirts of Constantinople at night vigils on the eve of various church festivals.[31] These *kontakia*, as these hymns are now called, were stanzaic poems, performed by one soloist who sang for all the characters, while the audience closed each strophe with a one-line refrain. Romanos's *kontakia* retold biblical stories from the margins. Major events of Jesus' ministry and death were told from the perspective of his mother, but also from that of characters like the leper, Peter, Judas, Doubting Thomas, and even anonymous women Jesus encountered. They all assumed vibrant voices in these dialogues. Some of his most vociferous characters, however, were Hell, Death, and Satan.

Of the sixty hymns that survive today, Romanos composed no less than six about Jesus' underworld journey, a theme he would revisit throughout his

30. *Hymns on Nisibis* 35.1; 36.11; 38.1; 39.6, cited in Paul Féghali, "La déscente aux enfers dans la tradition syriaque," *ParOr* 15 (1988–89): 127–41, esp. 133–34. To what extent Romanos was influenced by this Syriac tradition is a scholarly debate that is far from settled but need not concern us here. For a helpful overview of the debate, see Averil Cameron, "Disputations, Polemical Literature and the Formation of Opinion in the Early Byzantine Period," in *Dispute Poems and Dialogues in the Ancient and Mediaeval Near East: Forms and Types of Literary Debates in Semitic and Related Literatures*, ed. Gerrit Jan Reinink and Herman L. J. Vanstiphout, OLA 42 (Leuven: Peeters, 1991), 91–108, esp. 92–93.

31. José Grosdidier de Matons, "Liturgie et Hymnographie: Kontakion et Canon," *DOP* 34/35 (1980–81): 31–44, esp. 37–39; Herbert Hunger, "Romanos Melodos, Dichter, Prediger, Rhetor—und sein Publikum," *JÖB* 34 (1984): 15–42; José Grosdidier de Matons, *Romanos le Mélode et les origines de la poésie religieuse à Byzance* (Paris: Éditions Beauchesne, 1977), esp. 37–47, 103–8; Derek Krueger, *Writing and Holiness: The Practice of Authorship in the Early Christian East*, Divinations: Rereading Late Ancient Religion (Philadelphia: Pennsylvania University Press, 2004), 159–88; Georgia Frank, "Romanos and the Night Vigil in the Sixth Century," in *A People's History of Christianity*, vol. 3, *Byzantine Christianity*, ed. Derek Krueger (Minneapolis: Augsburg Fortress, 2006), 59–78.

career.[32] Romanos devoted many dialogues to the underworld's anticipation of Christ's arrival. Although Christ's descent to hell was associated with the end of Holy Week, either Good Friday or Holy Saturday, Romanos's subterranean dialogues reached farther back in liturgical time. His audiences would have first heard Hades and Death squabbling as Christ raised Lazarus from the dead, an event commemorated on the day before Palm Sunday. They commented on Christ's agony, trial, and torture, with empty reassurances that they had sufficient allies aboveground to ensure Christ's defeat.[33] Their underworld conversations continued on the day Christ died in a hymn called "The Victory of the Cross."[34] The Easter vigils often showcased Hell, Satan, and Death's slow and agonized realization of their own demise.[35] Taken together these dialogues form a running underground commentary that will shape the faithful's perceptions of Jesus' final days.

Two hymns in particular describe events prior to Christ's descent. "Lazarus 1" and the "Victory of the Cross," offered extended dialogues between Hades and Death, and thereby reshaped perceptions of the Easter drama. The raising of Lazarus is the subject of two *kontakia*, one sung in the church and the second sung during a procession to a shrine dedicated to Lazarus. These two locations allowed the poet to postpone Christ's arrival at the tomb until the final stanzas of the first *kontakion*. Romanos reserved the actual raising of Lazarus for the second hymn of the pair. This delay opened a narrative space in which to introduce the underworld and let its inhabitants speak. Thus "Lazarus 1" follows Jesus as he walks to Judea, not on the path, but from below, for Hades hears the sound of Christ's footsteps above ground. In hushed tones he asks his companion, "What are those feet, O Death, which march over my head?"[36] Unable to bear the thought of losing another prisoner to Christ, Hades laments his loss of the widow's son and his impending loss of Lazarus. These losses, however, are presented as a bad case of indigestion, for Hades ingests his dead and cannot keep them down. "You bring me the bound dead," he complains to Death, "and when I swallow them, I vomit" (*Kont.* 26.9; trans. Carpenter, 1:144). Death shows no sympathy, pointing out that Hades could have spared himself this malaise if he had not swallowed

32. José Grosdidier de Matons, ed. and trans., *Romanos le Mélode, Hymnes*, vol. 4, *Nouveau Testament* (XXXII–XLV), SC 128 (Paris: Éditions du Cerf, 1967), 566.

33. E.g., SC 37. The Greek text of Romanos used here is José Grosdidier de Matons's five-volume edition in the SC series (vols. 99, 110, 114, 128, 283). Another fine edition, *Sancti Romani Melodi Cantica: Cantica Genuina*, ed. Paul Maas and C. A. Trypanis (Oxford: Clarendon, 1963), numbers the hymns differently. I follow the SC edition hymn and strophe number, with the Oxford [Oxf.] hymn number supplied in brackets in the first citation of any given hymn.

34. SC 38 [Oxf. 22], in Ephrem Lash, ed. and trans., *St. Romanos the Melodist, Kontakia: On the Life of Christ* (San Francisco: HarperSanFrancisco, 1995), 155–63; hereafter Lash.

35. SC 41 [Oxf. 24]; 42 [Oxf. 25]; 43 [Oxf. 28], esp. 17–32; 44 [Oxf. 26]; 45 [Oxf. 27].

36. *Kontakia* 26.8, in *Kontakia of Romanos, Byzantine Melodist*, trans. Marjorie Carpenter, 2 vols. (Columbia: University of Missouri Press, 1970, 1973), 1:144; hereafter Carpenter.

mortals like water. This depiction of resurrection as regurgitation is a common theme in Romanos's hymns. In "On the Resurrection 3" (SC 42:3), he recalls how a corpse he was prepared to eat sat up, strangled him, and caused him to regurgitate his dead. In another resurrection hymn, Christ descends as if he were manna from heaven, but once in Hell functions more like a fishhook, piercing Hades's insides (SC 44:7). More than premonitions about Christ's victory, Hades feels Christ's effects in his gut, literally.

In retelling the story of Lazarus's death, Romanos combines Hell's visceral response with a keen sense of hearing. As Death warns, "For the feet which you hear, and I see they are threatening, are footsteps of one who is raging . . . as he draws near the tomb, he kicks at your gates and searches for the contents of your belly" (*Kont.* 26.11; trans. Carpenter, 1:145). He senses Christ's approach audibly, visibly, and viscerally, like a strong purgative coursing through his bloated body. As putrefaction gives way to perfume, Lazarus's limbs begin reassembling as the worms beat a hasty retreat (*Kont.* 26.12; trans. Carpenter, 1:145). These words shake Death to his core, as he cries, "the fragrance of the Son of God permeated his friend. . . . It reordered his hair and reconstructed his skin, and put together his inner organs, and stretched out his veins so that the blood could again flow through them, and repaired his arteries" (*Kont.* 26.13; trans. Carpenter, 1:145). The detail of this remade body is striking, not least for its close attention both to the hairs of the head and to the intricate crafting of the body's interior: veins, arteries, and organs. We have here mortuary practice reversed, as Jesus demummifies Lazarus. This reembodiment of Lazarus prompts Hades and Death to launch a wailing lament for their lost dominion: "The tomb has become like a dye which changes corruption to life" (*Kont.* 26.13; trans. Carpenter, 1:146). Now the laughing stock of the living, this pair comes to realize in retrospect what Elijah and Elisha's raising of the dead meant. The awful truth is that "no one of the faithful will die, but he will live, especially whenever he is connected with the bodies of the saints" (*Kont.* 26.16; trans. Carpenter, 1:147). That connection to the body prefigures Christ's eventual descent to Hell, for the poet links Hades's visceral response to Christ's revisceration of Lazarus. To see the resurrection as bodily means that even Hades' body must be punished so that it can be taken into account, its clinging hands, its distended stomach, and even its vomit. If Christ is to rescue the devoured dead, Romanos acknowledges the embodied devourer.

Hades' body is the subject of another poem by Romanos, "The Victory of the Cross," composed for Good Friday.[37] Here the poet links the crucifixion to Hades' body, as in the first strophe, which is worth quoting at length:

---

37. A more detailed discussion of this hymn appears in Georgia Frank, "Dialogue and Deliberation: The Sensory Self in the Hymns of Romanos the Melodist," in *Religion and the Self in Antiquity*, ed. David Brakke, Michael L. Satlow, and Steven Weitzman (Bloomington: Indiana University Press, 2005), 163–79, esp. 171–74.

> Three crosses Pilate fixed on Golgotha,
> two for the thieves and one for the Giver of life,
> whom Hell saw and said to those below,
> "My ministers and powers, who has fixed a nail in my heart?
> A wooden lance has suddenly pierced me and I am being torn apart.
> My insides are in pain, my belly in agony,
> my senses make my spirit tremble,
> and I am compelled to disgorge Adam and Adam's race.
> Given me by a Tree, a Tree is bringing them
> *again to Paradise."* (*Kont.* 38.1; trans. Lash, 155–56)

By these words Romanos begins with the elevated site of three crosses and rapidly plunges the audience into the subterranean prison. What joins these two realms is a piercing wound, first Christ pierced *on* the cross, simultaneous with Hell pierced *by* that cross. Middle Byzantine artists would capture that scene in a tenth-century ivory plaque, showing how the cross pierces the earth's surface and reaches down to puncture a recumbent Hades.[38]

Like early Jewish and Christian "tours of hell," the *kontakia* retain graphic depictions of bodily punishments and wails of lamentation. The victims, however, are Hades and Death. The righteous dead suffer no bodily pain, nor, for that matter, does the serpent, who lacks a body and is spared physical torment. Instead, the serpent offers a cerebral response to the death of Christ. As the cunning one explains, Christ cannot plunder Hell; for the serpent personally crafted the cross and enlisted "the Jews" to nail Christ to it (*Kont.* 38.2). His smugness only aggravates the solitude and pain of Hell's visceral anguish. He cries to the serpent, "Run, open your eyes and see the root of the Tree inside my soul. It has gone down to my depths, to draw up Adam like iron" (38.3). The breakdown of communication between the serpent and Hades would be comical if it weren't so tragic. To dispel the fear of punishment, the serpent recalls the pierced bodies of Christ, Haman (Esther 7:10), Sisera (Judg. 4:21–22), or the tyrants slain by Joshua (10:26–27). Proud of the catena of the impaled, the serpent misses the obvious: the pierced belly of Hades. The serpent's obtuseness is the audience's witness to Hell's bellyache.

Why locate Hades' suffering in the belly? Students of Roman satire may recall the mocking depictions of the gluttonous rich who suffer "death by dinner." Satirists such as Persius and Juvenal described symposiasts so bloated by food that they died in their own vomit or suffered a sudden heart attack in the bath.[39] Euripides ridiculed Polyphemus, who declared his belly "the

---

38. Metropolitan Museum, accession number 17.190.44; see *The Glory of Byzantium: Art and Culture of the Middle Byzantine Era, A.D. 843–1261*, ed. Helen C. Evans and William D. Wixom (New York: Metropolitan Museum of Art/Harry N. Abrams, 1997), §97, pp. 151–52; also found online at www.metmuseum.org/collections.

39. Persius, *Sat.* 3.98–103; Juvenal, *Sat.* 1.143–46; quoted in Willi Braun, *Feasting and Social Rhetoric in Luke 14*, SNTSMS 85 (Cambridge: Cambridge University Press, 1995), 39n52.

greatest of divinities" (*Cyclops*, 323–41; LCL 98–99).[40] Moral philosophers also targeted gluttons. As Cato famously remarked, "It is indeed difficult . . . to talk to bellies which have no ears" (quoted in Plutarch, *Mor.* 996D; LCL 12:562–63). And the apostle Paul condemned enemies whose "god is the belly" (Phil. 3:19; cf. Rom. 16:18; Titus 1:12). This is no less the case with Hades, whose wounded belly renders him deaf.

Beyond signaling the glutton, the belly also evoked the underworld. As mentioned earlier, Cyril effectively somatized Hell when he called attention to Jonah's sojourn in the belly of the great fish. At the resurrection, then, Death would "disgorge those it had swallowed up." (*Cat.* 14.17; FC 64:43). By somatizing the figure of Hell, Cyril also evoked patristic images of redemption as the victory over digestion.[41]

To give back and to give birth were closely related images for Christian homilists who compared the underworld to a womb. According to Isaiah 26:19, "the earth will give birth to those long dead." This image appeared in Jewish speculations on bodily resurrection (e.g., *4 Ezra* 4.41–42; *b. Sanh.* 92a), which liken the place of the dead to a womb and thereby interpret resurrection as birth.[42] Similarly the Syriac priest Jacob of Serugh (ca. 451–521) understood the incarnation as the Savior's entry into a series of three wombs: first, Mary's; next, the Jordan River's upon baptism; then Sheol's at death.[43] Many believed that Jesus' birth was painless for Mary.[44] A century before Romanos sang of Hell's belly wounds, Proclus, Bishop of Constantinople, also marveled at Mary's "birth pang without pain," to signal the reversal of God's curse on Eve (*Hom.* 3.5.38; VCSup 66:200; cf. Gen. 3:16).[45] Yet Proclus himself also regarded pain as a proof of incarnation, such that he invoked Mary's "virginal birth pangs" (*Hom.* 4.1, 12; VCSup 66:226) to show that

40. On this theme, see Karl Olav Sandnes, *Belly and Body in the Pauline Epistles*, SNTSMS 120 (Cambridge: Cambridge University Press, 2002), esp. 38.

41. The apologist Athenagoras devotes considerable attention to the connection between poisons and regurgitation in his discussion of the resurrection (*De res.* 4.1–6.5, in *Athenagoras: Legatio and De Resurrectione*, ed. and trans. William R. Schoedel [Oxford: Clarendon, 1972], pp. 96–103). Further examples include: Tertullian, *De res.* 4; Augustine, *Serm.* 127, 5.6, discussed in Caroline Walker Bynum, *The Resurrection of the Body in Western Christianity, 200–1336* (New York: Columbia University Press, 1995), esp. 41, 102–4; cf. plates 12, 13, 14, 16, 28, 32.

42. Bauckham, *Fate of the Dead*, 269–89, esp. 277.

43. Sebastian Brock, "Baptismal Themes in the Writings of Jacob of Serugh," *OrChrAn* 205 (1978): 325–47, esp. 326. Nicholas Constas, ed. and trans., *Proclus of Constantinople and the Cult of the Virgin in Late Antiquity: Homilies 1–5, Texts and Translations*, VCSup 66 (Leiden and Boston: Brill, 2003), 318.

44. *Ascension of Isaiah* 11.14, *OTP* 2:175, cf. 2:150; cf. Isa. 66:7 ("Before she was in labor, she gave birth; before her pain came upon her she delivered a son"); cf. 54:1 ("Sing, O barren one who did not bear; burst into song and shout, you who have not been in labor"); *Protoevangelium of James* 19 (Elliott, 64), which mentions a midwife's postpartum examination but makes no reference to a painless birth. *Odes Sol.* 19.8, *OTP* 2:752. *Gospel of Pseudo-Matthew*, Elliott, 93.

45. Cf. VCSup 66:208–9.

divinity *could* remain undiminished by pain. In his words, Christ's "birth did not diminish him, nor did the pangs of birth alter his uncreated nature" (*Hom.* 2.4.40–41; VCSup 66:166). A sixth-century text, the earliest Greek narrative about Mary's dormition, suggests a painful birth: "I have painfully given birth first to you and then to all those who hope in you."[46] In Romanos's *kontakion* "On the Forty Martyrs of Sebaste," Mary cries, "As I again bear in my arms the One whom I bore in pain, / So I shall now point to my shoulders as a second womb" (Oxf. 57.17; trans. Carpenter, 2.275–76). These examples are too few to point to a parallel between Hades' belly and Mary's womb. At the very least, however, they suggest another connection between the womb and underworld in narratives of resurrection.

The nocturnal setting also played a role in staging this apocalyptic drama. As historian of Greek religion Peter Struck remarks of ancient incubation centers, "the dream served primarily as a vehicle for the god to perform an invasive procedure and manipulate the patient's body parts."[47] Like the ailing dreamer, the Melodist's Hades found his body pierced and his organs exposed. Singing of Christ's descent in the dreamtime of the night vigil, worshipers gave voice to those who heard the footsteps overhead as they breathed in the incense wafting through the church. In a visceral villain like Hades and his gut-wrenching pain, worshipers found a poetry that would render an unseen event like Christ's descent audible, palpable, and thereby knowable. Hades' belly, then, condensed and evoked a host of resurrection metaphors: from regurgitation to birthing, all pointing to the matrix of that pain.

Conclusion

What began as a story told by and about Jesus would develop into a tale narrated by a host of voices of those who simulated Jesus' journey. This proliferation of witnesses meant that the *Gospel of Peter*'s baffled Roman guards above ground would find their story corroborated by those who simulated the journey, as in twin Jewish witnesses from the *Gospel of Nicodemus* or the defiant Bartholomew who interrogated Satan about the events. Multiple narrators meant that Christian audiences discovered multiple paths to the underworld, much as simulated ritual descents did for non-Christians. As tours of hell, however, these descent tales diverged from earlier apocalypses,

46. Stephen J. Shoemaker, *Ancient Traditions of the Virgin Mary's Dormition and Assumption*, OECS (Oxford: Oxford University Press, 2002), 357, §11, esp. n. 13. I thank Prof. Shoemaker for this reference.

47. Peter Struck, "Viscera and the Divine: Dreams as the Divinatory Bridge between the Corporeal and the Incorporeal," in *Prayer, Magic, and the Stars in the Ancient and Late Antique World*, Magic in History (University Park: Pennsylvania State University Press, 2003), 125–36, esp. 126. For seventh-century examples of such invasive dream visitations, see *The Miracles of St. Artemios*, ed. and trans. John Nesbitt, Virgil Crisafulli, and John Haldon (Leiden: Brill, 1997).

in that the dead—whether the righteous or the wicked—neither experienced nor even anticipated physical punishments. Rather, Jesus' tour of hell pointed to one victim: Hell.

I have focused on Romanos's underworld dialogues, in particular, to examine a later convergence of these traditions of descent and punishment and how they became ritualized through the night vigil in sixth-century Constantinople. As Evagrius once advised ascetics, "A stomach in want is prepared to spend vigils in prayers."[48] Hades' bloated belly was a grotesque counterpart for the fasting faithful gathered in Romanos's church to sing of Jesus' descent. Unlike Livy's Bacchants, Romanos's audiences did not need caves, but chose instead to fashion the church as the echo chamber of those events. Late Antique Christians may not have devised the likes of a Plutonium or Trophonium, but through storytelling they discovered multiple points of entry into hell by following the voices.

---

48. *On the Eight Thoughts* 1.12, in Robert E. Sinkewicz, trans., *Evagrius of Pontus: The Greek Ascetic Corpus*, OECS (Oxford: Oxford University Press, 2003).

12

THE EARLY CHRISTIAN
DANIEL APOCALYPTICA

LORENZO DITOMMASO

The closing of Jewish and Christian Bibles barely affected the ongoing composition of literature revolving around the prophet Daniel. There are over fifty postbiblical Daniel apocrypha,[1] representing three types of literature. The *legenda* are third-person narratives, in the mold of the court-tales of Daniel 1–6 MT, which rework, explain, amplify, or augment the biblical story. The *prognostica* are first-person forecasting manuals, like the *Somniale*

An early version of this essay was presented at the First Pappas Conference in October 2004. It is based on material that has since appeared in the present author's *Book of Daniel and the Apocryphal Daniel Literature*, SVTP 20 (Leiden and Boston: Brill, 2005), and in essays that focus on specific aspects of the corpus: "Biblical Genre, Form, and Function in the Post-Biblical Historical Apocalyptica," *The Reception and Interpretation of the Bible in Late Antiquity: Proceedings of the Montréal Colloquium in Honour of Charles Kannengiesser, 11–13 October 2006*, ed. Lorenzo DiTommaso and Lucian Turcescu, Bible in Ancient Christianity 6 (Leiden: Brill, 2008), 145–61; and "The Armenian *Seventh Vision of Daniel* and the Historical Apocalyptica of Late Antiquity," forthcoming in *After the Apocalypse: The* Nachleben *of Apocalyptic Literature in the Armenian Tradition*, ed. Sergio La Porta. The research has been funded by a multiyear grant from the Social Sciences and Humanities Research Council of Canada.

1. Not counting the additions to LXX Daniel and the Aramaic Dead Sea "Pseudo-Daniel" texts. Both groups of texts are products of pre-Christian Judaism, so the label "postbiblical" is conceptually and chronologically inappropriate.

Danielis, which although lacking a biblical model derive their inspiration from the figure of the wise Daniel of the court-tales. The *apocalyptica* are first-person revelations, resembling the visions of Daniel 7–12 MT, which present new disclosures about history and its end.

This essay surveys the chief issues in the study of the Daniel apocalyptica. Late antique in origin, these texts subsequently enjoyed a period of composition and circulation that stretched over a millennium, outlasting even the Eastern Empire. Despite their popularity, however, it was not until the end of the Victorian century that scholars such as Vassiliev, Klostermann, Macler, and Istrin isolated and edited a small collection of *apocalypses apocryphes* ascribed to Daniel.[2] After World War I academic interest in these texts resumed its slumber, reawakening only in the 1970s as part of a broad renaissance in pseudepigrapha studies. Since knowledge of the corpus had not altered greatly in the interim, several late-nineteenth-century assumptions about the apocalyptica lingered into the late twentieth. It was believed, for instance, that these texts were little more than theological curiosities, largely of folk provenance, which numbered perhaps eight or nine textually discrete compositions, all or most of which derived directly from a common Greek *Vorlage*.

Recent research has revealed the true extent and diversity of the corpus.[3] This in turn has challenged nearly all the old assumptions about them. Twenty-four Daniel apocalyptica are now known, not counting those that still require verification by autopsy in MS. Most are Christian compositions, but several Jewish and Islamic examples exist. Many are written in Greek, but three are extant in Arabic and three more in Slavonic, two each in Syriac, Hebrew, and Persian, and one each in Coptic and Armenian. One Arabic text is a translation from Coptic, while two of the Greek texts are preserved in Slavonic versions.[4]

An adverse result of their long history of academic neglect is that, alone of these twenty-four texts, only the *Diēgēsis Daniēlis*[5] can claim familiarity with

2. Afanasii Vassiliev, *Anecdota graeco-byzantina* (Moskva, 1893); Erich Klostermann, *Analecta zur Septuaginta, Hexapla und Patristik* (Leipzig, 1895); Frédéric Macler, *Les apocalypses apocryphes de Daniel* (Paris, 1895); and idem, "Les apocalypses apocryphes de Daniel," *RHR* 33 (1896): 37–53, 163–76, 288–309; 49 (1904): 265–305; and Vasiliĭ Mikaĭlovich Istrin, "Виденія Даниил," *COIDR* 182, no. 3 (1897): 253–329; 184, no. 1 (1898): 135–62.

3. Florentino García Martínez, *Qumran and Apocalyptic*, STDJ 9 (Leiden and New York: Brill, 1992), 137–61; Jean-Claude Haelewyck, *Clavis apocryphorum Veteris Testamenti*, CCSL 82 (Turnhout: Brepols, 1998), 203–11; Albert-Marie Denis, *Introduction à la littérature religieuse judéohellénistique* (Turnhout: Brepols, 2000), 1291–1303; and Lorenzo DiTommaso, *The Book of Daniel and the Apocryphal Daniel Literature* (Leiden and Boston: Brill, 2005), 87–230.

4. The scope of this essay does not permit a description of these compositions, nor can it outline their affiliation with other historical apocalyptica of the fourth to fourteenth centuries. See Bernard McGinn, *Visions of the End: Apocalyptic Traditions in the Middle Ages* (1979; repr., New York: Columbia University Press, 1998).

5. DiTommaso, *Apocryphal Daniel Literature*, 130–41.

scholars other than specialists in early Christian apocalypticism. The subject of K. Berger's fine commentary,[6] the *Diēgēsis* is also the sole representative of the corpus included in James H. Charlesworth's influential anthology, *The Old Testament Pseudepigrapha*.[7] Like all the Daniel apocalyptica, the *Diēgēsis* presents an *ex eventu* review of history and a forecast of eschatological events. Authorities have dated its present form to the eighth or ninth century; the year 797 or 798 perhaps best fits its historical allusions.

According to Berger (and subsequent scholarship as well), the *Diēgēsis* survives in three Greek MSS from the fifteenth or sixteenth century: Oxford, Bodleian Library Canonicus gr. 19 (SC 18472), fols. 145–52; Montpellier, Bibliothèque de la Faculté de médicine 405, fols. 105–15; and Venice, Biblioteca Marciana gr. VII.22, fols. 14–16. The Venetian MS is the only one that claims Daniel as its author. The Oxford copy credits Methodius, while the Montpellier MS is titled *Diēgēsis peri tōn hēmerōn tou Antichristou to pōs mellei genesthai kai peri tēs synteleias tou aiōnos*. Actually, the Venetian text differs so much from that of two other MSS that Berger, who took it to be a variant expression of the *Diēgēsis*, edited it separately. As a result, most of his learned commentary on the *Diēgēsis* is based on the text of the Oxford and Montpellier codices, and is informed by the Venetian text only in the places where it contains overlapping material.

This Venetian text, however, is not a third copy of the *Diēgēsis*, insofar as the notion of a "copy" is normally understood. Rather, it appears to be a Greek version of another composition, *The Vision and Revelation of Daniel*, which survives in a Slavonic MS.[8] Although the Greek and Slavonic texts are not precisely identical, they preserve a similar composition. Yet the Venetian text also overlaps portions of the *Diēgēsis* as it is represented in its Oxford and Montpellier witnesses. In other words, this Venetian MS, which is not an anthology, is a copy of one document but contains portions of text from another document. Its relationship to the Oxford and Montpellier MSS and to the Slavonic *Vision* reflects in miniature the textual affiliation among the majority of the Daniel apocalyptica, and illuminates the principal object of our investigation, namely, the development and function of the genre apocalypse in late antiquity and the early medieval period.

According to most scholars, compositions such as the *Diēgēsis Daniēlis* are apocalypses, a view that is supported by the designation *horasis* in the title or *incipit* of the MSS themselves. However, Matthias Henze has determined

6. Klaus Berger, *Die griechische Daniel-Diegese: Eine altkirchliche Apokalypse. Text, Übersetzung und Kommentar*, StPB 27 (Leiden: Brill, 1976).

7. George T. Zervos, "Apocalypse of Daniel," in *OTP* 1:755–70.

8. Ed. Istrin, 159–62, and trans. E. Folco in Agostino Pertusi, *Fine di Bisanzio e fine del mondo. Significato e ruolo storico delle profezie sulla caduta di Costantinopoli in oriente e in occidente* (Roma: E. Morini, 1988), 81–89. See DiTommaso, *Apocryphal Daniel Literature*, 141–44.

that although these compositions all contain an apocalyptic eschatology,[9] only a few conform to John J. Collins's definition of an apocalypse as "a genre of revelatory literature with a narrative framework, in which a revelation is mediated by an otherworldly being to a human recipient, disclosing a transcendent reality which is both temporal, insofar as it envisions eschatological speculation, and spatial as it involves another, supernatural world."[10] An evaluation of the extended corpus of Daniel apocalyptica indicates that the issue of their genre is even more complicated. Nine of the twenty-four compositions are apocalypses by definition, demonstrating that the genre is well represented among this literature. The remaining texts, though, correspond to all the parameters and implications of Collins's definition save the one specifying that the revelatory information is mediated by an otherworldly being (usually an angel). Instead, the information in these texts is communicated directly to the reader through a series of pronouncements typical of those in the *Sibylline Oracles* and cognate texts. Essentially these texts are "apocalyptic oracles." The category "apocalyptica" thus includes formal apocalypses plus texts like apocalyptic oracles or testaments, which, while lacking this one element of the definition, functioned as apocalypses. Collins also identifies two types of apocalypses: otherworldly, which incline to cosmological speculation and heavenly ascents, and historical, which are marked by *ex eventu* revelations about the past, present, and future. All twenty-four Daniel apocalyptica are historical in orientation, reflecting their antecedents in the biblical book of Daniel.

On closer inspection, it is clear that apocalyptic oracles also differ from apocalypses in ways beyond the formal definition of the genre. Consider the biblical book of Daniel, which is an apocalypse. Three of its four revelations contain a vision followed by its interpretation: Daniel is granted a vision, which an angelic figure must interpret. This structure is typical of all ancient apocalypses of the historical type. Daniel 8, for example, begins:

> In the third year of the reign of King Belshazzar a vision appeared to me, Daniel, after the one that had appeared to me at first. In the vision I was looking and saw myself in Susa the capital, in the province of Elam, and I was by the river Ulai. I looked up and saw a ram standing beside the river. It had two horns. Both horns were long, but one was longer than the other, and the longer one came up second. (Dan. 8:1–3 MT)

The rest of Daniel's vision unfolds until its end, at which point the narrative resumes:

9. Matthias Henze, *The Syriac Apocalypse of Daniel: Introduction, Text, and Commentary*, STAC 11 (Tübingen: Mohr Siebeck, 2001), 6–7.
10. John J. Collins, *The Apocalyptic Imagination: An Introduction to Jewish Apocalyptic Literature* (Grand Rapids: Eerdmans, 1998), 5.

> When I, Daniel, had seen the vision, I tried to understand it. Then someone appeared standing before me, having the appearance of a man, and I heard a human voice by the Ulai, calling, "Gabriel, help this man understand the vision." So he came near where I stood; and when he came, I became frightened and fell prostrate. But he said to me, "Understand, O mortal, that the vision is for the time of the end." As he was speaking to me, I fell into a trance, face to the ground; then he touched me and set me on my feet. He said, "Listen, and I will tell you what takes place later in the period of wrath; for it refers to the appointed time of the end. As for the ram that you saw with the two horns, these are the kings of Media and Persia." (Dan. 8:15–20)

Contrast the structure of the biblical text with the opening sentences from a postbiblical Daniel apocalypse, the Slavonic *Vision of the Prophet Daniel*:

> (1) The angel Gabriel came to the prophet Daniel and spoke as follows: Daniel, beloved man, I have been sent to you to announce and show you the last days. Do place them in your heart and listen to what is going to happen to the human race because of the sins of those who will live in them [i.e., the last days]. The angel took me and placed me on a high mountain where there was no trace of a human being. And the angel said to me: Place this in your heart and listen! Behold four large beasts coming out of the sea. These are the four winds. And I said to the angel: My lord, what are these beasts that have come out of the sea? (2) And the angel said to me: These are the great empires in the last days.[11]

Whereas Daniel 8 presents the full vision followed by its interpretation, the *Vision* weaves both elements together, stressing the visionary component. It also reduces the amount of subsidiary data, such as the biography of the seer or the geographic setting of the narrative.

The streamlining of form is more drastic still in the apocalyptic oracles. Compare, for example, the opening sentences of the *Diēgēsis Daniēlis*:

> According to the God-spoken word which says: "*When you hear of wars and rumors of wars, nation will fight against nation, and kingdom against kingdom, earthquakes* [cf. Mark 13:7–8], plagues and deviations of stars." Then the bush which restrains the sons of Hagar will dry up. And three sons of Hagar will go forth into great Babylonia, (whose) name(s are) Ouachēs, and another Axiaphar, and the third Morphosar. And Ishmael will come down the region of the land of swift passage. And he will establish his camp in Chalcedon across from Byzantium.[12]

The narrative here immediately commences with the *vaticinium ex eventu*. There is no indication that the seer has had a vision that requires interpretation,

---

11. English translation *apud* Paul Julius Alexander, *The Byzantine Apocalyptic Tradition* (Berkeley: University of California Press, 1985), 65. See DiTommaso, *Apocryphal Daniel Literature*, 145–51.

12. English translation by Zervos, *OTP* 1:763.

and details concerning his temporal and spatial coordinates are lacking entirely. Typical visionary formulae, such as "And I saw" or "The angel/He showed me," are also conspicuously absent.

The postbiblical Daniel apocalyptica (both apocalypses and apocalyptic oracles) also differ from the biblical book of Daniel in their microstructures. Indeed, the recurrent appearance of such microstructures in the MS tradition suggests that, contrary to the standard view, the Daniel apocalyptica cannot be interpreted solely in terms of the composition, reception, and transmission of texts and copies of texts. Instead, these processes engaged a series of interactions that occurred on three levels: the motif, the oracle, and the text.

Motifs in the Daniel apocalyptica are nearly always eschatological, since this goes to the purpose of this literature (see below). Surprisingly few, however, derive from the book of Daniel itself. More common are those that germinated or ripened in the postbiblical era, including the end-time appearance of Enoch and Elijah, the last Roman emperor, and the Antichrist/Armilos, and expectations about Gog, Magog, and the enclosed nations. Not every Daniel text contains all such motifs, nor are they unique to the Daniel apocalyptica. Rather, to express the idea in broad terms, the congress of these motifs formed a conceptual storehouse of expectations. Literary critics sometimes refer to a "myth kitty"—a common depot of myths and mythic language from which authors partake. Such depots are shaped by evolutionary forces: neither myths nor motifs are static, nor are their forms immutable or their continued relevance assured. But the evidence connotes that there was a measure of stability to the motifs that continually appeared in the various Byzantine-era apocalyptica and that distinguished them from other types of literature. This stability also resulted when motifs became affixed within larger structures like oracles.

Oracles are the principal method of data transmission among all the Daniel apocalyptica, particularly the apocalyptic oracles, which are arranged as a series, strung together like a string of pearls. Unlike pearls, however, oracles were reused in other compositions, not only individually, but also in fixed sequence with other oracles. Since oracles contain one or more motifs, when the oracle was reemployed, so too were its ingredient motifs. As with motifs, oracles were neither automatically stable nor immune from obsolescence: those who composed/redacted the apocalyptica were not archivists but authors, writing for audiences with priorities. Whatever material was required was used, and what was used was required and expected. The message of these texts was principally one of consolation and exhortation, normally in response to an urgent political or military crisis. They derived their authority from their pseudonymous accreditation to the figure of Daniel, who, through the visions in the biblical book bearing his name, was accepted as an authority on such crises. The name of Daniel the Prophet was the guarantee of the authenticity of his revelation.

The oracles were strung together to form a text. But what does one mean by a "text"? Consider the *Last Vision of the Prophet Daniel*,[13] preserved in twenty-five Greek MSS plus many Slavonic ones. All the MSS are copies of the *Last Vision*: replicas of an identifiable composition, possibly redacted and certainly subject to scribal errors, yet the same composition. Multiple versions of such compositions might exist, or even families of versions, but there is a holistic unity to all the copies, whose diachronic interrelationship we can visualize stemmatically and retrace to an autograph, hypothetical or confirmed. These summary statements are not meant to address the issue of texts and their definition in their entirety, and there are exceptions to the rule. But for the purposes of the argument, the key characteristic of such a composition is that it was received and reproduced as an identifiable entity. In the case of the apocalyptic oracles, this would imply that its sequence of oracles was reproduced in another copy. The composition could be critically edited, even with multiple additions, subtractions, or emendations among its copies, or in cases where its versions differ enough to require synoptic printing.

In contrast to such identifiable compositions are assemblages of similar yet different compositions, like the three MSS once considered copies of the *Diēgēsis Daniēlis*. These share various oracles and perhaps were assembled from portions of the same sources, but are not copies of the same text. Rather, they are new texts, each of which might have its own tradition history, depending on the MS evidence.[14] In such cases critical editions can do no more than identify and sequence the microstructures—the component oracles.

We can now restate the textual situation of the Daniel apocalyptica with more clarity. A persistent coherence of macro- and microstructures (texts and oracles) indicate a complex process of creation, dispersion, and reception that drew freely on these structures. Each MS represents the literary precipitate of a historically dynamic compositional process. Sometimes the MS represents a copy of a composition with a tradition history, real or presumed. Other times it was created spontaneously from portions of older texts. For scholars familiar with biblical books, patristic writings, or classical literature, where Isaiah is neither Jeremiah nor Ezekiel, and where Cicero's *De re publica* must not be confused with his *Philippics*, the concept that texts might have

---

13. Often called *The (Greek) Apocalypse of Daniel*. See DiTommaso, *Apocryphal Daniel Literature*, 186–92.

14. This multilevel process of composition and transmission is not unknown. It has been suggested that the Hekhalot texts of medieval Jewish mysticism are products of the ongoing reassembly of blocks of received tradition. See Peter Schäfer, *Hekhalot-Studien*, TSAJ 19 (Tübingen: Mohr Siebeck, 1988); idem, *The Hidden and Manifest God: Some Major Themes in Early Jewish Mysticism*, trans. Aubrey Pomerance (Albany: State University of New York Press, 1992). Cf. the cycle of medieval texts concerning Mary and Pilate stemming from the *Protoeuangelium Iacobi*, the *Euangelium Pseudo-Matthaei*, and *De natiuitate Mariae*.

been disassembled and reassembled to form new texts may be difficult to envision. But the MS evidence suggests that many Daniel apocalyptica were composed from the storehouse of motifs and oracles, and even if they were copied again as discrete texts, they were just as likely to be disassembled and their oracles repeatedly cannibalized to make other texts.

The potential complexity of the relationship among the full corpus of twenty-four Daniel apocalyptica and their MS evidence is additionally complicated by the fact that texts and oracles common to the apocalyptica are not proprietary to the figure of Daniel. MS copies of Daniel apocalyptica were attributed to figures such as Methodius (like the Oxford copy of the *Diēgēsis*) or left anonymous. Similarly, oracles embedded in Daniel apocalyptica, whether as singletons or in suit with other oracles, also appear in compositions ascribed to different figures. Common examples are the *Revelations* of Methodius and the *Oracles* of Leo the Wise, texts that also have their own complicated tradition histories. At the panoramic perspective, therefore, one must imagine a Daniel complex of traditions, which on the level of oracle and text partially overlapped the Methodius and Leo complexes, and which on the level of motif shared a larger terrain with the postbiblical Sibylline complex and the other historical apocalyptica of the period.

Such complexities potentially occlude dates of composition. Every apocalyptic review of history transforms into eschatological speculation normally after what for the author (or redactor) is his present time, and is marked by a change in the degree and acuity of the historical detail. Eschatological predictions are described less precisely than incidents from the author's present,[15] while the distant past is painted with broad strokes. The turning point from history to prediction thus indicates the date of a text's composition. However, whenever older oracles were recycled, as they were with the Daniel apocalyptica, their historical references were overwritten by new references appropriate to the current situation of the new composition. Thorough redactions erased original referents, leaving the date of a text's final form potentially clear. Some apocalyptica, though, imperfectly edited by later hands, retain leftover turning points, vestiges from the oracle recycling process, which can cause chronological confusion.[16]

Notwithstanding such problems, a *terminus post quem* must exist for each text and every oracle. Many authorities consider the *Revelations* of Pseudo-Methodius the source of many motifs and oracles typical to the medieval apocalyptica of the post-Islamic era. Its significance is beyond

15. One would think that the appearance of eschatological motifs in the text would be enough to indicate the switch from history to prediction. But sometimes such motifs can be historicized, i.e., applied to a past or current event.

16. Apocalyptica are notorious for describing historical figures and events in cryptic language, which can obscure their identities—for modern scholars, not the intended audience—and thus subvert the process of dating them.

doubt: Pseudo-Methodius is the most important apocalyptic text written in the eleven centuries between the Revelation of John and Joachim of Fiore. Its Syriac original, however, was composed at least a century after the Armenian *Seventh Vision of Daniel*, which is a translation of a lost Greek original of the late fifth century,[17] and over two centuries after the *Vision of Daniel on the Island of Cyprus* and the *Vision of Daniel on the Blond Race*, two fragments that are preserved in MS as independent oracles.[18] While the relationship between the Daniel and the Pseudo-Methodian complexes has yet to be clarified, as a class, the Daniel apocalyptica clearly antedate Justinian. Some authorities even believe that they are products of Second-Temple Judaism. H. Schmoldt argues as much for the oldest portions of the Syriac *Vision of the Young Daniel*.[19] Henze, more prudently, suggests that in message, language, and genre, the Syriac *Revelation of Daniel the Prophet* resembles the classic Jewish historical apocalypses of the period.[20] While such evaluations possess a degree of subjectivity, and for this reason are difficult to disprove, the evidence for accepting a Second Temple date is slight.[21] Moreover, as was mentioned, even in their earliest exemplars the Daniel apocalyptica contain vocabulary, themes, and interests that reflect a late antique milieu.

A late antique date presumes that the earliest Daniel apocalyptica were Christian, not Jewish. Both Jews and Christians ceased writing historical apocalypses by the middle of the second century. With Judaism, the failure of three rebellions against Rome, culminating in the Bar Kokhba revolt of 132–135, might have caused the rabbis to abandon interest in full-blown apocalypses.[22] The MS evidence also indicates that Jews of the era were less interested than their Christian counterparts in preserving Second-Temple apocalypses other than the biblical Daniel. There is no evidence, either, to suggest that early medieval Jewish apocalypses like *Sefer Elijah* and *Sefer Zerubbabel* were composed before the middle of the millennium.

In contrast, late antique Christianity produced a full slate of apocalypses, but almost invariably of the otherworldly type. As David J. Frankfurter observes, *vaticinium ex eventu* was not a compositional feature of early Christian apocalyptic literature.[23] This statement may be tempered in light of the *Apocalypse of Adam* and in view of ongoing Christian composition and redaction

17. See the arguments in DiTommaso, *Apocryphal Daniel Literature*, 103–4.

18. Ibid., 97–100.

19. Hans Schmoldt, "Die Schrift 'Vom jungen Daniel' und 'Daniels letzte Vision': Herausgabe und Interpretation zweier apokalyptischer Texte" (PhD diss., Hamburg, 1972).

20. Henze, *Syriac Apocalypse of Daniel*, 17–22.

21. DiTommaso, *Apocryphal Daniel Literature*, 110–13, 118–21.

22. See further Lorenzo DiTommaso, "Apocalypses and Apocalypticism. III. Judaism," in *Encyclopedia of the Bible and Its Reception*, 30 vols., ed. Hans-Josef Klauck, Bernard McGinn, et al. (Berlin and New York: de Gruyter, forthcoming).

23. David J. Frankfurter, "Early Christian Apocalypticism: Literature and Social World," in *The Encyclopedia of Apocalypticism*, ed. John J. Collins (New York: Continuum, 1998), 1:415–53.

of the *Sibylline Oracles*, but its overall sentiment is valid, and the reasons for the temporary retreat of historical apocalypticism remain incompletely understood. The situation persisted until the last decades of the fourth century, when the westward irruption of the Huns initiated a chain reaction of barbarian migrations and invasions that terminated with the retreat of imperial authority in the West. It was during this period of catastrophic upheaval that one of the classic historical apocalyptic texts of the postbiblical age, the *Tiburtine Sibyl*, was written. It was also, as the MS evidence signifies, the era of the earliest Daniel apocalyptica.

The foregoing observations on the genre, structure, and historical context of the Daniel apocalyptica inform issues related to their function, development, and distribution. We begin with two postulates concerning the division between apocalypses proper and apocalyptic oracles. The first postulate is that the division is generic, not functional. Although the formal characteristics of any sufficiently well-established genre will communicate its function, the device of angelic mediation, which uniquely distinguishes apocalyptic oracles from formal apocalypses, is neither the sole nor central component of this process. Moreover, the function of the genre is a property of the underlying ideology that stands behind all the Daniel apocalypses and apocalyptic oracles equally. As noted, their cardinal message is to assure audiences that history remains under God's control. It was particularly, though not exclusively, formulated for communities facing military threat or under intense political, social, or religious oppression. Critical to its consolatory and paraenetic purposes was the reassurance that, no matter their intensity, present-day tribulations were part of a divine plan that would culminate in an eschatological resolution.

The second postulate is that the genre apocalypse underwent a transformation in its early Christian contexts. The evidence for this is the apocalyptica themselves, especially, as has been repeatedly underscored, the apocalyptic oracles, the most visible effects of which are structural hallmarks like the streamlining of form and loss of the *angelus interpres*. This transformation was likely adumbrated by a similar development of the *Sibylline Oracles* over the same period. Whatever the case, the evolution of historical apocalyptica from a point not later than the last quarter of the fourth century was caused by an overuse of the genre apocalypse. This resulted from a tension between the authority of the canon and the requirements of a text that could at once accommodate past history, explain present crises, and communicate future hope.

To explain further, we must recall that every early Jewish and Christian apocalypse is a discrete composition. Wholesale reprocessing of microstructures did not occur: entire chapters of Daniel, for example, are never recycled in later apocalypses or in the Sibyllines. This is true even when texts were products of an accretive process, like Daniel or *1 Enoch*, or when the original prophecy went unfulfilled. In the latter instances, rather than importing, updating, and embedding a long section from Daniel (for example) in a new composition, believers could and did consider apparent discrepancies between past revelation and present reality an interpretative matter.[24]

However, while reification of past revelation did not disappear after Bar Kokhba, within a few centuries it was accompanied by a new method of composition, of which the Daniel apocalyptica are parade exemplars, where microstructures such as oracles were reused and reworked for historiologic purposes. True, the canonical status of the book of Daniel imposed a measure of stasis on the contents of its visions, and authors subsequently devoted much energy to relating its revelatory material to their present-day exigencies. At the same time, other authors evidently found that this enterprise did not address their communities' specific needs (a situation that partly explains the development of eschatological motifs in the postbiblical age). From the fourth century through the Byzantine period, the empire experienced constant military threat, particularly, after the mid-seventh century, from Islam. As new apocalyptica were composed to address each calamity, their eschatological expectations, through initial application and then familiarity, became part of the collective consciousness. The apocalyptic format was reused time and again as the storehouse of texts, oracles, and motifs were constantly refitted to current historical *realia*. Such overuse bred expectation, conversancy, and ultimately transformation. This is indicated by the number (and MS copies) of the historical apocalyptica and political prophecies, as well as corroborating evidence from men like Liudprand, bishop of Cremona, who after his embassy to Constantinople in 968–969 declared, "The Greek and the Saracens have books, which they call visions of Daniel, but which I call Sibylline books, in which are foretold how many years each emperor will live; the events of his reign, peace or war; [and] whether fortune will favor the Saracens or the reverse."[25] In sum, the Daniel apocalyptica bear witness to an evolutionary phenomenon that, although not unique to these texts, found in them its best representative. The genre apocalypse did not vanish in late antiquity, but was transformed structurally and, more significantly, was accompanied by this

---

24. Dan. 9 reinterprets the prophecy of the seventy weeks of Jer. 25:11–12 and 29:10, the Eagle Vision of *4 Ezra* 11–12 reinterprets the vision of the fourth beast of Dan. 7, while several New Testament passages denote a creative exegesis of historical allusions of Dan. 7–12 in response to the Jewish war with Rome. On the last, see Adela Yarbro Collins, "Christian Messianism and the First Jewish War with Rome," in *Biblical Traditions in Transmission: Essays in Honour of Michael A. Knibb*, ed. Charlotte Hempel and Judith M. Lieu, JSJSup 111 (Leiden: Brill, 2006), 333–43.

25. "Habent Graeci et Saraceni libros, quod ὁράσεις, sive visiones, Danielis vocant, ego autem Sibyllanos, in quibus scriptum reperitur quot annis imperator quisque vivat, quae sint futura eo imperitante tempora, pax an simultas, secundae Saracenorum res an adversae" (*Relatio de legatione Constantinopolitana* §39, in *Liudprandi Cremonensis: Antapodosis, Homelia Paschalis, Historia Ottonis. Relatio de legatione Constantinopolitana*, ed. Paolo Chiesa, CCCM 156 [Turnhout: Brepols, 1998], 204).

new form, the apocalyptic oracle, wherein expressions of revelation became streamlined, oracular, and, in general, briefer.[26]

Details about the *Sitz im Leben* of these apocalyptica remain enigmatic. Their message presumes a situation of political distress or military threat, real or perceived. However, studies of ancient apocalyptic literature demonstrate that the underlying ideology cannot be restricted to a single social movement or milieu. Apocalyptica are often perceived as folk or populist literature, disseminated perhaps by itinerant preachers and holy men, and designed largely for an uneducated, provincial population. Many texts, however, address urban populations like Constantinople under military siege, and we cannot dismiss Liudprand's report of the influence of these texts within Byzantine court circles. Similarly, while apocalyptica could serve marginal communities, apocalyptic historiography need not be restricted to the peripheral aspects of society, when it so obviously linked the empire with the divine plan for history. Its teleological orientation carried an immediate appeal for any social group considering itself the special object of history. The innate nationalism of apocalyptic literature clearly could serve official interests, particularly when political power was causally linked to the greater, divinely controlled order.

What is most striking about the audience of the Daniel apocalyptica is implied by the number and distribution of the MSS. These were extremely popular texts for a wide variety of communities over a long period of time. True, this literature was entirely a phenomenon of the Eastern Mediterranean world. Unlike the Pseudo-Methodius and the *Sibylla Tiburtina*, the Daniel apocalyptica were never translated into Latin or the vernacular languages of the West. On the other hand, while the majority of the apocalyptica are Christian compositions, there are, as noted, Islamic and Jewish examples,[27] the latter a result of "back-borrowing" from Christianity.[28] Apocalyptic literature crossed boundaries among Christianity, Judaism, and Islam with impunity. This is not a new proposition, to be sure. But the expanded corpus of Daniel apocalyptica provides us with a rich cross-section of related texts, the study of which might lead to further insights into the dynamics of late antique and early medieval interreligious contacts. Good work has

---

26. Although there is discussion whether macroforms stood at the end of the complex processes of composition and transmission of the Hekhalot literature (see n. 15 of this chapter), the manuscript evidence suggests that apocalyptic oracles were a part of late antique historical-political apocalyptica (Danielic or otherwise) from the start.

27. DiTommaso, *Apocryphal Daniel Literature*, 151–55, 162–70, 171–72, 184–85, 193. On Islamic apocalypses, see David Cook's very useful *Studies in Muslim Apocalyptic*, SLAEI 21 (Princeton, NJ: Darwin Press, 2002).

28. The term "back-borrowing" is itself borrowed from Annette Yoshiko Reed, who in her book, *Fallen Angels and the History of Judaism and Christianity: The Reception of Enochic Literature* (New York: Cambridge University Press, 2005), discusses how early medieval Jews back-borrowed Enochic traditions from their Christian neighbors.

been accomplished in this area, but the diverse elements have yet to be collated coherently.

Finally, the expanded corpus of the Daniel apocalyptica, their cross-religious distribution, and the model of the multilevel process of their composition and circulation have abrogated the standard view that most or all derive from a single Greek *Apocalypse of Daniel*.[29] Many formal apocalypses are independent compositions: the Genizah *Nuvu'ot Daniel*, for instance, is not the *Fourteenth Vision of Daniel*, and neither is a version of the *Diēgēsis Daniēlis*. As for the apocalyptic oracles, we have demonstrated that a more probable model of their literary affiliation envisions a complex system of revision and recycling involving motifs, oracles, and texts. The relationship among the entire corpus of apocalyptica thus is as much radial as it is linear. This would explain the correspondence among compositions such as the Armenian *Seventh Vision*, the Greek *Last Vision of Daniel*, and the Slavonic *Vision of Daniel*, without resorting to the theory that they are versions of essentially the same text. The new picture is far less elegant, but probably more closely reflects reality.

29. See further DiTommaso, "The Armenian *Seventh Vision of Daniel.*"

13

TEMPLE AND ANGEL

Apocalyptic Themes in the Theology of St. John Damascene

ELIJAH NICOLAS MUELLER

St. John Damascene was clearly living in a difficult time for the Christians of Palestine and Syria. Even when we approach apocalyptic in a simply political, eschatological sense, the Damascene had ample justification for scorning the hopes of this world. He lived in a "disestablished" Christian community that, by the time he was writing most of his works, had been under Islam for nearly one hundred years, with no end in sight and with Christian political influence such as his family had wielded in the earlier times of the Umayyad Caliphate waning. In fact, the Damascene clearly does see his political environment in apocalyptic terms: the religion of the "Ishmaelites," or Islam, he calls "forerunner of the Antichrist" (*Heresies* 100.1).[1] For a man who lived his early life in high political circles and would have known the

---

1. Throughout I quote from Bonifatius Kotter, ed., *Die Schriften des Johannes von Damaskos*, 5 vols., PTS 7, 12, 17, 22, 29 (Berlin: de Gruyter, 1969–88), 22:60; hereafter designated by PTS vol. no. On the other hand, Sidney Griffith seems to think that this is not the work of the Damascene. See Sidney Griffith, "'Melkites', 'Jacobites' and the Christological Controversies in Arabic in Third/ Ninth Century Syria," in *Syrian Christians under Islam: The First Thousand Years*, ed. David Thomas (Leiden: Brill, 2001), 22.

meaning of the anti-Trinitarian inscriptions on the Dome of the Rock[2]—
perhaps fitting the category of "Antichrist" belief (1 John 2:22–23)—and who
would have seen the rise of iconoclasm, certainly the conditions would seem
explicitly and literally eschatological. However, the character of his work is
by no means political like modern "rapture" theology.

A concern with returning to scriptural, Old Testament imagery certainly
is key for much of the Damascene's thought. Who else among the post-
Nicene fathers has to write against circumcision (*Orthodox Faith* 98; PTS
12:230–32)?[3] Indeed, he fights iconoclasm (or perhaps Islamic, or Islam-
influenced local iconoclasm)[4] on a firm basis of belief in Christ and a return
to a pre-Nicene style of christological apologetic based in Old Testament
typology and refitted for the defense of icons.[5] It is interesting to note that not
only is the Quran a poetic challenge that would have required poetic answer
from the Christians, but also Judaism saw an increase in the collection and
writing of hymnography, with many of the most famous and imitated poets
roughly contemporary with John Damascene and the other Damascene and
Palestinian canon-writers.

This apologetic turn revives some apocalyptic themes in order to engage
in Christian dogmatic dispute: meditation on the mystical presence of God in
the inner sanctum of the temple, the furnishings (and even the sacrifices) of
the temple, and the iconic role of angels or angelomorphic[6] beings as initia-

---

2. See Oleg Grabar, *The Formation of Islamic Art* (New Haven: Yale University Press, 1973),
48–67. Also Shelomo Dov Goitein, "The Historical Background of the Erection of the Dome of the
Rock," *JAOS* 70 (1950): 104–8.

3. Though clearly a feature of the seventh- and eighth-century polemic literature covered by David
Olster, *Roman Defeat, Christian Response, and the Literary Construction of the Jew* (Philadelphia:
University of Pennsylvania Press, 1994), 120–21.

4. Which is the main thrust of Griffith's treatment of the Damascene ("'Melkites,' 'Jacobites,'"
26–34).

5. I will be arguing for the direct influence of Origen and perhaps Clement and Justin on the
Damascene's use of the "angel" as a christological title. This sense of a traditional topos is exactly
what is lacking in the presentation of Glenn Peers, *Subtle Bodies: Representing Angels in Byzantium*
(Berkeley: University of California Press, 2001), 104–16. Peers makes the valuable point that angels
serve as a mediating third between God and humanity, that provides a useful parallel to Christ's entry
into the world and notes the connection with polemics against Judaism. What Peers is pointing out is
clearly the same sort of angelology and Christology that we find in pre-Nicene authors before Arius
problematizes it. Others have noted an increase in polemics with Judaism after the fall of Roman
power in the Near East to the Arab forces; see Olster, *Roman Defeat*. The "adversus Judaeos" form of
apologetic clearly goes back to earlier apologetic and polemic with Judaism, such as Justin Martyr's
Dialogue with Trypho. Similarities (though not dependence) between the Damascene's and Justin's
approach to the second commandment have already been pointed out by Jaroslav Pelikan, *Imago
Dei* (Princeton, NJ: Princeton University Press, 1990), 52–53.

6. This term should not really pose any difficulty from an Orthodox Christian standpoint.
Angelomorphic simply means that someone or something is depicted as angelic: a very typical
patristic way of depicting what we speak of through a less visual modality when we use the terms
"divinization" or *theosis*.

tors into the mysteries or even as veiled appearances of Christ and perhaps even the Spirit. None of this is really new in the history of the church, but we often have a tendency to denigrate the early pre-Nicene themes with the label "theological experiment," "spirituality," or "ascetic speculation," and not to give it the renewed theological, ideological import that the Damascene himself gave it. Asceticism as angelic life is very explicitly central to his notion of what the human being's final destiny is, as we shall see below.

Angels/Angelic Themes, Temple Imagery in Recent Biblical Studies

Clearly the Damascene himself is not a writer of apocalyptic literature. He imports from apocalyptic only broad themes, a certain inclination toward angelic and temple imagery, and an emphasis on the experience of the vision of God.

Building off the work of Christopher Rowland on apocalyptic and Gershom Scholem on Jewish mysticism, Jarl Fossum endeavors to show us that "mysticism is 'vertical' apocalypticism. It supplements eschatology, 'linear' apocalypticism by dealing with mysteries of the heavenly world and the ways in which man can gain knowledge of those mysteries."[7] As others of the "New History of Religions School," he traces both mysticism and apocalyptic back at least as far as Ezekiel and his vision of the throne-chariot or Merkabah and the anthropomorphic or angelomorphic figure on the throne.[8] Alan Segal provides us with a great deal of rabbinic evidence for the dispute over divine powers and angels—a dispute that is troubled most over apocalyptic texts.[9] These scholars are also concerned with the transformation of the seer of the vision, often into an angelic form, and understanding the temple and its furnishings.

As I see it, these traditions are really the more biblical way of speaking of the divine energies and in the case of angelomorphic humans, *theosis*; but they do this in a way that is more phenomenological and less natural science–based

7. Jarl E. Fossum, *Image of the Invisible God: Essays on the Influence of Jewish Mysticism on Early Christology* (Freiburg, Schweiz: Universitätsverlag and Göttingen: Vandenhoeck & Ruprecht, 1995), 1. See also Christopher Rowland, *The Open Heaven: A Study of Apocalyptic in Judaism and Early Christianity* (New York: Crossroad, 1982), 9–48; and Crispin H. T. Fletcher-Louis, *Luke-Acts: Angels Christology and Soteriology* (Tübingen: Mohr Siebeck, 1997), 1–18. For a survey of Second Temple themes and typologies, see Crispin H. T. Fletcher-Louis, *All the Glory of Adam: Liturgical Anthropology in the Dead Sea Scrolls* (Leiden: Brill, 2002), 1–86. Work on these apocalyptic themes in a number of church fathers has been done in many articles by Fr. Alexander Golitzin.

8. Fossum, *Image of the Invisible God*, 7–8.

9. Alan F. Segal, *Two Powers in Heaven: Early Rabbinic Reports about Christianity and Gnosticism* (Leiden: Brill, 1977).

than with the Greek philosophical terminology.[10] The apocalypses provide imagery not only or primarily to describe an end-time scenario, but rather to reveal mysteries of mystical experience in iconographic form, using the understanding of heavenly angelic ministries and the temple imagery. An apocalyptic sense of the experience of God explains how the Damascene's defense of the icons comes not just from a dry reading and exegesis of temple and angel traditions in the Bible, but rather a living sense of vision. To speak of a "prototype," such as the Damascene does, from this perspective, goes back (via apocalyptic and mystical experience) to a very biblical notion of the correspondence of heavenly pattern or figure and earthly worship, and not primarily to Platonic or Neoplatonic theories (though there is clearly mixture with these via the medium of the Greek language and his Greek antecedents).

Angels, Eschatology, and Monastic Life in the Damascene's Thought

The Damascene's use of angels in his theology is very important for us to understand, because his notion of humanity is very highly colored by angels and angelic life. The ultimate destiny of the human is to be in angelic communion with God through sight: "They see God to such an extent as is possible for them, and this is their food. . . . They take whatever form the Lord may command, and thus they appear to men and reveal divine mysteries to them" (*Orthodox Faith* 17:59–60, 62–64; PTS 12:47; FC 37:207–8).[11]

In a later chapter of *On the Orthodox Faith*, a very closely corresponding imagery is given for human eschatological communion: "They [the eucharistic gifts] are called antitypes of things to come . . . because it is through them that we participate in the divinity of Christ now, while then it will be by the nous and through vision alone" (*Orthodox Faith* 86:180–82; PTS 12:198; FC 37:361).

Clearly these quotes bear great comparison to the rabbinic notion of "feeding on the light of the Shekina," an interpretive topos based on Exodus 24:9–11.[12] Using the categories of the New History of Religions School, this

10. Sebastian Brock expresses this as the difference between a "philosophical approach" that uses definitions and a "symbolic approach" that uses paradoxes such as we encounter in trying to correlate human, angel, and Word; see Sebastian Brock, *The Luminous Eye: The Spiritual World Vision of Saint Ephrem the Syrian*, CS 124 (Kalamazoo: Cistercian Publications, 1992), 23–25.

11. The English is from Saint John of Damascus, *Writings*, trans. Frederic H. Chase Jr., FC 37 (Washington, DC: Catholic University of America Press, 1958); hereafter FC 37.

12. See chapter 5, "'Nourished by the Splendor of the Shekinah': A Mystical Motif in Rabbinic Midrash," in Ira Chernus, *Mysticism in Rabbinic Judaism: Studies in the History of Midrash* (Berlin: de Gruyter, 1982), 74–87. A New Testament application of these motifs can be seen in Fletcher-Louis, *All the Glory of Adam*, 63–70.

is a claim for an angelomorphic destiny of the human. Clearly this notion ties in (through the visual logic of Christian liturgy) with the temple (Rev. 4; 7:15; 14:15–18, et al.), veil (Rev. 15:5; 19:11) and door (Rev. 4:1) imagery so important to apocalyptic and also evident in the letters of Paul as the explanation of the deepening of revelation through the seeing of the Lord (2 Cor. 3:12–18).

Angels themselves are "made . . . after his own image in a bodiless nature" (*Orthodox Faith* 17.3–4; PTS 12:14; FC 37:205) even though we are superior to angels in our closer sharing of the glory of the Son through the incarnation (*Divine Images* 3.26.42–62; PTS 17:133–34; *On the Two Wills of Christ* 16.30; PTS 22:199). And the human is also by rank or reflection somehow angelic (as in *Orthodox Faith* 26.24–26; PTS 12:76; FC 37:235; he quotes from Gregory Nazianzus, *Oration* 38.11): "And God made man . . . as a sort of miniature world within a larger one, another adoring angel." This particular quotation very clearly echoes what is found in *2 Enoch* 30.10, where Adam is described as microcosm and a second angel. It is worth noting that Gregory Nazianzus the elder was originally part of a Judeo-pagan cult, which could easily have had similar scriptures. The quote from Nazianzus also makes much use of the idea that the human is a *zōon* ("living creature," *Orthodox Faith* 26.32) or *ousia zōsa* ("living being," 26.44). In the use of this term Nazianzus and the Damascene are paradoxically using a type of angel (from Hab. 3:2 LXX, probably associated with cherubim, perhaps the two overshadowing the temple's altar) to portray the human's two-part nature as making the human mobile and like the chariot or *merkabah* of God, and perhaps, by means of applying angelic imagery to the human, showing the human to be above angels, or a higher angel.

All this ties in very well with the Damascene's concern not just to shore up Christianity against the dominance and influence of Islam, but also the position of monasticism as a paradisial and angelic life that indicates human angelomorphic destiny against the pressure of a vulnerable Christian community, which seemed to have felt the need to procreate to keep up their numbers (*Orthodox Faith* 97.1–3, 52–61, 70–72; PTS 12:227–30).

Defense of Icons: Angelic Iconography of the Angelomorphic Word

It should be no surprise, when we see how explicit the Damascene is on the angelic destiny of the human being, that we can understand this whole manner of describing spiritual experience as more iconic and less natural science, and yet fairly consistent and systematic as imagery. One of the strongest examples of angelic themes intruding into the Damascene's arguments is when he says, "It is therefore because of the Holy Spirit that we know Christ, the Son of God, and God, and in the Son we behold the Father; for by nature the *Logos* [Word] is an *angelos* [angel] of the *Nous* [Mind] and the Spirit discloses the *Logos*" (*Divine Images* 3.18.25–29; PTS 17:127; Louth, 97).[13]

Now this could be a patristic/philosophical, natural scientific explanation for the process of expressing mind through thought and breath. And it clearly has one such root (as a psychological analogy for the Trinity), as noted by Andrew Louth in his translation (Louth, 97n61). But it also has clear precedent (another root) in Clement of Alexandria's *Paedagogos*:

> Who could educate us more philanthropically? For therefore, at first, on the one hand, for the elder people there was an older covenant and the law educated the people with fear and the *Logos* was an *angelos*, but on the other hand with the new people a new and young covenant is given and the *Logos* has been born and fear has been changed to love and that mystical *angelos* has been born. (*Paedagogus* 1.7.59.1)[14]

In nearby passages Clement also deals with the important Scripture regarding Jacob's wrestling with the angelomorphic figure, and acquiring the name "Israel," with Clement taking his cue from Philo and perhaps much older tradition.[15] This is a very powerful story for the Damascene as well and provides one of his surely most heated and bold exclamations of the *Divine Images* (1.22.4–9; PTS 17:11; Louth, 36):

> I have seen [*eidon*] the human form [*eidos*] of God, "and my soul has been saved" (Gen. 32:30). I see the image of God as Jacob saw it, if in another way. For he saw an immaterial image, proclaiming beforehand what was to come to the immaterial eyes of the intellect [*nous*], while I have seen the image of one seen in the flesh that enkindles the memory."

Origen also is a precedent for what the Damascene says in *Divine Images* 3.18:

13. I have used the English translation of Andrew Louth, *St. John of Damascus: Three Treatises on the Divine Images* (New York: St. Vladimir's Seminary Press, 2003); hereafter Louth. I have, however, reinserted the Greek words to show that the sense of this passage is that the Logos is *angel*, specifically because we are not talking about a purely auditory word but rather a logos as icon or icon as angel.

14. Clementis Alexandrini, *Paedagogus*, ed. Miroslav I. Marcovich (Leiden: Brill, 2002), 37.6–11; my translation. This same passage is mentioned, without much comment, as evidence of angelomorphic Christology in Charles Gieschen, *Angelomorphic Christology: Antecedents and Early Evidence* (Leiden: Brill, 1998), 194.

15. If Exod. 23:17 has the verb vocalized as active not passive, we get the sense of Israel as those who see God (ritually, on pilgrimage). See Gary Anderson, "Towards a Theology of the Tabernacle and Its Furniture." This article is labeled "not for citation" but is easily found in at least three locations on the Internet and is a fine study that deserves to be properly published; see http://orion.mscc.huji .ac.il/symposiums/9th/papers/AndersonPaper.pdf.

But the Son also may be called the *Logos* because he reports the secret things of his Father who is *Nous* in the same way as the Son who is called the *Logos*. For as with us the *Logos* is an *angelos* of those things which the *Nous* sees, so the *Logos* of God, knowing the Father, since no created being can approach him without a guide [*hodēgos*], reveals the Father whom he knows. For no one knows the Father save the Son. And he to whomsoever the Son reveals him and inasmuch as he is the *Logos*, he is the *angelos* of great counsel, who has the government upon his shoulders; for he entered his kingdom by enduring the cross. (*Commentary on John*, 1.38.277–78)[16]

This passage shows the earlier patristic precedent for combining psychological analogy (albeit without the Spirit) and scriptural christological typology, clearly intending the Word to be depicted as *angel* and not just a generic messenger or a spiritual neuron.

However, the Damscene does not stop with what already is a strongly angelomorphic statement about Christ, but I believe he extends it further. Having said that the Logos is an angel of the Mind, he then says that "the Spirit is therefore the like (*homoia*) and undeviating image (*aparallaktos . . . eikōn*) of the Son, being different only in proceeding; for the Son is begotten, but does not proceed" (*Divine Images* 3.18.29–32). While this is clearly traditional Trinitarian theology, there is something else at play. He has just before this called the Word an angel; if the Spirit is "like an undeviating image" of the Word then perhaps the Spirit is also, as icon of the Son, angel. Such a thing seems to be implied by the description of Spirit revealing Son/Word revealing Father/Mind. But where would we have such a dual angelic revelation of God? The "mercy seat" with its two angels is such an image and a justification of icons in itself, and perhaps it corresponds on a theological level of interpretation to the two "Living Creatures" (which we saw above in anthropological interpretation) of Habakkuk 3:2 LXX: "*en mesō dyo zōōn gnōthēsē*" ("in the midst of two living creatures you will be known"). And within Second Temple and early Christian and rabbinic literature, including apocalyptic or apocalyptically tinged thought, this temple icon already has moved toward a divine status; we need only refer to Philo's *On the Cherubim* 27–28; Irenaeus, *On the Apostolic Preaching* 1.9–10; *b. Yoma* 54; *The Ascension of Isaiah* 9.31–40; and perhaps Origen, *On First Principles* 1.3.4. The Damascene in *Divine Images* 1.15.6–13 (PTS 17:88) treats the temple icons of the cherubim as created and circumscribable angels, not God, but then says that they are overshadowed by the "divine mysteries," perhaps thus taking on a higher, prefigurative image of the Eucharist, but also perhaps of revelation of the Trinity—surely something that is in any case not missing from the theology of the Eucharist.

16. Origène, *Commentaire sur Saint Jean*, trans. Cécile Blanc, SC 120 (Paris: Éditions du Cerf, 1966), 198; my translation.

Canon: Experience of Vision and Ascent?

John Climacus, whose *Ladder* the Damascene may have known, says in the *Shepherd*, clearly not a writing for the novice (cf. 93–100 for description of the shepherd's apocalyptic gnosis) but rather for an "elder," "A certain man beloved of God told me that although God always rewards his servants with gifts, yet he does so especially on the yearly festivals and the feasts of the master" (*Shepherd* 17; Paraclete, 386; Holy Transfiguration, 234).[17] We have no need to list all the somewhat apocalyptic (remembering the definition of apocalyptic given above, by Fossum) visions that are associated with appearances of saints (simply consult *Divine Images*) or with the day of the death of a saint—which would, with canonization, become a festival. If this is true then long, extended hymns on feasts should be evidence of, or seeking of, gifts.

The Damascene has numerous canons; we will simply pick a few points from several. In the Damascene's Christmas canon we observe an attempt to see at once both heaven and earth. This is not simply hyperbole, but an exhortation to ascension: "O Christ . . . come to us and grant us cleansing; make the path easy for us, whereby we may ascend and so attain to glory" (Ode 5.1; *Anthologia Carminum*, 206; *Festal Menaion*, 275).[18] His canon on the theophany is a cosmic song of victory over the powers of chaos depicted in mythic terms (*Anthologia Carminum*, 209–13; *Festal Menaion*, 367–82). The canon for pascha calls, "Let us purify the senses, and in the unapproachable light of the resurrection we shall see Christ shining forth" (Ode 1.2; *Anthologia Carminum*, 218; Lash, 1).[19] The departed saints stand among the faithful as angelomorphic: "Let the Prophet Avvakoum, inspired by God, keep the divine watch with us, and show forth the radiant Angel, who with resounding voice declares, 'Today is salvation for the world, for Christ has risen as omnipotent'" (*Anthologia Carminum*, 219; Lash, 2).[20] The whole of the paschal canon is awash in light and assurance that Christ is present and

---

17. No critical text exists yet. I have used the Greek text: Ἰωάννου τοῦ Σιναΐτου, Κλίμαξ, ed. Archimandrite Ignatius Oropos (Attika: Monastery of the Paraclete, 1997). For the English I have used the only edition with the *Shepherd*: St. John Climacus, *The Ladder of Divine Ascent* (Boston: Holy Transfiguration Monastery, 2001). The issue of the Damascene's use of Climacus is complex. I will give the short explanation: the Damascene quotes from step 11 (Paraclete, 175) in his *Homily on the Transfiguration* (9.16–17; PTS 29:448) and seems to make use of Climacus's warnings against visions (steps 3 and 26) in his treatment of Muhammad in *On Heresies* 100 (PTS 22:60–67).

18. The closest to a critical text of the canons is in *Anthologia Graeca Carminum Christianorum*, ed. Wilhelm von Christ and Matthaios K. Paranikas (Leipzig: Teubner, 1871). The English translation is from Mother Mary and Kallistos Ware, *Festal Menaion* (London: Faber and Faber, 1969).

19. English translation with notes by Archimandrite Ephrem Lash, http://anastasis.org.uk/Paschal%20Canon%20Noted.pdf; hereafter Lash.

20. This comes from Gregory of Nazianzus's *Oration* 45.1 on pascha. In Gregory's oration, Habakkuk's "watch" refers to Hab. 2:1; but he expresses the desire to respond to the angel's annunciation in a way that echoes Hab. 3:2, when combined with *Orat.* 45.7 (which repeats the same content as *Orat.* 38.11 mentioned above). In other words, the angel in the canon is one of the δύο ζώων of Hab. 3:2

shedding his presence on the worshipers in a way that could be described as angelomorphic or even perhaps cherubic.

However, the most remarkable canon in apocalyptic/mystical terms is the transfiguration canon, which can be compared to his homily for the same feast. The homily definitely shows an ascent to discussion of the summit event on Mount Tabor and then descends again to mundane concerns. However, the canon for the transfiguration begins on Sinai and conflates it with Tabor (Ode 1), then moves to the tabernacle and the experience of God there to Tabor again (Ode 3). The canon goes from the burning bush to Tabor (Ode 4), and then goes from the creation of man to Isaiah's vision of the "live coal of the Godhead that consumes sins while it enlightens souls" (Ode 5.4; *Mēnaion Augoustou*, 93; *Festal Menaion*, 487).[21] The canon continues in a similar vein throughout, until the end where we are exhorted, "[Let us go] up into the holy and heavenly mountain, let us stand in spirit in the city of the living God and let us gaze with our minds at the spiritual Godhead of the Father and the Spirit, shining forth in the only-begotten Son" (Ode 9.3; *Mēnaion Augoustou*, 98; *Festal Menaion*, 494). However, it is the last troparion of the canon, which is later taken into many collections of eucharistic prayers, that seems to justify the sense that the hymn and the hymnographer himself are taking part in the theophany(ies) on the mount(s): "You have taken me captive with longing for you, O Christ, and have transformed me with your divine love. Burn up my sins with the fire of the Spirit, and count me worthy to take my fill of delight in you, that dancing for joy I may magnify your two comings" (Ode 9.4; see paschal canon, Ode 9, *Mēnaion Augoustou*, 98; *Festal Menaion*, 494). I believe that this last troparion shows us that the writing and singing of these canons are more than an imaginative exercise or static "icons" but rather a straining past these things to real mystical and apocalyptic experience, as the experienced elder told John Climacus.

Conclusion

For the Damascene, the liturgical life has an abiding iconography that is both central to the living scriptural sense of the inner mystery of approach to God through the temple and really relates the worshiper to the heavenly liturgy, and thus continues as an ongoing eternal and thus ever-present structure to mystical experience. This is not to deny that which is "new" in the incarnation, but to say that it is all the structure of one liturgy. Old Testament and New Testament are one in experience of the mystical vision of Christ, using the

to which we are to move to imitate with purified senses and filled with light, as we, with the angels, make cherubic altar space for Christ's appearance.

21. No critical text for this particular canon; see Μηναῖον τοῦ Αὐγοῦστου (Athens: Apostolike Diakonia, 1993).

mediation of angels, angelic states of humanity, icons, and the angelomorphic appearance of the Word and Image of God. In this "temple" of experience and vision of God, the angel mediates as an image or icon of God and human, which parallels the human movement from earth to heaven as bearer of the Word and Image of God.

14

IMAGES OF THE SECOND COMING
AND THE FATE OF THE SOUL
IN MIDDLE BYZANTINE ART

NANCY PATTERSON ŠEVČENKO

When, forty days after the crucifixion, Christ ascended into heaven, the Bible relates that "while he was going, and they (the apostles) were gazing up toward heaven, suddenly two men in white robes stood by them. They said, 'Men of Galilee, why do you stand looking up toward heaven? This Jesus, who has been taken up from you into heaven, will come in the same way as you saw him go into heaven'" (Acts 1:10–11). These very words, referring to Christ's second coming, were often inscribed directly onto Byzantine paintings of the Ascension, a reminder of his promise to return.

The prospect of the second coming of Christ, the *deutera parousia*, and of its central event, the terrible day of judgment, was considered very real indeed in the medieval period.[1] Though the Apocalypse was not fully accepted as a canonical text in Byzantium until somewhere around the middle of the fourteenth century,[2] and it was not illustrated until the post-Byzantine

---

1. For the theological aspects of the Last Judgment, see the various papers presented in 1999 at a symposium at Dumbarton Oaks on "Byzantine Eschatology: Views on Death and the Last Things, 8th to 15th Centuries," published in *DOP* 55 (2001).

2. Johannes Leipoldt, *Die Geschichte des neutestamentlichen Kanons* (Leipzig: Hinrichs, 1907; repr., Leipzig: Zentralantiquariat der Deutschen demokratischen Republik, 1974), 51–103; Josef Schmid,

period, images of the Last Judgment were being painted as early as the ninth century. These images can enhance our understanding of how the Last Judgment and the fate of the soul immediately after death were envisaged in the Middle Byzantine period.[3]

Images of the Second Coming

I shall start by presenting a typical Last Judgment composition of the Middle Byzantine period, and by describing one by one its basic components.[4] For convenience and clarity, I have chosen an icon of the Last Judgment on Mount

---

Studien zur Geschichte des griechischen Apokalypse-Textes, part 2 (Munich: Karl Zink Verlag, 1955), esp. 31–43. The text was therefore not routinely included in New Testament manuscripts, and not illustrated when they were. Readings from the Apocalypse never entered the liturgy. This is not to say, as shall become clear, that certain elements of the Apocalypse imagery did not make their way into depictions of the Last Judgment.

3. The research here has been stimulated by several fundamental studies: those of Beat Brenk on the Last Judgment, "Die Anfänge des byzantinischen Weltgerichtsdarstellung," *ByzZ* 57 (1964): 106–26; idem, *Tradition und Neuerung in der christlichen Kunst des ersten Jahrtausends. Studien zur Weltgerichtsbilder* (Vienna: Böhlau in Komm, 1966); and idem, "Weltgericht" in *Lexikon der christlichen Ikonographie*, ed. Engelbert Kirschbaum et al. 8 vols (Rome: Herder, 1968–76), 4:513–23; that of Miltiades K. Garidis, *Études sur le Jugement Dernier post-byzantin du XVe à la fin du XIXe siècle. Iconographie-Esthetique* (Thessalonike: Hetairea Makedonikon Spoudon, 1985); that of Rainer Stichel on late- and post-Byzantine mortality images, *Studien zum Verhältnis von Text und Bild spät-und nachbyzantinischer Vergänglichkeitdarstellungen*, Byzantina Vindobonensia 5 (Vienna: Böhlau in Komm., 1971); and the essay of Hans-Georg Beck, *Die Byzantiner und ihr Jenseits: Zur Entstehungsgeschichte einer Mentalität* (Munich: Verlag der Bayerischen Akademie der Wissenschaften, 1979). See also the works cited in the following note. Shortly after this paper was delivered, a fine article by Marcello Angheben appeared in print: "Les Jugements derniers byzantins des XIe–XIIe siècles et l'iconographie du jugement immédiat," *CaA* 50 (2002): 105–34; this article deals with many of the same monuments and issues as mine. I have included references to it wherever relevant but do not venture to debate its theological arguments. See also the recent (since this writing) volume of studies on the theme of the Last Judgment: *Alfa e Omega: Il Giudizio Universale tra Oriente e Occidente*, ed. Valentino Pace and Marcel Angheben (Castel Bolognese: Itaca, 2006). Recent studies involving Last Judgment images in the West are those of Jérôme Baschet, *Les justices de l'au-delà: Les représentations de l'enfer en France et en Italie (XIIe–XVe siècle)* (Rome: École française de Rome, 1993); and idem, *De l'art comme mystagogie: L'iconographie du Jugement dernier et des fins dernières à l'époque gothique*, ed. Yves Christe (Poitiers: Université de Poitiers, 1996).

4. For works of the Byzantine and post-Byzantine period, see Garidis, *Études*; Desanka Milošević, *The Last Judgment* (New York: Taplinger, 1964); Doula Mouriki, "An Unusual Representation of the Last Judgment in a Thirteenth-Century Fresco at St. George near Kouvaras in Attica," *DCAE* 4, no. 8 (1975–76): 145–71, pls. 70–93; Paul A. Underwood, *The Kariye Djami*, 4 vols. (New York and Princeton, NJ: Bollingen Foundation, 1966–1975), 1:199–212; 3:pls. 368–407; Sirarpie Der Nersessian, "Program and Iconography of the Frescoes of the Pareclesion," in Underwood, *Kariye Djami*, 4:305–49, esp. 325–31; Anne-Mette Gravgaard, "How to Paint the Day of Judgement," *SSMG* 7–8 (1983–84): 67–78. See also *Contribution à l'étude du jugement dernier dans l'art byzantin et post-byzantin*, ed. Tania Velmans, *CaB* 6 (Paris: Publications Langues 'O, 1984); Juliette Renaud, *Le cycle de l'Apocalypse de Dionysiou* (Paris: Presses universitaires de France, 1943), 1–17.

Sinai, an icon that probably
dates to the twelfth century
(fig. 14.1).[5] There are, incidentally, only three painted
icons of the Last Judgment
that survive from the Byzantine period, all of them in
the monastery of St. Catherine on Mount Sinai.[6]

The composition con-
sists of a variety of parts,
many of them unrelated.
Across the top, spreading
across two columns, so to
speak, is Christ seated in
his mandorla, having ar-
rived to judge the quick and
the dead. He is flanked by
the twelve apostles seated
on high-back thrones, and
is surrounded by a body-
guard of angels, their lances
flashing, and an archangel
clad in the jewelled imperial *loros*. Next to Christ are
the traditional two figures

Figure 14.1. Mount Sinai, Monastery of St. Catherine: icon
of the Last Judgment.

of the *deesis*, the Virgin and John the Baptist, interceding with him on behalf

5. Georgios and Marie Soteriou, Εἰκόνες τῆς μονῆς Σινᾶ, 2 vols. (Athens, 1956, 1958), 1:pl. 151;
2:130–31 (hereafter Sinai 151); Kurt Weitzmann, *The Icon: Holy Images—Sixth to Fourteenth Century*
(New York: Braziller, 1978), pl. 23 (in color); Panagiotes Vokotopoulos, Βυζαντινὲς Εἰκόνες (Athens:
Ekdotike Athenon, 1995), pl. 20 (in color). See too the careful analysis of the traditional Last Judgment composition by Angheben, "Jugements derniers."

6. Soteriou and Soteriou, Εἰκόνες, 1:pl. 150; 2:128–30 (hereafter Sinai 150; twelfth century); John
Galey, *Sinai and the Monastery of St. Catherine* (Garden City, NY: Doubleday, 1980), fig. 106 (late
fifteenth century). Sinai 150 and Sinai 151 were both apparently originally parts of polyptychs, whose
adjoining panels in one case comprised calendar cycles, christological scenes, and Virgin icons
(Sinai 150), in the other, twelve regular feast scenes, two Virgin feasts, and holy portraits (Sinai 151):
Kurt Weitzmann, "Byzantine Miniature and Icon Painting in the Eleventh Century," in his *Studies
in Classical and Byzantine Manuscript Illumination*, ed. Herbert L. Kessler (Chicago and London:
University of Chicago Press, 1971), 297–306; figs. 301–3 (Sinai 150), and 304–7 (Sinai 151). Sinai 150
has inscriptions in both Georgian and Greek on the Last Judgment panel, and poems in Greek by a
certain monk John that run along the backside of all six related icons; for the texts, see Soteriou and
Soteriou, Εἰκόνες, 2:123, 128, 130. See also the carved wooden Last Judgment from Iceland: Selma
Jónsdóttir, *An 11th Century Byzantine Last Judgment in Iceland* (Rejkjavik: Almenna Bókafélagio,
1959), with good photographs of the Sinai icons, and Angheben, "Jugements derniers," fig. 6.

of those who are about to be judged. Below Christ are the fiery wheels seen by the prophet Ezekiel in his vision of God in majesty.[7]

From under Christ's feet flows the river of fire of the book of Daniel, a narrow stream that widens as it flows off to the right to become the lake of fire. Below, still on the central axis, is the prepared throne, the *hetoimasia*, on which rest the cross and Gospels; it is adored by Adam and Eve, the first sinners of all, who are prostrate before it and, fully clothed, await Christ's final judgment.[8] Below are the figures of two angels and a pair of devils preparing to weigh on the scale between them the deeds of someone about to be judged, though no one in particular is standing by. The angels trumpet to wake the dead across land and sea (the latter personified by a female figure seated on a marine monster); the exotic quadrupeds, including that fiercest of carnivores the elephant, the birds and fish disgorging parts of human bodies, represent earth and sea giving up the dead they had devoured, proof that God can reassemble all particles, however dispersed, into the resurrected body.[9] The angel rolling up the scroll of heaven shows these events are occuring at the end of time, when, as the book of Revelation says, "The heaven departed as a scroll."[10]

The rest of the composition shows the stark contrast between the condemned and the saved. The condemned on Christ's left, our right, who wait their time of judgment, are pushed and bob around helpless in the lake of fire. These figures are mostly crowned kings, court officials, bishops and abbots: secular or ecclesiastical authorities. Below the fire are those who are apparently eternally damned, clustering in tight groups that represent the gnashing of the teeth, the worm that never sleeps, the unquenchable fire, and the outer darkness, all features of the punishments awaiting the sinner as described in Matthew 24–25 and elsewhere. Suffering in their company is Plousios, the rich man of Christ's parable in the Gospel of Luke, who refused to give water to the poor man Lazarus, and who is now condemned to burn in hell in eternal thirst. The figure of Hades, lord of death, sits in a corner adjacent to the lake of fire, the ruler of a dark domain under the earth; he holds on his lap a condemned soul, probably the soul of

7. For the biblical sources, see Brenk, *Tradition*, 79–103, esp. 91; Underwood, *Kariye Djami*, 1:199–211.

8. On the *hetoimasia*, see Thomas von Bogyay, "Zur Geschichte der Hetoimasie," *Akten des XI internationalen Byzantinistenkongresses, München 1958*, ed. Franz Dölger and Hans-Georg Beck (Munich: C. H. Beck, 1960), 58–61; *Oxford Dictionary of Byzantium*, ed. Alexander P. Kazhdan, 3 vols. (New York: Oxford University Press, 1991), 2:927 (Annemarie W. Carr).

9. Caroline Walker Bynum, *The Resurrection of the Body in Western Christianity, 200–1336* (New York: Columbia University Press, 1995), esp. chaps. 1 and 2; Angheben, "Jugements derniers," 121–22.

10. Isa. 34:4; Rev. 6:14. See the rich study of Victoria Kepetzis, "Quelques remarques sur le motif de l'enroulement du ciel dans l'iconographie byzantine du Jugement Dernier," *DCAE* 4, no. 17 (1993–94): 99–112; H. Hunger, "'Ελιγήσεται ὁ οὐρανὸς ὡς βιβλίον," *Kleronomia* 1 (1969): 79–82.

Judas, the one sinner whose chances of redemption would seem extremely dubious indeed.[11]

On Christ's right are the happy elect, neatly arranged groups of apostles, prophets, martyrs, bishops, monks, nuns, and female saints.[12] Each group is headed by its most familiar and prominent representatives, for example, David the prophet, Stephen the martyr, Basil and Chrysostom the bishops, Antony the monk, and Mary of Egypt the ascetic. It is labeled a "choir"—*choros*—and in their arrangement they evoke the various groups of officials and dignitaries summoned to the emperor's court, as described in the books of imperial ceremonies.[13] The elect here come into the presence of Christ exactly as the officials come into the presence of the emperor: in groups according to rank, each group led in by its highest ranking member (the *spatharioi* led by the *protospatharios*, etc.). The elect here are undoubtedly the elite.

Below is the gate of paradise, barred by the fiery angel to a group approaching with St. Peter. Paradise itself is a pleasant horizonless grove of vines (often fruit trees) within which sits the Old Testament patriarch Abraham, with the soul of an innocent on his lap (sometimes identified as the poor man Lazarus of the parable); Abraham is flanked by the souls of baptized children who died too young to even think about sinning, depicted almost as schoolboys in clean identical tunics.[14] Above him sits the Virgin on a lovely throne flanked by two angels; she, of course, had proceeded directly to paradise upon her death. In paradise, too, stands the good thief with his cross, for Christ told him just before he died, "Truly I tell you, today you will be with me in Paradise" (Luke 23:43).[15]

As is clear from even this quick tour, the elements of the composition of the Last Judgment derive from a variety of biblical sources, from both Old and New Testaments and from the book of Revelation. Most of the imagery comes from the Gospels, especially that of Matthew, and from Isaiah and Daniel: the angels trumpeting to round up the elect, Christ on his throne of glory, the gathering of the court and the opened books, the river of fire, the everlasting fire, the gnashing of the teeth, the worm that never sleeps. The

11. On this section of a Last Judgment, see Angheben, "Jugements derniers," 122–27.

12. The women are sometimes divided into two groups: female martyrs and female ascetics, as on Sinai icon 150 (see n. 6 of this chapter).

13. In the *De Ceremoniis*, the word used is βῆλα (lit. a banner), translated by Vogt as "entrée" (*Le livre des cérémonies*, ed. Albert Vogt, 2 vols., 2nd ed. [Paris: Les Belles Lettres, 1967], vol. 2 passim). On the elect, see Angheben, "Jugements derniers," 120–21.

14. Angheben interprets these youths as souls who have left their bodies ("Jugements derniers," 116).

15. On paradise see Henry Maguire, "Paradise Withdrawn," in *Byzantine Garden Culture*, ed. Antony Robert Littlewood et al. (Washington, DC: Dumbarton Oaks, 2002), 23–35; Angheben, "Jugements derniers," 115–17 (Abraham), 117–18 (good thief), 118–20 (Virgin); Jean Daniélou, "Terre et Paradis chez les pères de l'église," *ErJb* 22 (1953): 433–72. On Angheben's reading of the paradise imagery, see n. 21 of this chapter.

rolling up of the scroll of heaven, and the earth and sea giving up their dead come from Revelation. A few components, such as the weighing of the soul, have no clear biblical sources behind them, but do have a visual tradition that dates back to the ancient, pre-Christian world.[16] Though the works of Ephrem are the most complete and have been often thought a prime literary source, there is no single text that contains all these elements and that could have provided an immediate base for the composition.[17]

The striking lack of coherence in this composition is something unusual in Byzantine art. When there is a conflation of events in a Byzantine composition—in scenes of the Nativity, for example, the birth of Christ, his bath, the annunciation to the shepherds, the adoration of the magi, are presented as all happening at once—the scene is usually given a rational coherent setting, whether it is set indoors or outdoors in a structured landscape.[18] No such spatial coherence is evident here. Nor is there a temporal coherence, in the form of some kind of easily readable narrative, such as we find in some contemporary hagiographical cycles or miniatures of the *Romance of Barlaam and Joasaph*.[19] There are several things going on here, but are they all taking place at once? Which of the events shown here precede Christ's arrival and his judgment, and which are the result of it? Take the bishops rounding the hill and approaching paradise: these can be easily identified by their facial features as Gregory, Basil, and John Chrysostom. These same three figures head the line of bishops above, which does suggest some sort of narrative

16. Leopold Kretzenbacher, *Die Seelenwaage: Zur religiösen Idee vom Jenseitsgericht auf der Schicksalswaage in Hochreligion, Bildkunst und Volksglaube* (Klagenfurt: Verlag des Landesmuseums für Kärnten, 1958). The first surviving image of the weighing of the souls in a Last Judgment context is apparently that at St. Stephen in Kastoria (ninth century): see pp. 259–60 and n. 33 below. See also Angheben, "Jugements derniers," 127–29.

17. Georg Voss, *Das Jüngste Gericht in der bildenden Kunst des frühen Mittelalters* (Leipzig: E. A. Seamann, 1884), esp. 64–75. But see Brenk, "Anfänge," 109–14. The hymnography for the Sunday of the Last Judgment (the Sunday of Apokreas, or Meatfare Sunday), found in the Triodion, was crucial for the transmission of the vivid imagery of the Early into the Middle Byzantine period; it has been translated by Mother Mary and Kallistos Ware, *The Lenten Triodion* (London and Boston: Faber and Faber, 1978), 150–67. Little is known about when this feast began and what texts were originally involved—it is the only feast devoted entirely to an event that has not yet taken place! A critical study of its tradition would help clarify the relation between the literary and the visual imagery of the Last Judgment. See B. Guerguiev, "Le Jugement dernier et le Triode de Carême," *CaB* 6 (1984): 281–88.

18. An extreme example of this is the icon of the nativity season, now on Sinai, which has ten episodes unfolding in a unified landscape: Soteriou and Soteriou, Εἰκόνες, 1:pl. 43; 2:59–62; Hans Belting, *Likeness and Presence: A History of the Image before the Era of Art*, trans. Edmund Jephcott (Chicago and London: University of Chicago Press, 1994), 279–81, fig. 168.

19. Hagiographical cycles: e.g., *Panegyrikon*, Athos, Esphigmenou 14; *Barlaam and Joasaph*, e.g., Athos, Iveron 463: Stylianos Pelekanides et al., *The Treasures of Mount Athos: The Illuminated Manuscripts*, 4 vols. (Athens: Ekdotike Athenon, 1973–1991), 2:figs. 327–36, 53–132; *The Glory of Byzantium: Art and Culture of the Middle Byzantine Era. A.D. 843–1261*, exhibition catalog, ed. Helen C. Evans and William D. Wixom (New York: Metropolitan Museum of Art, 1997), no. 164.

sequence is involved. But if so, in which direction does the story go? Have all the elect above already passed through the gates, and stand interceding with Christ for us? Or are they still pleading with him for their own salvation, still awaiting permission to approach the gates of paradise, which permission only the three bishops so far have received? It may be relevant here that none of the "saints" has a halo: that is reserved for the seated apostles, the punishing angels, and for the figures already in paradise.[20]

But despite the absence of the usual spatial and temporal guides to this action, some residual principles of symmetry may help us read the composition.[21] The judging Christ appears over a fragmented landscape divided into areas for paradise and hell. The lowest level, even if it is shared by earth and sea, seems to be the area of final solutions, both good and bad. It would seem that paradise to our left and the chambers of hell to our right both depict ultimate states, places for the truly damned and the truly saved.[22] The middle level can be seen as the intermediate state, the area reserved for the elect or blessed, those who went to heaven when they died but have to wait for this last day actually to enter paradise, and for the condemned, those who are not yet damned for all eternity but who have been sent upon death to Hades, where they also await final judgment in rather less pleasant circumstances: for them there is the lake of fire and the deathly domain of Hades. The implication is that they still have a chance to be saved by the intercession of the Virgin and John the Baptist above. The figures clustered above the fire are a puzzle: do they correspond to the groups of the elect on their level at the left, or to the group of three bishops who await entrance into paradise? Either way, it seems that their fate has already been determined and that they are doomed. Once the condemned in the lake of fire have been judged and found wanting, they are truly damned and will join the skulls below to live forever anonymous, devoured and mutilated, in dark pits, where the light of Christ and his angels never shines.

One thing is sure: the disjunctions we experience here are intentional. The usual conventions for depicting time and space in Byzantine painting have been deliberately ignored. Paradise looks like no other Byzantine landscape with which we are familiar, not just in its fruitfulness, but in its white background, and its lack of horizon. The black boxes in hell are hard even to describe, being virtually devoid of any spatial reference at all. We need only to compare our composition as a whole to some splendid pages from the illustrated homilies of James Kokkinobaphos of the first half of the twelfth

20. But see the case of Paris, Bibl. Nat. gr. 74, fig. 14.3 below.

21. Angheben comments on these more puzzling aspects of Byzantine Last Judgment compositions, and concludes that in two works (the Paris manuscript and Torcello), a distinction was being made between the earthly paradise, what he calls the "paradis d'attente," and the kingdom of heaven at the end of time, but that the distinction later got blurred: "Jugements derniers," esp. 108–15.

22. Here my reading differs from that of Angheben (see previous note).

century, where a valiant attempt is made to cope with the underworld in a logical way.[23] On one page (fol. 20v), we see the prophets awaiting Christ's arrival on earth, tucked up in various levels of Hades; they eagerly question newly arriving souls: "Have the signs begun yet? Is our time about to come?" Another page shows not only the *anastasis*, but an angel giving impatient souls the devastating news that they must still wait, that the time for them to rise has not yet come, and then it shows Christ taking Adam and Eve and the prophets up into paradise, walking up a ramp that leads from the darkness of hell to the garden of paradise, and leaving Adam and Eve at the feet of the Virgin.[24] In short, a landscape *could* be invented, with different levels and degrees of darkness. Although in the famous and familiar Byzantinizing mosaic on the west wall of the church of the Virgin at Torcello, outside Venice, an attempt was made to regularize this composition, its strict zoning and rigorous symmetry is not found in any purely Byzantine Last Judgment.[25]

Beat Brenk has compared the Last Judgment composition to a florilegium for its apparent random assemblage of parts; Jane Baun compares it to works of visionary literature for its lack of coherent structure.[26] She and others have stressed how the composition makes most sense when its diverse elements are distributed over a three-dimensional space, on the east, west, north, and south walls of a church. Take the late twelfth-century frescoes in the crypt of the ossuary church at the monastery of Bačkovo in Bulgaria: here a certain unity is forged from the viewer's own experience of space.[27] Painted on the walls of the narthex, as this composition often was, the elements surround the viewer on all sides, giving the spatial referents missing on the flat pro-

23. Bibl. Vat. gr. 1162, fols. 20v, 48v: Facsimile: Irmgard Hutter and Paul Canart, *Das Marienhomiliar des Mönchs Jakobos von Kokkinobaphos: Codex Vaticanus Graecus 1162* (Zurich: Belser Verlag, 1991). See also Cosimo Stornajolo, *Miniature delle Omilie di Giacomo Monaco* (Rome: Danesi, 1910).

24. Homily 2. Hutter and Canart, *Marienhomiliar*, Introduction volume, 29–30, 36–38. For the text, see PG 127:576–77, 593–95.

25. Anna D. Kartsonis, *Anastasis: The Making of an Image* (Princeton, NJ: Princeton University Press, 1986), esp. 159–64, 221–26; Irina Andreescu, "Torcello. I. Le Christ inconnu. II. Anastasis et Jugement Dernier: Têtes vraies, têtes fausses," *DOP* 26 (1972): 185–223; idem, "Torcello III. La chronologie relative des mosaiques pariétales," *DOP* 30 (1976): 245–345, esp. 245–76.

26. Brenk, *Tradition*, 102–3; Jane Baun, *Tales from Another Byzantium: Celestial Journey and Local Community in the Medieval Greek Apocrypha* (New York: Cambridge University Press, 2007). See also idem, "Middle Byzantine 'Tours of Hell': Outsider Theodicy?" in *Strangers to Themselves: The Byzantine Outsider*, ed. Dion Smythe (Aldershot and Burlington, VT: Ashgate Variorum, 2000), 47–60.

27. On this theme, see Karoline Papadopoulos, *Die Wandmalereien des XI Jahrhunderts in der Kirche* Παναγία τῶν χαλκέων *in Thessaloniki* (Graz and Cologne: Böhlau, 1966), 67; cf. Robert Ousterhout, "Temporal Structuring in the Chora Parekklesion: Iconographic Program for the Byzantine Church St. Savior in Chora, Istanbul," *Gesta* 34 (1995): 63–76. For Bačkovo (the frescoes are in the narthex of the crypt of the ossuary church), see Elka Bakalova, *The Ossuary of the Bačkovo Monastery* (Plovdiv: Pygmalion, 2003), 63–65, color pls. 23–38, sketch figs. 7–10.

jection, enabling the viewer to enter the corner of the blessed or that of the damned by simply moving about. That this kind of composition originated in monumental painting cannot be doubted.

Let us look for a moment at what is missing in this composition on the Sinai icon (see fig. 14.1). We have virtually no trace of the many vivid and imaginative elements found in Byzantine visionary literature: no tollgates or custom booths, no individualized punishments for private sins (those will come later), no soul waiting by the balance scale (that too will come later).[28] And where is the saintly intercessor, whom we assume will be there to pray for us on the terrible day?[29] The Virgin and John the Baptist are there, pleading on behalf of mankind, but is there no private advocate?

Who, in fact, are these compositions addressing? I would argue that in this early period of their development, at least, these Last Judgment compositions have more of a political agenda than we might suspect, that they do not primarily address the individual sinner but are designed above all to strike terror in the hearts of those who administer the highly structured Byzantine world.

One of our earliest references to a Last Judgment image is contained in an eighth-century treatise directed at the iconoclast emperor Constantine V, probably written around 770.[30] If you look at a representation of the Second Coming of Christ, says the author, addressing the emperor:

> you would see how He comes in His glory, and (you would see) the myriad crowd of angels standing before His throne with fear and trembling, the river of fire that flows from the throne and consumes the sinners; if you then see the joy and gladness of the righteous on the right hand of God, and how they rejoice before the Bridegroom, could you then in mind and in heart remain hard and stubborn, and your heart not be pierced by that fearsome hour?[31]

28. On the visionary literature, see John Wortley, "Death, Judgment, Heaven, and Hell in Byzantine 'Beneficial Tales,'" *DOP* 55 (2001): 53–69; Baun, *Tales*; Lennart Ryden, *The Life of St. Andrew the Fool* (Stockholm: Uppsala University, 1995); Evelyne Patlagean, "Byzance et son autre monde: Observations sur quelques récits," in *Faire croire: Modalités de la diffusion et de la réception des messages religieux du XIIe au XVe siècle* (Rome: École française de Rome, 1981), 201–21; George Every, "Toll Gates on the Airway," *ECR* 8 (1976): 139–51. On the personified sins, see Pavle Mijović, "Personnification des sept péchés mortels dans le Jugement Dernier à Sopoćani," in *L'art byzantin du XIIIe siècle*, Symposium de Sopoćani, ed. Vojislav Djurić (Belgrade: Faculté de philosophie. Departement de l'histoire de l'art, 1967), 239–48. On the individualized punishments, see Miltos Garidis, "Les punitions collectives et individuelles des damnés dans le Jugement Dernier (du XIIe au XIVe siècle)," *ZLU* 18 (1982): 1–17; Sharon Gerstel, "The Sins of the Farmer: Illustrating Village Life (and Death) in Medieval Byzantium," in *Word, Image, Number: Communication in the Middle Ages*, ed. Santa Casciani and John Contreni (Florence: Sismel, 2002), 205–17. See also the works cited in n. 51 below.

29. See Henry Maguire, "From the Evil Eye to the Eye of Justice: The Saints, Art, and Justice in Byzantium," in *Law and Society in Byzantium: Ninth–Twelfth Centuries*, ed. Angeliki E. Laiou and Dieter Simon (Washington, DC: Dumbarton Oaks, 1994), 217–39.

30. *Oratio adv. Constantinum Cabalinum*: PG 95:309–44, esp. 324–25.

31. Brenk, "Anfänge," 110.

One hundred years later, the image of the Last Judgment was again invoked, we are told, to impress another ruler, this time Tsar Boris of Bulgaria, around 864. Boris, still a pagan, and looking to decorate what seems to have been one of his palaces or hunting lodges, summoned a Greek painter, a monk by the name of Methodios. Boris told the painter to forego the usual themes for palace decoration, and

> to paint not the killing of men in battle or the slaughter of wild beasts, but anything he might wish, on condition that the sight of the painting should induce fear and amazement in its spectators. The painter, who did not know of any subject more apt to inspire fear than the Second Coming of the Lord, depicted it there, with the righteous on one side receiving the reward for their labors, and the sinners on the other, reaping the fruit of their misdeeds and being harshly driven away to the punishment that had been threatened to them. When he had seen the finished painting, he [Boris] conceived thereby the fear of God, and after being instructed in our holy mysteries, he partook of divine baptism in the dead of night.[32]

The impressive frescoes in the narthex of St. Stephen at Kastoria in northwestern Greece (fig. 14.2) now thought to date to the ninth century, are located in a town that was under Bulgarian domination in just this period, and they are therefore probably the closest we can get to the type of Last Judgment that would have been painted for Boris.[33] The Last Judgment frescoes at St. Stephen concentrate almost entirely on the judgment aspect of the event,

32. *Theophanes continuatus*, 4:15, ed. Immanuel Bekker (Bonn: E. Weber, 1838), 163.19–164.16, trans. Cyril Mango, *The Art of the Byzantine Empire 312–1453: Sources and Documents* (Englewood Cliffs, NJ: Prentice Hall, 1972; repr., Toronto: University of Toronto Press, 1986), 190–91. According to Symeon the Logothete (*Chronographia* of Leo Grammaticus, ed. Immanuel Bekker [Bonn: E. Weber, 1842], 664–66), who relates the same story, the painting was done after Boris's conversion. But he, too, implies the image was in a royal dwelling. See also Francis Dvornik, "La conversion des Bulgares," chap. 6 in *Les Slaves: Byzance et Rome au IXe siècle* (Hattiesburg, MS: Academic International, 1970), 184–95, esp. 188.

33. According to Brenk this is the earliest surviving Byzantine Last Judgment composition (*Tradition*, 80–82). Kastoria may not yet have been under Bulgarian control in the time of Boris (852–889), but was more surely so under Symeon (893–927): cf. Ann W. Epstein, "Middle Byzantine Churches of Kastoria: Dates and Implications," *ArtB* 62 (1980): 190–207, esp. 201n58. On the Church of St. Stephen, see Stylianos M. Pelekanides, Καστορία, I. Βυζαντιναί τοιχογραφίαι, Makedonike Bibliotheke 17 (Thessalonike: Hetaireia Byzantinon Spoudon, 1953) pls. 87–101, esp. 87–88; Stylianos M. Pelekanides and Manoles Chatzedakes, *Kastoria* (Athens: Melissa, 1984), 6–21, figs. 4, 6–7; Anastasios K. Orlandos, *ABME* 4 (1938): 107–24; N. K. Moutsopoulos, Ἐκκλησίες τῆς Καστοριάς 9ος–11ος αἰώνας (Thessalonike: Paratetetes, 1992), 202–305, esp. figs. 200, 236–48, pls. 19–20. The narthex frescoes were in part left unfinished: some of the faces were only half painted, others almost not at all (Pelekanides and Chatzedakes, *Kastoria*, note p. 7, who wonder whether some untoward event prevented the completion of the Last Judgment frescoes). A damaged inscription painted between the legs of Hades has been taken to refer to the painting of the figure of Hades and to give the date 889 (Moutsopoulos, Ἐκκλησίες, 299).

especially on the twelve apostles seated each with an imperial angel behind his chair. The barrel-vaulted roof of the narthex is low, the apostles loom very large overhead. In one corner of this narthex we find a figure of Hades as a giant draped in flames, shown as though mounting the staircase in search of prey; there is also an angel with a balance, and one with a fiery sword. But the main emphasis here is not on the visionary landscape of heaven and hell, but on the justice being administered by the apostles' court.

The image painted for Boris, it should be noted, was not in a church but in one of the tsar's own private residences. Such an imperial use of the Last Judgment theme occurs again later, in the time of Emperor Alexios I Komnenos, who, according to the poet Kallikles, commissioned in the early twelfth century an image of the second coming inside the palace itself.[34] Here Alexios sees himself in the fire, awaiting judgment from the supreme judge. And he takes this opportunity to warn his representatives, his own judges, lest they be caught misusing their authority.[35] Alexios returned to the theme

Figure 14.2.
Kastoria, St.
Stephen, narthex:
Last Judgment.

34. Nicolaus Kallicles, *Carmi*, ed. Roberto Romano (Naples: Bibliopolis, 1980), 101–2, no. 24; Paul Magdalino and Robert S. Nelson, "The Emperor in Byzantine Art of the Twelfth Century," *ByzF* 8 (1982): 123–83, esp. 124–26; Victoria Kepetzis, "The Vlacherna Palace Revisited: An Image in the Text?" (forthcoming). The image should perhaps be understood in the context of Alexios's deep feelings of guilt and desire for penance after his bloody takeover of the capital at the inception of his reign in the early 1080s.

35. "The thrones set up, the opened books, the trumpet raising the lid of every tomb, and the Spirit giving life to the dead: the thousands of praying spirits and the myriads of worshipping angels indicate, O Christ, your final coming. . . . Judges, as you look upon these things, put aside all consideration of persons and of gain, and keep the scales of justice balanced. 'In what measure ye judge (Matt. 7:2), ye shall be judged by me'; the saying is God's, and to be believed. This is what I have to say and paint for you, I Alexios Komnenos, King of the Ausonians." Translation by Magdalino and Nelson, "Emperor," 124–26. The language of the poem echoes the hymnography for the Saturday of the Last Judgment (see n. 17 of this chapter).

of the Last Judgment again toward the end of his life, in his *Mousai*, poems addressed to his son and heir, the future John II, cautioning him to maintain justice in office.[36]

In a famous Gospel book in Paris thought to have been painted in the monastery of St. John of Stoudios in Constantinople in the third quarter of the eleventh century, there are *two* Last Judgment compositions in the one manuscript.[37] The first of these, a miniature painted at the end of the Gospel of Matthew (fig. 14.3), is an impressive, mul-

Figure 14.3. Gospel book (Paris Bibl. Nat. gr. 74, fol. 51v): Last Judgment.

tilevel composition. The ingredients are familiar, except that the earth and sea here are separated from each other; there are bodies still in their winding sheets emerging from sarcophagi at the sound of the trumpet, and but one

36. *Mousai* 1:105–17, 123–25, 225–38: Paul Maas, "Die Musen des Kaisers Alexios I," *ByzZ* 22 (1913): 348–69. I wish to thank Ruth Macrides for calling my attention to this poem, and Robert Jordan and Charlotte Roueché for kindly sending me a copy of the new edition and translation they are preparing. See also Paul Magdalino, *The Empire of Manuel I Komnenos, 1143–1180* (New York: Cambridge University Press, 1993), 27–29; Michael Angold, "Alexios I Komnenos: An Afterword," in *Alexios I Komnenos*, ed. Margaret Mullett and Dion Smythe, BBTT 4.1 (Belfast: The Queen's University, 1996), esp. 409–10.

37. Henri Omont, *Évangiles avec peintures byzantines du XIe siècle*, 2 vols. (Paris: Impr. Berthaud frères, 1908); Iohannis Spatharakis, *The Portrait in Byzantine Illuminated Manuscripts* (Leiden: Brill, 1976), 61–67, figs. 29, 31, 33, 36; Irmgard Hutter, "Theodoros βιβλιογράφος und die Buchmalerei in Studiu," *BollGrott* 51 (1997): 177–203, esp. 202–3, figs. 3, 6; Sirarpie Der Nersessian, "Recherches sur les miniatures du Parisinus Graecus 74," *JÖB* 21 (1972): 109–17, figs. 1–7; Angheben, "Jugements derniers," figs. 1, 7, 12, 14–15, 18, 20. The dissertation by Erika Baumgärtner, "Die byzantinische Weltgerichtsdarstellung in Evangelienhandschriften und ihre Ausläufer" (PhD diss., Heidelberg, 1947), was unfortunately unavailable to me. The Last Judgment is rarely found in illuminated manuscripts, but see the "paradise" page in the manuscript of Acts, Epistles, and Revelation in Moscow, University Library gr. 2280, fol. 311v (dated 1072 and made for the emperor Michael VII Doukas; the page is inserted but is presumably contemporary with the other miniatures in the manuscript. The miniature, labeled ὁ παράδεισος, shows the Virgin and the good thief in paradise: Mikhail V. Alpatov, "Un nuovo monumento di miniatura della scuola Costantinopolitana," *StB* 2 (1927): 103–8, fig. 8; V. G. Pucko, "Miniatjura 'ὁ Παράδεισος' v grečeskom 'Apostole' 1072 goda iz sobranija biblioteki Moskovskogo Universiteta (2280)," *BSl* 29 (1968): 327–33, fig. 1. I wish to thank Georgi Parpulov for calling this miniature to my attention.

angel trumpet. The group of the blessed about to enter paradise seem to be all martyrs, not bishops. As for the damned, they are in vaulted chambers this time, some of them miserable shivering nude figures who remind us of real prisoners in dungeon cells. In the lake of fire can be seen a king, a bishop, and men in court dress, along with Plousios, the rich man burning with thirst.

The second image of the Last Judgment in this manuscript is painted at the end of the Gospel according to Mark (fig. 14.4). It is smaller in scale; abandoned are the figures of Hades, of Adam and Eve, and the resurrection of the dead. The number of the elect and damned have each been reduced to three groups. In the lake of fire are again only secular powers, the figures of an emperor and members of his court.

The image of paradise in this second miniature is remarkable, for within its walls is a group of monks, led by a dark-haired abbot with a halo, which is blue in color. This is the only Byzantine Last Judgment I know where any group or individual member of the elect is shown actually inside paradise.[38] In fact, the usual choir of monks is missing from above where the elect await judgment; it has been shifted into paradise. Furthermore, the monks are led not, as they are usually, by one of the venerable long-bearded heroes of Egyptian or Palestinian monasticism, such as Antony or Sabas, but by the figure of a contemporary abbot.[39]

There are other curious elements in this Gospel manuscript (fig. 14.5). Following each Gospel is an image of this same haloed abbot interacting in some way with the relevant evangelist.[40] The abbot, labeled *ho kyr hegoumenos*, the Lord Abbot, is being given a book by Matthew; Mark discusses him with Christ in a dialogue, and at the end of the manuscript he is being given the staff of office by the evangelist John. After each image comes a poem that stresses the nature of the abbot's responsibility to his flock and the divine source of his authority.[41]

38. There is a large sixteenth-century Cypriot icon of the Last Judgment that shows a bishop alongside the throne of the Virgin in paradise; see Athanasios Papageorgiou, *Byzantine Icons from Cyprus*, exhibition catalog Benaki Museum 1976 (Athens, 1976), no. 62.

39. He stands with hands outstretched toward the Virgin, his pose echoing that of the choirs of saints above him, and that of the Virgin and John the Baptist near Christ; he is presumably approaching the Virgin on behalf of his monks, asking her to intercede with Christ.

40. Paris, Biblio. Nat. gr. 74, fols. 61v, 101v, 213v: Omont, *Évangiles*, 56, 91, 187.

41. The poems have been transcribed and translated by Spatharakis, *Portrait*, and by Dirk Krausmüller, "Abbots and Monks in Eleventh-Century Studios: An Analysis of Rituals of Installation and Their Depictions in Illuminated Manuscripts," *REB* 65 (2007): 255–82, esp. 270–81. Omont reproduces the miniatures but not the poems. I wish to thank Dirk Krausmüller for some enlightening discussions regarding this manuscript. At the end of the manuscript, on fol. 215v, there is a fifth poem, this one a prayer to Christ on behalf of the emperor and his family. Spatharakis (*Portrait*, 67) and Hutter ("Theodoros," 202–3) suggest that the Gospels originally had an imperial portrait as a frontispiece, as does the later relative of this manuscript, the Gospels of Tsar Ivan Alexander (see p. 264 below). See also Jeffrey Anderson, "On the Nature of the Theodore Psalter," *ArtB* 70 (1988): 550–68, esp. 567–68, who interprets the contemporary Theodore Psalter of 1066, another Studite manuscript, as a sort of mirror of abbots, an equivalent to the literary mirror of princes.

Figure 14.4. Gospel book
(Paris Bibl. Nat. gr. 74,
fol. 93v): Last Judgment.

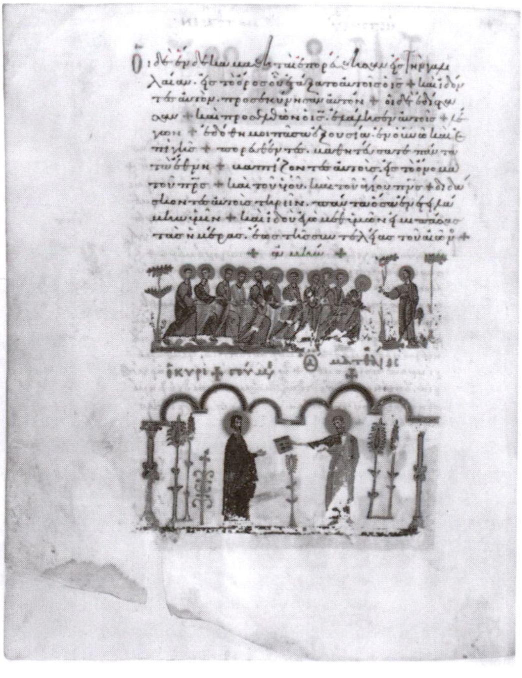

Figure 14.5. Gospel book
(Paris Bibl. Nat. gr. 74,
fol. 61v): Abbot and
evangelist Matthew.

These themes, responsibility in office and a direct line to God, have been connected by Dirk Krausmüller with contemporary disputes involving the independence of the monasteries from outside control.[42] Who exactly is this *kyr hegoumenos*, the Lord Abbot, in Paris 74?[43] The absence of a proper name, or even of the common phrase "our holy father," suggests that the *kyr hegoumenos* here should be seen as a generic abbot, rather than the patron of the manuscript. In monastic foundation documents of this period, abbots are frequently enjoined to act responsibly, or they will have to face the monastery's founder in court on the last day.

Most Byzantine Gospel books lack any such programmatic, even political, thrust, and are devoid of any image of the Last Judgment. But in a fourteenth-century Slavic Gospel book very like Paris 74 in format and probably copying a model like it we find the theme repeated: in the so-called Gospels of Tsar Ivan Alexander, now in the British Library (B. L. Add. 39627), a miniature of the Last Judgment comes at the end of the Gospel of Mark, just as it does in Paris 74[44] (fig. 14.6). But here the lucky resident of paradise is not an abbot but the tsar, Ivan Alexander. The poems about the abbot as administrator are omitted in the Slavic Gospels, but the miniatures accompanying them were copied, with the tsar again taking the place of the abbot.[45] The royal use of the Last Judgment theme continues into the post-Byzantine period: a Romanian Gospel book of the sixteenth century commissioned by Voivode Alexander II repeats the compositions first found in Paris 74 and again shows the ruler (and his sun Mihnea) with the evangelists (Sucevita 23, fols. 83v, 140v, 303v).[46] The fact that the individual in paradise can be so easily shifted from abbot to ruler suggests that they were both viewed as administrators with high official responsibilities, individuals who can be judged only at the highest level, by Christ himself. The acts for which they are to be held responsible are not their own personal failings but the deeds of their administration.

42. Dirk Krausmüller, see the previous note. See also Rosemary Morris, *Monks and Laymen in Byzantium 843–1118* (Cambridge and New York: Cambridge University Press, 1995), esp. 145–65; John Thomas, *Private Religious Foundations in the Byzantine Empire*, DOS 24 (Washington, DC: Dumbarton Oaks, 1987).

43. Though he is haloed, he does not resemble St. Theodore of Stoudios: Doula Mouriki, "The Portraits of Theodore Studites in Byzantine Art," *JÖB* 20 (1971): 249–80.

44. London, British Library Add. 39627, fol. 124r: Ekaterina Dimitrova, *The Gospels of Tsar Ivan Alexander* (London: British Library, 1994), fig. 58; Spatharakis, *Portrait*, 67–70, fig. 32. On the relation between the two manuscripts, see Sirarpie Der Nersessian, "Two Slavonic Parallels for the Greek Tetraevangelion, Paris 74," *ArtB* 9 (1927): 223–74. This relationship and the political implications of the Bulgarian Last Judgment composition have been further analyzed with great insight by Elka Bakalova, "Society and Art in Bulgaria in the 14th Century," *BBulg* 8 (1986): 17–72.

45. Fols. 86v, 134v, 212v (Luke), 272v: Dimitrova, *Gospels*, figs. 31–33 and title page; Spatharakis, *Portrait*, figs. 30, 34–35, 37; Bakalova, "Society and Art."

46. Gheorghe Popescu-Valcea, *Romanian Miniatures* (Bucarest: Editura Eridiane, 1998), 35–42, figs. 30, 32, 63.

Figure 14.6. Gospels of Tsar Ivan Alexander. London, B. L. Add. 39627, fol. 124r: Last Judgment.

The imagery of the Last Judgment was deeply embedded in the consciousness of Byzantine rulers, so much so that to a degree art and reality came to be envisaged each in terms of the other. One night the tenth-century emperor Romanos I Lekapenos, who had assumed the throne in place of his son-in-law, the legitimate Constantine Porphyrogennitos, had a terrifying vision: two white-clothed eunuchs were taking him by the hand to a place in the palace called the Trikymbalon, from which he could see a pit ablaze with a great pyre, which was being stoked by dozens of henchmen.[47] He had to watch as his own son Constantine and the metropolitan of Herakleia, Anastasios, were led out by servants and thrown into the flames. When he awoke, Romanos discovered that both men, his son and the bishop, had in fact died that very night. He reacted to this alarming vision with acts of penance himself and pleas to monks all over the empire to pray for him.[48]

47. *Theophanes continuatus*, 6:4, Bekker, 438.20–440.14; Steven Runciman, *The Emperor Romanus Lecapenus and His Reign: A Study of Tenth-Century Byzantium* (Cambridge: Cambridge University Press, 1929; repr., 1988), 235–36. See also Paul Magdalino, "Obervations on the Nea Ekklesia of Basil I," *JÖB* 37 (1987): 63n70.

48. The prompt action on the part of the monks led to the happy discovery by one of them that the list of sins that Romanos had circulated to the monasteries on sheets of parchment had been completely erased.

Punitive fires, above all for heretics, really were lit, some within the palace complex itself. Emperor Alexios I Komnenos may have imagined himself being consumed by the flames in that image he had had painted on the walls of his palace. But he himself did not hesitate to prepare flames for others, and he sat with his court as the judge who condemned them to the pyre. Anna Komnena, the daughter of Alexios and author of the biography of her father known as the *Alexiad*, was a witness to the intimidation and eventual death at the stake of the heretic Basil the Bogomil and his followers around the year 1100.[49] Alexios's stage-managing of the events seems almost like a deliberate evocation of the Last Judgment. Anna writes that her father took his seat on the imperial throne, flanked by senators and members of the clergy. To test the faith of the Bogomils, pyres were lit nearby within the palace grounds, at just the spot, incidentally, where Emperor Romanos I had seen the fiery pit in his dream two centuries earlier.

Last Judgment images became more numerous as time went on. Rarely appearing in manuscripts or icons, they developed into large-scale dramatic compositions spread out over the four walls of a narthex or funerary chapel, designed to envelop and overwhelm the viewer. In the famous Chora monastery in Constantinople of the early fourteenth century (fig. 14.7), the viewer

Figure 14.7. Istanbul, Church of the Chora, parecclesion: Last Judgment.

49. *Alexiad*, 15:9–10, ed. Bernard Leib, 4 vols. (Paris: Les Belles Lettres, 1967), 3:224.1–228.29; trans. Edgar R. A. Sewter, *The Alexiad of Anna Comnena* (Harmondsworth: Penguin Classics, 1969), 496–504.

Figure 14.8. Asinou (Cyprus), Church of the Virgin Phorbiotissa, narthex: Last Judgment; punishments of the damned.

Figure 14.9. Asinou: Last Judgment; soul waiting to be weighed.

enters the actual space of the Last Judgment events, sees the scroll of heaven being rolled up in the vaulted ceiling overhead, stands before the very throne of judgment and witnesses others being thrown into the pyre.[50] It is Byzantine public art at its grandest, a composition that originated and found its finest expression in monumental painting, a bold and dramatic set-piece designed more and more with the ordinary viewer in mind. Depictions of the individual punishments for individual crimes, long familiar from written texts, slowly enter the iconographic repertory (fig. 14.8).[51] And the weighing of the individual soul, entirely absent in the Middle Byzantine period,

50. Underwood, *Kariye Djami*, 3:pls. 335–520.

51. Garidis, "Punitions"; K. P. Chatziioannou, "Αἱ παραστάσεις τῶν κολαζομένων εἰς τοὺς βυζαντινοὺς καὶ μεταβυζαντινοὺς ναοὺς τῆς Κύπρου," *EEBS* 23 (1953): 290–303; Maria Basilakes, "Οἱ παραστάσεις τῶν κολαζομένων γυναικῶν στὶς ἐκκλησίες τῆς Κρήτης," *Ἀρχαιολογία* 21 (1986): 41–46. The condemned include corrupt surveyors, falsifiers of weights, etc., cf. Gerstel, "Sins of the Farmer."

becomes an essential element of the grand
compositions (fig. 14.9).

The Fate of the Soul

This is not to say that the fate of the individual soul was not a matter of concern in
Byzantium: it is merely manifested outside
the context of the Last Judgment.[52] Images of the eleventh and twelfth centuries
show how this "Middle State," the period
between death and the second coming, was
envisaged.[53]

First came the separation of the soul from
the body. Not everyone could hope for a moment of death as beatific as those depicted
in two images of the eleventh and twelfth
centuries, one a miniature in a manuscript
of the Heavenly Ladder of John Climacus, in

Figure 14.10. Heavenly Ladder of
John Climacus. Princeton University,
Garrett 16, fol. 63v: death of a monk.

Princeton, dated 1081 (fig. 14.10), the other
a fresco in the refectory of the monastery of St. John on Patmos (fig. 14.11).
In the miniature, an angel grasps the soul firmly by the wrist to wrest it out
of the body through the mouth, while on the fresco a group of angels reaches
out to embrace the soul as it leaps out of the body on its own.[54]

The immediate aftermath of separation of body and soul is revealed in a
sequence of images prefacing a psalter now in the Dionysiou monastery on
Mount Athos (Dionysiou 65), a manuscript dating probably from the second quarter of the twelfth century.[55] On fol. 11r (fig. 14.12) we see a monk

52. Nicholas Constas, "'To Sleep, Perchance to Dream': The Middle State of Souls in Patristic
and Byzantine Literature," *DOP* 55 (2001): 91–124; Wortley, "Death, Judgment," 53–69.

53. Angheben, "Jugements derniers," believes that the Last Judgment images do relate to this
period between the death of the individual and the second coming.

54. John R. Martin, *The Illustration of the Heavenly Ladder of John Climacus* (Princeton, NJ:
Princeton University Press, 1954), 28–29, fig. 36. For another example, see London, B.L. Add. 19352,
fol. 137r (Theodore Psalter of 1066): Sirarpie Der Nersessian, *L'Illustration des psautiers grecs du
moyen âge, II: Londres, Add. 19.352* (Paris: C. Klincksieck, 1970), fig. 220. Some sources relating to
the arrival of the angel to take the soul have been collected by Annemarie W. Carr in Evans and
Wixom, *Glory of Byzantium*, no. 512. On the visual sources, see Branislav Todić, "Freske XIII veka u
paraklisu na pirgu sv. Georgija u Hilandaru," *HilZb* 9 (1997): 35–70 (English summary 71–73), esp.
64–65; Christopher Walter, "Death in Byzantine Iconography," *ECR* 8 (1976): 113–27, esp. 117–20.
Note too contemporary debates on the soul, E. Stéphanou, "Jean Italos: L'immortalité de l'âme et la
résurrection," *EO* 32 (1933): 413–28; and Constas, "To Sleep."

55. Athos Dionysiou 65, fols. 11r–12r: Pelekanides, *Treasures*, 1:figs. 118, 121–22, pp. 419–21;
Stichel, *Studien*, 70–75, esp. 71; figs. 7–9; Chrysanthe Mauropoulou-Tsioume, "Οἱ μικρογραφίες

Figure 14.11. Patmos, Monastery of St. John, refectory: death of a monk.

contemplating the eternal fire as though in a vision. Above him is Christ and his angelic escort; Christ's left hand is extended, presumably poised to condemn. On the following page, fol. 11v (fig. 14.13) we see the individual soul at its moment of death, when the angel again wrenches it with effort from the body. Two angels then escort the soul to a sort of preliminary hearing that seems to have no direct connection with the Last Judgment, imagery that suggests that some sort of judgment was thought to take place almost at the moment of death: even though the angel has received the soul, there is still a reckoning ahead. The two angels carry rolls recording the good deeds of the anxious naked soul, but they are being challenged by the furious activity of the myriad black demons crowding forward

Figure 14.12. Psalter, Mount Athos Dionysiou 65, fol. 11r: Christ in glory; a monk sees the eternal fire.

τοῦ ψαλτηρίου ἀρ. 65 τῆς μονῆς Διονυσίου," *Kleronomia* 7 (1975): 131–71; figs. 1–12. The date of the manuscript has been controversial, but a twelfth-century date is now generally accepted; see Spatharakis, *Portrait*, 49–51; idem, "The Date of the Illustrations of the Psalter Dionysiou 65," *DCAE* 4, no. 8 (1975–76): 173–77, pls. 94–99; Georgi R. Parpulov, "Texts and Miniatures from Codex Dionysiou 65," *Twenty-fifth Annual Byzantine Studies Conference, Abstracts* (Washington, DC: University of Maryland, 1999), 124, has identified the verses that surround these prefatory miniatures with a poem published by Athanasios Papadopoulos-Kerameus, "Βυζαντινὰ Ἀνάλεκτα. A. Ἀλφάβητος Οὐρανοῦ μαγίστρου," *ByzZ* 8 (1899): 66–70. I wish to thank Dr. Parpulov for sharing this information with me in advance of his paper. The manuscript also contains a text describing how the soul departs from the body.

Figure 14.13. Psalter, Mount Athos Dionysiou 65, fol. 11v: Angel receiving a monk's soul; the weighing of the soul.

Figure 14.14. Psalter, Mount Athos Dionysiou 65, fol. 12r: Condemnation and salvation.

with rolls of their own to put on the scales, rolls on which presumably a rather different record of events has been inscribed. This is not, however, the second coming: Christ is absent, and the immediate fate of the soul is evidently about to be settled first in a lower court, a matter for the angels and devils to determine, at least for the time being. On the third page, fol. 12r (fig. 14.14), the alternatives are presented: if the soul is wicked, it is destined for a black and dank pit; if good, it receives a sort of blessing by two angels. This series of images, with its unique iconography, is the closest we come in Byzantine art to a visual representation of the challenges facing a soul immediately after its departure from the body.[56]

Another cycle involving the travails of the soul immediately after death can be found in a *horologion* of the late twelfth century, a manuscript on the island of Lesbos (Leimonos monastery 295, fols. 321-45).[57] The *horologion* includes

56. Angheben, "Jugements derniers," 108–15. The famous fresco in the burial chamber of St. Neophytos, founder of the monastery on Cyprus that bears his name, shows him apparently being borne aloft by two angels; Neophytos's words, which are inscribed on the fresco, express his wish that his "schema" (pose?) will come to pass (turn out to be true?): Cyril Mango and Ernest Hawkins, "The Hermitage of St. Neophytos and Its Wall Paintings," *DOP* 20 (1966): esp. 165–66, figs. 66–68 and color plate.

57. Panagiotes Vokotopoulos, "Ή εἰκονογράφηση τοῦ κανόνος εἰς ψυχορραγοῦντα στὸ Ὡρολόγιον 295 τῆς μονῆς Λειμῶνας," *Symmeikta* 9 (1994): 95–104 (with English summary on 105–6).

a relatively rare text, the *akolouthia eis psychorragounta*, a canon for the soul struggling to leave the body at death.[58] Each verse of each ode of the canon has its own page, and each is accompanied by a miniature, except for the verses of the ninth ode.[59] These miniatures, now flaked and fragmentary, recount the journey of the soul from its departure from the body to a clearly envisaged possibility of salvation. The cycle opens with scenes of the dying of the monk and shows the angel wresting his soul from the body. The *theotokia*, verses addressed to the Virgin at the end of each ode of the canon, are illustrated with miniatures showing the dying monk addressing himself to an icon of the Virgin. After death, the abandoned body is devoured by birds and beasts (the beasts that presumably will disgorge the parts at the Last Judgment), while the naked soul is brought by angels to an icon of Christ and weighed by them again in the presence of demons attempting to tip the scales.

Monastic life, of course, was conceived as a form of death to the world, a death in life that becomes a life in Christ, not in the hereafter, but in the here and now. For a monk, then, the possibility of salvation or damnation did not necessarily have to wait until the moment of physical death. The image of the "ladder of divine ascent," based on a text known as *The Heavenly Ladder* by the seventh-century writer John Climacus and here exemplified by an icon on Mount Sinai (fig. 14.15), concentrates on the possibility of success and failure in this life. It shows graphically how missing out on even one step in the ascent to Christ during life can lead to perdition, while at the same time reassuring the monk that the attempt can be crowned with success even in this lifetime. Hades here is present, but as a kind of cave in the mountainside or a black sinkhole with a large mouth at its entrance, a place into which we might stumble somewhere in the landscape.[60]

58. Jacobus Goar, Εὐχολόγιον *sive Rituale Graecorum* (Venice, 1730; repr., Graz: Akademische Druck, 1960), 585–87; Incipit: Δεῦτε συνάχθητε πάντες οἱ εὐσεβῶς ἐν τῷ βίῳ ζήσαντες. See Stichel, *Studien*, 74–75. The text itself, attributed to Andrew of Crete, is not found in standard *euchologia*. But see Paul J. Fedwick, "Death and Dying in Byzantine Liturgical Traditions," *ECR* 8 (1976): 152–61, esp. 153–54; Placide de Meester, *Rituale-Benedizionale Bizantino*, Liturgia bizantina, libro II, parte VI (Rome: Tipografia Leonina, 1929), esp. 73–77.

59. Illustrating the same canon are some mid-thirteenth-century frescoes in a tower in the walls of the Chilandari monastery on Mount Athos (the tower of St. George), unfortunately heavily damaged: Todić, "Freske," esp. 55–70, figs. 12–17 and sketch 11; Vojislav Djurić, "Fresques médiévales à Chilandar," *Actes du 12e Congrès international des études byzantines* (Belgrade, 1997), 3:59–98, esp. 65–71, figs. 8–15; Dimitrije Bogdanović, Vojislav Djurić, and Dejan Medaković, *Chilandar*, 2nd ed., (Belgrade: Monastery of Chilandar, 1997), 62, figs. 41–42. The cycle runs along the west and south facades of the chapel. The verses of the canon are written on the frescoes but are not included in the sketches of the frescoes that appear in the publications cited here. There is also a fourteenth-century cycle in the church of St. Sophia in Ochrid (exonarthex, gallery level): Cvetan Grozdanov, *Ohridsko zidno slikarstvo XIV veka* (Belgrade: Institut za istoriju umetnosti, Filozofski fakultet, 1980), 87–91, 193–94, schema 24, figs. 60–61. For post-Byzantine illustrations of the canon, see Stichel, *Studien*, 75.

60. Evans and Wixom, *Glory of Byzantium*, no. 247. For the Greek text of the *Heavenly Ladder*, see PG 88:632–1160. For an English translation, see John Climacus, *The Ladder of Divine Ascent*, trans.

Figure 14.15. Mount Sinai, Monastery of St.
Catherine: icon of the Heavenly Ladder.

Figure 14.16. Heavenly Ladder of John Climacus,
Bibl. Apost. Vat. gr. 1754, fol. 6r: theotokion of the
third ode of the Penitential Canon; the Virgin addresses the monks.

The steps of the Heavenly Ladder offered the monk a clearly defined means of
ascent to Christ within his own lifetime. A manuscript of the *Heavenly Ladder*
in the Vatican (fig. 14.16) illustrates another means of ascent: here, in images
that accompany the text of the penitential canon included in this manuscript,
a group of monks, after performing a sequence of grisly penances, succeed
in passing through the fiery gates into the light of paradise, where they find
the Virgin occupied with intercession.[61] It should be noted that no death has
occurred, no judgment: their penitential practice alone has won these monks
access to paradise. There is no implication here that this is something for which
they will have to wait until the end of time, or even have to wait until after death:
for these monks, this entry into paradise can happen in the here and now. If
the grand Last Judgment images address a special and fearsome warning to the
public at large, especially those in positions of authority, these private manuscript images of the twelfth century not only reveal to the individual monastic
viewer the threat of the eternal fire, but also show him the ways by which he
can, even in this life, move forward step by step into paradise.

Colm Luibheid and Norman Russell (New York: Paulist Press, 1982). For the illustrated manuscripts
of this text, see Martin, *Heavenly Ladder*.
    61. Martin, *Heavenly Ladder*, 128–49, 181–83, figs. 246–77.

ABBREVIATIONS

ABME	*Archeion tōn byzantinōn mnēmeiōn tēs Hellados*
AGJU	Arbeiten zur Geschichte des antiken Judentums und des Urchristentums
AL	Analecta liturgica
Ambrogio e Agostino	387 d.c.: *Ambrogio e Agostino: Le sorgenti dell'Europa.* Milan, 2004
ANF	*Ante-Nicene Fathers*
ANTC	Abingdon New Testament Commentaries
ArtB	*Art Bulletin*
Aug	*Augustinianum*
AV	Analekta Vlatadon
BAC	Biblioteca de autores cristianos
BAR	*Biblical Archaeology Revue*
BBC	Blackwell Bible Commentaries
BBTT	Belfast Byzantine Texts and Translations
BBulg	*Byzantino-bulgarica*
Bib	*Biblica*
BollGrott	*Bollettino della Badia greca di Grottaferrata*
BSl	*Byzantinoslavica*
ByzF	*Byzantinische Forschungen*
ByzZ	*Byzantinische Zeitschrift*
BZNW	Beihefte zur Zeitschrift fur die neutestamentliche Wissenschaft
CaA	*Cahiers archéologiques*
CaB	*Cahiers balkaniques*
CCCM	Corpus Christianorum: Continuatio mediaevalis. Turnhout, 1969–
CCSG	Corpus Christianorum: Series graeca. Turnhout, 1977–
CCSL	Corpus Christianorum: Series latina. Turnhout, 1953–
COr	*Cahiers d'Orientalisme*
CS	Cistercian Studies
CSCO	Corpus scriptorum christianorum orientalium. Paris, 1903–
CurTM	*Currents in Theology and Mission*
DCAE	*Deltion tēs christianikēs archaiologikēs hetaireias*

DDD	*Dictionary of Deities and Demons in the Bible*. Edited by Karel van der Toorn, Bob Becking, and Pieter W. van der Horst. Leiden and New York, 1995
DOP	*Dumbarton Oaks Papers*
DOS	Dumbarton Oaks Studies
DS	*Dictionnaire de spiritualité*. Paris, 1980
ECR	*Eastern Churches Review*
EEBS	*Epeteris Hetaireias Byzantinon Spoudon*
EECh	*Encyclopedia of the Early Church*. Edited by Angelo di Berardino. Translated by A. Walford. 2 vols. New York, 1992
EO	*Echos d'Orient*
ErJb	*Eranos-Jahrbuch*
FC	Fathers of the Church. Washington, DC, 1947–
GCS	Die griechische christliche Schriftsteller der ertsten [drei] Jahrhunderte
GO	Göttinger Orientforschungen
Herm	*Hermathena*
HilZb	*Hilandarski Zbornik*
HR	*History of Religions*
HTR	*Harvard Theological Review*
JAOS	*Journal of the American Oriental Society*
JECS	*Journal of Early Christian Studies*
JETS	*Journal of the Evangelical Theological Society*
JJS	*Journal of Jewish Studies*
JÖB	*Jahrbuch der Österreichischen Byzantinistik*
JSJ	*Journal for the Study of Judaism*
JSJSup	Journal for the Study of Judaism: Supplement Series
JSNT	*Journal for the Study of the New Testament*
JTS	*Journal of Theological Studies*
LCC	Library of Christian Classics
LCL	Loeb Classical Library
LIMC	*Lexicon iconographicum mythologiae classicae*
LXX	Septuagint
MBT	Münsterische Beiträge zur Theologie
MRTS	Medieval and Renaissance Texts and Studies
MS/MSS	manuscript/manuscripts
MT	Masoretic Text
Mus	*Muséon: Revue d'études orientales*
NIB	The New Interpreter's Bible
NovT	*Novum Testamentum*
NTOA	Novum Testamentum et Orbis Antiquus
NTS	*New Testament Studies*
OCP	*Orientalia christiana periodica*
OECS	Oxford Early Christian Studies
OLA	Orientalia lovaniensia analecta
OMT	Oxford Medieval Texts
Or	*Orientalia*
OrChr	*Oriens christianus*
OrChrAn	*Orientalia christiana analecta*
OTM	Oxford Theological Monographs

OTP	*Old Testament Pseudepigrapha.* Edited by J. H. Charlesworth. 2 vols. New York, 1983
ParOr	*Parole de l'orient*
PBR	*Patristic and Byzantine Review*
PG	Patrologia graeca. Edited by J.-P. Migne. 162 vols. Paris, 1857–1886
PL	Patrologia latina. Edited by J.-P. Migne. 217 vols. Paris, 1844–1864
PLS	Patrologia latina supplementum
PO	Patrologia orientalis
PS	Patrologia syriaca. Rev. ed. I. Ortiz de Urbina. Rome, 1965
PTS	Patristische Texte und Studien
RAC	*Reallexikon für Antike und Christentum.* Edited by T. Klauser et al. Stuttgart, 1950–
RB	*Revue biblique*
REAug	*Revue des études augustiniennes*
REB	*Revue des études byzantines*
RevPhil	*Revue de philologie de littérature et d'histoire anciennes*
RHR	*Revue de l'histoire des religions*
RTAM	*Recherches de théologie ancienne et médiévale*
S./SS.	San/Santa; Sans/Santas
SA	Studia anselmiana
SBLDS	Society of Biblical Literature Dissertation Series
SBLSP	*Society of Biblical Literature Seminar Papers*
SC	Sources chrétiennes. Paris: Éditions du Cerf, 1942–
ScrB	*Scripture Bulletin*
SJ	Studia Judaica
SJLA	Studies in Judaism in Late Antiquity
SJSJ	Supplements to the Journal for the Study of Judaism
SLAEI	Studies in Late Antiquity and Early Islam
SNTSMS	Society for New Testament Studies Monograph Series
SSMG	*Scandinavian Studies in Modern Greek*
STAC	Studien und Texte zu Antike und Christentum
StB	*Studi bizantini*
STDJ	Studies on the Texts of the Desert of Judah
StPatr	*Studia Patristica*
StPB	Studia post-biblica
StudMon	*Studia monastica*
SVTP	Studia in Veteris Testamenti pseudepigraphica
TD	*Theology Digest*
TRE	*Theologische Realenzyklopädie.* Edited by G. Krause and G. Müller. Berlin, 1977–
TSAJ	Texte und Studien zum antiken Judentum
TU	Texte und Untersuchungen
TUGAL	Texte und Untersuchungen zur Geschichte der altchristlichen Literatur
TZ	*Theologische Zeitschift*
VC	*Vigiliae christianae*
VCSup	Supplements to Vigiliae christianae
WBC	Word Biblical Commentary
WUNT	Wissenschaftliche Untersuchungen zum Neuen Testament
ZLU	*Zbornik za likovne umetnosti*

LIST OF CONTRIBUTORS

Bogdan G. Bucur, assistant professor of theology at Duquesne University, is the author of the forthcoming *Angelomorphic Pneumatology in Early Christianity: Clement of Alexandria and Other Witnesses* from Brill. His current research project explores the exegesis of Old Testament theophanies in patristic literature.

J. A. Cerrato, rector of Saint James' Episcopal Church in Greenfield, Massachusetts, is the author of *Hippolytus between East and West* (Oxford University Press, 2002) and other Hippolytan studies.

Brian E. Daley, SJ, the Catherine F. Huisking professor of theology at Notre Dame University and executive secretary of the Catholic-Orthodox Consultation for North America, is the author of numerous patristic publications including *The Hope of the Early Church* (Cambridge University Press, 1991; Hendrickson, 2003) and *Gregory of Nazianzus* (Routledge, 2006).

Robert J. Daly, SJ, professor of theology emeritus at Boston College and former editor of *Theological Studies*, is the author of several works on the meaning of Christian sacrifice and related issues (the Eucharist, the atonement, etc.) and of the forthcoming book *Sacrifice Unveiled* with T&T Clark.

Lorenzo DiTommaso, assistant professor of theology at Concordia University in Montréal, is the author of several books on apocalyptic and apocryphal literature. He is presently writing *From Antiquity to Armageddon: The Architecture of Apocalypticism*, to be published by Oxford University Press.

Georgia Frank, associate professor in the department of religion at Colgate University, is the author of *The Memory of the Eyes: Pilgrims to Living Saints in Christian Late Antiquity* (University of California Press, 2000).

Dragoş-Andrei Giulea earned a PhD in philosophy from the Institute of Philosophy in Bucharest and is currently completing a PhD in religious studies at Marquette University in Milwaukee, Wisconsin. His areas of research interest include Second Temple traditions, early Christianity, and patristics, areas in which he has published several articles in peer-reviewed journals.

Alexander Golitzin, professor of theology at Marquette University, specializes in the origins of Eastern Christian ascetical and mystical traditions, especially in their relationships with Second Temple Judaism and Rabbinic Judaism, and their subsequent developments in Greek- and Syriac-speaking Christianity. Among his numerous works on this theme is *Et introibo ad altare Dei: The Mystagogy of Dionysius Areopagita* (Thessalonika, 1994).

John Herrmann Jr. is emeritus curator of classical art at the Museum of Fine Arts in Boston. His numerous publications include, authored with his wife Annewies van den Hoek, the exhibition catalog *Light from the Age of Augustine: Late Antique Ceramics from North Africa (Tunisia)*, 2nd ed. (Institute for the Study of Antiquity and Christian Origins at the University of Texas at Austin, 2003).

Bernard McGinn is the Naomi Shenstone Donnelley Professor emeritus at the Divinity School of the University of Chicago. He is currently at work on the fifth volume of his history of Christian mysticism under the general title *The Presence of God*.

John A. McGuckin, the Nielsen Professor of Late Antique History at Union Theological Seminary and professor of Byzantine Christianity at Columbia University, has written extensively in early Christian history and theology. His latest book is *The Orthodox Church: An Introduction to Its History, Doctrine, and Spiritual Culture* (Blackwell-Wiley, 2008).

Elijah Nicolas Mueller, Orthodox Christian Campus Minister at the University of Chicago, parish priest of an Orthodox Church in Chicago's Hyde Park neighborhood, and a doctoral candidate in theology at Marquette University, is working on a dissertation on angelology and temple imagery in John Damascene's theology and hymns.

Ute Possekel received her PhD from Princeton Theological Seminary and lives and teaches in the Boston area. She is author of *Evidence of Greek Philosophical Concepts in the Writings of Ephrem the Syrian* (Peeters, 1999).

Nancy Patterson Ševčenko is a Byzantine art historian living in Vermont. She is the author of *The Life of Saint Nicholas in Byzantine Art* (Torino, 1983) and numerous other works on illustrated lives of the saints and the relation of Byzantine art and liturgy.

Theodore Stylianopoulos, the recently retired Archbishop Iakovos Professor of Orthodox Theology and professor of New Testament at Holy Cross Greek Orthodox School of Theology, is the author of several books including *The New Testament: An Orthodox Perspective* (Holy Cross Press, 1997).

Annewies van den Hoek, lecturer on Greek and Latin at Harvard Divinity School, has published extensively on Clement, Philo, and Origen and also works with her husband John Herrmann in Greek, Roman, and early Christian archaeology. Her current work is a commentary on Philo's *De Cherubim* and a revision of Clement's *Stromateis*.

Subject Index

MODERN AUTHORS INDEX

ANCIENT SOURCES INDEX

Scripture

Old Testament

Other Ancient Sources